MONOPOLY'S MOMENT

The Organization and Regulation of Canadian Utilities, 1830–1930

TECHNOLOGY AND URBAN GROWTH,

A Series Edited by

BLAINE A. BROWNELL

MARK S. FOSTER

ZANE L. MILLER

MARK ROSE

HOWARD J. SUMKA

JOEL A. TARR

MONOPOLY'S MOMENT

The

Organization

and

Regulation

of

Canadian

Utilities,

1830–1930

CHRISTOPHER ARMSTRONG / H.V. NELLES

Temple

University

Press,

Philadelphia

Temple University Press, Philadelphia 19122
© copyright 1986 by Temple University. All rights reserved
First published 1986
Printed in the United States of America

Library of Congress Cataloging-in-Publication Data

Armstrong, Christopher, 1942–
Monopoly's moment.

(Technology and urban growth)
Includes bibliographical references and index.
1. Public utilities—Canada—History.
I. Nelles, H. V. (H. Viv), 1942–
. II. Title.
III. Series.
HD2768.C37A75 1986   363.6′0971   85-26178
ISBN 0-87722-404-8

For
Our
Parents

Contents

Tables

Figures

Series Preface

Historical scholarship in the United States is profoundly uninformed regarding developments in Canada. Although several American universities offer programs in Canadian studies, and the Canadian government routinely sponsors post-doctoral study for American as well as international conferences, American scholars, nonetheless, lack a disciplined portrait of the Canadian experience.

This gap is peculiar and it merits special attention. Part of the lacuna flows naturally from the conventions by which historical knowledge in the United States is organized. Histories of cities, politics, business firms and technologies, the topics of this book, are bound within the traditional categories of nation and period and further shaped by specialized training. Studies of public transit or electrification, as examples, are difficult to compare with earlier work. Historians of technology emphasize the factors guiding inventive activity; those studying the development of public policy write knowingly of the social bases of political life; and among business historians, attention has turned toward the study of organizations and their environments, especially their political relationships. The urge to locate certitude in specialized knowledge has encouraged strenuous and detailed research in manuscript collections as well as the accumulation of immense sets of unique data. Scholarship, as a consequence, is more closely focused in terms of a topic and within a period of time and geographical area. A remarkable paradox of contemporary research is that the search for patterned behavior among large numbers of actors is yielding a literature verging on the idiosyncratic, perhaps the solipsistic. Our own historiographical moment has thus created a set of assumptions uncongenial to the inclusion of Canadians as consequential figures on the North American scene.

Comparative scholarship, including perhaps Canada, has of course assumed a lofty place in the dialogue of the scholarly life. But still another set of conventions militates against its development. By the 1960s, the social sciences, especially sociology, had emerged as a major component in the rhetorical and cognitive styles of historians. In principal, the study of group experiences, social structure, and social processes transcend political boundaries. But the language and methods of the social sciences and in particular their emphasis on discrete units of observation reinforced the tendency to produce monographic literature offering portraits in miniature. The absence of major sources of funds for large numbers of American scholars to conduct this form of research on Canadian sites permitted the tendency toward localism to continue; and the inability of Canadian scholars to secure the attention of American colleagues for the results of their own social scientific history proved an additional barrier to comprehending the Canadian scene. The fact that Canada is one of the two most accessible points at which to conduct "cross-cultural" studies only highlights in another way its absence from our understanding of the North American experience.

Nor have Christopher Armstrong and H. V. Nelles escaped their own backgrounds. They are bound by the traditions of Canadian historiography and the conventions of Canadian life. This book, like many in the field of Canadian business, is about political economy, and in particular about the development of large-scale organizations and their relationships with regulatory apparatus. Armstrong and Nelles grant the sovereignty of parliament, and want to know how corporations were able to hedge it about. In Canada, as Armstrong and Nelles demonstrate, "parliamentary sovereignty plainly permitted control of any and all undertakings without demanding that due process be observed." Creation of regulatory agencies, they argue, was "the means whereby powerful economic institutions participated in a legitimizing process by rendering themselves accountable to some judgement other than that of the owners." By contrast, the American version of that question has assumed the legitimacy of an autonomous commercial system and a passive state, leaving scholars to explain the development of intrusive government. These competing approaches to the creation of regulatory processes are reflected in the distinctive mentalities of Canadian and American historians in the field of government and business relationships.

Yet the diverse traditions of these two nations and their respective scholars overlap in this study, particularly because Armstrong and Nelles ask questions of trans-national interest. They place Canada squarely in the middle of several of the most important issues facing democratic and capitalist nations during the early years of the twentieth century. How did Canadian entrepreneurs organize their firms with a view toward handling employees and customers by the thousands? What was the significance of new technologies such as telephones and trolleys housed in nationwide and abundantly-capitalized firms for political agencies organized on the local level? Did the outcomes of political action vary according to province and city, suggesting the presence of regional styles of politics that shaped technological systems? On the national level, Armstrong and Nelles find that "the technology transferred to Canada was undeniably American, but the pattern of regulation that evolved might be thought. of as mid-Atlantic, relying more upon public ownership than the United States but less so than Europe." But at the urban and provincial levels, they identify a variety of outcomes ranging from public ownership to modest regulation, a function from place to place of shrewd or insensitive owners, inter-regional competition, business leaders seeking to promote economic development, and politicians with an eye on the main chance. Much like the studies published earlier in this series, Armstrong and Nelles locate no imperatives as Canadians sought to find resolutions for these questions. Politics, defined in the broadest sense to include the allocation of prestige and resources, conditioned the organization of each technology differentially and according to local circumstances.

An added strength of this book is that it is located squarely in the recent literature on these subjects. Practitioners will recognize the influence of Alfred D. Chandler, Jr., Leslie Hannah, Ellis W. Hawley, Thomas P. Hughes, Thomas K. McCraw, and Sam B. Warner, Jr. But Armstrong and Nelles are not in the habit of parading the names of illustrious scholars across their pages. Instead, the secondary literature guides analysis, informing a group of interpretive schemes always subtle, witty, and loaded with the ironies and contradictions of the human experience. Even more, *Monopoly's Moment* departs from earlier studies by emphasizing the contingent relationships among politicians, technologists, urbanites, and business leaders who had to deal with the industrial and urban changes taking place throughout the West. The urban technologies, they argue, "were the vaulting ambitions and subsequently the hallmarks of bourgeois civilization." This book comprises an addition to the literature exploring the social and political development of the Atlantic Basin.

Monopoly's Moment is the fourth book in the Technology and Urban Growth series. Authors and editors seek to expand our understanding of the critical role of technology in the city-building and urbanization processes. Armstrong and Nelles maintain that tradition with their attention to cities such as Montreal, Toronto, and Vancouver and the politics of gas, electric, water, telephone, and trolley development. They also enhance a second dimension in the series with their attention to provincial and national affairs. National and provincial parliaments were the loci of authority that fixed the frameworks and styles of political action and economic activity and also settled, adjusted, postponed, and altered decisions rendered locally. The editors look forward to the publication of books that will hasten the maturation of both of these paths of scholarly endeavor.

The Editors, Technology and Urban Growth Series.

Acknowledgments

Our thanks go to the staffs of the archives mentioned in the notes, who met our requests for innumerable documents. In particular, we owe a debt of gratitude to the employees of those enterprises, both public and private, who accomodated our applications for access to their records, sometimes at considerable inconvenience to themselves. This book has been a long time in the making, and we have accumulated many obligations, of which we can repay only the most pressing here. The Canada Council and the Social Sciences and Humanities Research Council of Canada have provided funds to permit us to undertake the research and writing, and the Social Science Federation of Canada has awarded us a grant in aid of publication. York University supplied secretarial and other assistance in the preparation of the manuscript. Mark Rose, as one of the editors of the series on Technology and Urban Growth, provided thoughtful criticism; and the staff of Temple University Press, in particular Michael Ames, laboured long and hard to improve the quality of our prose. Any errors are entirely our own responsibility, and we hope that when our friends discover them they will keep quiet.

C.A.
H.V.N.
Toronto,
October, 1985

INTRODUCTION
COMMUNITY PROPERTY

Community Property

On those rare occasions when the power goes off, the buses and subways stop, and the telephone goes dead, we are forcibly reminded of the importance of things often taken for granted. Urban life depends upon a complex of interconnections and technological systems, most of which remain invisible to us as we go about our daily business. The services that pervade our lives are the subjects of this book.

Communications, light, power, mobility: these are fundamental attributes of urban life in the modern era. The essential organizations that developed to supply these services were created by public law; they used public property; they delivered public services and so became *public* utilities with all of the claims to control (if not ownership) that the phrase implies. They were, to that extent, community property. Like other property accumulated through partnership, utilities often became the object of passionate discord when their performance did not equal expectations. But this kind of community property could not be divided up as a result of such disputes; rather it had to be effectively regulated.

Utilities, which scarcely existed in the mid-nineteenth century, rapidly became some of the biggest business enterprises in the country. Today Hydro-Québec and Ontario Hydro are the two largest companies (measured by assets) in Canada; Bell Canada, the largest telephone corporation, ranks fourth.[1] In writing the history of the utilities sector we are surveying a terrain of institutional mammoths. Encompassing such sums of capital as they did, utilities played a key role in the development of the Canadian capital market. Utilities not only provided essential services to their users; they also supplied vast quantities of stocks, bonds, and other high-quality securities upon which finance capitalism depended.

Canadians even developed an international specialization in the promotion of companies of this sort. Before World War I, many of the principal figures in the development of Canadian utilities were also responsible

3

for organizing similar ventures in Great Britain, the United States, Brazil, Mexico, Cuba, Puerto Rico, Jamaica, and Spain.[2] In Canada this sector gave rise to that most typically Canadian of all economic institutions, the "Crown corporation." Some observers have been led to the conclusion that this form of enterprise embodies the national economic character.[3] Others have viewed the massive intrusion of the state into business as a major national problem, a predilection of government to be curbed.[4] A large public sector anchored by huge provincial utilities remains one of the most distinctive features of Canadian industrial structure.

For many years the study of the management of utilities was primarily the concern of the institutional economist, the regulatory lawyer, the engineer, and the accountant. Recent debates about regulation have produced an abundance of writing, chiefly by political scientists and economists, aimed essentially at dismantling the inefficient regulatory state and replacing it with more market-sensitive institutions.[5] We have not adopted the vocabulary or the analytical perspectives of these disciplines, but we have borrowed from them whenever we thought it appropriate. In return we hope that our analysis of the historical evolution of this sector and its regulatory process will contribute grist for other disciplinary mills. In this endeavour we are encouraged by a growing body of historical literature dealing with regulation of economic activity in general[6] and the control of public utilities in particular.[7] At the very least, we hope that our book will make it possible for Canada to be more easily included in any further international comparisons of public policy in this sector. Moreover, our study differs from much of what has gone before in Canada and elsewhere by attempting to include all major utilities within the frame of analysis: gas, water, electricity, public transit, and telephones. It is not a history of these industries, only of the organizational and regulatory problems common to them all.

Everywhere in the utilities sector, entrepreneurial drive, profit-making opportunity, technology, and economic structure pointed in the direction of monopoly from the beginning, but the response to monopoly varied greatly from city to city and region to region. Different societies found different resting points on the spectrum of regulation, nor was there any necessary progression from the pole of private ownership to that of state enterprise. In Canada the outcome was plural: telephones fell under public ownership on the prairies but elsewhere remained in private hands under federal or provincial regulation. From Nova Scotia to British Columbia hydroelectric and transit companies came under different kinds of regulatory regimes, ranging from the Public Utilities Commissions so familiar in a U.S. context to radical experiments with provincewide public ownership.

Regulation, even more than monopoly, was a social and political product.[8] We have purposely set out to study the problems of technology transfer, company promotion, industrial organization, and public choice in regulation within a regional or local context. For better or for worse, ours is the view from the city hall basement, from the company minute book, from private correspondence, and from archives and local newspapers. We have tried to build up a comprehensive "national" picture of this key industrial sector on a city-by-city, case-by-case basis. Thus, while we are eager to expose the structural context of events, we also want to stress the importance of chance, choice, will, and frequently error and ignorance in the shaping of institutions. Determinism is more obvious in retrospect.

Before we begin, some information needs to be sketched in for readers unfamiliar with the municipal geography of Canada. At the end of the War of 1812, none of the urban centres in the British North American colonies exceeded 15,000 inhabitants, but with postwar immigration these towns began to swell into genuine cities by mid-century (Table 1). As immigrants pushed westward into the interior, new settlements like Toronto, Hamilton, and Ottawa grew rapidly along with the undisputed metropolis of British North America, Montreal. Farther east, Quebec City, Halifax, and Saint John expanded but at a slower rate. After Confederation in 1867 the new Dominion of Canada gained control of the far western territories beyond the Great Lakes, and once railway links were established, a trickle of new settlers found their way to the prairies and the Pacific coast beyond. After 1900 the cities of western Canada underwent a sudden burst of rapid growth not unlike that which their eastern counterparts had experienced during the Irish famine

TABLE 1

POPULATION OF MAJOR EASTERN CANADIAN CITIES, 1851-1931

Year	Halifax	Saint John	Quebec	Montreal	Ottawa	Toronto	Hamilton
1851	20,749	22,745	42,052	78,331[b]	7,760	30,775	14,112
1861	25,026	27,317	59,990	118,015	14,669	44,821	19,096
1871	29,582	41,325[a]	59,699	144,044	21,545	75,903[c]	26,716
1881	36,100	41,353	62,446	193,171	27,412	113,128	35,961
1891	38,437	39,179	63,090	277,525	44,154	207,450	48,959
1901	40,832	40,711	68,840	360,838	59,928	238,080	52,634
1911	46,619	42,511	78,118	554,781	87,062	409,925	81,969
1921	58,372	47,166	95,193	724,205	107,843	611,443	114,151
1931	59,275	47,514	130,594	1,003,868	126,872	818,348	155,547

Sources: George Nader, *Cities of Canada*, vol. 2, *Profiles of Fifteen Metropolitan Centres* (Toronto: Macmillan, 1976); Leroy O. Stone, *Urban Development of Canada* (Ottawa: Dominion Bureau of Statistics, 1968).
[a]Includes Portland, annexed in 1889.
[b]Island, not city, of Montreal.
[c]Metropolitan area.

migrations of the late 1840s and early 1850s (see Table 2). By the eve of the First World War, Canada's 14 largest cities contained about 1,750,000 inhabitants.

Halifax and Saint John were old shipping and commercial cities that struggled to develop an industrial base in the late nineteenth and early twentieth centuries. Montreal and Toronto were both regional industrial centres and rival national metropolises. The second-rank cities in their hinterland—Quebec City, Ottawa, London, Hamilton, Port Arthur, and Fort William—had more specialized bases in administration, transportation, heavy industry, or wholesaling. Winnipeg yearned to be the Chicago of Canada, gateway to the West where regional finance, wholesaling, grain shipping, meat packing, and railways, converged. Before the Great Depression, Regina, Edmonton, Saskatoon, and Calgary never became much more than large central places for a broadly dispersed agricultural economy, the first two combining provincial administrative functions with regional commerce. Vancouver emerged after the 1890s as the principal port city of the west coast, coordinating the fishing, logging, mining, transshipment, and wholesaling functions where the transcontinental railway met the Pacific ocean. The provincial capital of Victoria on Vancouver Island remained primarily an administrative centre.

Regional specialization characterized the Canadian economy before 1930. The head offices of manufacturing, banking, and finance were concentrated in Ontario and Quebec, primarily at Toronto and Montreal. American capital penetrated the economy through these two points, and in the tight triangle formed by Toronto, Ottawa, and Montreal the basic national economic decisions were made. Under this hegemony the Maritimes attempted with diminishing success to shift from agriculture, fishing,

TABLE 2
POPULATION OF MAJOR WESTERN CANADIAN CITIES, 1881–1931

Year	Winnipeg	Regina	Saskatoon	Calgary	Edmonton	Vancouver	Victoria
1881	12,154[a]	—	—	—	—	—	5,925
1891	29,543	—	—	3,876	—	13,709	16,941
1901	47,969	2,249	113	4,152	2,626[b]	29,432	20,919
1911	156,163	30,213	12,004	43,704	24,900	120,847	31,660
1921	228,035	34,432	25,739	63,305	58,821	163,220	38,727
1931	293,300	53,209	43,291	83,761	79,197	246,593	39,082

Source: George Nader, *Cities of Canada,* vol. 2, *Profiles of Fifteen Metropolitan Centres* (Toronto: Macmillan, 1976).
[a] Metropolitan area.
[b] Excludes Strathcona.

forestry, and mining to industry. Wheat farming and its related services, its shipping and marketing activities, predominated in the prairie West. On the Pacific Coast large-scale exploitation of the coastal and mountain resource base had only just begun before World War I. Each region thus possessed its own distinctive economy and social organization—partly a function of different development patterns and partly a function of differential migration—and its own location in the evolving political and economic hierarchy.[9]

By 1911 not only Montreal (with over 500,000 residents) and Toronto (with over 400,000) but also smaller places like Halifax and Calgary (each with about 45,000 inhabitants) presented rich markets for such urban services as lighting, transportation, gas, and water supply. As elsewhere in the industrializing world, a whole new sector sprang into existence to supply these needs. Industries that had barely existed in the 1850s now absorbed huge quantities of capital, employed thousands of people, and serviced millions of customers. Entrepreneurs seized their opportunities; in maximizing their returns, they made monopolies.

Once made, however, these monopolies passed through two perilous decades of insecurity following 1905 when their legitimacy came to be questioned. This moment, when powerful popular and financial interests struggled over the regulation of monopoly, is the subject of this book.

Part One, The Invention of Necessity, surveys the history of the first urban utilities in the nineteenth century. The transformation wrought by electricity and modern capitalism is the main concern of Part Two, The Transfer of Technology and Technique. Monopoly's moment comes in Part Three, Regions and Regulations, which examines the political crisis of the private industry. The organizational and regulatory history of the Canadian utility sector reflects the pronounced economic and social diversity of Canada. The final section, Mediation and Legitimacy, analyzes the different outcomes of the regulatory process, but focuses upon the common result.

PART ONE
THE
INVENTION
OF
NECESSITY

Gas and Water Capitalism

Fire and darkness forced city dwellers everywhere to protect themselves and their property. Until the nineteenth century this had remained largely an individual responsibility. Householders provided their own security as best they could, the usual precautions being wells, cisterns, latches, shutters, night watches, masonry walls, and slate roofs. But not everyone could afford the luxury of safe passage at night or untroubled sleep at home, especially in the overcrowded port cities of Canada, where urban colonists lived in constant peril, hostages to their neighbours and often a danger to themselves.

Coal and iron, the grimy progenitors of the industrial revolution, greatly enhanced public safety. Water forced through iron pipes by stream pumps afforded a much more reliable means of fighting the inevitable fires than watercarts. Gas released from coal could also be channeled through iron mains so that brighter streetlights could banish the gloom from public thoroughfares. Each system offered side benefits that were desirable in and of themselves. The mains carrying water to fire hydrants could also bring a continuous supply of fresh water into residential neighbourhoods, thus displacing backyard wells that were rapidly becoming contaminated, and the gas lines could be tapped to brighten shops, commercial establishments, and private parlors as well as streets.

Water and gaslight were symbols of progress, metaphors for life and illumination. Light for those abroad at night banished dread; for those indoors it lengthened the day. Clean water, protection against fire, the safety of well-lit streets: those were the vaulting ambitions and subsequently the hallmarks of bourgeois civilization. Obtaining these amenities was as much a social and political accomplishment as a technological triumph.

By the 1840s the means of improvement were generally known. Famous gas and water undertakings in London, Manchester, Paris, Hanover, Philadelphia, Baltimore, New York, and Boston proclaimed the feasibility and unquestioned benefits of such services. The broad principles of these technologies were readily understood; it remained to transfer them to the British North American colonies. The colonies would have to import the technicians and—just as important—develop the social forms, the institutions and organizations, to operate the technologies. There might be water everywhere, but for social rather than technological reasons, it was not always freely available or fit to drink.

These technologies were inherently collective. Iron pipes welded fiercely independent households into communities of consumers, thereby giving concrete expression to the notion of a distinct public interest that transcended individual interest. The demand for gas and water and the technology to supply them appeared in British North America at a time when capitalist organizations and municipal corporations were both in their infancy. Into this world of rudimentary institutions the first utilities insinuated themselves; once established, they demanded regulation.

———————   Joseph Frobisher, a leading member of Montreal's fur-trading elite, organized the Company of Proprietors of the Montreal Water Works with five associates in 1801. The charter granted him by the government of Lower Canada included the exclusive privilege of piping water into the city for a period of 50 years. The company decided against drawing water from the St. Lawrence—which would have required pumps—preferring the simpler task of conveying the flow from a spring pond down the slopes of Mount Royal through several miles of wooden pipes to two large wooden tanks and a half-dozen pumps located in the principal squares.[1] Thus Montreal obtained water privately from its leading businessmen, using an organizational form with which they were thoroughly familiar as fur traders: a government grant of monopoly rights.

By the early nineteenth century the citizens of some North American cities had concluded that the community had a more direct interest in the provision of urban services than merely licensing private agents. In Philadelphia, for instance, the city council—with strong support from the mercantile community—pledged municipal credit to build an expensive, technologically advanced project to expand the capacity and improve the reliability of their waterworks. The Schuylkill was dammed and the waterpower created was used to pump the water up from the river to a huge reservoir on Fairmount Hill. The ingenious and beautifully landscaped Fairmount waterworks completed in 1823 were soon renowned as one of the greatest technological wonders and civic adornments of the age.[2]

Montreal, much smaller and less advanced, struggled along with the wooden pipes that the Proprietors of the Water Works had laid down. But in time the springs gave out and the pipes began to rot. Nevertheless, in 1816, Thomas Porteous paid out £5,000 pounds for the company's charter and rebuilt the system from scratch; unlike the Philadelphians, he used his own money. After Porteous's death in 1832 the charter was sold to M. J. Hayes for $60,000. Soon the 11 miles of pipes were supplying 250,000 gallons a day. Private enterprise seemed to have met the test successfully, and in 1839 a local chronicler could boast that "Montreal is better supplied with water than any other city on this continent with the exception of Philadelphia."[3]

Private efforts filled the demand for streetlighting in Montreal, too. In 1815, Samuel Dawson and his well-off neighbours banded together to erect 22 oil lamps on St. Paul Street. Not to be outshone, householders on other streets formed similar voluntary associations, and in 1818 the colonial legislature established a night watch whose duties included the trimming and lighting of these lanterns. By that time in Britain and Europe these flickering oil lamps had already begun to give way to brighter coal-gas lamps. The Montreal Gas Light Company, promoted by Albert Furniss in 1836, was the first such enterprise in British North America.

Furniss began operations at a particularly unpropitious time, for in 1837 part of the francophone population of Lower Canada rose in revolt against the oligarchy that controlled the colonial government. British officials responded to the emergency by suspending civil government altogether, including the local government of Montreal, thus removing the most likely consumer of gas for streetlighting. The disorders, which continued for over a year before being brought under control militarily, were attended by a commercial panic that bankrupted many merchants. Not until 1841 was Furniss able to negotiate an agreement with a temporary city council to light the streets, but within a year his 300 streetlamps had become a source of considerable civic pride, like the waterworks.[4]

That gas and water mains made their first appearance in British North America at Montreal is hardly surprising; with 40,000 people by 1840, the city was the undisputed metropolis of the St. Lawrence trading system. From Montreal these technologies were diffused westward to smaller centres; Toronto, just commencing a period of extraordinary growth, depended upon Montrealers for the organization of the company that first supplied water and gas. Local entrepreneurs had tried to raise enough capital for a gas company in the late 1830s but failed. The city, hampered in its efforts to borrow and lacking the technical know-how, gratefully accepted Furniss's offer to build both a gas and a water system. The Toronto Gas Light and Water Company began to light the streets in the summer of 1842 and started pumping water out of Lake Ontario the following year.

Almost at once, however, the first Canadian utility companies became the object of bitter quarreling and widespread public complaint. Inevitably, cases arose where the city would just finish paving a street when a gas or water crew would dig it up again. More serious complaints rained down upon the operators when the water supply failed, or when it proved inadequate to fight large fires, as was the case in 1843 in Toronto. The continued presence of puncheons in Montreal and watercarts in Toronto was a constant reminder of the unreliability and expense of service from the water companies. Even those who could afford to pay criticized the quality of the water. In Montreal, M. J. Hayes freely admitted that his intake, located downstream from the city, was poorly situated. Albert Furniss blamed the problem on the Toronto city council, which, in 1845, located a main sewer outfall next to the waterworks intake.[5]

With gas, the major objections seemed to be the rates and the brazen behavior of Albert Furniss's two companies. Once established in Toronto, for example, Furniss raised the price of streetlighting from $24 to $28 per lamp. When the city council refused to pay the increase, the proprietor shut off the gas and plunged the city into darkness. Vigilant residents in Montreal caught the gas company charging for streetlamps that were not lit, and the indignant city council deducted $1,000 from its bill. Customers also complained of the poor illuminating quality of the gas, but more particularly of its expense. Knowledgeable critics could not understand why Montreal gas prices were between 200 and 300 percent higher than rates in Great Britain. Furniss habitually brushed aside the problems, or blamed them on the city or the ignorance of his critics.[6]

Once gas and water became readily available, the service alone was not enough. Consumers inevitably compared their rates and service with standards prevailing elsewhere and just as inevitably found local conditions unsatisfactory. The rapid growth of the cities placed impossible demands upon the companies to keep pace. During this first phase of gas and water development, a peculiar market situation regulated the industry. Monopoly was counterpoised against monopsony: a single supplier served markets dominated by a large buyer. Expenditures for fire protection, streetlighting, and the illumination of public buildings made the city itself the major customer of both gas and water companies. At the same time the city licensed the companies to use the streets for their distribution systems. In arriving at its streetlighting agreement, the city negotiated on behalf of the community in two ways: it sought the lowest price in the interest of the taxpayers, and it used its bargaining power to minimize rates for other users. Streetlighting contracts, for example, usually specified the maximum rates that might be charged private customers, and domestic water rates were set when the city and the water company came to terms over the price of service to the fire hydrants.

Haggling between a city and its private utilities had serious shortcomings as a regulatory technique. Ultimately, the private companies rather than the public authorities had veto power, as the unrelieved darkness in the streets of Toronto so bluntly revealed in 1845. Moreover, the private companies *were* constrained by their ability to raise money and the public willingness to pay. Bargaining over price alone was unlikely to produce the necessary improvements and major capital expenditures. Two other alternatives suggested themselves: the city might take the unusual step of operating the business itself, or, by licensing new companies, it might try to bring the normal discipline of competition to bear. Eventually, both Montreal and Toronto experimented with public ownership *and* competition, in the process learning of the limitations of both regulatory techniques.

"Fires are great promoters of waterworks," a civil engineer once shrewdly observed. On January 14, 1843, the Montreal *Gazette* replaced its front page advertisements with a large table giving details of the £17,366 ($69,464) lost in 18 major fires the previous year. Two weeks later Alderman Benjamin Holmes urged his fellow councillors to consider the advantages to the health and comfort of the citizens of a municipally owned waterworks, pointing out that the gas and water companies were busy undoing the paving efforts of the municipal corporation. Holmes was no rootless demagogue. An alderman in a city with such a narrow franchise had to be a man of substance. In fact, Holmes was the chief executive officer of the most important bank in the colony, the Bank of Montreal. His voice was that of property and capital.[7]

The owner of the waterworks, M. J. Hayes, could not have been more cooperative. He opened the books of his company to the subcommittee of council struck to examine the matter, frankly admitted the difficulties he had been having, and laid out the major capital projects he considered necessary to upgrade the quality and reliability of the water supply; eventually, he even offered to sell his company to the city for £50,000 ($200,000). In the summer of 1843, Alderman Holmes's subcommittee recommended that the city petition the provincial government for authority to operate a municipal waterworks and that it buy Mr. Hayes's company at the asking price.[8]

When the full city council turned its attention to the committee's report, the fate of the waterworks became bound up in the tangled politics of the post-Rebellion era. The political divisions within the Montreal city council mirrored those of the colonial legislature, partly owing to overlap in personnel. On the 1843 council the Tories or supporters of the Governor, consisting mainly of English-speaking merchants and landlords, held a slight majority. They were opposed by the Reformers, predominantly—although by no means exclusively—French-speaking professionals and men of affairs. In this fiercely divided polity, Benjamin Holmes was something of a renegade, having been elected to the provincial assembly in 1841 as a Tory and to the Montreal city council in 1842 with Reform support. A Reform attack on the water committee report—objecting mainly to the price rather than the principle—momentarily stalled any action, but a few weeks later, under Holmes's gentle prodding, the city council reversed itself by a slim majority and agreed to meet Hayes's terms.[9]

It then fell to Benjamin Holmes, as one of the two Montreal members of the provincial assembly, to shepherd the municipal waterworks bill through the colonial legislature. The statute that received Royal Assent on December 9, 1843, gave the mayor, aldermen, and citizens of Montreal authority to purchase, acquire, and hold the property known as the Montreal Water Works.[10]

Progress toward municipal ownership then stalled for more than a year. In the mid-1840s, elections in Montreal were decided chiefly by organized violence. Armed gangs of nonvoters roamed the streets, intimidating electors and occupying key polls in force to prevent rivals from casting their ballots. On the Tory side, secret societies like the Orangemen, the mounted Cavaliers and the Loyal Patriotic Society (L.P.S.) disported themselves at election time. The French Canadian Reformers, having recently suffered a crushing military defeat in the abortive rebellion, lacked any organized paramilitary force; nevertheless, they were aided and abetted from time to time by Irish canal laborers. The Reform council elected in December of 1843 declined, during its term of office, to carry out the Tory plan to purchase the waterworks.[11]

Even by Montreal standards, 1844 was a remarkably violent year. Troops had to be called out to quell vicious riots set off by a provincial by election in April and a general election in October. These left plenty of scores to be settled during the municipal election called for Monday, December 2. On the Saturday night before the election an L.P.S. militant shot and killed one of the four Irish toughs who had beaten him up. The Irish sought revenge on election day, storming a poll in Queen's ward and killing one of the Cavaliers in the melee. Owing to clash of Orange and Green, Reform voters were effectively excluded from the polls in Queen's, St. Lawrence, and St. Mary's wards. At a cost of two killed and dozens wounded, the Tory faction regained control of the city council. In a matter of weeks, negotiations resumed over the purchase of the waterworks, and by April, 1845, it was firmly under municipal control.[12]

Even though violence had determined the victors, no heads were broken or lives lost over the water question itself. The Tories, in this instance represented by Holmes, argued that the municipal government should use its credit to enhance services to property in the broader interest of promoting economic expansion. As a banker, Holmes must also have seen the issue from another perspective—the growing demand within the rising capitalist economy for secure, interest-bearing securities, which municipalities with their taxing power could supply. The Reformers did not dispute the desirability of improved public services; rather they focused upon the expense and questions of timing. Reformers were more cautious about forging ahead, suspicious of burdening the community with debt, and reluctant to sanction the enlargement of the bureaucracy.

The city pushed the intake farther out into the harbour to obtain cleaner water; new pumps were installed, more pipes laid, and a new reservoir built. Nevertheless, these marginal changes still left the city woefully equipped. Even in neighbourhoods that were connected to the system, pressure and quantity proved to be inadequate. In 1852, as the city council began to address the question of what should be done, two fires in rapid succession leveled more than 1,000 buildings.

The city council commissioned T. C. Keefer, a civil engineer well known in the community, to advise on what kind of waterworks Montreal ought to build. Keefer's report began by noting the obvious difficulties with the existing system: the expense of steam pumps, the frequent breakdowns, and the polluted harbour from which the city drew its water. To overcome these problems, he proposed a radical new design, clearly based upon the model of the Fairmount works in Philadelphia, which would bring fresh water from above the Lachine Rapids to the west of the city, down $4\frac{3}{4}$ miles of aqueduct to a hydraulic pumping station where, in effect, the water would pump itself up to enlarged storage reservoirs on Mount Royal. With characteristic grandiloquence Keefer proclaimed the ingenuity of his scheme: "One of the largest and purest rivers in the world flows at the very feet of your city—affording not only an illimitable supply for consumption but the cheapest power for elevating this supply to the highest parts of City." This would necessarily be a costly undertaking (Keefer estimated £150,000, or $600,000), but the five-million-gallon daily capacity would be sufficient for a city twice the size of Montreal. He closed his brief with an argument keyed to the private calculus of the largely Scots mercantile community. The recent fires had raised the total fire insurance premiums for the city from $100,000 to over $160,000 per annum. A more reliable water supply, he claimed, could reduce those premiums by at least 20 percent.[13]

Initially the city fathers expressed skepticism about Keefer's plan on two grounds: economy and engineering. The sums involved were unprecedented. Nor could the council conceive of a waterworks without steam pumps, and no less than three outside consulting engineers were called in to give their opinions. Two of the three gave Keefer's design their blessing with minor changes. The third, a British expert, insisted that steam pumps would be more reliable and just as cheap. With professional opinion divided the city council nonetheless decided with some trepidation to go ahead with Keefer's scheme in May of 1853.[14]

Toronto, meanwhile, had placed its hopes for a better water supply on competition rather than public ownership. When relations with Albert Furniss soured in the late 1840s, the city council lent its weight to the charter application of a rival company organized by Charles Berczy, the city postmaster and a prominent businessman. Furniss confounded these plans by simply selling out to his supposed competitors. Unfortunately, Berczy defaulted on his interest payments in 1853, and Furniss, the mortgage holder, was reluctantly compelled to repossess the property.[15]

That same year, the Metropolitan Gas and Water Company, the brainchild of two controversial railroad promoters, obtained a charter from the legislature. The appearance of the Metropolitan scheme, coming as it did on the heels of previous disappointments with private competition, split the city council. Furniss offered his waterworks to the city on the same terms he had sold to Berczy, but some members of the council thought the price too high, given the condition of the physical plant and the conduct of the owner. Advocates of the Metropolitan project insisted the city would obtain a first-class water system for little or no capital investment if it simply bought shares in the company or allowed it to collect water rates from all homeowners within its territory. Opponents, completely disillusioned with private enterprise and especially suspicious of the promoters behind the speculative Metropolitan venture, preferred to get on with building a new municipal waterworks. In 1854, with this last group in the ascendancy, the city actually held a competition for the design of an ideal public plant.[16]

Each municipal election altered the balance of power between the various factions. In 1856, for example, the Committee on Fire, Water and Gas recommended construction of a public system, but the full council voted by a narrow margin to deal with the Metropolitan company. The next year the council changed its mind, choosing instead to buy out Furniss and operate a public system. The legislature eventually approved a municipal waterworks for Toronto, but with the proviso that the city not levy a general water tax as long as private companies also continued to operate. Thus, the city was merely given power to become a competing water supplier until such time as it came to terms with the existing companies. Nevertheless, Toronto might well have proceeded with the plan in 1858 but for the withering depression that descended upon the colony and dried up municipal credit.

By default, therefore, Albert Furniss continued to supply Toronto with water for another decade or more. In 1864, 1868, and 1870, the city and the company renegotiated domestic water rates and hydrant charges. The bitterness surrounding those discussions finally drove the city council to reconsider the water question in the early 1870s, when a buoyant economy and a growing market for municipal bonds made radical change feasible. In 1872 new legislation was obtained, the ratepayers gave their approval, and after a good deal of ill-tempered haggling over price with the executors of the Furniss estate, the city at last purchased the waterworks for $220,000 cash.[17]

Toronto would soon discover, like Montreal, that public ownership and even massive investment would not necessarily solve the water problem. The Montreal waterworks had commenced operations in the summer of 1856 with a spectacular display of the capacity and pressure of the new system. City fire companies shot plumes of water over the 110-foot spire of Notre Dame church—as close an identification of faith and fire insurance as could be conjured. But the project had been plagued by cost overruns and miscalculations, and ended up requiring more than twice as much as the $600,000 Keefer had originally estimated. Moreover, the system would not work to capacity at certain times of the year; cold weather and seasonal variations in the flow of the St. Lawrence River greatly affected the efficiency of the machinery. In the dead of winter and in high summer the pumps lacked sufficient power to keep the reservoirs filled, and temporary water shortages ensued. Even after constructing an expensive municipal system, Montreal still had need of its puncheons.[18]

In less than a decade the city was already consuming the five million gallons daily that Keefer's system was theoretically designed to supply. Three years later, amidst acute embarrassment, the water commission installed—temporarily—a supplementary steam pump. But it was abundantly clear that the waterworks needed a major overhaul. In an atmosphere thick with recrimination and innuendo, the city council invited three eminent engineers, T. C. Keefer included, to propose remedies. Keefer thought that relatively minor changes to the intake at Lachine and the installation of new turbines would prove adequate. Walter Shanly, a Canadian, and James B. Francis of Lowell, Massachussets, called for a major widening and realignment of the aqueduct and the addition of permanent steam-pumping capacity at an estimated cost of over $2,000,000. Presented once again with divided professional opinion, the city council leaned toward the majority view but balked at the price. Gradually, however, the water commissioners abandoned Keefer's hydraulic plan. First one, then two additional steam-pumping engines were added, and in the process the canal was turned into an aqueduct. By 1896 more than 65 percent of the 43,000,000 gallons consumed daily was pumped by steam.[19]

The mounting expense and unsatisfactory performance of the Montreal waterworks had an ironic outcome: the reappearance of private ownership. "I mean to say," wrote Thomas F. Miller in 1868, "the lack of water to wash with makes me feel the want of it, and so my reason asserts the scheme of Mr. Keefer as being a failure." Miller and his associates hoped that the hostility toward T. C. Keefer, the water commission, and public ownership, would advance their private scheme to pipe water into the city from works on the Back River. Nothing came of these plans immediately, but later in the 1880s another group of promoters revived the charter of Miller's company and actually negotiated contracts to supply water to the 14 independent municipalities surrounding the city. The Montreal Water and Power Company pumped its water from the St. Lawrence and bought water wholesale from the city—though it frequently refused to pay for it—to supply customers in the suburbs at roughly half the rates prevailing in the city. This thriving private company, which continued to operate into the late 1920s, was an implied rebuke to municipal enterprise and telling evidence of the inability of the city to meet public expectations.[20]

Unhappiness with the new and enlarged municipal system in Toronto also created a glimmering opportunity for hardy entrepreneurs. Dirty tap water drawn from the harbour and frequent, sometimes comic, interruptions occasioned angry complaints.[21] A syndicate consisting of a former mayor, a theatrical city alderman and a Liberal party boss concocted a scheme to bring water into the city from Georgian Bay via Lake Simcoe and a navigable canal. In this way Toronto would simultaneously obtain direct shipping connection with the upper Great Lakes, pure water, and cheap hydraulic power within the city limits where the canal descended into Lake Ontario. Too clever by half, far beyond the financial capacity of the company, and condemned by the quixotic reputation of the principals, the proposal of the "Aqueductors" was ultimately rejected by the city council, though not without a four-year struggle. The scheme was finally laid to rest in 1896 when a distinguished British engineer pronounced it unworkable, and the city council voted instead to upgrade the existing works.[22] An excess of ambition and a shortage of capital thus prevented a private company from capitalizing upon Toronto's water supply problem.

The experience of these two cities showed that there was no necessary progression from private through public ownership to consumer satisfaction. In the matter of water supply, the choice of the regulatory instrument depended upon a shifting perception of available municipal credit, public need, and the willingness of the ratepayers to approve expenditure. Keeping rapidly growing cities supplied with water in the late nineteenth century proved to be technically more difficult and infinitely more expensive than anyone had imagined. Albert Furniss understood: he scrimped along where others failed by resisting pressure to sink too much capital into his system. But need and expectations overwhelmed the early private owners. Then even the municipalities, with their much greater credit and compulsory taxing power, had trouble meeting the demand. Despite efforts that strained the patience and pocketbooks of ratepayers, the poor quality of the water supply in both cities at the turn of the century was still a public scandal.[23]

――――――――― Gaslight was as desirable an amenity to city dwellers in the mid-nineteenth century as a reliable supply of water. "Darkness is the friend of vice," William H. Atherton reminded readers of his chapter on Montreal's municipal services.[24] The efficiency of firing coal in closed retorts to produce gas, which was then stored under pressure, steadily improved, and the gas mantle demonstrated its indisputable superiority over coal-oil lamps or candles. The cities themselves were far and away the largest gas consumers. Councilors used every weapon they could command to procure low-cost streetlighting, including the threat of public ownership. Moreover, the high price of gas ensured that its domestic and commercial customers were almost exclusively drawn from the local elites. Paying to light their shops, offices, and homes gave these people a keen interest in low rates. Thus a monopoly that served an influential few proved as liable to threats of a public takeover as a poor water service, with which many more people had to suffer.

Gas companies proved more resourceful and more recalcitrant than water companies, however, when it came to dealing with public hostility and political pressure. For one thing their proprietors were notably less eager to sell out under duress, once their companies were well established, because they owned something well worth keeping—relatively stable, remunerative businesses that readily multiplied their capital. Thus the resilience of the owners, the availability of substitutes, and a narrow clientele made for a substantially different regulatory equation in the late-nineteenth-century Canadian gas business.

Montreal, where the gas industry began, was also the city where consumer resistance first forced changes in organization. John Mathewson, a businessman and former city councilor, led the assault on Albert Furniss's Montreal Gas Light Company. Armed with statistics and information supplied by a British manufacturer of gas fixtures, Mathewson denounced the extortionate rates charged by the company, accused the management of incompetence, and condemned its arrogant conduct in an attempt to convince the city of the need to construct a gasworks of its own. Impressed by Mathewson's campaign, the city council's Light Committee actually did propose municipal ownership early in April, 1845. But the movement lacked broad ratepayer support, and the idea of a municipal gasworks evaporated.[25]

That left the critics no alternative but to go ahead on their own. Claiming a "public duty" and abjuring all "vindictive feeling," Mathewson invested his promotion with the most exalted public purposes. If these public-spirited individuals were permitted to carry out what Mathewson called "their patriotic designs," gas costs would be reduced from $5.00 per thousand cubic feet (MCF) to $2.50 and street lighting from $24 to $16 per lamp. When Furniss angrily pronounced these rates a fiction, he was read a lesson in public utility economics: "The Montreal Gas Company, like most other persons, do not see that the profits would be greater in the aggregate, by lowering the price, from the increased consumption—it is proved so in every instance in this country,. . . . The apparatus and workmen being more fully employed, the gas is made cheaper."[26]

In 1846, Mathewson and twelve associates supported by the city council petitioned the legislature for a charter to incorporate the consumer-owned New City Gas Company. Furniss, of course, attempted to refute what he considered the irresponsible claims of the promoters and to block their charter. Pathetically, he reminded the legislature that he had persevered in a hard climate with a hazardous enterprise. He had suffered many setbacks and purchased his experience at great expense. A rival company with a small, centrally located plant could skim the cream off the business, leaving him to serve the outlying districts. Would it not be churlish of the government to allow competition now that his company was at long last a going concern? Besides, he argued, Montreal gas was as cheap as any in North America, as the mischievous city council knew. This touching appeal—one that has been sounded by monopolists before and since—failed to move the legislature, which was more impressed with the strong feeling running against Furniss's company.[27]

Thus, the first step away from monopoly toward competition in the gas industry was taken by the joint-stock equivalent of a consumers' cooperative. In actual fact, however, rivalry did not occur. Perhaps by way of compensation the legislature also allowed Furniss to increase the capitalization of his company, and with that bargaining tool in hand he promptly sold out to what he must have considered his foolhardy competitors. The long list of those connected with the new company showed that it had strong support in the city's flourishing Scots merchant community.[28] If the New City Gas Company did cut gas rates as promised in the early 1850s, by mid-decade charges had been restored at close to the old levels. Streetlighting still cost $24, but domestic rates—reflecting the subtle balancing of interests among the shareholders—stood at approximately 70 percent of Furniss's schedule.[29]

Much the same thing happened in Toronto. In 1847 a group of irate customers of the Toronto Gas, Light and Water Company, some of whom had eagerly welcomed Furniss to town only a few years earlier, gathered to organize a competing company. The promoters advertised their proposal as "a mutual company wherein all consumers participate in the surplus profits." To ensure that power within the company would not be dominated by one individual, the draft charter contained restrictions on the numbers of shares owned and votes cast by shareholders. To guarantee low rates, dividends could not rise above 10 percent of the paid-up capital. The city council endorsed the project, and in March, 1848, the Consumers' Gas Company of Toronto obtained its charter. A few months later Albert Furniss sold his Toronto gasworks as well to the Consumers' Gas Company to avoid ruinous competition.[30]

The change in ownership brought a new form of industrial organization to the gas industry in Toronto and Montreal, the quasi-cooperative. In 1850, when the Consumers' Gas Company had 369 customers and over 300 shareholders, the company was in effect customer-owned. This was abundantly clear in the fall of 1848 when a deputation of shareholders demanded that Consumers' Gas honour its pledge to reduce prices.[31] However, as the number of customers increased beyond the circle of shareholders, the new companies began to draw the same criticism as their much-maligned predecessors and had to respond in such a way as to avoid a similar fate.

Consumers' Gas did reduce its domestic rates in January, 1849, and again in the spring of 1851—but not enough to suit some complainants When the directors momentarily hesitated to bring rates down further, uncertain of the increased expenses and reduced profits that might result, the critics sped off to Quebec City—then the capital of the Province of Canada—to incorporate the Metropolitan Water and Gas Company.[32] Their motives may well have included lower gas prices, but they were also intent upon a speculation and hoped to swing civic support and capital behind their venture. At any rate, the promoters were warmly received by the legislators. One influential member, Henry Sherwood, welcomed both the particular application and the principle it represented: "I intend to give the application my support. Competition in this as well as other matters generally is productive of good."[33]

The directors of the Consumers' Gas Company recognized the danger; these were the very tactics they had used to break Albert Furniss's monopoly. Alarmed at the prospect of competition, the company sent Samuel Alcorn, one of its directors, to Quebec City to protect its interests. He persuaded the Private Bills Committee to insert a clause in the charter placing a ceiling of $2.50 per MCF on the rates the company might charge, hoping thereby to wound the promotion if not kill it.[34] The board of Consumers' Gas then swallowed its own apprehensions and cut its rates to $2.50 to forestall the competition.

The financial damage from the gas rate reduction was not nearly as great as had been anticipated—in fact, the number of customers increased almost 45 percent, while revenues rose 35 percent for the year ending September 30, 1854—but profits remained stagnant. Accordingly, the $3.00 rate was restored in 1855, producing a 70 percent jump in gross income while profits more than doubled (see Table 3). The complaints of consumers encouraged the Metropolitan Company promoters to revive their plans in 1857. A local monopoly (as Furniss had already learned) was a constant temptation to potential competitors. O. G. Steele of the Buffalo Gas Company observed to Henry Thompson, General manager of Consumers' Gas, "As for opposition companies we are perpetually threatened with them. . . . We must simply take them as they come and defend ourselves like good Christians against the assaults of the devil." In this case the management of Consumers' contented itself with writing to the English underwriters who dealt in the market for colonial securities to remind them of the danger of challenging a prosperous, well-established company.[35]

Having beaten back two attempts to set up a rival concern, the shareholders of Consumers' Gas could enjoy their monopoly during the prosperous years of the mid-1850s—as did their counterparts in Montreal's New City Gas Company. In the process Consumers' had been subtly transformed from a form of cooperative into a regular profit-maximizing joint-stock corporation. As a monopoly the company had only one source of serious concern: in the words of Steele of Buffalo Gas, "it does seem as if city corporations and gas companies were natural enemies. Certainly, they are almost constantly at war."[36]

In the absence of competition, city councils kept a vigilant if not

TABLE 3

CONSUMERS' GAS COMPANY, TORONTO, 1849–80

Year[a]	Gas Consumers	Street lamps	Gas Production[b]	Net Rate per MCF	Gross Revenues[c]	Net Revenues
1849[d]	317	164	5,774	$5.00[e]	$ 22,546	$ 9,883
1850	369	175	6,546	3.33	20,284	10,702
1851	424	183	7,390	3.33[f]	24,180	11,077
1852	578	196	9,206	3.00	25,238	11,757
1853	641	255	9,868	3.00[g]	28,311	14,104
1854	924	352	13,954	2.50	38,209	15,177
1855	1,119	415	22,000	3.00[h]	57,525	20,445
1856	1,409	484	45,186	3.00	97,352	44,653
1857	1,694	675	65,347	3.00	121,132	43,839
1858	1,796	834	47,848	3.33[i]	119,942	47,511
1859	1,763	964	47,597	3.33	119,709	52,626
1860	1,755	977	42,931	3.33	111,355	53,667
1861	1,657	546	39,661	3.00[j]	103,262	53,957
1862	1,420	546	33,937	2.50[k]	84,435	44,910
1863	1,370	549	31,228	2.50[l]	70,234	37,643
1864	1,265	549	32,440	3.00	79,808	43,239
1865	1,188	549	30,014	3.00	73,870	38,866
1866	1,233	549	27,122	3.00	75,973	38,099
1867	1,250	559	34,330	3.00	83,166	42,741
1868	1,254	572	38,596	3.00	90,875	47,914
1869	1,291	577	39,571	3.00	98,512	54,232
1870	1,403	613	45,548	2.67[m]	108,677	53,632
1871	1,566	650	52,595	2.67	117,040	48,400
1872	1,791	701	60,938	2.50[n]	130,587	47,521
1873	2,050	740	71,838	2.50	156,039	61,061
1874	2,292	990	78,956	2.50	177,680	59,984
1875	2,508	1,151	100,122	2.50	224,329	79,876
1876	2,620	1,562	108,074	2.50	238,989	113,901
1877	2,945	1,803	121,397	2.00[o]	242,694	101,954
1878	3,285	1,975	124,118	2.00	237,279	60,073
1879	3,547	2,057	135,185	1.75[p]	251,597	105,016
1880	3,906	2,136	140,383	1.75	236,888	117,337

Source: *Annual Reports,* Consumers' Gas Company.

[a] Fiscal year ending September 30.

[b] In Mcf.

[c] Includes sales of byproducts like coke and tar.

[d] Covers 15 months from July, 1848.

[e] Cut to $3.33 on Jan. 1 1849.

[f] Cut to $3.00 on April 1, 1851.

[g] Cut to $2.50 on July 1, 1853.

[h] Date of price increase unknown.

[i] Increased to $3.33 on Jan. 1, 1858.

[j] Cut to $3.00 on April 1, 1861.

[k] Cut to $2.50 on July 4, 1862.

[l] Increased to $3.00 in September, 1863.

[m] Cut to $2.67 in April, 1870.

[n] Cut to $2.50 on April 1, 1872.

[o] Cut to $2.25 on Jan. 1, 1877 and to $2.00 on April 1, 1877.

[p] Basic rate cut to $1.75 in October, 1879, and discounts introduced for large consumers.

openly antagonistic watch upon the affairs of their gas companies, particularly whenever the streetlighting contract came up for renewal. The aldermen wanted to drive the hardest possible bargain, while management had to calculate how much the city's large and steady demand for gas was worth. Implicit in such negotiations was the prospect that the city itself might be driven into the role of competitor should an agreement prove impossible. During the 1850s, the legislature of the Province of Canada had also authorized amendments to the Municipal Act, permitting cities and towns to raise money to erect their own gas and waterworks. At that time the existing companies did nothing to oppose the bill openly. At Consumers' Gas, for instance, the directors calculated that the requirement of approval by two-thirds of the ratepayers would render municipal ownership unlikely.[37]

Negotiations in Toronto were complicated by the very serious depression after 1856 which reduced civic revenues so severely that drastic measures had to be taken to cut expenditures. In this time of stress for both company and city, the streetlighting agreement came up for discussion. A great deal of haggling produced a three-year agreement almost halving the number of lamps.[38] Over the next five years gas consumption fell by more than 30 percent, despite another decrease in the price to $2.50 per MCF, and only the most rigid economies managed to keep the company's profits at acceptable levels (see Table 3). Fiscal restraint forced the gas company in Hamilton to sell at a loss to the city in order to keep its business. Thomas Littlehales of the Hamilton Gas Light Company explained the origins of the punitive rate of $15 per lamp that prevailed in his territory:

> Some few years ago the almost bankrupt condition of the city induced the Corporation to abandon gas and light the city lamps with coal oil, and the directors of this company being anxious to meet the Corporation as far as possible offered a price which they knew was unremunerative in order to get the lighting again, but I must tell you that when this contract expires this comp[an]y will not renew it on the same terms.[39]

With the return of better times, the streetlamps winked on again in Toronto one by one. Lower rates and a growing sense of need strengthened civic demand. The endless bickering that went on over streetlighting on moonlit nights further underscored the transition of gas from a luxury to a necessity. E. S. Cathels of the New City Gas Company observed that there were always complaints when moonlit evenings clouded over, particularly "if the newspaper editors happen to find it dark going home, late or early."[40]

Persistent demands for better service, equalled only by the clamour for lower rates, placed the companies in an even more dangerous position. As part of the skirmishing that preceded the 1874 round of streetlighting negotiations in Toronto, for instance, the Fire, Water and Gas Committee tabled a damning indictment of the Consumers' Gas Company. The committee pointed out that there was no other city of the magnitude and importance of Toronto on the continent "at the mercy of a single gas company." Buoyed up by its recent success in taking over the waterworks, the city council then voted to apply for the power to build a publicly owned gasworks.[41]

The city clearly possessed the credit and perhaps the ratepayer support to make good its threat. The directors of the Consumers' Gas Company lost no time in drawing up a counterpetition defending its record. Allegations of narrow self-interest were rejected with the argument that the company was a "consumers'" concern whose dividends had never exceeded 10 percent and whose rates had fallen 50 percent since Albert Furniss's day. Meanwhile, the company had been expanding its works to accommodate a city of 150,000, even though Toronto had just 56,000 inhabitants according to the 1871 census. Neither competition nor municipal ownership would benefit consumers, the company argued. Gas was already cheaper in Toronto than in those cities where private competition prevailed. As for the purported benefits of public ownership on the model of the waterworks, there was no compelling parallel, given that

> there is a very plain and obvious distinction between the supply of water and that of gas, the one being an article of necessity and the other of comparative luxury, and that regulations which could properly be made and justified on sanitary and other grounds respecting a water supply are not applicable to the supply of gas, and that rates which could properly be imposed and willingly paid by all classes of the community for the former would, if imposed for the latter, be regarded as a grievous burden by those who are not gas customers and who form a large portion of the ratepayers of the city.[42]

There the jousting ended. Instead of pressing ahead, the city withdrew its legislation and triumphantly accepted a ten-year contract containing considerable reduction in streetlighting costs. Despite the municipal bluster and the company's apparent submission, in truth Toronto settled for no more than the going rate in other large cities. Thomas Littlehales congratulated Henry Thompson, general manager of Consumers' Gas, on his coup: it was, he wrote, "a very good price and I only hope we may be able to get as much out of the Corporation of Hamilton."[43]

In 1876 another rival, the People's Gas Company, sprang up in Toronto. Consumers' Gas felt confident that the private opposition could be contained, but it took the threat of municipal competition more seriously. The company retained a well-connected young lawyer to lobby the provincial government for legislation preventing the breakup and piecemeal purchase of existing companies by municipalities. The Premier and the Attorney General of Ontario in due course granted the request that cities be required to buy out the total assets, if any, of companies such as Consumers'. In this way the gas company ensured that should it encounter an irresistible municipal takeover drive, it would be resolved on favourable terms. But to avert criticism of these flanking tactics, to curry favour with the city council, and to make headway more difficult for the People's Gas promoters, the company reduced its rates to $2.25 on January 1, 1877, and then to $2.00 in April.[44]

Customers frequently objected that they were not getting the amount of gas they paid for, or that the gas delivered was of inferior quality. During the early years these complaints were well justified. The brightness of the lights depended upon the quality of the coal used to manufacture the gas and upon the diligence of management. The first gas meters often failed, usually in winter, though that worked to the advantage of the customer. By the 1860s, however, better gas meters were available, which customers rented from the gas company. But who could tell that the company's meters were accurate? Customers harbored the darkest suspicions, sustained by the always unexpected quarterly bills and just enough incidents and accidents to justify skepticism.[45] To head off these disagreements over the quantity and quality of gas delivered to the consumer, the gas industry proposed limited regulation.

As early as 1860 the management of Consumers' Gas had concluded that it was "desirable that a good bill appointing a meter inspector should be passed, as there appeared to be a great feeling of dissatisfaction amongst gas consumers everywhere as to the correctness of their meters." Despite considerable lobbying, renewed in both 1861 and 1862, no measure of this kind was passed into law at that time.[46] When the new federal government took its first steps to specify a uniform system of weights and measures for Canada in 1873, however, the Consumers' Gas Company saw a chance to insert provisions covering the measurement and the illuminating power of gas. Not only did management have "no objection" to the appointment of federal gas inspectors, but "the Directors of this Company are fully of the opinion that the appointment of such officials will be beneficial rather than injurious to the interests of the Companies and will do much towards satisfying the public mind with regard to the quality of the gas and the accuracy of the meters." Consumers' Gas organized a delegation of executives to lobby for the bill in Ottawa and to see that no clauses "objectionable" to the industry were included. The resulting enactment seems to have provided satisfactory protection against angry consumers and municipal politicians.[47]

In 1873, Professor Thaddeus S. C. Lowe demonstrated a process in the United States that greatly reduced the cost of manufacturing gas from coal. This "carburetted water gas" had several advantages: caloric values could be adjusted, the coke byproducts could be sold or used to heat the retorts, and the equipment required fewer inputs and less labour.[48] Consumers' Gas acquired rights to the Lowe process in 1879, but it took some time for the operating staff to perfect the technique. Rates were lowered to ease the introduction of the new water gas; nevertheless, the many production difficulties aroused a storm of protests—some abusive, some exasperated, some threatening, and some mildly humorous. "Permit a long-suffering consumer of the material which you supply for the purpose of making darkness visible to remonstrate," wrote one J. Oiler. "You have been graciously pleased to promise us a reduction in price, but what with the extra quantity which I am obliged to use, and the cost which I foresee I must soon incur of spectacles (for the light is most ruinous to my eyes), I do not see much prospect of economizing. . . . If the present stuff is the result of some new experiment, pray return to the old paths and old prices."[49]

Managers of gas companies in the region watched the trials of water gas with sympathetic interest. By February of 1880 the Toronto company seemed to have the new system working properly, and the reduction in costs allowed the company to slash rates. In 1875 over $80,000 worth of coal had been required to make gas that sold for $197,000, whereas in 1880—even though gas rates had been lowered 30 percent in the interim—Consumers' Gas was able to produce gas that retailed at $227,000 from materials that cost only $51,000.[50]

As Table 3 shows, the demand for gas in Toronto had risen steadily during the 1850s, particularly after 1853. However, the long depression following the panic of 1857 reduced consumption by nearly 60 percent from the peak. The city fixed the number of streetlamps at around 550 for eight years as an economy measure; domestic customers disconnected or cut back sharply on the amount of gas used; and in the midst of this dramatic collapse of demand, the company lost one of its larger customers—the colonial government, which moved out of the city. Business began to pick up once again in 1867 when the city again became provincial capital, and within a few years production surpassed the predepression peak as the city relit the streetlamps and added new ones, as old customers resumed service and new ones signed up. During a period of rising incomes, streetlighting and house lighting were affordable. The year 1879 marked the beginning of a transition period in both prices and technology, during which the company experienced a major reduction in expenses as a result of the falling cost of coal and the introduction of the Lowe process requiring less coal (see Tables 3 and 4).

During the eight years of expansion in the 1850s, the company came very close to maximizing output and net revenue. It did not, however, always earn a 10 percent dividend on its capitalization, and to that end it increased its prices in 1858. In normal circumstances this might have been a terrible mistake, but in the ensuing depression the demand curve shifted so sharply that Consumers' Gas was disproportionately rewarded for each MCF *less* it produced. During the first phase of the collapse, costs fell more rapidly than income. In 1865, for example, the company made more money per MCF producing less gas than it did in 1860. When demand sud-

TABLE 4
CONSUMERS' GAS COMPANY, TORONTO, 1849–80

Year	Average Cost per MCF	Average Revenue per MCF	Average Return per MCF	Book Value of Assets	% Return on Assets[a]
1849	$2.19	$3.90	$1.71	$ 127,823	7.7%
1850	1.46	3.10	1.64	131,437	8.1
1851	1.77	3.27	1.50	141.706	7.8
1852	1.46	2.74	1.28	164,879	7.1
1853	1.44	2.87	1.43	206,044	6.8
1854	1.65	2.74	1.09	242,298	6.3
1855	1.69	2.61	0.92	382,082	5.4
1856	1.17	2.15	0.98	488,468	9.1
1857	1.18	1.85	0.67	570,871	7.7
1858	1.51	2.51	1.00	597,528	8.0
1859	1.41	2.52	1.11	578,299	9.1
1860	1.34	2.59	1.25	565,818	9.5
1861	1.24	2.60	1.36	560,352	9.6
1862	1.19	2.49	1.30	533,195	8.3
1863	1.04	2.25	1.21	552,537	6.8
1864	1.13	2.46	1.33	558,456	7.7
1865	1.17	2.46	1.29	528,735	7.4
1866	1.40	2.80	1.40	515,622	7.4
1867	1.18	2.42	1.24	520,179	8.2
1868	1.11	2.35	1.24	518,950	9.2
1869	1.12	2.48	1.36	507,619	10.7
1870	1.21	2.39	1.18	521,743	10.3
1871	1.31	2.23	0.92	505,307	9.6
1872	1.36	2.14	0.78	498,096	9.5
1873	1.32	2.17	0.85	564,011	10.8
1874	1.49	2.25	0.76	712,009	8.4
1875	1.44	2.24	0.80	731,493	10.9
1876	1.16	2.21	1.05	715,249	15.9
1877	1.16	2.00	0.84	739,936	13.8
1878	1.43	1.91	0.48	722,092	8.3
1879	1.08	1.86	0.78	762,679	13.8
1880	0.85	1.69	0.84	985,596	11.9
1881	n.a.	n.a.	n.a.	n.a.	n.a.
1882	0.83	1.51	0.68	762,679	10.8
1883	0.86	1.54	0.68	985,596	11.2
1884	0.85	1.45	0.60	1,481,724	9.8
1885	0.80	1.37	0.57	1,466,291	10.7
1886	0.80	1.16	0.36	1,514,309	7.2
1887	0.68	1.14	0.46	1,771,920	9.3
1888	0.74	1.13	0.39	2,204,862	7.3
1889	0.68	1.15	0.47	2,481,893	8.7
1890	0.65	1.06	0.41	2,607,618	8.1

Source: *Annual Reports,* Consumers' Gas Company.
[a] Net revenues as % of book value.

denly improved in the 1870s, it would seem that Consumers' Gas continued to charge higher prices than necessary to maintain efficient markets. Significantly, it was during this period that criticism of the gas company from both municipal authorities and individual consumers intensified alarmingly. As far as price was concerned, the complaints appear to have been fully justified. The company abused its monopoly position to restrict consumption. The data for the period 1877 to 1880 probably reflect the problems associated with the introduction of the new technology. But as costs fell, the company not only lowered its rates 30 percent but also eliminated meter rental charges and introduced discounts for large consumers.

From the point of view of the shareholders, companies like Consumers' Gas performed admirably, returning a regular 8 to 10 percent dividend annually in good times and bad. They generated sufficient income to pay for a good deal of their own expansion and to raise money in the financial markets. By the late 1860s, for instance, Consumers' Gas shares traded at a premium. However, gas markets characterized by monopoly on the one side and monopsony on the other did not perform efficiently, if the Consumers' Gas record is anything to go by. Despite the bulldog tenacity of city council negotiating committees, domestic prices were not driven down as rapidly as they could have been, and the companies captured unwarranted rents.

Thus by the 1880s the existing form of regulation was not working and was seen not to be working. Public criticism focused upon the fact that gas companies earned high profits from selling poor-quality gas at prices that seemed too high. City councils, as in the case of Toronto, fought efforts by the company to tuck away in reserve accounts income earned in addition to the 10 percent dividend and began to think seriously once again about taking over the gas business in the public interest. Rival private promoters lurked just offstage. Gas companies that might at one time have been quasi-cooperative ventures were, by the 1870s, plainly the property of a small elite. A vague conviction had begun to form that something would have to be done to bring the gas monopoly to heel. The government of the province of Ontario, which had formerly been most sympathetic to Consumers' Gas and other companies like it, began to change its tune. In 1880 a cabinet minister confidentially warned Consumers' Gas that if the quality and price of its product did not improve, the government would take steps to make its own gas or charter competition. "Some members would also appear to think it necessary that some interference on behalf of the public is called for," Arthur S. Hardy threatened.[51] In this dangerous situation the private companies scrambled to outflank public criticism by means of further rate reductions.

By the turn of the century most Canadian cities owned and operated their own waterworks and received gas service from a private company, usually a monopoly. The private water company in Halifax, which started up in 1848, was taken over and enlarged by the city in 1861. The local custom of letting taps run all winter to keep them from freezing had complicated the task of the private company, and even after several expansion programs the city experienced some difficulty in keeping pace with demand. Nevertheless, municipal management of the Halifax waterworks proceeded uneventfully, marked only by the occasional debenture bylaw, until eels began slithering out of the taps in 1905. Apparently the creatures had managed to hurl themselves up and over the intake screens into the reservoirs. With commendable understatement and barely concealed pride, the city engineer reported: "All the eels taken out were large and a great many were washed out through the hydrants, numbers of them being caught in the street sprinkling carts."[52]

Few cities could record such an arresting form of water contamination as eels wriggling in the gutters, but most relived the more mundane experience of disappointment with private ownership leading to municipal control followed by major capital expansion. Usually a fear of fire prompted the municipal initiative—Winnipeg serves as a notable example[53]—and only much later did public health concerns bring about a concerted effort to improve water quality. As late as the 1880s, for instance, Winnipeg, Calgary, and Vancouver all negotiated contracts with private companies mainly because these recently organized municipalities lacked the financial and technical capacity to operate waterworks themselves. In doing so, they attempted to take into account the experience of their eastern Canadian forerunners. Summing up what he had learned after 30 years, T. C. Keefer advised the city of Calgary in 1888 to provide for the recapture of the system within eight years.[54] In each of the three cases the company received a short franchise that would allow the cities to reacquire the works at a price to be settled by arbitration.

Private ownership proved even less satisfactory in the West than the East. Vancouver briefly toyed with the idea of helping to finance a competitive water company along the lines of the Metropolitan company in Toronto.[55] But after a great deal of petty wrangling, Vancouver bought out its waterworks in 1892; Winnipeg took control in 1898, and Calgary a year later. In all cases public ownership was a vehicle for reconstruction and enlargement of the systems, but the change in ownership and more aggressive expansion plans did not necessarily produce pure water or public satisfaction. In Winnipeg, for example, the inadequacy of immediate water supplies eventually led the city and eight surrounding suburban municipalities to organize themselves into a Greater Winnipeg Water District in 1912 to bring clean water into the city through an aqueduct from the Lake of the Woods region.[56]

Some cities did not go through the private phase of water development at all. In 1845, Quebec City advertised for tenders from private capitalists to supply the city with water; when none were forthcoming, the city had no choice but to proceed with a municipal system. When the Hamilton city council examined the water supply problem in the mid-1850s, no private company had come forward to ask for a franchise; therefore, with a clear field to itself, the city built a pumping system designed by T. C. Keefer—as did the city of Ottawa.[57] In the West, Regina had a municipal system from the very beginning.[58]

In the gas distribution business, there was far less local variation amongst Canada's larger cities. In 1843 a representative sampling of the Halifax commercial elite organized the Halifax Gas Light Company; it flourished for the next forty years, regularly paying its shareholders an 8 percent dividend.[59] Similar local monopolies were formed in St. John, Quebec City, Ottawa, Kingston, Hamilton, London, Winnipeg, and Vancouver as in most American cities. As a rule these companies were organized and owned by members of the local business establishment. In the later 1890s some of these concerns were bought out by metropolitan financiers, who folded the gas utilities into a street railway or electric lighting operation. Gas development lagged in Calgary and Regina, as well as other prairie cities. When gas did make an appearance in the West, electricity already dominated the lighting market and the locally abundant natural gas was used mainly for heating and cooking.[60]

By the turn of the century, water supply had ceased to be a capitalist undertaking in most Canadian cities. One by one, municipal governments purchased or built waterworks and found a ready market for the debentures issued to finance these socialized capital projects. To that extent, therefore, water supply passed from private ownership to private investment secured by public credit. Gas companies, by virtue of the smaller amount of capital required (gas could be produced and distributed more cheaply than a fluid)[61] and the higher charges that could be levied on a comparatively small number of users—a significant proportion of whom were shareholders—tended to produce an attractive rate of return from the very beginning. Steady profitability, the discretionary nature of consumption, and the relative penury of overburdened municipal governments insulated these gas monopolies against public ownership. The companies (and their customers, too) acquired a further layer of protection from federal regulation of gas-measuring devices and lighting quality—an early intrusion by the federal government into the realm of business regulation that was promoted and eagerly welcomed by the gas industry itself.

Nevertheless, Joseph Chamberlain had made a name for himself in the 1870s as mayor of Birmingham, England by taking over that city's two gas companies and operating a profitable public enterprise. The city of Philadelphia remained a notable beacon of public gas ownership in the United States. And the dramatic amalgamation of seven rival New York City gas companies into one huge combine again called attention to the dangers of unregulated private monopoly. Canada's gas monopolists, hearing the mounting clamour in the 1880s and recalling the fate of the water companies, came to realize that if they hoped to hang on to their property against this tide of history, they would have to submit to some further measure of public control.

Transportation and Its Discontents

As the mid-nineteenth-century city spread into the surrounding countryside, pushed from within by a growing population and drawn outward by the taste for space, nature, privacy and status which rising personal incomes allowed, the horse-drawn tram gradually insinuated itself into an ever more prominent place in the lives of a dispersed citizenry.[1] This new freedom of an enlarged city was purchased at the expense of a growing reliance upon a technology that lurched forward according to its own inherent logic. The streetcar permitted the city to burst its spatial bonds but also imposed a disturbing new order upon all those who came in contact with it.

Everyone wanted service in comfort, with unlimited capacity, at all times (though there was some question about Sundays), in every direction, at minimal fares. Owners of tramways, whatever their good intentions, quickly learned that they could not be all things to all potential customers and hope to survive. Indeed, the limits of the possible fell woefully short of public expectations. The street railway, more particularly the street railway *company,* had imperatives of its own. The margin between success and failure, profit and loss, especially during the early years, was extremely narrow. Dependence upon this new technology was further complicated by its control through that most suspect of economic institutions, a private monopoly. People either paid their five cents and took what was offered, or they walked. And throughout the last half of the nineteenth century, it must be said, the majority chose to walk.

Citizens who depended upon the trams, as well as those who were denied service, built up a powerful store of grievances on the basis of daily personal experience. The very act of turning street railways into profitable enterprises also turned their patrons and employees against them. City councils, which had licensed the tramway companies in the first place, were invariably compelled to mediate between the various interests contending on city streets: passengers, shareholders, drivers, conductors, teamsters, carters, pedestrians, suburbanites, merchants, ratepayers—and last, but by no means least, the horses. The successful conversion of public transportation into profitable business eventually precipitated a revolt during the 1880s, first by street railway workers and then by city councilors. This outbreak coincided with a general upsurge in labour militancy, a weakening of monopoly power as the original franchises approached their termination dates, and a broadening of the social base and institutional responsibility of the municipal corporation.

The street car made a less than triumphal entry into Canada's two largest cities, despite extremely favourable advance publicity. When promoters appeared around 1860, they were not welcomed with open arms. In both Toronto and Montreal, the street railway had to overcome two obstacles before it could be put into service: the hostility of vested interests and the wariness of municipal politicians. Neither proved an insuperable barrier, but together they held up the horsecars for more than a year.

Almost simultaneously the city councils of Montreal and Toronto became embroiled in debate over street railways, as the former got down to the business of writing precise terms and conditions for a franchise and the latter ruminated upon the propriety of granting a contract. In the ensuing struggles, which reached new heights of vituperation even by nineteenth-century standards, virtually identical factions and arguments surfaced in both cities.[2] Violent disagreement arose from the fact that street railways divided both city councils into three main groups: the implacable foes, the impatient boosters, and a mediating majority of cautious negotiators.

The interests most threatened by the new technology—the carters, cabmen, omnibus proprietors, and teamsters, who would have to share the streets and compete for fares with the streetcars—were well represented on both councils. The veiled opposition of this group frayed tempers and prolonged discussion beyond endurance. The evident popularity of streetcars and their demonstrable utility precluded a frontal attack. Instead, the opponents struck from cover: they complained about congestion that streetcars would only aggravate; they became extremely solicitous of the views of property owners on the streets the tracks would traverse; they questioned the city's ability to keep its streets adequately paved; they warned ominously that taxes would have to be raised to compensate for revenues lost as householders fled beyond the city limits with the aid of the street railway. At key moments they withheld the required quorum; they insisted upon impossible terms, filibustered, and embarrassed their opponents by revealing the favours received by street railroad enthusiasts on council. Only occasionally were their underlying fears openly expressed. Alderman Carruthers, a Toronto carter, lost his patience during a particularly heated exchange and blurted that "he would be one to head a body of citizens to tear up the rails as they were laid down. . . . He had paid his taxes for twenty years, and he would allow no man to tear up the streets and lay down rails."[3]

Councillor Jodoin in Montreal expressed the boosters' response to these critics who argued that the new technology would ruin the carters and carriage makers: "Were all the clamour raised against every improvement listened to," he claimed, "we would be existing in the primitive ways of the Feejees and other benighted mortals"; the caterwauling of vested interests should not be allowed to impede progress. Enthusiasts like Councillors Jodoin and Bernard in Montreal and Aldermen Baxter and McMurrich in Toronto deplored the long-winded debates, the solemn investigations, the grudging tone and glacial pace. The promoters, after all, were prepared to shoulder all of the risks. Why not press ahead as quickly and with as few strings attached as possible in order that the citizens might immediately enjoy the inestimable benefits of improved transportation?[4]

Nonetheless, the majority on both councils demurred. The Montreal city council spent the spring and summer of 1860 composing a draft contract and then debated it for over a month. Toronto moved with even greater deliberation; Mayor Adam Wilson believed that the council was being asked for a valuable privilege, that it was dutybound to negotiate a comprehensive agreement protecting the interests of all citizens, and that it should exact a handsome license fee in the process. Above all, he and others argued, the city should wait, study the question in detail, correspond with other cities, and clear up the legal confusion before proceeding. The Toronto city council backed him in October, 1860.[5]

The *Toronto Globe* and others caught up in the street railway excitement could only mutter furiously, question the integrity of those involved, and retreat to the high ground that improved transportation was merely a matter of time. But the decision taken by the Toronto city council was prompted by more than the footdragging of disgruntled interests. After all, street railways did transfer wealth from one group of citizens to another through a public franchise; they did pose questions of law, public safety, and regulatory responsibility.

It is possible to detect the emergence of a new notion of public interest in these animated discussions, a concept whose appearance marked the transformation of Montreal and Toronto from towns into cities. Proposals were no longer acceptable simply on their own terms but had to be weighed against the general good. In this process, of course, the painful relations with the gas and water companies had been a continuing school of what might be called civic sensibility. However much this middle group of councillors wanted the new technology, they wanted it on terms they deemed favourable to the city as a whole. Toronto and Montreal were now seen as a collection of interests held together by a larger public interest, which the municipal corporation articulated and protected. This was most certainly a classbound view, but it was more than mere personal calculus, and for those not directly affected, a community interest was a salient consideration.[6] It remained to give this abstract notion concrete expression in the precise language of a contract. Here the city officials entered the imperfect world of bargaining, compromise, and making do with the best that could be obtained under the circumstances.

The two bylaws passed by Montreal in September, 1860, and in Toronto the following March bore a striking resemblance. Each contract granted the franchise to certain individuals (Alexander Easton in Toronto; William Molson, John Ostell, Thomas Ryan, William Dow, et al. in Montreal), specified the streets to be used, established deadlines for completion, required approval of plans before construction and supervision of work by the city surveyor. Each insisted that the company pave and maintain the street between and on either side of its tracks, use flat rails installed at street level, and undergo inspection by city officials before commencing business. Each council imposed a time limit on the franchise: 40 years in Montreal and 30 in Toronto. At the end of 20 years, the Montreal city council had the option of recovering the road from its owners at a price to be arbitrated plus a 10 percent premium, an option that would recur every five years thereafter. The Toronto contract would expire at the end of 30 years and be automatically renewed if the option were not exercised; a municipal purchase would not involve payments over and above the value established by arbitration. During the debate in Montreal, however, an amendment to prohibit Sunday running was defeated 15 to 6, whereas in Toronto a clause declaring "no cars shall run on Sunday" carried unanimously.[7] Apart from this militant sabbatarianism—a cultural difference that distinguished Protestant, anglophone Toronto from an increasingly Catholic, French Canadian Montreal—the terms of the two street railway bylaws were essentially the same.

Alexander Easton, who had just finished a similar job in Milwaukee, set to work immediately grading and laying track down Yonge Street, Toronto's central artery. The businessmen and industrialists behind the Montreal City Passenger Railway Company proceeded at a more stately pace. Early in the summer of 1861 they opened a stock subscription book (3,000 shares at $50, half payable in five monthly calls); when enough capital had been pledged, they went looking for someone who would build them a railway. The enterprising Easton came down from Toronto in the fall, and after a certain amount of haggling he contracted to build and equip a six-mile line for $79,166, half in cash and half in fully paid up stock.[8]

In a furious summer of activity, Easton managed to tamp down enough track in Toronto to hold a grand opening on September 10, 1861— a somewhat premature celebration, as it turned out, marred by derailments but marked nonetheless by good humor and extravagant congratulations all around.[9] Amazingly, the Montreal line was declared fit for use on November 26, 1861. At noon under grey skies, four cars loaded down with civic dignitaries, shareholders, and hangers-on traversed the city to the delight of thousands of gaping spectators, then returned to the stables, where Alexander Easton invited his guests to christen the enterprise by sprinkling the track with champagne. Newspapers commented on the ease with which the cars negotiated the slushy, crowded streets. Only the Montreal *Witness* chose to rain on the parade with a brief notice that concluded: "Many persons have remarked that the horses appear to be too hard worked."[10]

The Montreal street railway flourished. In 1862, 1863, and 1864 the directors were able to pass a 12 percent dividend after paying expenses, allowing for depreciation, and even setting aside a small sum in a reserve account. By the end of 1864 the company was carrying almost a million and a half passengers annually on road, track, and equipment valued at $230,000.[11] In Montreal at least—less so in Toronto—the street railway era got off to an auspicious beginning.

First impressions proved quite misleading: street railways did not automatically disgorge satisfied riders one end and put out profits at the other. Even before the last rails had been laid, both companies began to experience wrenching financial difficulties. In 1865 the Montreal City Passenger Railway Company omitted its dividend, and by the end of the decade the Toronto Street Railway Company was in receivership. As proprietors scrambled to regain control over enterprises that seemed to be slipping towards bankruptcy, the ruthless retrenchment they instituted naturally alienated their employees, turned that initial fund of public goodwill to anger, and wounded the pride of the city councils.

The travails of management do not usually receive much attention from academic historians. The residual influence of the muckrakers and progressives and the recent ascendancy of working-class historians have cast a veil of indifference or disdain over such subjects. But these bourgeois struggles were important nonetheless and need to be understood, if for no other reason than that taken collectively they represented challenges met and, for better or for worse, a new world made.

The problem in Montreal was very simple: too much track and not enough business. Under the terms of its agreement with the city, the street railway constructed another six miles of line in the north end during 1864, almost doubling its size but increasing its earnings only marginally. More men, cars, and horses and more miles of track requiring maintenance ate into an only slightly higher gross, which of course drastically reduced net income. Between 1864 and 1865, expenses as a proportion of income rose from 62 to 80 percent. The company had almost expanded itself into extinction.

Angry stockholders, expecting the customary 12 percent dividend, demanded an explanation. An embarrassed management tried to explain without revealing the grim particulars. The simple truth, the newly elected president confided to his board early in 1866, was that all but one of the company's lines were losing money, but for political reasons—namely, the threat of losing the franchise if it failed to operate the routes specified in the bylaw—the company could not contemplate abandoning tracks.[12] Still, there was hope, President Charles Geddes told the sixth annual meeting of shareholders in November, 1866:

> A new undertaking of this kind was naturally subject to many drawbacks and disappointments, which were not foreseen and guarded against by the projectors of the Company or previous Boards of Directors. For instance, sufficient allowance was not made for the great length and severity of our winters; had this been duly appreciated it is certain that some of the lines now built, portions of which scarcely pay their expenses even in summer, would not have been built or contemplated for many years to come; but nevertheless, as already stated, your Directors are now hopeful that the worst period of the Company's career is passed, and that a fair share of prosperity may be expected for the future as it is manifest that the public require the great accommodation furnished by the cars, and will doubtless patronize them more and more as well from habit as from the increase of the population.[13]

If the company could economize, hang on, and hope for the best, it would be rescued by the eventual growth of the city. *La survivance,* however, would require a major transformation of the board from a figurehead group to an effective working body.

The men who had organized the Montreal City Passenger Railway Company were not primarily, or even secondarily, interested in street railways. They were brewers, manufacturers, bankers, and wholesalers with wide-ranging interests in shipping, industrial, and financial institutions.[14] Men like these had been needed at the beginning, of course, to wheedle the franchise, to steer the necessary legislation through the city council and the legislature, and above all to supply the confidence needed to attract capital. As the venture got off the ground, they dropped off the board one by one, pleading the press of other business and selling their shares for a modest profit. By the time of the shareholders' uprising in November, 1865, the last of the original directors had just assumed the presidency; he was unceremoniously kicked out. Charles Geddes, the new president, and the four men elected to the board with him all had significant investments at risk and were obviously prepared to devote a great deal of time and energy to company business. All became long-serving directors.

The board controlled the company through two principal officers: a secretary, who prepared monthly cash flow data, handled the money, and looked after corporate communications; and a superintendent, who actually ran the railroad. The division of labour and hierarchical relationship between the two was never very clear and caused a certain amount of needless bickering. The superintendent, by virtue of his greater responsibilities, eventually emerged as the chief executive officer, but the board dominated activity so thoroughly that both officers were more or less equally subordinate. The superintendent operated though foremen who headed functionally differentiated units of conductors and drivers, stablemen, maintenance workers and repairmen, carpenters and construction crews. In addition, he personally supervised every aspect of day-to-day activity from the printing of tickets, scheduling, buying horses and equipment, hiring and firing men to the letting of the stable-cleaning contract. The directors scrutinized his every move at its regular Friday meetings and reviewed every policy decision down to and including the price to be paid for oats.

The street railway operated more like a large partnership than a modern corporation, and in that respect it probably resembled most of the incorporated businesses in Montreal at the time. For a small, single-purpose business, the system was sufficient and reasonably efficient. It did at least have the virtue of placing decision-making in the hands of those with the most at stake, which was commendable as long as those people were conscientious and competent.

Thus in 1865 the new board of directors, hovering over a harried superintendent, set out to restore the fortunes of the City Passenger Railway Company. Committees were struck to examine the causes of "the present unsatisfactory conditions of the company's performance compared with past years," to treat with the city over hours of running and service on certain routes, and to investigate all possible economies.[15] All accounts were gone over, every single employee had his status and wages reviewed, new banking arrangements were settled, and certain tasks—such as harness repairs—were contracted out. Some things, however, could not be tampered with. The old board, in attempting to economize on the care of the horses had once cut back rations with disastrous results. Horses were capital, after all, and had to be well fed and properly cared for. It was false economy as well as bad public relations (people wrote letters to the newspapers about the thin and overworked animals) to tamper with the health and appearance of the horses.[16]

That meant the directors had to look elsewhere to effect economies. Dividends were halted for a year and a half. Most of the free passes normally handed out to helpful politicians, newspapermen, and other fixers were revoked—exceptions being made for the mayor, city clerk, city surveyor, and the chief of police. Extensions to the physical plant were cancelled; service was drastically reduced on underutilized portions of the system; a moratorium was declared on all but absolutely essential repairs and paving.[17]

Not surprisingly, the wage bill, the most important variable cost, came in for the deepest cuts. Wages represented the company's largest single outlay, accounting for 46 percent of all expenses before 1866. At the height of company optimism in 1864, the board had adopted a daily pay schedule linked to seniority in order to encourage "long and faithful service" by its conductors and drivers. A year later these increases were withdrawn and wages reduced. Then in May, 1866, the company imposed different pay scales for each route depending upon the volume of traffic. At first large numbers of men were simply laid off in winter; later, everyone was kept on but at reduced wages. When business picked up in the late 1860s, the company more readily gave in to pressure for increases from the conductors, drivers, stablemen, and carpenters, but by the mid-1870s street railway wages still stood at roughly the same levels as a decade earlier.[18]

The men who remained on the company payroll were set to work in a progressively more disciplined, more closely supervised fashion. Strict operating procedures were laid down, codified in printed rule books, and enforced with fines and suspensions. The company retained detectives to spy on employees, warn of imminent strikes, and provide the names of the ringleaders. For routine violations of company rules, the directors could rely upon passengers' complaints. Inspectors began recording the arrival and departure times of cars on each line to secure obedience to the prearranged schedule; no longer could conductors keep cars waiting to allow someone to dash into a shop, or linger for regulars who might be late. In 1866, with several brewers present, the directors had resolved "that in future none but men of total abstinence habits (teetotallers) should be employed as conductors on the cars,"[19] Nonetheless, the minute books of the company are dotted with instances of dismissals for intoxication on the job. Peculation, something the board worried about a good deal, was much less of a problem. (It should be added that insobriety and dishonesty infected the ranks of management as well. In 1868 the company secretary was seen drunk in the afternoon just before he disappeared with $286.65 from the cash box.)[20] As befitted a more regimented troop of employees, conductors and drivers were required to wear distinctive caps in the 1870s (the men supplying the caps and the company the red bands for them); later they wore uniforms and badges.

Regular layoffs and wage reductions, a steady tightening of managerial control of the workplace, and frequent summary dismissals naturally provoked anger, open defiance (drinking on the job), little acts of rebellion, passive resistance, and strikes. Although the workers were not organized into formal unions, the camaraderie of the stables and the depots supplied the ambiance necessary for collective action when company edicts became intolerable or when market conditions shifted in labour's favour. The stablehands responded to the first round of wage cuts by going out on strike in May of 1866, and the car drivers joined them. On this occasion chief of police F. L. Penton, ex-superintendent of the City Passenger Railway, urged the company to resist; he then marched down to the depot along with the president to harangue the workers in a symbolic association of police and corporate power that effectively broke the strike.[21] In the spring of 1873, with good weather and better business in the offing, the feisty stablemen and drivers (the lowest paid workers) went out again demanding wage increases. In a tighter labour market and amidst hopes of a really profitable season, the company quickly agreed to certain concessions. But when the higher-paid conductors asked for a raise soon afterward, the board turned them down flat.[22]

Union activity joined theft, drunkenness, and insubordination as grounds for dismissal. A threatened strike in 1880, for example, fizzled out when the company fired the organizers. With the exception of the 1873 strike, these uprisings usually failed in their objective and normally cost participants their jobs. Interruptions of service were brief and tended to go unnoticed in the press.[23] The Montreal labour market overflowed with unskilled workers and boys off the farm who knew how to look after horses and were prepared to accept the company's rules in return for a regular wage. In the absence of a citywide trade union organization and without working-class cohesion, this large reserve army simply overwhelmed the sporadic protests of the street railway employees.

Each week, petitions from ratepayers begging for extensions into their neighbourhoods, and angry communications from city hall demanding improved service piled up on the table in front of the directors. But the board members kept their eyes firmly fixed on "the running" (receipts compared to the same period in the previous year) and ignored pleas and threats alike. By 1870 matters had improved sufficiently for the president to contemplate extending the system, but the company decided it would go nowhere without a subsidy. Residents and developers along St. Catherine Street West, for example, successfully persuaded the street railway to extend its track in return for a private right-of-way and a cash bonus of $3,000. A group of landlords in Lachine induced the company to run a line in their direction with a gift of free land and a $10,000 subsidy. Other districts might have had a better claim upon public transportation, but those who could afford to pay received it.[24]

Complaints from passengers about long waits between cars and the grievances of districts with no service at all opened up an opportunity, of course, for competition. The City Passenger Railway did not have an exclusive contract for the whole city, only for those streets listed in the 1861 agreement. And there were lucrative possibilities awaiting development beyond the city limits. The City Passenger Railway Company, however, fought competition with the same fierce determination—and success—with which it smothered trade union activity. In 1869 the board bought out an omnibus proprietor operating in the northern suburbs, mainly to enlist his influence in tying up streets in that district for future use.[25] Promoters seeking a franchise to build a belt line railway around

Mount Royal and the Montreal Road Steamer Traffic Company both ran up against City Passenger's considerable legal and political might.

In the mid-1870s several omnibus companies began to do a thriving business running buses on the paved streets parallel to the streetcar routes, and business on the street railway fell off alarmingly. In 1875 two of those companies merged and applied to the city and the provincial legislature to build a competitive street railway. City Passenger's lobbyists scurried to city hall, where the councillors understandably remained unmoved by their defense of monopoly, and to the legislature at Quebec City, where the Private Bills Committee—under the subtle suasion of the company's influential lawyers and the constant watch of Charles Geddes himself—proved much more amenable. Meanwhile, representatives of the two groups met privately to seek an accommodation. An embarrassing public exposé of these secret negotiations complicated matters; nevertheless, Charles Geddes confidently predicted (for the ears of his shareholders only) that the Omnibus Company would soon be willing to sell and that "this company would ultimately have all the city to itself." Geddes and his political allies in the legislature had managed to insert some impossible conditions into the new company's charter without giving the appearance of killing it. Though the precise terms are unclear, the Montreal Omnibus and Transfer Company passed out of existence, and its assets ended up in the hands of the proprietors of the City Passenger Railway Company in the spring of 1876.[26]

Charles Geddes and the men who presided over the Montreal street railway from 1865 to 1877 had every reason to be pleased with themselves and the performance of their company. Costs had been reined in without wearing out the physical plant; horses, track, and equipment remained in first-rate condition throughout the austerity. By 1870 the company could issue $100,000 of new stock to its shareholders at par, which represented an attractive discount from the quoted market price. Dividends were resumed in the late 1860s at 6 percent, and in the years that followed a 2 percent bonus was sometimes added when the running seemed to warrant it. And through it all the company had been able to maintain its effective monopoly over public transportation.

Table 5 shows the steady growth in passengers and gross revenue over this period—1866 and 1869 being exceptions—and the success achieved by management in reducing operating expenses as a proportion of total income. The figures in Table 6 reflect the relative decrease effected in the wage bill. Although the managers did not themselves calculate earnings and expenses per car mile (preferring the rough-and-ready measure of how they had done this year compared with this time last year), it is clear from Table 7 that managerial decisions combined with a growth in ridership made for a more efficient, profitable company. Revenue per passenger remained almost constant as a result of the five-cent ceiling on fares, whereas revenue per car mile increased 34 percent between 1867 and 1873 and net revenue

TABLE 5

MONTREAL CITY PASSENGER RAILWAY COMPANY, 1864–73

Year	Revenue	Expenses	Ratio[a]	Passengers	Miles Run
1864	72,136	44,975	62.3	1,485,725	
1865	85,197	68,904	80.2	1,768,092	
1866	80,953	61,525	76.0	1,667,384	
1867	96,113	66,864	69.6	1,933,497	471,229
1868	103,773	71,986	69.4	2,097,357	473,176
1869	100,384	71,305	71.0	2,031,390	473,176
1870	109,186	66,256	60.7	2,217,311	474,540
1871	122,634	76,393	62.2	2,519,461	499,060
1872	136,806	86,957	63.5	2,827,254	507,454
1873	152,349	108,073	70.8	3,133,529	557,177

Source: MUCTCA, CPR, MB, Annual Meetings.
[a] Expenses as % of revenue.

TABLE 6

MONTREAL CITY PASSENGER RAILWAY COMPANY WAGE BILL

Year	Wages as % of Expenses
1865	46.0
1866	46.3
1867	44.5
1868	42.2
1869	41.9
1870	45.9
1871	43.8

Source: MUCTCA, CPR, MB, Annual Meetings.

per car mile by 28 percent. By 1874 the railway was doing so well that its president urged the shareholders not to print the annual report. Two years later these figures disappeared even from the minutes of the annual meeting.

Similar methods wrought similar results in Toronto. In 1869, William T. and George Washington Kiely bought the bankrupt Toronto Street Railway from its demoralized bondholders for $48,848, although it was said that only $7,500 actually changed hands. The Kiely brothers quickly whipped the street railway into shape, and soon the Toronto property

TABLE 7

MONTREAL CITY PASSENGER RAILWAY COMPANY PERFORMANCE RATIO, 1864–73

Year	Revenue per Passenger (¢)	Revenue per Car Mile (¢)	Expenses per Passenger (¢)	Expenses per Car Mile (¢)	Net per Car Mile (¢)
1864	4.85		3.03		
1865	4.82		3.90		
1866	4.85		3.69		
1867	4.97	20.39	3.46	14.19	6.20
1868	4.95	21.93	3.43	15.21	6.72
1869	4.94	21.21	3.51	15.06	6.15
1870	4.92	23.00	2.99	13.96	9.04
1871	4.87	24.57	3.03	15.31	9.26
1872	4.84	26.95	3.07	17.13	9.82
1873	4.86	27.34	3.45	19.37	7.97

Source: MUCTCA, CPR, MB, Annual Meetings.

began producing regular dividends. By 1881 street railway fortunes in Toronto had recovered to such a point that Frank Smith, a prominent Conservative politician and Canada's largest liquor wholesaler, assumed a controlling interest in what became known as "Senator Smith's Goldmine."[27]

By the mid-seventies, therefore, cost-conscious managers had restored the street railroads in Toronto and Montreal to financial health mainly by extracting greater productivity from labour. They had also been saved by the rapid population growth of the two metropolises.[28] In time the Montreal City Passenger Railway, and Toronto Street Railway, along with Consumers' Gas and the New City Gas Company common shares became the most attractive and most sought after non-bank securities available on the informal stock exchanges of the two cities. Thus before 1880 these utilities were firmly established fixtures of urban life. Equally important, the organization and the manner of their management also produced the interest-bearing, capital-appreciating securities which were more generally necessary to an evolving capitalist economy. Their utility lay in two realms.

In a narrow business sense, tough-minded executives in Toronto and Montreal had succeeded in their primary goals, but by the late 1870s they were the only people in their respective cities who were at all satisfied with their performance. By focusing so intently upon profits, the managers of these two street railways had lost public confidence, antagonized organized labour, and earned the undying emnity of their only serious potential competitors, the city councils. In a relentless dialectical fashion, the very methods that had saved the companies in the 1870s precipitated major crises in their relations with both city governments in the 1880s.

What had taken place on the street railway was probably not much different from what was going on in shops, offices, and factories all over the cities. Under the goad of competition and technological change, costs were cut, production reorganized and mechanized, and labour brought under more direct managerial control. But a street railway was not just one among many private enterprises: it occupied a special place in the lives of the many workers, shoppers, merchants, clerks, tradesmen, and middle-class business people who had come to depend upon it. Though nominally private, it was necessarily a public undertaking whose inadequate accommodations, harsh working conditions, and outward indifference were directly felt and intimately understood by millions of riders annually.

The owners, preoccupied with their own financial imperatives, adopted an air of disdainful detachment toward their customers and routinely brushed aside reasonable requests for improvements; they expected that cramped riders, people lacking service, and congenitally discontented municipal politicians would grouse. A visitor to any city during the last quarter of the nineteenth century quickly became conscious of the intense and seemingly endless quarrelling between the municipal government and the holders of its street railroad franchise. In Montreal, for example, the company and the city argued for more than a decade following 1874 over revenue sharing, extensions, fares, and the quality of service. In Toronto bitter labour relations and an irrepressible conflict over street paving provoked the crisis. But at another level these cities and companies fought about the same thing: tempering businesslike management with some kind of regulation in the public interest.

The fact that the municipalities and the street railway companies fell into fierce combat during the 1880s is not in itself noteworthy. Nor should the details of those disputes detain us long. What concerns us at this point is the broader political question: what factors promoted mediation and led to at least temporary resolution of such conflict, and what prevented eventual accommodation? How did the Montreal company manage to minimize the damage inflicted by the municipal insurgency and come to a mutually satisfactory agreement with its adversary? Why did the same thing not happen in Toronto?

At the outset, relations between the City Passenger Railway Company and the municipal corporation were exceedingly amicable from a company point of view. During the difficulties in 1865, the city proved remarkably understanding when approached by deputations from the struggling company: extensions specified in the contract were deferred, taxes reduced temporarily, and the street-paving obligations were narrowed.[29] Relations soured when the company chose to ignore requests for improved service after it seemed to be in a financial position to meet those demands, and when it became apparent that the granting of concessions was a one-way street.

Led by George Washington Stephens, a blue-blooded municipal reformer, in late 1873 the Montreal city council launched an all-out assault upon the street railway company that continued throughout the following year. Stephens convinced his fellow councillors to approve a bylaw compelling the company to lay grooved rails of the English type, pave and water the streets in a specified fashion for three feet on either side of its rails, carry only as many passengers as could comfortably be seated, clear snow and repair the roadway, open its books for examination, and pay one-half cent to the city for each passenger carried. When the company objected, Stephens warned: "If you don't accommodate the public someone else will. A new company will take the streets you neglect, and take them upon the terms of the council. There is no doubt but that will be the case. There are a good many more capitalists than are represented on the company."[30] In the ensuing conflict the financial provisions of the municipal bylaw were amended to require an annual payment to the city of $20,000, or roughly 12 percent of gross income.

For its part the company was already investigating the possibility of laying flatter rails that would interfere less with other traffic, but it vehemently resisted the additional changes. Councillors sympathetic to the company received briefings detailing the many benefits conferred by the railway upon the city, pointing out the "financial impossibility" of the municipal proposals, and gently suggesting terms on which the company and the city might agree. Provincial politicians, including the Attorney General, reported their willingness to oppose the $20,000 tax (later reduced to $12,000 by the city). The company's president informed the board that confidential agreements had been made with *La Minerve* and the *Sun,* "a French and English paper in this city to advocate the interests of this company when desired." Company directors as individuals took an unusual interest in the election of certain councillors, and discreet emissaries slipped into city hall to scout out some basis for negotiation.[31]

The controversy had boiled up at an altogether unfortunate moment as far as the company was concerned. In the first place, Stephens was right; there were capitalists—such as those behind the Omnibus Company—all too willing to take advantage of the street railway's misfortunes and strike a deal on terms dictated by the city. Second, dividends had been set at 11 percent in 1875 and would rise to 12 percent the next year. The profitability of the company was a matter of public notoriety. Then, at the very height of the storm, the shareholders in the street railway began to fight amongst themselves.

In 1876, President Geddes and his board announced their intention of issuing another $600,000 worth of stock, a 150 percent increase. Dissident shareholders rose in revolt, demanded and received the resignations of Geddes and the board, and launched an independent audit of the company books which revealed that previous dividends had not been earned. The new and somewhat inexperienced directors had to scramble to raise $100,000 to meet current expenses. Mismanagement by the old board, unprofitable extensions, and a mild recession conspired to exhaust the financial resources of the company just at the moment the city council and the general public believed them to be boundless.[32] Once again the cycle of retrenchment and recrimination was set in motion. Outsiders believed that the company was exaggerating its difficulties for tactical reasons, but this was not the case. Moreover, the city's first opportunity to assume ownership of the road under the original contract was rapidly approaching. Competitors could be bought out; the Private Bills Committee of the provincial legislature could be prevailed upon to deflect the most punitive measures; lawyers could be retained to keep the taxation question more or less permanently before the courts. But September, 1880, imposed an inescapable deadline: on that date the city could, if it chose, exercise its option to buy.

Meanwhile, the two sides arrived at an angry deadlock that served no one's interests: the company absolutely refused to contemplate any extensions to its system until what it called "the corporation question" had been settled; the city just as stubbornly refused to give the company permission to improve service on any of its lines until it agreed to come to terms. The company therefore decided to lie low and let matters unfold at city hall, and just before the civic elections in February, 1881, the council voted to assume control of the street railway as permitted under the franchise. The next council reaffirmed that resolution during the summer, but when the aldermen reconvened in the fall, they reversed the decision.[33]

Throughout all of this excitement the company maintained an air of Olympian detachment, but shareholders grew restive. At the annual meeting in 1882 a number of them rose one after another to complain about the poor quality of street railway service in Montreal compared with other cities. The president's attempt to pin all the blame upon the uncooperative municipal government was not accepted by this minority, nor by another disgruntled group who thought the railway needed to be managed more efficiently. The shareholders, and in time even the board of directors, came to believe that the company ought to be able to provide better service and to make some positive move to improve relations with the city as a first step toward enhancing its earning power.

The immediate threat of takeover had passed—though it would come up again briefly in 1885—and the time had come to negotiate with yet another Select Committee of city council. On April 19, 1883, the president tendered his resignation and noting "the advantage of having at the present juncture a French member of the board."[34] He was immediately replaced by Louis A. Senécal, a notorious railroad and company promoter, political fixer, and leading Conservative organizer in the province of Quebec.[35] The new president actually took little or no direct interest in the company, nor did he participate in the detailed bargaining over terms and conditions which then commenced in earnest. His symbolic importance, however, was enormous: his presence signalled an eagerness to settle the long-standing dispute. A francophone president improved the odour of the company amongst the French Canadian majority on city council (the harshest critics of the company were mainly, though by no means exclusively, anglophone), and Senécal's standing with the provincial government telegraphed to the city that it could not expect much support at a higher level.

With Senécal up front though often out of town, Vice-President Hingston and the other English Canadian directors reopened discussions with the city. In the summer and fall of 1885, the company and the city finally concluded a comprehensive new agreement.[36] For its part the company promised to build a long list of extensions and to double-track its more important routes; it continued to pay an annual license fee of $20 for each two-horse car and $10 for each single-horse car; and it agreed to pay an annual tax of $1,000 for the first five years of the franchise, to be increased at five-year intervals to $5,000 during the fifth quinquennium. Fares remained fixed at five cents, although sheets of tickets were to be made available at a slight discount. In most other respects the new agreement followed the lines of its predecessor. Certainly it imposed no heavy burden, financial or otherwise, upon the company; indeed, the taxation conditions were less stringent than the company's own offer to the city in 1878. The City Passenger Railway Company emerged from its dangerous encounter with the municipal government in the 1880s with a perfectly satisfactory contract from its point of view and a new 25-year lease on life.[37]

Yet in Toronto, when the street railway franchise came open for the first time in 1891, the city seized the opportunity to buy back the road. The dispute began with the Toronto Street Railway Company's refusal to meet its street-paving obligations, as the city interpreted the 1861 agreement. The city's first attempt to sue the company met defeat in the courts. A blatant attempt by the company to get the Ontario legislature to convert its agreement into a perpetual franchise heightened suspicion and bad feeling. A populist press exaggerated the profitability of the company, attacked its performance, and invariably took the municipal government's side in the numerous disputes.[38]

In 1886 an unusual sequence of events brought this simmering crisis to a head. When spies informed management that a union organization drive was underway in the winter of 1885, Senator Frank Smith ordered his men to sign yellow-dog agreements that prevented them from joining a trade union. About 30 employees refused, and Smith fired them one by one.

Those still on the payroll bided their time until March, 1886, when—with the aid of Toronto's Knights of Labour organizers—they secretly formed another union. This time management delayed assigning drivers and conductors until the ringleaders could be rooted out. On March 10, 1886, almost all of the street railway employees walked out in protest.[39]

This strike-lockout produced a most extraordinary show of support from carters, cabmen, organized and unorganized workers, and pedestrains. When strikebreakers attempted to operate the streetcars, teamsters (mainly coal carters) blocked their way, mobs derailed a few cars, and rowdy sympathizers simply unhitched the horses and sent them back to the stables. On the second day the street railway ground to a halt. Unlike most strikes during that period, this one acted as a lightning rod for public antipathy *toward the company*. The moral economy of the mob spoke unequivocally on behalf of the strikers. So, surprisingly, did the mayor, W. H. Howland. A businessman, a moral reformer elected on a wave of municipal reform enthusiasm with the support of labour, Howland publicly blamed Senator Frank Smith for the strike and its consequences: "This action of yours having produced the difficulty, and being the cause of the annoyance under which the citizens are labouring, I hold you and your company responsible for it, and hereby demand that you restore to the city the order which existed and to the citizens the convenience they have a right to, as they existed before your action disturbed them."[40] On the third day more than 100 police, accompanied by a mounted detachment, drove corridors through the crowds to permit the cars to operate once again on a reduced and erratic schedule. Meanwhile, conciliators from the city council persuaded company management to take back the striking employees; thinking they had won the right to unionize, the employees voted overwhelmingly to return to work.

But Smith had no intention of letting his men join a union. He had agreed to take the men back but, he believed, on the same terms as before the strike: namely, under the yellow-dog agreements. One by one the strike leaders and union men were let go on various pretexts. It was all too familiar—the company agreeing to something only to renege later, or so it seemed to the public. In May the employees struck the company once again but with disastrous consequences. Public enthusiasm for demonstrations of the sort that had marked the first strike had been dampened considerably by the intervening events in Haymarket Square, Chicago, and the mayor and the police made much more forceful efforts to preserve the public order in advance of the strike, threatening heavy fines and jail terms for perpetrators of violence. As a result the strikers' call for a public boycott failed to receive the overwhelming support expected from the riding public. A month of picketing, marching, and attempting to run a competitive bus service inflicted little damage upon the street railway, which, fully staffed by strikebreakers, maintained its schedule throughout. The strikers lost their jobs, and the Knights of Labour lost a good deal of working-class support.

In the longer run the strike served another grim purpose: Senator Frank Smith had won. He had beaten organized labour in plain view of the entire city, overpowering it in the same way as he crushed protests about company policies emanating from city hall. It was now abundantly clear that he would brook no opposition in his determination to deliver street railway service to the people of Toronto on his own terms. In the aftermath of their respective defeats, labour and the city council—not to mention the majority of the street railway's sullen patrons—vowed that he would not get his own way when the franchise expired in 1891.[41]

By 1890 a popular new mayor, E. F. Clarke, and a more determined city council had steeled themselves to clear up the street railway mess once and for all. On June 21, 1890, the ratepayers voted 5,385 to 427 to authorize the city's purchase of the street railway the following year. The newspapers reported a particularly heavy vote against the company in "the outside wards and the most remote portions of those near the centre of the city. . . . The people living there are the ones who ride the cars."[42] Meanwhile, the arbitrator assigned to determine the price to be paid by the city reduced the size of the company's claim for its property from $5,500,000 to a mere $1,453,788.

Thus on May 16, 1891, as the clock in the steeple of St. James' Cathedral chimed midnight, Mayor Clarke led a small band of politicians and city officials to the street railway office just as Senator Frank Smith came into view, sauntering along King Street with George Kiely. Blandly refusing to surrender the key, Smith forced the civic worthies to retire to city hall in disarray, an event captured in the *Toronto World*'s poetic portrait of the embattled proprietor:

I'm purty rich and I'm mighty sly,
I've a stiff old spine in my back;
I've a heavy hand and a searching eye,
I'm a tough old nut to crack.[43]

But crack he did a few days later when, armed with a court order, Mayor Clarke and the City took command of the street railway. Smith then retired in good humour to his mansion with his generous settlement.

The Montreal owners worked out a deal; their Toronto counterparts had their property taken from them. There was not much to choose between the two companies. They operated more or less according to the same rules; they were both ruthlessly anti-union, for example, and similar working conditions applied in the two places. The Toronto company was no more profitable than the one in Montreal—if anything a little less so. The fact of the matter is that street railway profits were by no means extraordinary when compared with those of other successful late nineteenth-century commercial ventures. Had the newspapers and city councils known more about the rate of return on capital invested in department stores and packing plants, they might well have been less excited about the street railway. But there was an inescapable problem confronting the street railway proprietors: their businesses were by nature public, their activities the frequent subject of comment and caricature.

The Montreal directors consciously decided to close the distance between themselves and the hostile city council. The symbolic importance of Louis Senécal's appointment cannot be overemphasized, and the owners seemed to know what they needed to give in order to get. Whether through company influence or not, there remained a cadre of councillors who wanted to continue the company's franchise if in return the company would accept certain minimal conditions. In Montreal, because both city officials and company directors were willing, negotiation was possible.

In Toronto, by contrast, the close identification of Frank Smith with the company posed a major impediment to negotiation. A Catholic liquor merchant could not expect to arrive easily at terms with a fiercely Protestant, largely evangelical, and in some cases brilliantly Orange city council. The symbolism was all wrong. Moreover, Smith lacked the influence in municipal and provincial politics (even though he was a cabinet minister in the federal government, he was a nonelected senator) to compensate for his weak negotiating position. Organized labour was more influential in municipal politics in Toronto than in Montreal. The memory of the abortive 1886 strike imparted a certain passion to the street railway question in Toronto labour circles. And there was a self-righteous, uncompromising quality to Toronto political culture that may well have had something to do with the militant Protestantism of the town; once the street railway crossed some unstated and invisible line of correct behaviour, there could be no more dealing with it.

One need not put much weight upon this last point, for there was an even more compelling reason for heightened civic interest in the street railway in Toronto. Ironically, precisely because the Toronto Street Railway had done as well as it had, it had become a more important institution in the lives of Torontonians than the City Passenger Railway Company had become for Montreal. The data presented in Tables 8 and 9 indicate this differential level of social dependence on street railways in the two cities.[44] Even though Toronto was a smaller city than Montreal, its street railway carried about the same number of passengers at the beginning of the period and fully 64 percent more by the end; indeed, it could be said, on the basis of the index of riders as a proportion of the labour force, that the Toronto system was more than twice as important as a means of public transportation. These figures must be used cautiously, given the differences in terrain and number of operating days between the two cities; nonetheless, the

TABLE 8

STREET RAILWAY USE IN MONTREAL, 1881–92

Year	Population	Passengers Carried	Daily Return Trips	Riders as % of Labour Force
1881	193,171	3,953,405	5,830	5.4%
1882	201,606	4,146,265	6,115	5.5
1883	210,041	4,163,211	6,140	5.2
1884	218,476			
1885	226,911			
1886	235,346			
1887	243,781			
1888	252,216			
1889	260,651			
1890	269,086			
1891	277,525			
1892	285,856	11,631,386	17,155	10.6

Source: See note 44.

TABLE 9

STREET RAILWAY USE IN TORONTO, 1881–92

Year	Population	Passengers Carried	Daily Return Trips	Riders as % of Labour Force
1881	113,128	3,323,928	5,309	8.4%
1882	122,560	4,644,264	7,419	10.8
1883	131,992	5,142,516	8,215	11.2
1884	141,424	6,131,440	9,794	12.4
1885	150,856	7,386,208	11,799	14.0
1886	160,288	8,636,472	13,796	15.4
1887	169,720	10,545,112	16,813	17.7
1888	179,152	12,368,700	19,758	19.9
1889	188,584	14,414,960	23,027	21.8
1890	198,016	16,310,444	26,055	23.4
1891	207,450	16,818,413	26,866	23.0
1892	210,513	19,122,022	30,546	25.7

Source: See note 44.

dependency ratio is sufficiently spread to suggest very strongly that the street railway had become a more essential aspect of municipal life in Toronto than in Montreal. It certainly seems true that a greater proportion of the Toronto labour force used the street railway, and greater dependency gave Torontonians a greater incentive to regulate the railroad in their own collective interests. Sensing this, Toronto politicians articulated popular grievances and acted decisively in accordance with the will of the majority expressed in a ratepayer plebiscite. Ironically, therefore, the comparatively poor service supplied in Montreal by the City Passenger Railway Company indirectly contributed to its salvation.

The introduction of a new technology is rarely, if ever, costless in a social sense. Useful devices become necessities and in the process subtly shape the world in their own image. So it was with the street railways that appeared in Canada at the beginning of the 1860s. The progress they represented required that their users surrender some personal freedom and replace it with greater social and institutional interdependence. A certain degree of misery was the natural product of advancing civilization.

Technology harnessed to business imparted a dual social imprint: first technology widened the realm of the possible; then business narrowed that realm to certain permissible particulars. The street railway raised hopes; its unusual economics limited satisfaction. Necessity, the benign mother of invention, thus also became the more forbidding parent of denial.

To the extent that the street railroad disciplined both its workers and its riders, it was a harbinger of the emerging social order. The trams, plainly visible on the city streets, offered a glimpse of similar organizational forms taking shape less obviously in shops, offices, and factories. A uniformed contingent of unskilled workers, closely watched by inspectors and controlled by a hierarchy of managers, marched steadily to the beat of the clock, day in and day out. Soon all the world would resemble a street railway.[45]

The revolt against discipline and disappointment necessarily pitted the cities against the companies, whatever the immediate source of discontent. At the moment of crisis in the mid-1880s, the cities had the choice of either renewing street railway contracts on different terms or of taking over the properties themselves. In Montreal the company shrewdly preserved enough influence with the city council to win a renewal of its contract; in Toronto the ownership wanted everything its own way. Frank Smith's pugnacity, as well as his success at building a service that was a daily necessity to a very large proportion of Toronto's citizens, called forth an equally determined response. The city of Toronto, almost as an act of revenge for the company's past sins, snatched the street railway from Smith's grasp even before it knew what it was going to do with it.

The question of how the public interest could be best served by horse-drawn transportation had not been fully answered in either city. But sometimes such problems are not so much solved as they are replaced. For even as councils and companies wrangled over the inadequacies of the old technology, a revolutionary new system of street railway transportation appeared that cast the question in an entirely new light.

PART TWO
THE
TRANSFER
OF
TECHNOLOGY
AND
TECHNIQUE

The Theatre of Science 3

No business was more dramatically affected by the technological changes set in motion by the inventor-entrepreneurs of the late nineteenth century than the emergent public utilities sector. In the mid-1870s and 1880s, a frantically competitive, international research effort successfully developed the telephone, electric light and power, and electric railroads.[1] In retrospect, the energy released by American and European inventors was matched only by the enthusiasm with which Western society embraced their revolutionary innovations.

The appearance of electrical utilities at this critical juncture helped prevent North America's industrial cities from collapsing under their own weight. Large cities could—and did—exist without such complex infrastructures. Edo, Japan, for example, with more than a million inhabitants the largest city in the world during the 1860s, conducted its affairs on foot without even very much assistance from the wheel.[2] With enough time and servants almost anything is possible. These utilities, however, made it possible for cities to contain within their expanding boundaries the tremendous productive power unleashed by simultaneous technological and organizational change in the manufacturing, transportation, distribution, and retailing sectors.[3] By rendering communications and travel easier and more efficient, these new technologies as systems converted urban "externalities" from potentially negative to positive forces, thereby tightening the linkage between urbanization and industrialization. The telephone, electric light and power, the electric street railroad and its vertical counterpart the elevator allowed the city to grow outward and upward, at the same time permitting larger, more coordinated flows of information and people within the city and between cities. Electricity lengthened the productive day; bright lights and job opportunities beckoned the migrant labour force.

Canadians participated in but were not in the forefront of this inventive activity. Alexander Graham Bell, whose parents had emigrated to

Ontario in 1870, did some of his theorizing and early tinkering at the family homestead near Brantford. Charles Van Depoele operated one of the very first electric street railways at the Toronto Exhibition in 1884 and again in 1885. But the fact remains that these systems were designed, developed, and manufactured for the most part in the northeastern United States. Canada, in common with the rest of the United States, was the scene of extraordinarily rapid technological diffusion.

In less than a year after Bell's first patent, at the same time as telephones were being tried out in Boston, they were also in use in Hamilton, Ontario. The Prime Minister of Canada became the proud possessor of two instruments in November, 1877. Telephones were commercially available within two years of their first manufacture in all the major North American cities and in a surprising number of smaller Canadian centres from Halifax on the Atlantic to Victoria on the Pacific. The same phenomenal acceptance greeted arc and incandescent lighting and the electric street railway. No sooner had the arc lights been invented (and well before they were perfected) than they were casting their white glare and deep shadows over streets, squares, and public buildings all over the continent. When Frank Sprague gambled on the electrification of the Richmond, Virginia, street railway in 1887, there were already 21 experimental electric transit systems in operation. Within two years of his well-publicized (though costly) success, more than 200 horse-powered lines had been converted to electricity, half of them to the Sprague system. These included operations in Victoria and Vancouver, British Columbia, which were about as far removed as possible from the centres of research and experimentation.[4]

How could these new systems sprout in such profusion more or less simultaneously, in cities of different sizes and stages of development, at widely separated points across a vast continent? The inventor-entrepreneurs themselves must be given much of the credit. They thought a good deal about their environment, its needs, and above all the cost of addressing deficiencies. Of all the problems they might have chosen to work on, they selected those of practical utility: they were market oriented as well as technologically driven. Though fully absorbed in the intricacies of their work and the process of puzzle solving, they nevertheless maintained a shrewd sense of what was needed, and they adapted existing scientific knowledge to meet those needs *at acceptable costs*. The invention of ingenious devices was not the goal. The great inventor-entrepreneurs were, in Thomas Hughes's apt phrase, "econotechnical,"[5] concerned as much with the requirements of commercial development as with scientific research per se.

In the breathless aftermath of his famous telephonic summons to Thomas Watson, Alexander Graham Bell scribbled down for the benefit of his father in Brantford the possibilities of his speaking telephone: "This is a great day with me. I feel I have at last struck the solution of a great problem—and the day is coming when telegraph wires will be laid to houses just like water or gas—and friends converse with each other without leaving home."[6] Bell was not content to invent a toy, which is what Elisha Gray, his most serious rival, thought he had done. Worldly success, which Bell privately craved, depended less upon invention than upon application. The potential for profit filled Bell with a most unscientific ambition as he awaited the judgement of the U.S. Patent Office in February of 1876: "If I succeed in securing that Patent without interference from the others *the whole thing is mine*—and I am sure of fame, fortune and success if I can only persevere in perfecting my apparatus."[7]

The gas industry inspired Thomas Edison as he grappled with the problem of creating an electric lighting system based upon central stations, and provided minimum standards of price and quality upon which he would have to improve. During the course of his experiments with incandescent lighting at Menlo Park, Edison also studied the cost structure, organization, and business practices of the gas industry. Because he set out to develop a fully patented system that would compete directly with gas in the growing commercial and domestic lighting markets, Edison was preoccupied with economic factors at every step of the way.[8] A year before he succeeded in getting his system to work, he told reporters that someday soon distribution mains would spread out from central generating stations in all major cities, and electricity would light private homes at a lower cost than gas.[9] It was not enough to invent the electric light bulb; that, after all, had already been done.[10] Edison's objective was technical and economic: the development of a competitive, commercial system of illumination.

The evident shortcomings of horse-drawn public transit presented the inventor-engineers with a more precisely defined but nevertheless technically difficult problem in applied science. The search for some kind of motive power to move the urban masses over increasingly greater distances had been underway for some time before Thomas Edison, Edward Bentley, Walter Knight, Charles Van Depoele, and Frank Sprague experimented with electricity. Here too the problem was econotechnical: any system of electrification would have to enhance street railway performance significantly—especially by lowering operating costs or increasing the size and speed of the cars—or it would not justify the higher capital costs. Edison and others failed this test, even though they invented workable, small-scale electric railroads. When Frank Sprague demonstrated more or less convincingly that his trolley system met these exacting commercial criteria, the electric street railway spread like wildfire.[11]

To bring such products to market required a good deal of faith and confidence on the part of the inventors and their backers. The Western Union Telegraph Company initially shared Elisha Gray's opinion that the telephone was only a curiosity. When Canadian newspapermen George

Brown and his brother Gordon were offered what amounted to world rights to the telephone before Bell had patented it, they turned the offer down on the strength of expert British scientific opinion.[12] Thomas Edison did not consider his electric street railway worth pursuing in view of its early costs. Gas industry executives regarded arc and incandescent lighting as harmless novelties at first.

Innovations had to be financed, manufactured, and sold. That required more than inventive genius. Charles Brush needed the financial support of a Cleveland telegraph equipment manufacturer to get his arc lighting system working and to mount attention-getting pilot projects. The research and development costs of Edison's incandescent lighting system rose to almost half a million dollars. Alexander Graham Bell's costs were more modest—he did not design a complete system—but still far beyond the resources he could personally command. Overcoming the inevitable "bugs"[13] also required considerable depth of capitalization. Edison's famous Pearl Street central electric station was a financial disaster, as was the Holborn Viaduct operation in London.[14] The first Bell Telephone Company was teetering on the brink of bankruptcy in 1879 when William H. Forbes, a Boston financier, rescued it. The electrification of the street railway in Richmond, Virginia, cost almost twice as much as Frank Sprague received for the contract.[15] Each of these inventor-entrepreneurs had business associates capable of raising the very large amounts of capital required to underwrite system development. Charles Coffin performed this function for Elihu Thomson and Edwin Houston; Edison had Henry Villard, Egisto Fabbri, and J. P. Morgan behind him. Bell depended upon Gardiner Hubbard, but successful commercial development of the telephone was accomplished by Forbes, his financial associates, and Theodore N. Vail.

Manufacturing and marketing presented further business challenges. The fact that these innovators successfully leapt over these hurdles partly explains the extremely rapid diffusion of telephone and electricial technologies in the 1880s. Forbes and Vail decided upon manufacturing their own equipment, licensing local operating companies, leasing equipment, operating the long distance lines, and continuing their commitment to telephonic research, all of which required the quantities of capital needed to build a railroad. These policies maximized central control and fortified monopoly, but they placed severe burdens upon the directors, merchant bankers, and shareholders. The electrical equipment companies also financed the sale of their equipment in order to maintain the necessary production volumes to make a profit. Thus to the capital-intensive manufacturing process was added the requirement of financing an aggressive marketing campaign. The cost reductions associated with large-scale production, and the willingness of manufacturers to take shares of local operating companies in partial payment for equipment, greatly speeded up the diffusion process. These corporate strategies, with their heavy emphasis upon marketing and the reliance upon middle managers to coordinate sales and production, demanded a genius in the financial and organizational realms at least the equal of the ingenuity embodied in the products themselves.[16]

The economic pressures to produce and sell are readily understood. But markets must also be made in minds. What made people want to buy? Price is only a partial answer, for purchasers often ended up paying more than they bargained for. In 1880 the city of Montreal paid $24,000 to light its streets with gas; a little more than a decade later the electric lighting bill for a not greatly enlarged city had risen to over $160,000.[17] Nor can compelling need offer a sufficient explanation. It was not mere necessity that induced the Jesuits to illuminate their Montreal Seminary in October, 1878 (the first demonstration of electric lighting in Canada), or the chief of police in Toronto to demand a telephone linking the police station, courthouse, and jail in 1879, or the Montreal Harbour Commissioners to install arc lights on the docks, or the millionaire George Stephen to light up his mansion with them, or courting Montreal couples to favour an electrically illuminated cruise boat, or the militia to parade beneath the sizzle of arc lights on the Champs de Mars, or a proud welcoming committee to string lights in the station for a ducal visit, or tram companies in Victoria and Windsor (two of Canada's smaller cities) to build the earliest electric street railways. Nor was it more opportunity alone that led a prosperous furniture manufacturer, J. A. I. Craig, to drop everything to become an electrical manufacturer, or—to take but one example—J. O. Hutton of Huttonville to buy an electric generator to light up his town.[18]

The public had become convinced through skillful public relations that technology verged upon the miraculous. The inventors were not just glorified mechanics; they were also the leading actors in a grand public spectacle, the theatre of science in the late nineteenth century. Electric power and the telephone generated tremendous public interest, which the inventors and promoters actively fed. At all levels the press avidly followed the development of each new invention. The Brantford *Expositor* and the Toronto *Globe* reports of Bell's long distance experiments in the summer of 1876 attracted the attention of *Scientific American*. Articles from metropolitan journals were carried in newspapers all over the world. The French language press in Montreal kept up with the progress of electrical experimentation just as eagerly as the English papers.[19]

Much of the sensation, of course, was carefully created by the inventors themselves, some of whom were consummate performers. Edison's New Year's Eve railroad excursion to a brilliantly lit Menlo Park was pure theatre, as was Alexander Graham Bell's dramatic demonstration of the telephone for Sir William Thomson and Dom Pedro, both of whom played their parts of dumfounded amazement to perfection. It helped a great deal that the process of mechanical improvement had been turned into a kind of scientific Olympics, complete with glittering international exhibitions in crystal palaces, head-to-head contests between rival pieces of equipment, panels of judges, cries of foul, and gold medals for the victors.[20] Between the main events there were plenty of claims and counterclaims of priority, slanders and innuendo in the magazines, and tense courtroom battles over patents to maintain the interest of the spectators. Rising above this rude clamour, the recognized "inventors" of the telephone, electric light, alternating current, and various appliances, emerged to be hailed, rewarded, interviewed, lionized, and never forgotten.

In the theatre of science hyperbole came naturally; the inventors became giants and their discoveries the wonders of the age. The star performers were invariably described as "great," their occupation a "romance of invention" or an "adventure." A new era required its own "industrial explorers." Though nominally still humble "eminent mechanics," the inventors were nonetheless renowned generals commanding a "conquest of invention." Above all, they were the true "makers of America."[21] The melodrama of invention stimulated a deep-seated desire to participate, to share in the process of discovery, to be part of a wildly successful endeavor—and of course there were parts available for everyone. This carefully contrived promotion and the willingness on the part of the inventors to be turned into living icons of individualism (when in fact they stood atop a pyramid of specialized knowledge and elaborate teams of researchers) satisfied another yearning, the need for heroes. And all of this was grist for the marketers' mill.

The desire to have or use these systems transcended the rational: the inventor and the huge enterprises to which he sold his name supplied a real but intangible psychic need. Novelty can be an object of desire and, once purchased, a source of considerable satisfaction. The delight of using a telephone, or the boast of the best-lit streets in North America, or the joy of zipping through familiar places on a clanging trolley may be thought of as frivolous luxuries. But, as Tibor Skitovsky has reminded us, we should not be too dogmatic about differentiating between the discretionary and the necessary: "The dividing line . . . between necessities and luxuries turns out to be not objective and immutable, but socially determined and ever changing, very differently drawn in different societies, by different people, and at different times by the same people."[22] In North America the anxiety to be up to date, progressive, is an appetite as basic as hunger. Novelty broke down initial market resistance; then, for an ever-growing number of people, luxury gradually became necessity.

But the theatre of science was more than a glorious public entertainment; in proper nineteenth-century fashion it was also a moral pageant. These systems attracted praise and admiration not just because they were novel, or even because they were useful, but also because they promoted social and intellectual betterment. The inventors were more than heroes of the moment; they became lasting symbols of what has been termed the "character ethic."[23] In both its British and North American canon, engineers and inventors figured as the foremost exemplars of "character" or "success." Edison, Bell, Stanley, Westinghouse, Sprague, and the rest were self-made men whose quest inspired others, who triumphed over adversity and created something of enduring value. It was possible to think of them as dedicated public benefactors because their devices advanced everyone's well-being. Moreover, their careers showed others of humble origin that success lay within their grasp. That the inventors should reap a fortune for their work was entirely fitting; that they should become the idols of success was certainly to be preferred to the worship of arcane knowledge, pelf, or power. This two-way reflection of mutually gratifying images between the inventor and his society served the additional function, however spontaneous and unintended, of advertising.

Salesmen cannot sell unless people are predisposed to buy. The theatre of science attracted capital to the manufacturing and utilities enterprises on the one hand while it greatly stimulated demand on the other. The salesmen quickly discovered that this new equipment could be sold without much difficulty in the most unlikely places. When a shopkeeper signed up for the lights he had heard so much about, or a businessman subscribed for stock in a promising electrical company, or a city council ordered up more streetlights or fussed impatiently over the delay in electrifying the street railway, they were all playing their parts in a moving and uplifting melodrama.

These were the general conditions, then, that pushed and pulled the new electrical technologies into the mass North American market at such a rapid rate: econotechnical systems, the production and distribution methods of managerial capitalism, and theatrical promotion that elicited enthusiastic audience participation. But our analysis must guard against making the process of diffusion appear too orderly. Electricity, the telephone, and the electric streetcar burst into a world already crowded with solidly entrenched gas, horsecar, and telegraph companies. Ironically, the demonstration effect of the old technologies alerted well-positioned businessmen to the possibilities of the new and released the animal spirits of competition.

At the beginning the technologies were plural: there were many telephones being offered, a multitude of electrical systems to choose from, and several different ways of electrifying street railroads. Equipment salesmen and company promoters planted a forest of poles in the streets and strung a riot of crisscrossing wires. And as utilities promoters competed, they all had to struggle with somewhat slower-moving and often menacing municipal governments, scarred and made wary by previous combat with private gas, water, and horsecar monopolies. The result was a two-level struggle for dominance: between competing companies and technologies, and between all the new utilities and the municipal authorities.

The telephone industry provides an excellent example of the way in which businessmen sought to capitalize upon these scientific wonders. The telephone *as a system* was not created by Alexander Graham Bell, although he visualized the possibility, and his two main patents eventually anchored it.[24] Rather, the telephone system was assembled from pieces supplied by many inventors working in competition with one another and often for rival commercial interests. William H. Forbes and Theodore N. Vail were primarily responsible: they negotiated the agreements that brought most of the major telephone patents under the control of one company; they laid out a comprehensive monopoly strategy, selected the best patents from the pool for development, manufactured the elements of completely integrated systems, and brought them to market through closely controlled local operating companies.

Alexander Graham Bell quite happily left the development of the telephone system to others. He abhorred commercial dealings and lacked business judgement. At almost the first opportunity he sold his patents and thereafter paid only desultory attention to the management of the corporation that bore his name—apart from vigorous participation in the defence of his patents, in which he played a decisive role.[25] But before taking leave of the business, Bell grandly divided the world up into telephone franchises, which he distributed among his friends and relatives. He gave a 75 percent interest in Canada to his father, Melville Bell, and the remaining 25 percent to his Boston equipment manufacturer, Charles Williams, in return for enough transmitters and receivers to launch the Canadian venture. Melville Bell then appointed his friend, the Rev. Thomas Henderson of Paris, Ontario (whose advice and help he had relied upon in emigrating), as general agent. However laudable as a filial gesture, Bell's dispensation was not best calculated to establish the telephone in Canada on a sound footing. Though renowned as an educator of the deaf, Melville Bell lacked capital, commercial experience, organizational ability, dynamism, and the necessary business connections. Not surprisingly, his main preoccupation during the time he owned Canadian rights to the Bell patents was with selling them.

Nevertheless, Thomas Henderson toured small-town Ontario during 1877 and 1878, leasing instruments for private line service. In Hamilton, Toronto, London, and Windsor, businessmen organized companies to supply Bell's patented service or added telephones to their existing telegraph operation. Hugh C. Baker, himself the youthful promoter of the Hamilton Street Railway and a local telegraph dispatch business, had the distinction of presenting the first formal demonstration of the telephone in Canada on August 29, 1877. By the end of 1878 there were Bell telephone agencies in 15 other Ontario centres and in the provinces of Nova Scotia, New Brunswick, Quebec, Manitoba, and British Columbia—a geographical dispersion that testifies more to widespread curiosity about the telephone and latent demand for communications than to any entrepreneurial energy on the part of the Canadian patentees.[26]

Of course, the Bell group did not possess complete control over telephone technology or its introduction into Canada. Thomas Edison, working for the Western Union Telegraph Company, developed another method of transmitting the human voice that worked even better than Bell's and authorized his friend F. H. Badger, superintendent of the Montreal fire alarm department, to license the use of the Edison and related patents in Canada. Badger promptly turned matters over to the most likely developer, the Montreal Telegraph Company, owned by shipping, banking, insurance, and transportation magnate Sir Hugh Allan. To meet the competition, Dominion Telegraph, with headquarters in Toronto, acquired rights to lease Bell equipment to its clients beginning in February, 1879. Thus the two main Canadian telegraph companies each had access to the new technology. Moreover, telephones were notoriously easy to make once the principles had been grasped. Thomas Ahearn, a young Ottawa mechanic, successfully copied Bell's design and put a few phones into service in the Ottawa area. A Quebec City jeweller, Cyrille Duquet, patented a modified version of the Bell transmitter in 1878 and began selling instruments of his own manufacture in Quebec.

The telephone, in its own curious way, held up a mirror to its adoptive society. It was introduced in different but quite fitting ways in various places. Hugh Baker, for example, assembled a crowd of bank managers and businessmen for his Hamilton inaugural. In Montreal, where a different ethos prevailed, the telephone was unveiled on September 28, 1877, in the main hall of the Roman Catholic seminary before a gathering of bishops and priests who listened to an inspirational program transmitted from a Mr. Lavigne's music room. The first telephones put into service in Montreal placed the seminary in direct communication with the cemetery on Côte des Neiges. In Nova Scotia they connected a mine with its office; in Hamilton, a merchant's home and his warehouse.

Those companies with the most to gain or lose from the introduction of the telephone responded sluggishly to both the opportunity and the threat. Even though Alexander Graham Bell had used Dominion Telegraph Company facilities for his 1875 and 1876 long distance experiments, that company and its Montreal rival remained unimpressed with the future possibilities of the telephone. Basically, the telegraph companies looked upon the telephone as a loss leader. They leased instruments at absurdly low rentals, or offered them free, to provide connections for high-volume telegraph users. The companies did not see the telephone as a substitute for the telegraph but as an expensive encumbrance that telegraphers would rather be rid of (later, of course, they would regret their shortsightedness). For these reasons Thomas Swinyard, general manager of the Dominion Telegraph Company, at first ignored and then summarily dismissed Melville

Bell's offer of exclusive rights to the telephone for a mere $100,000. In a bid to prevent the Canadian territory from going begging, William H. Forbes and the National Bell Telephone Company in the United States purchased Melville Bell's Canadian rights in the autumn of 1879.[27]

Seen from the Bell head office on Milk Street in Boston, the chaotic Canadian telephone situation needed to be taken in hand. Local companies had been allowed to spring up without any central coordination or control; competition was doing permanent harm to the business because of the uneconomically low rentals, duplication, incompatible equipment, and conflicting claims; and scarce capital was being wasted in unplanned dispersal and growth. William H. Forbes and Theodore N. Vail could allow themselves the luxury of thinking this way in the fall of 1879 because they had just concluded a triumphant agreement with the Western Union Telegraph Company that delivered all the rival telephone patents into their hands and gave them a virtual monopoly over the telephone business in the United States.[28]

Forbes and Vail could thus continue to consolidate their monopoly without serious opposition by following the plan they had already mapped out: renting rather than selling instruments to users; manufacturing their own equipment; forming locally owned regional operating companies in which they took a minority but controlling equity position and binding these companies with strict licensing and equipment purchase contracts; then building long lines linking the regional companies into a national system. As the Bell strategists organized and wired their vast territory, they also fenced and posted it in law by launching more than 600 actions against patent infringers, all their suits being sustained by the courts. Each element of this plan reinforced monopoly and centralized control, leaving the few remaining competitors isolated and weak by comparison.

Once National Bell had (somewhat reluctantly) assumed ownership of the Canadian patents, Forbes and Vail decided to develop their new territory, much like a region of the United States, and they commenced proceedings to incorporate the Bell Telephone Company of Canada. It then remained to chivy as many of the scattered and competing telephone interests as possible into a merger with Bell without committing too much cash in the process. Then a competent and dynamic manager, versed in the strategy and tactics of the head office, would be in a position to take charge of the Canadian situation and develop an integrated, defensible monopoly. To carry out this delicate mission, Forbes and Vail dispatched a 45-year-old former ship captain and insurance executive, Charles Fleetford Sise, to Montreal on March 8, 1880.[29]

Sise was in every way the ideal person for the job. As a merchant adventurer he was accustomed to assuming responsibility and acting decisively in the company interests. Since he had previously been the U.S.

agent for the Royal Canadian Insurance Company, Sise already had important Canadian business connections. Finally, despite his great ability, Sise had no future as a businessman in the northeastern United States. He had been hounded out of the insurance business by the rumors—all true— that he had married into a southern mercantile family, fought briefly and then served as a blockade runner for the Confederacy, and acted as a secret agent for the South in Liverpool during the latter stages of the Civil War. But these southern affiliations would do him no harm in Montreal; indeed, he would shortly introduce his friend Jefferson Davis to the Montreal commercial elite at the St. James Club. Above all, Sise had been thoroughly schooled in Vail's methods.

It would be tedious but possible to follow Sise's every step; his daily log and much of his correspondence with the head office in Boston and local agents in Canada survive in the company archives. The broad outlines of his campaign and the way he adapted Vail's strategy to the Canadian milieu will suffice, however, for our purpose.

Predictably, the people he relied upon in Canada were those with whom he was already associated: namely, the directors of the Royal Canadian Insurance Company. He persuaded his old friend Andrew Robertson, a prominent dry goods importer, chairman of the Montreal Harbour Commission, and head of the insurance company, to assume the presidency of the Bell Telephone Company. "His influence with the government alone would make him desirable," Sise informed Forbes, "but aside from that he is a thorough business man, who stands among the highest in the opinion of all parties and classes in the Dominion."[30] Sise also recruited other directors of the insurance company for the board of the telephone company: Thomas Davidson, a tinware manufacturer; Duncan McIntyre, a major importer and member of the Canadian Pacific Railway syndicate, and the Hon. J. Rosaire Thibaudeau, a Liberal senator and director of La Banque Nationale.[31] All of these directors were substantial men of exemplary rectitude, well connected financially and on both sides of politics; they represented both the English and French communities and, most important, were untainted by previous experience with telephones or telegraphs and so innocent of any bias in the ensuing touchy negotiations between rivals. Other board members included Hugh C. Baker and R. A. Lucas of Hamilton and, of course, Forbes, Vail, and Sise.

Given this powerful support and the predisposition of the telegraph interests to sell, Sise accomplished his major objective within the year: he was able to gather most of the existing Canadian telephone operations into his company. Nevertheless, tricky matters of protocol in dealing with the likes of Sir Hugh Allan, of the prices to be paid, and of subsequent employment for some principals took time to iron out. They also took money. Both the Dominion and the Montreal Telegraph companies wanted too much for their telephone properties, and they wanted too much of it in cash, causing Forbes to complain bitterly of the expense in July, 1880.[32] Eventually Sir Hugh Allan settled for $50,000 cash and $25,000 in Bell stock. The Hamilton, London, and Windsor companies joined the merger in 1880. During the first six months of 1881, Sise worked out deals to acquire the Toronto Telegraph Despatch Company phone service, the companies started in the Maritime provinces by the Western Union Telegraph Company, and a small operation in Winnipeg. After almost exactly a year's work Sise could report confidently, "We now have the entire field in Canada."[33]

It remained for him to weld these disparate pieces into a profitable, integrated system. Sise reorganized the company into regions, each headed by an agent.[34] Rentals were raised all over the system to recover costs and provide a substantial margin for expansion, reinvestment, and dividends to attract more capital. At $40 to $50 annually for residential service in the Quebec City exchange, for example, Sise calculated that net returns would increase more rapidly than subscribers over the next few years. Agents were encouraged to promote telephone development in the areas already occupied but discouraged from founding small, isolated exchanges. Sise wanted deeper market penetration in the already wired, more profitable urban areas.[35]

Operating procedures were tightened up, and Sise cancelled free telephone privileges for all but senior company officials. Standardized reporting schedules allowed him to maintain a close watch on comparative costs throughout the system. In March of 1883, for example, he pointed out to Hugh Baker that expenses as a percentage of gross revenues had been consistently higher in Ontario than in Quebec and the Maritime provinces, and he zeroed in on the key variable: the number of operators. The five major eastern exchanges employed one operator for 72 subscribers; the three Ontario exchanges averaged one operator to 39 subscribers. Nor could it be argued that the service was better, continued Sise in anticipation of a possible reply: "We hear as many complaints from Toronto with one operator to 35 subscribers, as we do from Quebec, where one operator works 82 subscribers. Or here [Montreal] where one operator has 61 subscribers to attend to."[36]

The Bell telephone must surely have been the first mass consumption product marketed by threats. Beginning in January, 1881, Sise placed small display advertisements in the major papers warning telephone customers to beware: only Bell service was "entirely FREE FROM RISK OF LITIGATION."[37] And Bell made good on that claim. Users and manufacturers of equipment deemed to infringe on Bell's exclusive patents were hauled before the courts and put out of business with injunctions—this was Duquet's fate in 1882, for example.[38] Such aggressive policing of company patents not only prevented poaching within Bell's operating preserve but also served to protect the market of its equipment manufacturing unit, which commenced operations—despite an acute shortage of skilled workers—in July, 1882.

The essential tactic in putting the telephone business on a solid, monopolistic footing was to occupy the territory fully and quickly. A head start and the denial of prime business to potential competitors gave Bell an advantage not easily overcome. To that end a few trunk lines were built linking centers in southern Ontario, but long-line development was severely constrained by a chronic shortage of capital.[39] Transborder connections linked the Canadian with the U.S. system through Maine, New York, Michigan, and Minnesota. Long distance service in advance of need was a key element in Vail's strategy: in cases of direct competition it gave Bell clients something the other companies could not provide—access to a vast national network.

Strong local exchanges served the long lines and vice versa. In times of crisis they held each other up. It helped as well that these lines in Canada, however attenuated by lack of capital, paid their way from the very beginning—much to the surprise of the telephone executives themselves, who invariably underestimated the demand kindled by their promotional efforts. Daily revenue from the Toronto-Hamilton line reached $6.50 soon after it opened in September, 1881, and shortly afterward exceeded $10 daily. Hugh Baker calculated that this line earned an average of $1.00 per mile per week in 1884 and the other lines about half that. It is little wonder, therefore, that the telegraph interests, themselves amalgamated in 1882 into a national monopoly (the Great North Western Telegraph Company) by Jay Gould and a mercurial Canadian entrepreneur, Erastus Wiman, began to express open concern about the loss of business to the telephones, and there were rumours of possible competition soon from that quarter.[40]

Sise took his instructions direct from Milk Street, which retained a controlling interest in the company. But in the care and feeding of his board of directors, Forbes and Vail deferred to Sise. From the very outset the head office had insisted upon encouraging local participation. "While we believe that the telephone business can be made of great value in Canada and that it has developed to a point where good management can make it profitable very soon," Forbes explained to Sise on July 13, 1880, "yet it is our policy there, as in the States, to bring in local capital, influence and management, since the whole field is far too large for us to undertake to cover."[41] Andrew Robertson and the others were not expected to take an active role in the direction of the company, nor was it desirable that they do so. Rather, they were to impart an aura of stability and respectability to the company and to induce others of their kind to join them in raising money and otherwise promoting the welfare of the business. The board members got along with each other; they took their stock allotments when called upon; and although they did not draw as much local capital into the enterprise as its founders might have liked, they kept the company out of the hands of speculators and more independent-minded corporate adventurers.[42]

Even though the Bell Telephone Company of Canada had acquired an effective monopoly as early as 1881, and under Charles F. Sise's careful management had taken steps that seemed likely to preclude the possibility of any damaging private competition, there was reason to be concerned about possible political interference. On the advice of J. J. C. Abbott, the leading corporation lawyer in the country, Bell Telephone acted to shore up its legislative breastworks against any public or private challenge long before there was public realization that a monopoly had been achieved. The company charter, passed by parliament in 1880, gave Bell its legal existence, granted it authority to operate its business, raise money, manufacture telephones, and so forth.[43] But exactly what powers a federal charter conferred within areas of provincial jurisdiction had not yet been settled. To be doubly sure, Bell obtained legislation reaffirming its authority to erect poles, string wires, and operate telephone exchanges from the Quebec and Ontario provincial governments.[44]

In 1882 the company returned to the federal government in Ottawa asking for somewhat broader powers, the authority to issue bonds in denominations of less than $100, and—for greater security—a declaration that Bell Telephone was "a work for the general advantage of Canada." The House of Commons passed the bill without amendment, but the Senate struck out the bond clause on the grounds that bonds of such small denominations might possibly be used to replace banknotes in general circulation. And there was some slight grumbling from two senators about "purely local undertakings" of this sort applying for a declaration of general advantage, but in the end that privilege was bestowed.[45] Such parliamentary legislation protected the company against political harrassment or confiscation of its property by provincial or municipal governments.

Thus the Bell Telephone Company was able to develop its market and build its system more or less according to its own plan during the early 1880s. Sise amalgamated the earliest companies at the very outset, then acquired the remaining major independents as opportunities presented themselves. In the meantime he strengthened managerial control over operations, established Bell stock in the very narrow Canadian capital market, and wired as much of his territory as available cash would prudently permit. He hounded patent infringers, slowly built up his manufacturing capability, and braced his monopoly fore and aft with legislation. Despite the relatively high rentals, business expanded at a steady, manageable pace of about 1,300 new subscribers per year. In 1882 the company tentatively commenced paying dividends, all of which were earned.[46]

Still, Bell dominance was by no means total. Not far from the head office, just south of Montreal, the Dominion Telephone Company somehow stayed in operation, embarrassing Bell with its lower rates. And the Toronto Telephone Manufacturing Company persisted in making instruments of its own design and offering them for sale to promoters with the promise that substantial profits could be made at much lower rates than those being charged by Bell. When threatened, the Toronto company decided to go on the offensive. In 1884 its lawyer owners applied to the Commissioner of Patents to negate Alexander Graham Bell's Canadian patents on the grounds that they had not been used for manufacturing in Canada as required by the Patent act. Bell's lawyers were sublimely confident that the case would be thrown out, but on January 26, 1885, Commissioner Joseph Taché found in favour of the Toronto company. That was literally a red letter day in Sise's log: he scribbled: "Decision against us in Ottawa," then added in vermillion, "voiding Bell's Patent on Telephone."[47] This, however, proved to be more a psychological than a financial blow.

Up to that point Theodore N. Vail's strategy had worked as well in Canada as it had in most regions of the United States. Bell Telephone had been able to swallow up all of the major existing companies, plant itself firmly, build complex defences, and defy all challengers. The pooling of patents under the control of one company as a result of the 1879 accord with Western Union was a key contributing factor to monopoly in both Canada and the United States. So too was the withdrawal of the telegraph interests from the telephone business, obsessed as they were between 1879 and 1882 with their internal affairs. Seizing that brief opportunity, Sise and Bell made the best of it while their strongest and best-equipped potential competitors were on the sidelines.

In addition, the telephone field could be occupied in Canada with relatively little investment, compared with gas, water, electricity, and street railways. The telephone business required no expensive power plant; its wiring was light; and though switching was expensive, outdated equipment could be reused in smaller exchanges. In the mid-1880s, when Bell Telephone controlled all the major markets in eastern Canada, it was capitalized at about the level of the Montreal Gas Company, which controlled only one market. Effective monopoly also meant that Bell could regulate the addition of new subscribers and thus accomplish many repairs, renewals, and extensions from cash flow. The small investment required and modern middle management techniques imported from Boston made it possible for a single company to envision controlling a vast area. The telephone men were able to rationalize and monopolize their industry without help or even much hindrance from others, and they were able to do so in advance of any powerful internal economic dynamic driving them to expand in order to capture economies of scale. They anticipated those forces before experiencing them, and so were able to reap the rewards offered in the theater of science.

Diffusion and Control 4

Electric lighting entrepreneurs did not acquire the same degree of market control, even locally, as the telephone promoters during the 1880s. In the first place they faced stiff price competition from entrenched gas companies who refused to abandon the field, as the telegraphers had done, in the face of a supposedly superior substitute. Second, technology in the electrical sector remained plural and experimental throughout the 1880s. Salesmen from more than a dozen companies swarmed about promoting rival systems, each with different technical and economic properties, but all available on easy terms. Diffusion, proliferation, and thus competition amongst local operating companies arose in part from the aggressive marketing practices of the manufacturers.

The electrical entrepreneurs could not themselves bring order out of this confusion. Assistance came from the most important consumers of electricity and de facto regulators of the business—the municipal governments. The tendency of one firm to rise above others in local markets did not depend upon superior technology, managerial ability, or impersonal market forces but was a matter of public choice. It was, in other words, a political product. Cities selected the dominant firms. Ironically, this occurred even in places like Toronto where politicians consciously strove to avoid such an outcome.

Canadian municipalities exercised an even more powerful influence over the adoption of electric traction. The street railway men were not allowed to weigh the relative merits of electrification calmly on the basis of their business and their balance sheets. Instead, the cities, some in full revolt against what was considered to be the abuses of the utilities, imposed themselves upon the process of technological diffusion in an effort to manage the development of the industry in the public interest.

Electricity followed several routes into Canada. The first, as it turned out, was not of lasting importance. J. A. I. Craig, the Montreal furniture manufacturer and a francophone despite his name, became thoroughly infatuated with electric lighting during his visit to the 1878 Paris Exposition. He engineered the first public display of electrical illumination in Montreal at the Jesuit College of Sainte-Marie in October, 1878. Later, he arranged various lighting spectacles and installed a few small lighting plants in and around the city as a sideline to his furniture business.[1]

There were others like Craig in Canada, and dozens of early arc lighting demonstrations occurred, such as those put on between 1879 and 1882 at McConkey's restaurant and Timothy Eaton's department store in Toronto. Inspired by the theatre of science, promoters and financiers who had no practical experience with electricity, but knew a good thing when they saw it, incorporated companies in anticipation of a coming boom.[2]

The actual takeoff of the electrical equipment and lighting industries awaited the arrival in Canada of business agents and trained technicians from the major U.S. companies. When the electrical equipment manufacturers commenced production, their sales representatives fanned out across North America, exciting interest in the new technology and inspiring the formation of electric light companies to whom equipment might be sold. Higher-level emissaries went abroad to register patents and found similar manufacturing ventures in overseas markets.[3] This process of technological evangelicalism established the electrical manufacturing and distribution industries in Canada on solid foundation. At first Canada was simply another sales region for drummers from the U.S. industry. Later it became a separate market, set apart for exploitation by locally owned companies operating under patents granted by American manufacturers.

Technology moves with people. J. J. Wright, a millwright who had emigrated to Canada from England in 1870, was the man primarily responsible for introducing electricity to Toronto. During a visit to the Philadelphia Exposition in 1876, Wright became sufficiently impressed by the electrical exhibits to move to the United States, where he obtained work with Professor Elihu Thomson in building his first streetlighting operation. Returning to Toronto in 1881, he persuaded about 15 downtown stores to install arc lighting supplied by a Thomson generator. In 1882 he lit up the Exhibition Grounds. The following year he incorporated the Toronto Electric Light Company and applied to light the city streets with electricity when the contract with the gas company expired. Wright possessed experience, technical ability, and connections with a major U.S. manufacturer, but he lacked capital. As he waited for the verdict of the city council, Wright convinced a group of Toronto businessmen headed by the young stockbroker Henry Mill Pellatt to buy into his company. Thus through the agency of J. J. Wright, U.S. technology migrated to Toronto, advertised itself, and fell under the sway of budding finance capital.[4]

A somewhat more complex episode of technology transfer occurred in Montreal at about the same time. Early in 1884 two other representatives of the Thomson-Houston organization, Henry E. Irvine and M. Lee Ross, settled in Montreal with the ambition of selling lighting equipment and setting up a Canadian manufacturing affiliate. It is interesting to note that the telephone company, a harbinger of the new technology, provided one of the key points at which electricity came in contact with the Montreal industrial and financial elite: Charles F. Sise chaired the meeting that formally organized the Royal Electric Company. He subsequently served as its vice-president until 1886, when he was replaced by another figure prominently associated with the Bell Telephone Company, the Hon. J. R. Thibaudeau. Elihu Thomson's brother Fred moved to Montreal to head up the manufacturing division; Irvine and Ross acted as combined managers and travelling salesmen.[5] Royal Electric was thus a hybrid: a central station lighting company and a miniature replica of the Thomson-Houston manufacturing company.

Royal was one of many lighting firms, of course; there were literally dozens being promoted and selling stock. J. A. I. Craig was already in the market; two prominent politicians, Louis A. Senécal and the Hon. Thomas Ryan, had an entry. Electrical companies were the penny mines of their time, the most speculative propositions of the early 1880s. Generally speaking, the Canadian business community greeted the wildly exaggerated claims of these stock flotations—Royal promised 10 percent dividends the first year, for example—with dour skepticism. Even as Charles Sise was helping to organize Royal Electric, the Toronto agent of the Bell Telephone Company wrote to inform him: "Of electrical companies there is no end, but there will be a sudden end to the shareholders' money in most cases."[6] Out of this welter of promotions, a handful of companies—usually operating under license from American manufacturers—actually did enter the electric lighting equipment business, including the Canadian Electric Light Manufacturing Company (Van Depoele), the Canadian Electric Company, the Fuller Electrical Company, the Ball Electric Company, and of course Craig.[7]

The successful companies had to be sufficiently well capitalized to make their own markets; that is, in order to sell equipment, agents would have to go out and organize a utility to buy it. Typically,these agents would apply to obtain a local streetlighting franchise, organize a company, contract with Royal for the necessary equipment, then—if all went well—sell out to a local syndicate. In 1884, for example, Royal started companies in Ottawa, Hamilton, Saint John, Halifax, Charlottetown, Fredericton, and Montreal. As soon as work commenced in Ottawa, negotiations for the sale of the plant began with local businessmen and the city council. Royal preferred to receive cash but usually had to settle for almost the entire purchase price (after a hefty markup) in the form of stock in the new company. The plants started in 1884—85 were for the most part sold by 1887. In the meantime, Royal agents had moved on to other places—Brantford, London, Galt, Moncton, Berlin, Goderich, Sherbrooke, and Winnipeg—to begin the cycle again. In cities like Quebec City, Chatham, and Toronto, where local entrepreneurs had already formed companies, Royal also supplied equipment for stock, and in time this became the regular pattern.[8]

The difficulty with this strategy, of course, was that it tied up scarce capital for long periods. Selling equipment by these methods proved relatively easy, finding the money to finance the sales rather more difficult. Banks could be persuaded to take some of the stock acquired in equipment sales as collateral for loans; then as local interest in lighting utilities picked up, some of these securities could be quietly sold—sometimes at a premium. Occasionally Royal Electric got stuck with a property it could not unload on local interests, as was the case with the Prince Edward Island Electric Company for the better part of a decade.[9]

Royal Electric experienced chronic financial troubles throughout the 1880s, some of which were of its own manufacture. Irvine and Ross took an unusually large chunk of stock at the outset ($200,000) in return for their Thomson-Houston rights. That severely constrained the company in its ability to raise capital. As a result the directors had to cosign for a $10,000 bank loan in 1884 to raise working capital, a practice that continued with discouraging regularity for the next three years.[10] Three directors and the president resigned in 1886, and J. R. Thibaudeau had to be more or less conscripted to keep the company afloat.

Nevertheless, the electrical market expanded rapidly. By 1890 one business directory listed more than 70 electric light companies operating in Canada, and hundreds of smaller isolated plants were at work illuminating hotels, office buildings, factories, freight sheds and train stations, sawmills and mines.[11] By then Royal Electric was selling about 25 plants a year and earning profits that its directors calculated to be 42 percent of sales.[12] At that point the embattled Thibaudeau felt confident enough to attempt to raise some new money. Royal increased its capitalization for the first time since its founding; new stock was offered to the public, and Thibaudeau managed to persuade two very prominent French Canadian financiers, F. L. Béique and L. J. Forget to purchase a substantial interest in the company.[13] Royal Electric survived and then flourished, more on the strength of its earnings as a local electric utility than its profits from electrical equipment manufacturing.

The first reaction of the gas companies to this wholesale invasion of their turf was to belittle the threat; their second was to take steps to meet it. The general manager of the Consumers' Gas Company of

Toronto returned from the 1878 American Gas Light Association convention with the comforting news for his board that

> Mr. Edison had not yet accomplished all that was claimed by him, and that the time when electric light would take the place of gas as a general illuminant was a good way in the future, if such were ever to be the case, and that gas companies had no serious cause for apprehension at present.[14]

Nevertheless, the company left nothing to chance. Late in 1878, accepting the view of Francis Clemow of the Ottawa Gas Company that it would be prudent for all such concerns to secure charter powers to supply electricity, Consumers' Gas sought such an amendment to its act of incorporation.[15] Jesse Joseph, president of the Montreal Gas Company (formerly the New City Gas Company), did the same.[16]

But just to be on the safe side, the owners of these established utilities decided to make the environment as inhospitable as possible for any newcomers. Both Consumers' and Montreal Gas began lowering their rates, a downward price spiral that accelerated once their rivals actually appeared on the scene. In Toronto, gas prices fell by 36 percent during the 1880s, from $1.75 per MCF in 1879 to $1.12 in 1889. For domestic lighting gas most certainly held its own against electricity, and Montreal Gas enticed big users—hotels and large stores—with discounts ranging from 5 to 12 percent if they would refrain from installing electric lights.[17] Francis Clemow competed so fiercely against electricity in Ottawa that the newcomers were willing to sell out on his terms. Even the electric companies had to admit—if only to themselves—that their lights were more expensive. In 1890, Royal Electric ran a controlled test comparing six gas jets with six light bulbs over 105 hours and found that the gaslight cost $4.90 and the electricity $6.20, a difference of 21 percent in favour of the old way.[18] In many respects the 1880s were years of rapid growth for the gas utilities as rates followed declining cost curves, while they invested in larger, more efficient plants, improved the quality of the light they provided, and reaped higher profits with much lower charges.

Even so, at one critical point the gas companies did find themselves on the defensive: arc lights provided much brighter streetlighting—2,000 candlepower, as compared with 16 or so per gas lamp. To install the same total candlepower would require fewer arcs but would space them far apart, creating pools of bright light with almost complete darkness between (since illumination decreases in proportion to the square of the distance from the source). Thus the electric companies had to provide much more light than the gas companies if they were to win streetlighting contracts—an expensive proposition. Nevertheless, the novelty alone was worth the premium, and it was a small price to pay to break the haughty gas monopoly.[19]

In the spring of 1884 as the streetlighting contract came up for renewal, the wily Toronto city council asked J. J. Wright's Toronto Electric

Light Company and a second tenderer, the Canadian Electric Light Manufacturing Company, to erect two 25-lamp systems for three months, agreeing to pay 62¢ per night for each arc light. At the end of this demonstration
period, the council voted to divide the streetlighting contract between gas
and electricity.[20] The Toronto Electric Light Company voluntarily reduced
its rates to 55¢ per night in 1886, when it put a more efficient plant into
operation, but even at those rates electric streetlights were approximately
30 percent more expensive than the gaslights they replaced. Clearly, they
were thought to be an improvement, however; city councils all over North
America willingly paid the difference, and electricity made steady inroads
against gas, especially in the downtown districts.

Notwithstanding Montreal's many spectacular electric lighting demonstrations and the urging of several city councilors for an investigation of
electric streetlights, the Montreal Gas Company got its streetlighting contract renewed in 1884 for ten more years, without any formal consideration
being given to electricity.[21] But popular enthusiasm for electric light and
pressure from interest groups could not be denied forever.

Early in 1886 petitions began arriving at city hall from the leading
English and French merchants. Lobbyists from Royal Electric, Craig, and
others worked the corridors, and in the spring bids were called for electric
streetlighting downtown. Le Systeme Craig D'Eclairage Electrique asked
$33,452 annually for a 140-lamp service. Royal Electric submitted a tender
of $24,747 for 113 lamps, and L. A. Senécal's Compagnie Canadienne pre-
sented a complex proposal mixing arc and incandescent lights over a 25-
year term. Technically, there was not much difference between the bids,
and all three companies were headed by French Canadians—which may
have accounted for the sudden rise to prominence of J. R. Thibaudeau in
Royal Electric in 1886. On May 4, 1886, Royal's board voted to supply him
with $17,000 in company stock "for the purpose of paying commissions
customary in such cases," and it is conceivable that at least some of this
found its way into aldermanic hands. In any event the Light Committee,
headed by H. B. Rainville (who would figure prominently in such affairs
subsequently), rejected the Senécal bid because it arrived too late (there
may have been collusion between Senécal and Thibaudeau as well), and on
May 10, 1886, the contract was awarded for five years to the next lowest
bidder, Royal Electric.[22]

The bids necessary to win in Toronto, Ottawa, Montreal, and Quebec
City left little margin for profit, although these contracts did give the winning company an advantage over its rivals by helping it plant its poles first,
cover the cost of wiring the city core, and purchase larger, more efficient
generating equipment. Still, if the first arc lights seemed less than impressive, so too did the income from them. Royal Electric found itself in such
straitened circumstances after winning the Montreal contract that its directors feared they could not raise the $30,000 necessary to get underway.

Thoughts turned immediately to selling the franchise to someone who could, which was the manufacturing company's standard practice in other places but a step to be taken reluctantly in the largest lighting market in Canada. Somehow the directors scraped together the money and were heartened by the early returns. With the addition of the streetlighting load (which in August, 1886, composed 55 percent of the company's electrical business), expenses as a percentage of gross income fell from 66 to 56 percent, leaving a corresponding increase in net revenue, or what the directors identified as profit in their minutes.[23]

In Toronto the directors of the Toronto Electric Light Company were less confident; apparently, they would have preferred to own gas company stock. Henry Mill Pellatt approached Consumers' Gas in 1888 with a proposition to sell Toronto Electric Light for 2,500 shares of gas company stock, but the board declined to pay such a price.[24] The low initial returns resulting from stiff competition with gas demoralized many company promoters and discouraged new entrants.[25]

By the late 1880s, however, Canadian gas companies had begun to reconsider their competitive position vis-à-vis electricity. Everywhere, it seemed, ratepayers and city councils wanted more electric lights, despite the expense; one by one, therefore, the gas companies took steps to meet the demand. Some newly chartered companies, like the Manitoba Electric and Gas Light Company, combined both technologies under one corporate roof from the very start.[26] In Ottawa, Francis Clemow achieved the same result by forcing the electric lighting company into submission. More gentlemanly conduct prevailed in Halifax, where the gas company bought the electric lighting company at a meeting of both boards on August 25, 1887.[27] A few months later on the Pacific Coast, the board of the Vancouver Gas Company resolved to purchase a controlling interest in the Vancouver electric Illuminating Company "if it could be obtained at a reasonable rate."[28] Even Jesse Joseph in Montreal revised his earlier harsh opinion of electric lights.[29]

The improved efficiency and rapid growth of their business had left gas executives with treasuries bulging—embarrassingly so in Toronto. Thus Henry Mill Pellatt's offer was refused by Consumers' Gas not because the directors were overconfident or set in their ways, or even because he was asking too much (they didn't even dicker). Rather, they themselves were on the verge of going into the electrical business, and it did not appear to them that Toronto Electric had the best technology. Instead, they acquired rights to what they considered the superior alternating current system just developed by Westinghouse.[30]

————————
    In the midst of their manoeuvring, utilities promoters ran up against a virtual revolt of the municipalities. It was as if city councillors suddenly woke up to discover that their streets had become forested with

poles, the sky overhead darkened with dangerous wires, and the public thoroughfares turned into battle zones slit with trenches dug for competing private interests. Telegraph, telephone, district dispatch, fire alarm, and electric companies all fought for position on the streets and lanes, while gas companies ripped open the roadways and street railways neglected to repair them.

The ensuing rumpus had its comic aspects. In Quebec City, municipal employees chopped down freshly planted Bell Telephone poles in 1881, an urban logging operation that went unpunished by the courts, which ruled that the federal charter did not apply (hence Bell's frantic determination to obtain provincial enabling legislation in 1881 and 1882). By day, work crews erected lines and poles; by night, municipal employees sawed them down. In addition, linemen from rival companies cut or shorted one another's circuits. In Halifax the city council tried to reduce the confusion with a pole tax.[31]

But there was a good deal more to this municipal uprising than a rebellion against clutter. The wholesale chartering of public service corporations by federal and provincial governments meant that cities as institutions had lost autonomy within their own jurisdiction. In adition to "home rule" concerns, the cities raised questions about the quality and safety of the service being provided. Furthermore, the swollen coffers of the gas companies provided a clear illustration of what lay in store for the other urban utilities, however straitened their present circumstances. Finally, there was the issue of concentrated power: would cities be able to cope with private corporations much bigger and more influential than themselves?

A few episodes in this municipal revolt deserve notice. The Toronto city council had always resisted the efforts by Consumers' Gas to establish a reserve fund, claiming that it was merely a means of maintaining high prices while piling up profits in excess of the 10 percent dividend limit. The company abandoned its first attempt in 1879 only to reopen the question in 1885. Guided by the provincial government, which perforce had to mediate the conflict, the two sides eventually arrived at a compromise. The company would be permitted to issue up to $1,000,000 par value of new stock, which would be sold at public auction. The premium received above par would be placed in a new reserve fund where the company would be permitted to accumulate up to half the value of its paid-up capital. In return, the company agreed to reduce gas rates whenever its surplus account rose above a certain level after dividends and reserves were covered. The city thought it had put a cap upon reserves and created an automatic mechanism for reducing gas prices.[32]

Soon it became apparent that the city had been duped. In the fall of 1888, a chartered accountant reported to Mayor E. F. Clarke that the gas company had effectively circumvented the much-touted agreement by borrowing the money necessary to expand its works. As a result the reserve fund was being maintained at a level $75,000 short of the point at which it would trigger the creation of the special reserve fund which would go towards lowering the price of gas. In the accountant's view the special reserve fund would never come into being.[33]

That is why the gas company encountered an unexpected obstacle to its proposed lighting venture—a hostile city. First, the council insisted that the gas company install its wires underground for reasons of safety and aesthetics. When the company reluctantly agreed, city councillors raised objections to the dangerously high voltages of the Westinghouse distribution system. The real source of antagonism lay in allegations that the company planned to use its gas profits to finance an electrical system instead of reducing gas rates. The city stuck to its guns that no gas revenues should be used to build an electrical utility; despite the fact that all six local newspapers supported the company, the municipal authorities effectively denied it the right to string the necessary wires, and Consumers' Gas was forced to drop its efforts to become a major force in the electricity supply field.[34]

A second and related episode in municipal regulation occurred in Toronto at the same time. With several firms bidding to supply electricity and the Bell Telephone Company extending its service, the city authorities became increasingly concerned about the jungle of wires and poles lining the streets. During 1889 the Toronto Electric Light Company and the newly organized Toronto Incandescent Electric Light Company signed a contract with the city to place their wires in buried conduits. These "Underground Agreements" gave the two firms the right to serve the central business district without fear of further competition for 30 years, at the end of which the city would have the option of purchasing their assets at a price to be arbitrated. The agreements also contained a provision intended to protect consumers from the monopoly: the franchises would become void if the two companies amalgamated. It was hoped that competition between them would regulate rates naturally.[35]

In Montreal the most prominent champions of the city and its citizens against corporate domination and monopolistic exploitation during the 1880s were councillors representing middle-class, predominantly English-speaking wards. This group, known by its supporters as "the Honest Minority," "the Noble Thirteen," and "the Faithful Anti-Monopolists," campaigned unremittingly to limit the abuses of the street railway, gas, and later electric light and telephone companies.[36] As a result, the French-speaking majority on the city council was cast—not always fairly—in the role of protector and promoter of the welfare of corporations. A public agitation for more electric street lights in 1888 (inspired in part by a disgruntled J. A. I. Craig and Jesse Joseph's gas company) provided yet another occasion for collision between these two factions.

Between September and December of 1888, the council's Light Committee pondered three possible courses of action. Should it grant a contract for the additional lights to a different company to encourage competition? Should the city light the streets itself? Or should Royal Electric be authorized to expand its system to service the entire city? Some municipal reformers thought that a municipal lighting plant was worth investigating. At the very least, they argued, public tenders ought to be called. Royal Electric contended that it held an exclusive franchise to light the city streets with electricity until the expiry of its 1886 contract (a point on which city lawyers concurred); if more lights were needed, Royal alone should supply them. But to justify its investment in a larger plant, Royal needed a ten-year renewal of its contract.[37]

The Light Committee decided the question amidst charges of irregular procedure and strong suspicion of corruption. F. H. Badger's September 25 report on the cost of a municipal system offered little comfort to the reformers: the city electrician calculated that it would require an investment of approximately $300,000 and annual operating expenses of roughly $85,000 to obtain lighting for which the city currently paid $87,000.[38] Most people on the council did not think the slight advantage justified the expense. So, it all boiled down to a choice between Craig and Royal. On December 4 the Light Committee passed over Craig's lower bid when it voted to extend the Royal Electric contract for ten years, paying the company $119,000 annually for 800 arc lights and 42¢ a night for each additional lamp ordered. The full council ratified a slightly amended agreement (a five-year term and 40¢ per additional light) on December 27, 1888, over the furious opposition of the anglophone reformers.[39] It was alleged at the time that Royal Electric had suborned F. H. Badger by offering him a job if Royal got the contract. True or not, Badger did resign to become an electrician for Royal soon afterward. Aldermen Rainville and Préfontaine, key figures on the Light Committee, were both known to be extremely close to J. R. Thibaudeau; afterward they became prominent shareholders in Royal Electric.[40]

But scandal should not obscure the fact that the outcome in Montreal was much the same as elsewhere. A company with an existing contract had a tremendous advantage—if only in political leverage—over its rivals in securing a subsequent contract. Whether they intended to or not, whether they profitted from it or not, city councillors played a key role in selecting the dominant firms in the electric lighting business. The prosperity of Royal Electric dates from this second contract, a triumph that Thibaudeau and the directors celebrated with bonuses and dividends.[41] The contract assured Royal a continuing monopoly of the streetlighting business, an opportunity to expand its distribution network, and a chance to invest in the most up-to-date technology. Two years later the Toronto city council went through the same exercise with the same results. The incumbent Toronto Electric Light Company had its contract extended (without a breath of scandal), and dividends began flowing there as well.[42]

Everywhere, these franchises raised ancient ethical questions, but corruption was really beside the point. To dwell for a moment upon the obvious, graft is a signal that politics is important, that it decides outcomes. If the electrical distributors bribed city councils on occasion, that very fact strongly suggests that the politicians momentarily controlled their fate.

Municipal regulation did influence the structure of the electrical industry during the 1880s and 1890s, whether that process was conducted by fair means or foul. The biggest customer for electricity—the city—in effect selected the eventual winner from among a host of competitors by its choice of a streetlighting contractor. Getting that first contract gave one company a virtually insurmountable advantage over its rivals; keeping it was a matter of corporate life and death, which explains the venality on both sides of the negotiations. The losers in these contests usually packed up and sold out to the victor, as Royal Electric did when it lost out in London, Ontario.[43] But in big markets like Toronto and Montreal, or where local waterpower supported several utilities (as in Ottawa), competitors hung on, hoping for a chance when the streetlighting contract came around again.

In Toronto, competition of sorts between arc and incandescent lighting technologies was guaranteed—or so it was thought—by a municipal ordinance. Regulations such as the Toronto Underground Agreements erected barriers to entry that served to discourage latecomers and restrict business to those already established. City councils in Toronto and Montreal also used their discretion in the granting of contracts to keep the powerful gas companies out of the electric lighting business, thereby preserving a measure of interfuel competition on the one hand and preventing a concentration of power on the other.

Toronto, Montreal, and Ottawa seriously considered the possibility of a municipal electric plant, only to reject it as too risky. Victoria did try it, and its failure after five years merely confirmed the conventional wisdom that these matters were best left to the private sector. In a few cities (Toronto and Ottawa, for example) the revulsion against the conduct of public utilities led to stricter regulation than elsewhere (like Montreal). But everywhere the outcome was the same: the selection of a streetlighting company established the dominant firm in the local market. Victory did not necessarily go to those companies with the best technology; rather, the winners then adopted the best available system.

═════════   The diffusion of electric street railway technology was less sudden than that of the telephone or the electric light. Greater control could be exerted over this business because its capital requirements (roughly $30,000 for a mile of single track and overhead wire in the early 1890s) tended to reduce the number of entrants. In the tradition of the capital goods sector, the traction equipment manufacturers placed less emphasis upon aggressive marketing and started fewer demonstration projects once the technology had proved itself. Rather than becoming embroiled in local franchise battles, the manufacturers preferred to hold back and sell their equipment (usually for stock) to companies with contracts already in hand. There were also fewer equipment companies, and they were greatly affected by the recession of the 1890s.[44] Thus the "push" from the manufacturing level did not necessarily lead to local competition.

The new technology appeared during a period of smouldering resentment against the old horsecar companies. Typically, it was thought that they had not kept up with the growth of their cities and that they provided inadequate, uncomfortable service on the few routes they did maintain. People suspected that the owners preferred nursing high dividends (which in the late 1880s had become quite common in the larger cities) to investing in needed improvements and expansion. Those given to passionate discourse could embroider this general bill of particulars with lurid charges of arrogance, meanness, dishonesty, corruption, stock watering, and cruelty to animals, employees, and passengers. The advent of the new technology presented an opportunity to establish public transportation on an entirely new footing. As often as not, the change from animal to electric traction also involved a change in management.

Just as the telegraph and gas industries in Canada seemed indifferent at first to the challenge of newer technologies, the established street railways, too, were slow to react. One can readily sympathize with the reluctance of some operators to innovate. Persistent losses had provided little incentive to further investment. T. C. Keefer, the venerable proprietor of the Ottawa City Passenger Railway, complained that just as his company had begun to make a little money after a long drought in the 1880s (during which he had twice tried to unload the property on an unwilling city council), he was unable to enjoy the profits because of threatened municipal competition. He wanted nothing more than some breathing room to recoup his losses.[45] But what deterred Jesse Joseph, since November of 1884 the president of both the Montreal City Passenger Railway and the Montreal Gas Company? Under his vigorous management the company (renamed the Montreal Street Railway in 1886) had improved its performance to the point of placing $300,000 worth of its bonds on the London market—one of the first Canadian industrials to do so—and to pay between 7 and 12 percent dividends on a much-diluted equity. Yet Joseph and his board approached technological change in the street railroad business and the gas business with the same trepidation. In the end, Joseph said he would rather resign than renegotiate the street railway contract with the city—and on

March 31, 1892, he did.[46] Thus both rich and poor held back, waiting for some indefinite moment in the future when the time would be right to think about electric power.

In Winnipeg, when the unpopular proprietor of the horse-drawn street railway proposed to change over to electricity, the city council objected. Then, after he went ahead and established electric service on a limited basis in January of 1891, the city proceeded to negotiate an agreement with an eastern Canadian syndicate, headed by William Mackenzie, for a much larger street railroad built according to specifications laid down by the council itself.[47] Old quarrels and a perceived record of poor performance prevented municipalities from doing business with existing companies in Winnipeg, in Toronto, and elsewhere.

This determination on the part of municipal politicians to start afresh and control the whole process is perhaps best examined in Ottawa, in 1890 a small city of 43,000 and seat of the federal government. There the municipality rejected the old company as a vehicle of modernization, made preparations itself to operate a system, explored the technical aspects of the question, led a provincial campaign to expand municipal power in the area, took a direct role in the selection of the appropriate technology, and simply refused to deal with companies who would not agree to its terms.

Ottawa was then a lumber town with booms, mills, kilns, and lumberyards centred on the Chaudière Falls, south of which clustered the houses of the mill hands and river men. On a bluff overlooking the mills and a sweeping curve of the Ottawa River perched the great gothic pile of the government of Canada. The politicians, bureaucrats, and merchants of the town spread themselves out on a rolling plateau, bisected by a picturesque canal, in front and to the east of the Parliament Buildings. The Ottawa City Passenger Railway Company had served the needs of the civil servants and the mercantile elite, but it had neglected the interests of the merchants along Rideau Street and the middle-class residential quarters that had grown up in the east and south—and of course the working-class districts had been totally ignored.

Several attempts to organize a second company having failed in the mid-1880s, in 1888 the city began investigating the possibility of operating a street railway itself. The council petitioned the Ontario legislature for the necessary authority, arguing that it ought to have the power to own street railways just as it had legislative authority to operate its own gas and waterworks.[48] At a convention of Ontario municipalities in November, 1889, the Ottawa delegation gathered significant support for its peitition from London, Hamilton, Toronto, Belleville, and Guelph. This municipal insurgency placed E. H. Bronson, Ottawa's Liberal member of the Ontario legislature, in an extremely delicate position. He was first and foremost a representative of the city and therefore under some obligation to promote legislation sent up to him by the council. On the other hand, he was also a shareholder in the Ottawa City Passenger Railway Company and a principal in a rising electric utility; he had the interests of his friends to consider. As a man of considerable property, he bore the usual reverence toward sunk capital and vested rights, a concern fully shared by Oliver Mowat, his Premier. Mowat agreed that legislation of the sort being sought by the city of Ottawa would have to be introduced, but "I would suggest your inserting in it such provisions as would seem to you reasonable for the protection of existing companies."[49] Accordingly Bronson sponsored and had passed a more restricted bill than Ottawa had asked for, one without the power of expropriation and with safeguards for the old company. At the same time Levi Crannell, Bronson's business partner and a member of the Ottawa council's Street Railway Committee, applied himself behind the scenes to dampen public ownership enthusiasm before it got out of hand.[50]

In April of 1890 the Street Railway Committee set to work in earnest. First it identified the streets on which lines needed to be built, then discussed what kind of railway should be built, what kind of traction should be employed, and how it should be operated. To answer these questions, a delegation visited the Thomson-Houston company in Boston and made an on-the-spot investigation of Henry Whitney's increasingly famous West End Street Railway. The Ottawa deputation returned from its trolley tour of Boston filled with enthusiasm and fully converted. Horses had been superseded by electricity, the committee reported to the council, and the overhead wire was the best means of supplying propulsion. Other systems, such as storage batteries, did away with the ugly poles, but they "suffered from excessive cost, great weight and rapid deterioration." With a clear view of what kind of street railway it wanted right down to the type of motors to be used, the committee laid down the terms on which it would let the franchise: an exclusive right for 20 years on specified streets; first refusal on additional streets; a $400 tax per mile of double-track and $300 for single to be paid to the city for paving; a five-cent fare with reduced rates for students and workingmen; and the posting of a $5,000 performance bond.[51]

A Toronto group led by ex-mayor W. H. Howland expressed interest but at length was driven off by what its members considered excessive municipal interference with business decisions.[52] The vast amount of information generated in the scuffle and greater familiarity with the advantages of the technology screwed up the courage of two local businessmen, Thomas Ahearn and W. Y. Soper. They offered to take over the contract on the same terms rejected by Howland and, as a token of good faith, they sent a $5,000 cheque in advance as their performance bond.[53]

The Ottawa case offers a clear example of the kind of municipal interventionism that marked the arrival of the street railway in Canada. A desire to avoid the errors of the past guided every step, as did an eagerness to obtain the fullest and most reliable information in order to make a decision in the broader public interest. While they mastered the technical details, city councillors also addressed the tactical requirements of getting what they wanted from private contractors. A vocal minority would have preferred public ownership from the very beginning—this was true as well in Toronto and Montreal—but the majority saw that option mainly as a means of extracting better terms from wily negotiators for private syndicates. Despite their best intentions they failed to draft the ironclad contracts they wanted, but the Ottawa council did make a sincere effort to gauge civic needs, avoid old quarrels, assess the existing technology, and obtain a reasonable contract to provide the most modern service at the lowest rates. Their negotiations also reveal the impatience and sense of outraged propriety of businessmen caught in a regulatory web for the first time. They found political meddling in their affairs annoying, and they had to give up rather more than they wanted. But if they refused to accept the restrictions, there were always others who were willing to do so.

It should be stressed that the gathering of information, the writing of detailed specifications, and the calling of tenders proceeded with deliberation. In Toronto this process went on at such great length that the council had not yet made up its mind when the time came to recover the old franchise from Senator Frank Smith. For a short time in 1891, therefore, the city of Toronto actually operated its own street railway, making respectable profits—which naturally amplified the enthusiasm for public ownership in certain real estate, labour reform, and radical circles. Eventually, however, the council settled on what it wanted (an annual paving tax of $800 per mile of track, a 30-year term, workingmen's fares, a minimum wage of 15¢ an hour and a maximum ten-hour day for employees, and a share of the profits) and twice rejected all the applicants before it received a set of tenders to its liking. In the final analysis the competing bids looked much the same.[54] The specification procedure more or less ensured this result.

Public ownership had looked best on paper—according to schedules prepared by the city's accountants, based upon hypothetical projections of revenue, expenses, and capital invested—but it was deemed unacceptable by the majority of the council and by Torontonians who were determined to relieve Frank Smith of his railroad but were decidedly opposed to running it as a public work. So it was a toss-up which bid was best. The companionship afforded some councillors by the mysterious "Clean Skater" and the comfort of his $40,000 in bribes merely helped certain obtuse aldermen see the advantages of the tender submitted by William Mackenzie, the railroad contractor, H. A. Everett, a street railroad expert from Cleveland originally retained by the city council to give professional advice, and George Washington Kiely, late of the unlamented Toronto Street Railway. It should be added that the majority of the Toronto aldermen came to the same conclusion without being bribed.[55]

Montreal politicians tried several techniques to quicken the pace of modernization. Annually, a group of anglophone reformers led by G. W. Stephens introduced motions calling upon the city to purchase the street railway from its lackadaisical owners. These resolutions invariably failed by large majorities.[56] But having signed a long-term contract as recently as 1886 with the Montreal Street Railway Company, the council had to confront the question of how an electrified street railway was to be obtained. In March of 1892 the city effectively forced the old company's hand. Municipal negotiators pointed out that the company could modernize on its own terms in its own good time, but then it faced the prospect of competition. Or it could negotiate a completely new contract with the city to perpetuate its monopoly. A number of veteran company directors would not countenance further negotiations and resigned from the board. L. J. Forget, a director since 1886 and a leading figure in the Montreal financial world, stepped in to replace the departing Jesse Joseph. He infused the board with new blood and the company with new capital, and set out in lusty pursuit of a revised franchise. Bargaining at this point focused on the percentage of gross receipts the bidders were willing to pay the city for rights. Forget submitted a proposal in the spring of 1892 but somehow learned in June that such a bid would not win the contract, so at his behest the board of the street railway sweetened the offer. The Montreal city council voted 24 to 12 to allow a revivified Montreal Street Railway to electrify and expand its existing plant.[57]

——————— Who arranged the transfer to electric street railway technology, and who ended up in control of it? As has been demonstrated, in many cases the cities themselves conducted much of the technological assessment, laid out the systems, and chose from among competing syndicates the owners of the municipally sanctioned and regulated monopolies. But, with a few exceptions, civic involvement ended there. Who carried these projects from design through to implementation? For small operations like the Vancouver street railway, the equipment supplier (Thomson-Houston in that case) set up the system on a turnkey basis.[58] In time, however, the Toronto, Ottawa, and Montreal companies provided a cadre of technicians. H. A. Everett of Cleveland was one of the key engineers who brought a detailed knowledge of the technical aspects of the business to Canada and helped train local apprentices. He had been hired originally by the city of Toronto to assess the relative merits of the tenders submitted, but as we have seen he subsequently teamed up with William Mackenzie and G. W. Kiely to win the contract. Mackenzie's silent partner in the Toronto franchise, James Ross, was also a major shareholder in the Montreal Street Railway; thus when the Forget group got the Montreal franchise H. A. Everett was recruited from Toronto as managing director during the construction, and William Mackenzie contracted to build the line. Everett would move on to modernize and consolidate street railways in

Detroit and London, Ontario.[59] Obviously, in the beginning there was a good deal of technical interchange, borrowing of personnel, and cross-ownership between the Toronto and Montreal street railways. At the technical and managerial levels, this movement continued even after ownership links had been dissolved. The Ahearn and Soper operation in Ottawa would also become a node of expertise and innovation, spinning off its own manufacturing and consulting engineering activities.

As a further step, the principals of these metropolitan ventures then applied their experience to organizing similar companies in the second tier of cities in their respective hinterlands, James Ross and R. B. Angus of Montreal bought and reorganized a bankrupt street railway in Saint John, New Brunswick.[60] William Mackenzie, James Ross, and some Toronto associates acquired the street railway franchise in Winnipeg, the metropolis of the prairie West; later they added gas and electric utilities. But metropolitan expansion in this sector did not proceed very far because there were not many urban communities of suitable size in Canada, and some were already occupied by local interests. The alternative then was to expand into foreign markets, which three clusters of entrepreneurs in Halifax, Montreal, and Toronto proceeded to do with almost reckless abandon.[61]

The fact that some Canadian cities had already been developed before Canadian metropolitan promoters could get to them suggests that there were other sources of technology and capital. The street railway in Halifax, for example, was electrified by Boston rather than Toronto or Montreal capitalists. H. M. Whitney had come to Nova Scotia for coal to fuel his New England power plants. Almost as an afterthought to the coal company he floated (with the help of a group of Halifax venture capitalists), Whitney and his chief engineer, F. S. Pearson, applied their knowledge to whip a small Halifax street railway promotion into profitable shape.[62] In this way, Halifax, Montreal, and Toronto financiers thus made contact with Pearson, who had been an engineer on both the Metropolitan Street Railway in New York and the West End Street Railway in Boston. He in turn would be one of the key techno-entrepreneurial adventurers who led Canadian capital into a series of electric traction, light, and power promotions in the Caribbean and Latin America.

Around these scattered electric street railway promotions in Canada, a loose network of engineers and capitalists gradually took shape. In 1891 the two dozen or so electrical engineers in the country formed the Canadian Electrical Association, and at their annual meeting they shared experience, swapped information, and kept up to date with developments in the electric traction, lighting, telephone, and telegraph industries. The *Canadian Electrical News,* revived about the same time, provided similar information on a monthly basis.[63] And although capital formed no national association and maintained no journal other than the weekly *Monetary Times,* something like a national capitalist community had begun to crystallize and establish links; in due course it created the formal institutions of a national capital market. This process had begun with the trunk railroads and chartered banks and would be extended by the electrical utilities, which would supply interest-bearing securities for consumption by Canadian financial intermediaries and ultimately by the British capital market.

Who were the men who made these connections? In the absence of a systematic prosopography, it might be ventured that the moving spirits behind the modernization and subsequent capitalization of the public transit sector were new men for the most part, creatures of the railroad era. Some got their start as railroad contractors, like Ross, Mackenzie, and (later) Herbert Holt. Others like Forget in Montreal and Pellatt in Toronto were financial specialists; they knew how to place securities in the narrow but rapidly expanding Canadian capital market. Banking and railroad experience brought these two groups into communication with British merchant banking houses. Promoters like Everett, Ahearn, Soper, and Pearson combined engineering and entrepreneurial ability. They too were new men, technological itinerants, some with formal university degrees—children of the telephone and electric light rather than the merchant's warehouse. As a group, these individuals formed part of a complex international network that linked the major sources of technological innovation with Canadian and later British pools of capital. It was thus to this loose alliance of new men plus a professional cadre of mechanical and electrical engineers that control over the new electrical and street railway technology flowed once the municipalities surrendered the franchises.

The telephone, electric light, and trolley took different routes into Canada, but they all came from the same place, entering the main Canadian cities in the first wave of diffusion from centers of innovation in the northeastern United States. Canada became tied into a continental technological network despite its strong political and economic connections with Great Britain; it was U.S. rather than European styles, standards, and systems that were transferred to Canada. In time, Canadian engineers and entrepreneurs would feed innovations and energy back into the U.S. sphere of technological influence.

Business structures were borrowed as well as technology. The telephone business was developed in Canada as it was in individual regions of the United States—under Boston's control using virtually the same monopoly strategy. Canadian electric lighting utilities were propagated by equipment manufacturers operating under license, or by branch plants using the same patents and marketing techniques as their U.S. parents. Canada thus bore the stamp of both U.S. technology and U.S. industrial organization.

The new technologies did not have to begin *de novo* in a primitive, indifferent, or unreceptive environment. The press and the theatre of science had already prepared public opinion and cultivated a taste for these symbols of modernity among private individuals, corporate bodies, and municipal corporations; existing institutions provided the footings for the new structures to be erected. We have observed, too, a certain amount of cross-ownership between the new utilities as individual capitalists became involved in more than one sector or more than one city. The telephone was organized nationally by a single company; the electric light and traction interests slowly evolved into an informal national network.

Only the telephone made it to market without regulation, though a case could be made that senior government legislation and the patent system provided important political props to the dominant organization. The electric light and the street railway industries depended more heavily upon municipal control to approach stable monopoly status. The regulatory process also gave rise to notions of alternative modes of industrial organization and vaguely adversarial relationship with private capital that would become open hostility in due course. But like the loosely associated groups of capitalists revolving around the new technologies, the local critics of private monopoly had yet to coalesce into an institutionalized national force.

Making Monopolies

Monopolies were made, not born. Competition did not wither away once dominant firms began to emerge in local utilities markets; indeed, the late nineteenth and the early twentieth century witnessed a surprising resurgence of competitive forces, which owners and managers of utilities had either to surrender to or surmount. These pressures varied in intensity from city to city, but they were present everywhere. At critical junctures monopoly was the product of purpose, choice, policy, influence, tactic, and human effort.

The underlying factors tending toward monopoly are familiar to students of introductory economics: patented processes, scarce raw materials, or long-run decreasing costs.[1] These were certainly present during the 1890s, but their effect was complicated by the persistence of certain countervailing forces. Patents sustained Bell Telephone during the early years, but in 1885 some of that protection was stripped away, and the remainder disappeared in the 1890s. Street railways holding exclusive franchises to the city core still had to cope with rapid population growth on the outskirts and guard against the penetration of their territories by suburban roads. Economies of scale had been enjoyed by the gas industry and had begun to be apparent in the electric sector as well, but it was still possible to build small, extremely competitive firms serving limited areas. The advent of hydroelectric generation and long distance transmission raised precisely the opposite problem: large producers in the countryside looked desperately for big urban markets. In the long run, hydroelectric technology would enhance corporate concentration by greatly increasing the scale of production, thereby placing a premium upon control over marketing and distribution.[2] But in the short run, the abundant waterpower within the metropolitan regions of many Canadian cities presented numerous openings for ambitious syndicates to challenge existing monopolies.

In short, the utilities entrepreneurs were not simply passive instruments of economic and technological dynamics. In specific historical circumstances where centrifugal and centripetal forces conflicted, capitalists had to make monopolies as an act of will, overcoming fissiparous tendencies in the face of strenous opposition.

In 1892 Ottawa had three electric light, two telephone, two gas, and two street railway companies. Within two years only one company remained in each market, and so it would remain for more than a decade. That pattern became familiar all over the continent, but it would not be the only one. Indeed, Ottawa provided an example of relatively weak concentration: the four companies remained institutionally separate, though they shared many directors and were managed by a cohesive group who often worked together in harmony on important questions. Cities at the other extreme included Halifax, Saint John, Winnipeg, and Vancouver, in each of which a single company supplied electricity, gas, and public transportation. And two of the three services were combined in Hamilton, Montreal, and Toronto. Leaving aside for a moment the telephone, which had been organized on a regional basis from the outset, we can identify three patterns of integration: complete unification, partial amalgamation, and unaffiliated development. To observe the making of these different kinds of monopolies more closely, it is necessary to examine a few specific cases.

Let us begin with Winnipeg, a booming new city in the West, whose population rose from around 30,000 in 1890 to over 100,000 by 1905. Against this background of burgeoning demand, a group of outside financiers from central Canada moved in during the 1890s and successfully monopolized all of Winnipeg's utilities. In 1892, as we have seen, a syndicate led by the Torontonian William Mackenzie obtained a franchise to build an electric street railway in the city.[3] Associated with Mackenzie and his partner, Donald Mann, in this enterprise were Montrealers W. C. Van Horne, R. B. Angus, and James Ross; H. A. Everett from Cleveland; and two Winnipeg businessmen, F. M. Morse and G. H. Campbell. When this group assumed control of the Winnipeg concession, there was already one other electric street railway in operation and at least two electric companies.

Characteristically, the impetuous William Mackenzie forced the issue. In 1894 he bought out A. W. Austin's rival line for $175,000 in cash, and consolidated street railway operations under one management.[4] Next he took aim at the tottering Manitoba Electric and Gas Light Company: his Winnipeg Electric Street Railway built its own power plant, large enough to go into competition with its former supplier. But it needed a distribution system: hence its interest in a failing competitor. Manitoba Electric, weakened by a burdensome floating debt and the loss of the municipal street lighting contract in 1895, stumbled toward receivership. Moving in for the kill, William Mackenzie managed to assume the company's major debts, then forced its sale to the Winnipeg Electric Street Railway for stock rather than cash.[5] Thus, in 1898, Winnipeg Electric acquired a distribution system, an additional power plant, and a very promising gas franchise. A year later MacKenzie engineered the purchase of his last remaining competitor, the small North West Electric Company, and closed down its obsolete plant.[6] By 1900 the Winnipeg Electric Street Railway had a complete monopoly of gas, electricity, and public transit in Canada's fastest growing city.

Some of Mackenzie's thinking on these matters may be gathered from a letter he wrote in 1895 to Charles Porteous, his business manager back in Toronto, when he was trying to negotiate a street railway franchise in Birmingham, England. If all the existing companies could be acquired, he explained to Porteous, "the cost of the separate management would pay a good dividend if put under one management and all the extra expenses saved. . . . I believe there is money in it by making the right combination which I think I can do."[7] Making the right combination—that might be considered Mackenzie's consuming ambition during the late 1890s. He had wanted to do the same thing in Toronto, but his associates James Ross and Charles Porteous cautioned him to avoid unnecessary trouble with the municipal authorities, the press, and the suspicious Toronto business community.[8] The achievement of complete fusion in Winnipeg at this time probably represented his ideal: the right combination at the right price in an expanding market.

Through his association with the American engineer F. S. Pearson, William Mackenzie had acquired rights to a much more economical means of gas production. Needless to say, the clamor being raised by the Board of Trade and the Winnipeg city council over exorbitant gas prices intensified when the company was absorbed by the street railway. To avert the threat of municipal competition and undermine support for a publicly owned system, Winnipeg Electric Street Railway quickly modernized its gas plant and cut rates. Each rate reduction was made to seem a hard-won municipal victory, but there is reason to believe that Mackenzie's costs fell much more dramatically than his returns.[9]

Economies of scale and technological improvements allowed Mackenzie to lower prices, increase output, and still improve profit margins in his Halifax, Winnipeg, and Vancouver gas operations. In Winnipeg these gas receipts enhanced cash flow, brightened the balance sheet, boomed the stock, and made capital easier and cheaper to obtain at a time when a great deal of it was required to finance electric and street railway expansion. By 1905, when net earnings were increasing at a rate of more than 30 percent annually and the company was returning more than 10 percent on its capital, the consolidated Winnipeg company was one of the most attractive utility investments in the country.[10]

Public expectations of service, price, and supply based upon experience in other Canadian markets stimulated potential opposition in two quite different camps: the city on the one hand, and speculative entrepreneurs on the other. Winnipeg remained in an almost constant state of excitement about Mackenzie's rates, and the demand for publicly owned gas and electric systems ebbed and flowed with price reductions and elections. The possibility of municipal competition had to be taken seriously, as did the threat of rivalry from private sources. There were plenty of hydraulic sites within easy reach of Winnipeg, which improvements in long distance transmission after the turn of the century immediately valorized. If Mackenzie's company did not take advantage of this new energy source, others certainly would. Mackenzie anticipated this, and in 1902 he joined forces with the principals of the Ogilvie Milling Company, a large bulk power user, to promote a hydroelectric venture on the Pinawa Channel of the Winnipeg River some 60 miles northeast of the city. Once this company had been organized and contracts for the delivery of hydroelectric power were signed with the street railway, it was then skillfully folded into Winnipeg Electric in such a way, an insider explained, "that all shareholders of the Street Railway Company derive a benefit without having to pay any cash."[11]

This brief résumé of Winnipeg developments prompts two general observations of broader relevance. First, the old technologies did not die. Gas markets expanded with urban growth and continued to offer opportunities for profit even as gas was being replaced by electricity in some applications. In Winnipeg, the bearers of the new electrical technology were also alert to the additional rents that could still be wrung from gas. Mackenzie and Pearson presided over the reconstruction of gas companies in Vancouver and Halifax as well. And there were certain advantages to being able to control the supply of gas and electricity in the same market. Gas could be made to underwrite other investments; prices could be adjusted to keep the growth of output within manageable proportions and regulate the demand between fuels, and profits could be juggled over time to produce a steady overall rate of return.

Second, a monopoly once made could be broken. Combining all the local utilities into one did not eliminate competition once and for all. New technology—in this case hydroelectricity—and political intervention could and did breach monopoly's defenses. City councils and public opinion also had to be managed. Prices could not be kept too high or technical innovation delayed too long without tempting the city, large power users, or venture capitalists to start up a rival waterpower company. In Winnipeg, Mackenzie took the threat of private competition seriously enough to swallow it up. He was less prescient in his judgement of other city councils.

—————   The guiding spirits behind the Vancouver utilities monopoly were much more security-conscious than Mackenzie, who, in time, came to be regarded as more than a little reckless. The fact that most of the tramway and electric light companies so proudly promoted in good times had, by the mid 1890s, collapsed into the hands of receivers sensitized owners to the perils around them. Nonetheless, the London merchant banking house of Sperling and Company saw an opportunity amidst this corporate carnage to combine the bankrupt utilities of Victoria, Vancouver, and New Westminster into one consolidated company, which could then be refinanced, integrated, and provided with enough working capital to flourish in the next cycle of growth. Locally, F. S. Barnard, federal member of parliament for Victoria, handled the purchase of the various companies and shepherded a charter through the British Columbia legislature in 1895–96. In London, R. M. Horne-Payne of the Sperling group presided over the organization of a small syndicate to refloat the amalgamated concern.[12]

The most attractive feature of this Pacific coast concern was its extremely broad mandate. In chartering the British Columbia Electric Railway (née the Consolidated Railway Company), F. S. Barnard had been at pains to confirm the company's rights under each of its predecessor's statutes. The charter also extended the company's rights over areas not yet organized into muncipalities, authorized it to enter almost any line of the utilities business (including telephones), and permitted it to merge and amalgamate with or own stock in similar enterprise.[13]

Nevertheless, a major defect marred the main franchise. The BCER's tram operations in Vancouver were licensed on a street-by-street basis with termination dates ranging from 1900 to 1918. Apart from its inconvenience and uncertainty, this arrangement gave the city an unusual amount of leverage with the company in establishing the terms of extensions. Unbeknownst to the city, the company also lacked explicit legal authority to operate an electric utility in the municipality. If the company were to be financed in the usual manner, these defects would have to be fixed, so the new owners immediately set to work plotting a strategy to regularize their Vancouver franchises and to reduce the power of the municipality.

The first step was to make certain that the city council could not enter the street railway, gas, or electric business without first buying out the BCER. To accomplish this, the company's local general manager, Johannes Buntzen, used his influence with the provincial government to have such a "protective clause" inserted in the City of Vancouver charter.[14]

The second step was to negotiate a new agreement with the city consolidating the separate contracts into one omnibus franchise with uniform terms, conditions, and a specified termination date. It required a five-year campaign to achieve a city wide contract, but despite the frustration of these on-again, off-again negotiations and the unbending line taken by the London board of directors, Buntzen secured a franchise consolidation agreement late in 1901 that was actually less favourable to the city than the one originally proposed. According to Buntzen, the BCER had finagled the lowest revenue-sharing agreement in Canada.[15] Finally, the company integrated operations in such a way as to make impracticable the disentangling of separate units for municipal purchase, thereby requiring that everything (if anything) be bought; so formidable an undertaking, it was believed, as to rule out municipal ownership altogether.

The British Columbia Electric Railway had to be concerned about possible municipal competition because its failing predecessors had desperately tried to unload themselves on their respective cities. Twice in the 1890s the ratepayers of Vancouver turned down requests to buy or help refinance the Vancouver Electric Railway and Light Company, not out of principle but rather because the costs were deemed excessive in the midst of a general recession. Thus, ideological barriers against public ownership were weak in British Columbia.

By 1901, however, the British Columbia Electric Railway had fully secured itself against municipal competition, regularized its Vancouver franchise, conceded less than any other major street railway had in the process, and successfully seized the regulatory initiative. The city could hardly hope to take over the system until 1919, and then only with great difficulty. The company also legalized its highly irregular electric lighting franchise by a subterfuge, adding a few harmless-looking clauses to an agreement with the city about another matter entirely. As Buntzen explained:

> I drafted it myself so that it should bear the marks of having been made out by a layman, as it might have called too much attention to the agreement if it had been issued from our lawyers, insignificant as the subject matter is. . . . The only thing of any interest in the agreement is that portion of the recital which says we have constructed and now operate an electric incandescent system in Vancouver, with the permission of the corporation. This . . . will stop the city from ever interfering with our polelines.[16]

By toughness, experience, determination, and guile, the BCER got what it wanted from a divided, confused, and perhaps overeager municipal government. Knowingly or not, the city council of Vancouver had effectively negotiated away an unusually powerful regulatory advantage.

The British management also addressed itself to neutralizing private rivals, including Mackenzie's gas company and a wildcat hydroelectric promotion. In 1897, Horne-Payne had considered buying the gas company to prevent competition, after Buntzen warned him that gaslight could be produced much more cheaply than electric light. The acquisition would have prevented the possibility of "ruinous rate-cutting," in Buntzen's opinion, but it also opened up the alarming prospect of a hostile takeover: the shares William Mackenzie and his Toronto associates would receive in such a deal, added to what they already had, would give them altogether too much influence over the British Columbia Electric Railway.[17]

Nevertheless, in 1902 the Vancouver Gas Company slashed its rates, and BCER felt compelled to follow suit whatever the cost. Delicate negotiations ensued in Vancouver to halt the downward price spiral, and in London—during one of Mackenzie's periodic visits—to reopen purchase discussions. It transpired that Mackenzie and other utility men felt betrayed by the BCER'S recent wage settlement and profit-sharing agreement with its employees. The generous terms of this contract had made life difficult for eastern Canadian managers, who were now determined to do everything in their power to punish the corporate maverick. Eventually the anger subsided, as Horne-Payne reported: "There are other businesses of much more importance to this group than the Gas Company or all the Electric Railway Companies in which they are interested. A recent threatened withdrawal on our part from the finance of these undertakings has had a salutory effect all around."[18] Early in 1904 the BCER finally did buy Mackenzie's Vancouver Gas Company.

While the purchase led to an immediate stabilization of gas prices, the BCER chose that moment to reduce its electricity rates. Price competition, with its attendant increase in output, had taught the company the lessons of economies of scale and the advantages of a diversified load.[19] The voluntary reduction took the sting out of the gas company merger, brought Vancouver rates into line with those prevailing in U.S. west coast cities, and could be publicly justified by the recent delivery of hydroelectric power to the city. Besides, Buntzen observed, reductions paid for themselves: "It has been our experience here that any reduction in rates is recouped within three months by people using more light on account of lower rates and by the number of new customers applying for lights who did not think they could afford them before."[20]

Competition from hydroelectric power was the last major threat to be overcome by the British Columbia Electric Railway in its pursuit of a complete monopoly of utilities on the lower mainland. The British directors remained skeptical of the potential of hydroelectric power. In fact, F. S. Barnard, as a local director of the company, appears to have organized the Vancouver Power Company to develop a waterpower site in 1898 without prior approval from London. After some delay, the BCER overcame its doubts and assumed control of the Vancouver Power Company (though it remained a separate corporate entity). A surge in demand for electricity in Vancouver fully justified the investment: the company took delivery of its first hydroelectric power in December, 1903, just in time to meet the need occasioned by the price war with the gas company.[21]

The BCER met the challenge of potential competition from the new hydroelectric technology by investing, somewhat reluctantly, in Vancouver Power. There were, however, other power sites close at hand and ambitious speculators poised to exploit them. In 1900 a group of Vancouver entrepreneurs incorporated a company to develop a waterpower concession at

Stave Lake. Competition from this quarter alarmed Buntzen, but Horne-Payne remained calm: he and his friends could "checkmate" the Stave Lake proposition in either the British or the Canadian capital market.[22] Nevertheless, the Stave Lake promoters clung to a tenuous existence, waiting for an opening either to launch their scheme or, more likely, to sell out to the BCER. The voluntary electricity rate reductions of 1904 had the additional justification of kicking the last remaining props out from under the Stave Lake scheme. If the BCER followed a policy of high prices, Buntzen reasoned, this would both stir up municipal hostility to the company and provide the Stave Lake promoters with an opportunity to exploit sentiment for municipal ownership to gain entry to the urban market. Lower prices preserved the monopoly better than higher prices. "You need not worry about anybody developing other power in the district," William Mackenzie reassured the company in mid-1904. "They had no market. Nobody will invest in anything of that kind."[23]

This brief glimpse inside the British Columbia Electric Railway reaffirms the points made earlier in a Winnipeg context. Gas continued to be profitable and menacing, and an established company had to be constantly on its guard against actual or threatened competition. The BCER managed to tie the hands of its most likely competitor, the city of Vancouver, with protective clauses, binding contracts, and consolidation agreements. Shrewdly advised by counsel and well served by its general manager, the BCER knew exactly what it was doing; the city, apparently, did not. The London connection brought additional advantages. Whenever the city did bestir itself against the company, the latter's influence with the provincial government and the Private Bills Committee ensured that the company rather than the city would prevail. So firmly entrenched was the BCER and so broad its powers that the leading corporation lawyer in the country advised that a federal charter, being eagerly sought by some eastern utilities, would be entirely superfluous.[24]

⎯⎯⎯⎯⎯⎯   Our final example of monopoly-making illustrates the process of consolidation against an excess of private competition. The largest and most notorious amalgamation took place in Montreal, where after 1903 the Montreal Light, Heat and Power Company and the Montreal Street Railway, both promoted by Senator L. J. Forget, controlled the territory. Montreal came to symbolize monopoly. But what is striking in retrospect is the persistent vitality of private competition.

The venerable Montreal Gas Company came under attack in the early 1890s. Its regular 12 percent dividend eventually inspired genuine competition from the Montreal Consumers' Gas Company, promoted by John Coates's engineering firm. At first Jesse Joseph, president of Montreal Gas, thwarted the competition by using his influence at Quebec City to deny the company a provincial charter. Coates and his backers obtained a charter from the federal government in Ottawa, garnered much goodwill in the process, and prepared to enter the gas business in defiance of Joseph. The many autonomous suburbs surrounding the city of Montreal provided Coates with the necessary streetlighting contracts to get started, and from this suburban base Consumers' Gas began penetrating the Montreal Gas Company's preserve. Public sympathy lay with the feisty newcomer which, it seemed, had magically reduced gas prices in the city by more than 25 percent. As the moment for renegotiating the all-important Montreal street-lighting agreement was fast approaching, the distressed shareholders of the Montreal Gas Company staged a minor revolt at the April, 1894, annual meeting, deposed the maladroit Jesse Joseph, and elected to the presidency the youthful Herbert S. Holt, whose meteoric rise as a railroad contractor, financier, and director of the Royal Electric Company was widely admired.

Holt first unleashed a brutal assault upon his rival in the streets and in the courts. He then changed his approach to the problem, adopting tactics that would become his hallmark. Holt quickly realized that it made more sense to buy out the competition than to fight it, and he did just that—though he had to pay a stiff price for control: the owners of Consumers' Gas received shares in Montreal Gas worth $817,950 on the open market for property valued at $520,000. With this newly reconstituted monopoly, lower rates (though not as low as those advertised by Consumers' Gas), and an offer to share 3 percent of the gross proceeds from gas sales with the city, Holt won a ten-year renewal of Montreal's gas streetlighting contract in 1895.[25] Holt understood that a monopoly in a market like Montreal was something worth preserving at almost any price.

Competition in the electrical business also flourished in the Montreal region during the 1890s. For one reason or another, the city of Montreal failed to annex any surrounding municipalities between 1883 and 1905. (By contrast, nineteen adjoining areas amalgamated with the city between 1905 and 1920.) These small, ambitious suburbs—eager for development, desperate for modern services to attract residents, and sometimes ignored by the hard-pressed Royal Electric Company—provided ideal circumstances for independent utilities promoters to get a start. Montreal, the commercial and financial capital of Canada, was also home to thousands of risk-taking businessmen at all levels, from local real estate developers, retail and wholesale merchants, manufacturers, and company promoters to finance capitalists with national and international connections. Some were merely speculators looking for any opportunity to embarrass, then sell out to, existing firms. Others took more substantial risks, sensing that the barriers to entry were low and that the dominant firm had weaknesses which could be turned to their advantage.

Royal Electric had succeeded in eliminating its most serious rival of the previous decade, J. A. I. Craig, by 1891. On the strength of a renewed streetlighting agreement with the city of Montreal, Royal acquired the base load necessary to justify investment in larger-scale, more efficient generating equipment, which in turn allowed it to take on more power and lighting customers. But no sooner had Royal's dominance been established than a half-dozen new companies popped up. After 1891 the Temple Electric Company, initially an isolated plant intended to serve the tenants of the Temple office building, turned itself into a central station and began to expand its radius of activities. The following year two disappointed bidders for the street railway concession founded the Citizens' Light and Power Company, the first to generate hydroelectric power in the city. Through a subsidiary, Citizens' extended its reach into the suburban municipalities of Sainte Cunégonde and St. Louis de Mile End. Two other companies, Imperial Electric Light on one side of the cultural divide and La Compagnie Electrique St. Jean Baptiste on the other, also carved out niches for themselves in the rapidly growing market.[26] Separately, these firms represented only a small nuisance to Royal Electric, which occupied itself with the more profitable task of wiring the commercial and industrial core of the city and radiating domestic service from its streetlighting lines. But in the mid-1890s, these small companies, some of which had been promoted by the same people, began to combine.

Hydroelectric technology and long distance transmission threatened the stability of established companies in all markets, but the problem was especially pronounced in Montreal because of the abundance of hydraulic sites surrounding the city. Not far away on the Ottawa, St. Lawrence, Richelieu, and Saint-Maurice rivers, waterfalls awaited development. Thus despite its higher capital requirements, hydroelectric technology added a new element to the competitive equation in Montreal.

In 1895 two electrical engineers, Thomas Pringle and MacLea Walbank, had joined forces with other Montreal businessmen to promote the Lachine Rapids Hydraulic and Land Company. They intended to build a major hydroelectric generating station at the Lachine Rapids of the St. Lawrence River, where a ten-foot fall could be made to produce as much as 12,000 horsepower of electricity. But how was this power to be distributed, and who would finance such a frankly speculative proposition? As a report to the board put it bluntly in 1896, "public opinion on the street was that as soon as we had spent our million dollars . . . it would be a soft snap for existing company's [sic], as our own company had no means of getting into town and had no customers for our own power in sight."[27] Nevertheless, Lachine Rapids managed to finance the first phase of this ambitious project—the equipment was supplied by the Canadian General Electric Company—and open officially on September 25, 1897. From then on Lachine was able to deliver electricity to its affiliates at less than $40 per HP, which forced the Royal Electric Company to reduce its rates by 33 percent in 1899.[28]

Part of Lachine's early success can be attributed to Royal Electric's blundering approach to the adoption of hydroelectric technology. It was not that J. R. Thibaudeau and his colleagues at Royal were indifferent to the new method of power generation, but rather that they were involved in another project at the expense of their company. Thibaudeau as an individual—along with fellow directors H. S. Holt and F. L. Béique, industrialists S. T. Willett and J. M. Fortier, lawyer-politician G. W. Parent, and two Montreal aldermen who had been of assistance during the streetlighting negotiations, H. B. Rainville and Raymond Préfontaine—had organized the Chambly Manufacturing Company in 1891 to develop a 20,000-HP site on the Richelieu River. This syndicate finally bestirred itself in 1895, probably stimulated by rumours of the Lachine promotion. The directors of Chambly then negotiated an agreement with the Royal Electric Company (themselves, in other words) whereby the latter company would purchase stock and bonds in the former and help finance it in return for a long-term agreement to purchase its power. Cost overruns and construction complications delayed the project and required the infusion of additional capital, and it was not until July of 1899 that Chambly hydroelectric power flowed into Montreal—almost two years after its competitor, Lachine Rapids, began delivery.[29]

Without a doubt the Chambly project was a state-of-the-art installation. The four generators built by Royal Electric and the 15-mile, 12,500-volt transmission line were thought to be the largest and longest in the world at that time.[30] Unfortunately, Chambly had to pay the price of innovation. According to Charles Porteous, president of the company after 1900, the dam and powerhouse were badly built, the wheels and generators defective, and the transmission line "not a great success." All of this could be repaired, of course, with more money. "The greatest disappointment was the quantity of water in the river," Porteous explained. "At times it was much less than anticipated and when the north wind blew capacity dropped from 18,000 HP to 2–3,000 HP. Sometimes the vacuum was lost in the draft tubes and the whole plant came to a standstill."[31] Modern and pathbreaking it might have been, but the Chambly plant was in the wrong place and didn't work well. Without a source of reliable, cheap hydroelectric power, Royal stood by helpless as the Lachine Rapids company poached on its territory.

Problems with Chambly and disagreements with management eventually inspired a rebel group of Royal Electric shareholders—led by Senator L. J. Forget, his nephew Rodolphe Forget, J. A. L. Strathy, and James Ross—to seize control of the company from J. R. Thibaudeau at the 1898 annual meeting. With Rodolphe in the president's chair, the Forget syndicate attempted to revive the flagging fortunes of what was still the preeminent electrical utility in the city. The Forget group, which already controlled the Montreal Street Railway, may also have been planning a complete rationalization of the utilities situation in Montreal, using Royal Electric as a base.

First, the Forgets raised new money to rebuild and expand the distribution network. The expensive and not very profitable electrical equipment manufacturing division was sold to Canadian General Electric. Then the new owners of Royal did an odd thing with the Chambly company; they sold it to themselves. Soon afterward they signed a long-term agreement with their street railway to supply 5,000 HP at $25 per HP. With that contract in hand, they concluded a second agreement with themselves, this time as directors of the Royal Electric Company, in which Royal leased the entire plant and output of Chambly for 50 years. The entire affair was fraught with multiple conflicts of interest. On the surface everyone gained from the deal: the street railway obtained base load power more cheaply than it could generate it itself; Royal got the cheap hydroelectricity it desperately needed to sell at a significant markup in the Montreal market, and Ross and Forget happily netted 16 percent on their investment in Chambly (their take rose to 23 percent eventually).[32]

Meanwhile, as the Forgets rearranged the furniture within the Royal Electric house, they turned their attention to the much broader question of what could be done to bring order to the competitive, uncoordinated utilities situation in the city of Montreal. As company promoters and financiers, they thought naturally of the advantages of mergers and recapitalization. In the spring of 1901, Royal Electric, the Chambly Manufacturing Company, and the Montreal Gas Company all leased their works for 98 years to a new firm, the Montreal Light, Heat and Power Company, shareholders of the old companies being guaranteed their dividends at the current rates.[33] The Forgets and James Ross also controlled the Montreal Street Railway, but apparently there were financial or other reasons for keeping that company a separate entity, despite its need for power and the common ownership. Herbert Holt brought the Montreal Gas Company into the consolidation on the understanding that he would be the president of the amalgamated enterprise, a point the Forgets readily conceded. Holt and Forget tried to convince the Lachine Rapids people to join as well, but they held out for much better terms than those offered, sensing that their reliable, nearby hydroelectric plant would be an extremely valuable component of the integrated system.

Even after consolidation, then, competition continued, much to the annoyance and embarrassment of the Montreal Light, Heat and Power management. After a year's operations, Holt told his board that the gas business remained excellent but that the returns from electricity were disappointing "owing to the nature of the competition encountered."[34] The stakes in this game were greatly increased with the appearance on the scene of yet another hydroelectric venture, the Shawinigan Water and Power

Company. Formed in 1897 by an alliance between Senator L. J. Forget and J. N. Greenshields of Montreal with an American, J. E. Aldred, this company planned to develop the massive hydroelectric potential of the entire Saint-Maurice River valley. Financing was easily arranged; the engineers retained were those who had designed the polyphase universal system at Niagara Falls and the pioneering transmission system at Telluride, Colorado; and construction commenced on a gigantic scale in 1899.[35] Yet Aldred lacked a market for all this power. He hoped to sell some of it locally to electrochemical industries attracted to the area by cheap power, but obviously the bulk of it would have to be transmitted 85 miles to Montreal. Aldred expected his associates Holt and Forget to buy it, but they surprised him early in 1902 by objecting to the price and choosing instead to add another small hydroelectric installation to their own system upstream from Chambly at St. Thérèse. Aldred countered in May, 1902, by negotiating a long-term contract with their rivals, the Lachine Rapids group, to distribute Shawinigan power in Montreal when the transmission line arrived in 1903.[36]

Superabundant waterpower intensified the already fierce competition between the two main electric utilities in Montreal. Even in this second phase of hydroelectric development, it was by no means clear which firm, if any, would emerge with a monopoly. For another year the two companies battled for customers in a booming market. Then disaster struck Montreal Light, Heat and Power in 1902 when a flood swept away the St. Thérèse plant and put the Chambly generating station out of commission.[37] To meet commitments to its customers, the company had to fire up all its old steam plants—and still it suffered the indignity of having to buy additional power from its competitor, Lachine Rapids. This ultimate embarrassment forced Holt and the Forgets to accept peace terms dictated by their rivals. In round numbers they had to raise $4,500,000 to purchase the generating station, distribution system, and Shawinigan power contract of the Lachine Rapids Hydraulic and Land Company in April, 1903.[38]

As the 1903 annual report of the Montreal Light, Heat and Power Company put it, with commendable understatement: "Your company is now supplying all the gas and electricity used in the city of Montreal and surrounding suburbs, and your directors expect that the company will realize considerable benefit from the economical operation of all the companies under one management."[39] Buoyant gas revenues and the ability to stabilize electricity prices allowed the conglomerate to pay a 4 percent dividend on its greatly swollen equity right from the start, rising to 6 percent in 1908. The case of Montreal demonstrates with brutal clarity that a monopoly could be broken by vigourous rivals and its own blunders. Only at great cost were Holt and the Forgets able to fight off a better-equipped rival and overcome their own mistakes. What lay behind their eventual triumph? Theirs may have been a technologically error-prone company, but they were best equipped to finance the acquisition of their rivals. They were also sufficiently powerful in the concentrated Canadian financial community to raise the money to bury their mistakes—the wrongheaded Richelieu River projects, the failure to bring Lachine into the combination from the start, and the curious handling of the Shawinigan contract.

Another kind of power, more properly called influence, sustained the Holt-Forget effort. Years of careful, usually circumspect attention to the concerns of the city council's francophone majority paid off at crucial junctures. For example, when the gas contract came up for renewal in 1900, all the sympathetic aldermen were "seen"—to use the euphemism of the insiders; even though there were no rivals bidding, the unlikely prospect of a municipal gas plant, a pet notion of the urban reformers, still had to be kept at bay. In this sense public ownership had its uses and value even to its political opponents. Political influence was a decisive factor also in 1901, when the crucial electric streetlighting contract was renewed. Had Lachine been able to wrestle this plum away from Royal, the outcome might have been much different. Even though Royal submitted a higher tender than Lachine, it won the contract amidst apparently justified imputations of corruption.[40] After 1901, with this municipal load secured, a wide domestic and industrial distribution network in place, and a contract with the street railway in hand, Montreal Light, Heat and Power commanded a much stronger market position, notwithstanding its great weakness as a primary producer. In the end, political influence, market control, and financial depth determined the outcome.

Holt subsequently bought out competition whenever he could. He also did his best to preclude the possibility of competition by following a policy of tying up the waterpower in the region, even though there was far more waterpower available within the Montreal area than even Montreal Light, Heat and Power, with all its financial resources, could control.[41]

The history of these three cities, Winnipeg, Vancouver, and Montreal, serves to illustrate some of the conflicting currents and countercurrents within which Canadian utilities promoters made their monopolies around the turn of the century. The same broad concerns would be apparent if other consolidations—the Halifax Electric Tramway, the Saint John Street Railway, the Quebec Railway, Light and Power, the Cataract consolidation promoted by the "five Johns" in Hamilton, or the Mackenzie-Nicholls-Pellatt syndicate in Toronto—had been selected for analysis, although local conditions governed timing and emphasis.[42] Everywhere, gas remained a vital force; competition from public and private sources had to be prevented or absorbed; and hydroelectric technology threatened the stability of existing electric concerns.

The Vancouver example also reveals how close William Mackenzie came to assembling a de facto national utilities conglomerate before the turn of the century. He was the principal owner of major companies in

Toronto and Winnipeg, and he shared in James Ross's Montreal ventures. From the bastion of his Vancouver and Halifax gas companies, he might have launched takeover raids upon the BCER and the Halifax Electric Tramway if he had wanted to. But as he positioned himself for attack, Mackenzie hesitated and then retreated, not out of timidity but because he got caught up in more interesting and audacious promotions elsewhere— railroads in western Canada and utility monopolies in Latin America. After the turn of the century he sold off his isolated gas companies, consolidated his Winnipeg and Toronto operations, and concentrated his energies on the demanding new ventures.

In most Canadian cities between 1890 and 1905, some degree of formal integration eliminated competition among and between urban utilities— Ottawa, with only informal collusion between owners, was an exception. Frequently, consolidation went as far as complete unification of transit, electric, and gas service within one company. Electric and street railway companies either merged or signed supply agreements that restricted the entry of one into the other's business. One way or another, markets were replaced by managers. As had been shown in the case of Winnipeg, Vancouver and Montreal, the establishment of these monopolies faced public and private opposition; but before 1905, at least, Canadian utilities managers met or anticipated these challenges. They helped make monopoly natural by first creating it.

The management of the Bell Telephone Company of Canada faced the challenge of preserving its monopoly after the Patent Commissioner canceled the seemingly crucial Alexander Graham Bell patents in 1885. This unexpected blow was "a serious matter for this Company and for me," Charles F. Sise confided to a friend at the Boston head office. "And I suppose that I shall come in for all the blame, although—as you know—I was merely the mouthpiece of the Am Bell in the matter, and acted throughout under the advice of our Counsel."[43] Canadian Bell was the first telephone company exposed to legal competition (the American Bell and its operating affiliates continued to enjoy full patent protection until the early 1890s). The U.S. management took a direct hand in shaping a new policy for Canada, and subsequently kept a close eye on the Canadian experiment to see what the future held for a telephone system facing competition.

Sise anticipated two different sources of rivalry: in small places poorly served by Bell on the one hand, and in profitable metropolitan markets on the other. More ominously, however, he thought that the telegraph companies, perhaps in combination with one or more of the major railways, might seize the occasion to promote another national system. How to contain these competitive forces was the question that drew Theodore N. Vail and John Hudson from the Boston head office and corporation lawyers

S. C. Wood and Z. A. Lash from Toronto to Montreal for talks with Sise and Hugh Baker on February 1 and 2, 1885, less than a week after the fateful decision.[44]

The strategy they worked out called for ruthless competition with rivals wherever they might appear within Bell's zone, a speeding up of the program of preemptive investment in long-line construction, and devolution of control over the Maritime region to permit concentration of company resources in central Canada and the West, where attacks were most feared. At the same time, Bell decided to enter tactical alliances with the railroads and telegraph companies in the form of service-swapping and pole-sharing contracts, as well as to sign revenue-sharing agreements with municipal governments in return for long-term, exclusive occupation of the most lucrative markets. Bell still owned some patents that had withstood the test of litigation, and these it continued to defend with its customary vigilance. But the defense of its monopoly increasingly depended upon these new measures.

The literature dealing with the Bell Telephone Company implies that its rivals simply folded up under the burden of their own recklessness and presumption. This may have happened in some instances, but when Bell considered its vital interests at stake, it was a ruthless competitor. In 1888 Bell, cut its Montreal prices by almost 30 percent to counteract a schedule being advertised by the Federal Telephone Company.[45] Sometimes Bell took price competition to ludicrous extremes: in Dundas, Peterborough, and Port Arthur the company offered free service to defeat its local rivals; once having done so, it jacked its residential rates back up to $35 a year.[46] Few competitors had the financial backing needed to survive for long against these predatory pricing policies.

On at least one occasion Bell even went so far as to compete with itself in order to eliminate a persistent rival. During the autumn of 1885 the businessmen of Winnipeg began to organize a cheaper cooperative telephone system. To sap support for it, C. F. Sise surreptitiously purchased some non-Bell equipment from a defunct Quebec competitor and sent a secret agent to Winnipeg to start up a third firm, the People's Telephone Company, that promised even lower rates. Over the winter the telephone situation in Winnipeg was in total disarray; but in the spring the legitimate rival collapsed. The People's Telephone Company then quietly disappeared, leaving Bell Telephone in full command of the situation at the old rates.[47]

Company legend has it that when Theodore N. Vail sized up the Canadian situation in February, 1885, he insisted that Bell Telephone begin immediately to build long distance lines connecting all the company exchanges within a 300-mile radius of Montreal and Toronto. When the Canadian directors quailed at the cost and wondered aloud if lines of this sort would pay, Vail is reported to have replied: "I did not say they would, but they will unify and save your business."[48] This may have happened; it seems consistent with Vail's general business policy. But the few surviving contemporary documents tell a slightly different story.

After Vail returned to Boston from Montreal, he counselled Sise not to worry too much about the loss of the Bell patents but to concern himself with other matters: "I am of the opinion that your company has all the patents that it wants, for if it must protect its business with the patents it has, patents will not avail much in the way of protection." He emphasized the tactical advantage of occupying the ground fully; nevertheless, the day after that letter was written, Vail could be found in his office, striking long lines and additional exchanges out of the list of construction estimates submitted by Sise and his board for approval. Any additional capital needed for such expansion would have to come largely from Boston, in view of the present state of the Canadian markets; "nor can we think that it is necessary to extend the trunk lines," Vail cautioned, "unless they are such as will greatly strengthen existing exchanges, or unless there is a very profitable field unoccupied." Thus the Boston head office actually restrained the Canadian directors, who seemed eager in 1885 to press ahead with long-line projects. Only when early returns in 1886 suggested more buoyant income was there authorization to commence an ambitious trunk-line development strategy in Ontario and southwestern Quebec.[49]

In 1887 the directors of the Bell Telephone Company came to the conclusion that they could not raise all the money needed to finance the industry for the entire country. British Columbia had been organized from the start by autonomous though friendly interests, the New Westminster and Burrard Inlet Telephone Company.[50] Sise and his board decided to set up a Maritime affiliate, the Nova Scotia Telephone Company, whose responsibility it would be to organize and finance locally the region's telephone business. This represented a partial evolution of Canadian Bell in the direction of the American Bell (now reorganized as the American Telephone and Telegraph Company) toward a national patent-owning holding company. The arrangement did not work out to anyone's satisfaction, however, and within a year a group of New Brunswick capitalists, quietly encouraged by Sise and his associates, founded the New Brunswick Telephone Company to purchase the business of the Nova Scotia Telephone Company in that province. Bell arranged similar terms with the new firm, in whose management it placed much more confidence.[51] Leaving these two companies and the much smaller Prince Edward Island Telephone Company in charge of service in this less profitable part of the country, Bell Telephone was free to focus its energies and financial resources on the more rapidly expanding markets of Ontario and the West.

At the company summit meeting of February 1–2, 1885, Vail and Sise had agreed upon a striking new plan to protect Bell Telephone against opposition. Beginning on February 11, Sise approached the Grand Trunk,

Canadian Pacific, and all other railroads great and small within his territory. He offered free telephone service in return for a limited number of passes for executives, permission to string wires on telegraph poles and bridges owned by the railroads, and the exclusive right to install telephones in train stations and freight depots. One by one the railroads signed up; by the turn of the century Bell Telephone was the only company allowed to string wires on railroad property or handle calls to and from railway stations anywhere in central or western Canada.[52] With these contracts Bell obtained cheap rights-of-way for its lines in cities congested with wires as well as through the countryside; it froze the competition out of vital communication with railway stations; its men moved about on company business free; and in some instances it even turned a profit on the deal.[53]

With the railroads sewn up, the Bell Telephone Company then came to terms with the cities and towns in its territory. Until 1891 the company had conducted its business entirely under powers granted by its federal and provincial statutes of incorporation, but during the late 1880s it came under increasing pressure in the larger cities, especially in Toronto, to bury its unsightly wires. Toronto tried various stratagems to force the company to run its cable in underground conduits, all of which the Bell lawyers easily confounded. Typically, the management of the company would search for a means of turning such a confrontation into an opportunity. On a visit to Toronto in April, 1891, C. F. Sise explored the possibility of offering the city a percentage of its gross revenues, rather than negotiating a general rate reduction, in return for exclusive rights in the city. To secure such a contract, he hired John F. Lash to "give his whole time to the Aldermen"; retained two men of unusual influence with some of the councillors (John Leys and James McWilliams); and summoned his most trusted agent, W. C. Scott, to Toronto "to work the Press." By the end of the month he had negotiated an agreement. The council made a public display of truculence, but the terms it consented to were essentially those offered by Bell.[54]

In this codicil to the earlier Underground Agreements, Bell Telephone undertook to pay the city 5 percent of its gross receipts for five years, install free telephones in city hall, fix maximum rates at $50 for businesses and $25 for dwellings, and press ahead with a program of placing its wires underground in the central business districts in return for a monopoly on telephone service during the life of the agreement. Sise calculated that the payment to the city would be the equivalent of a $2.14 reduction for each residential telephone and considered the expense of the underground work well worth the security purchased by it. By 1905, Bell Telephone had negotiated exclusive franchises of this type with 36 municipalities in Ontario and Quebec, most of which required no payments to the municipality at all.[55]

Thus, during the late 1880s, Sise followed an aggressive policy of fully occupying his territory. He decentralized the company in order to raise capital, attacked insurgents wherever they cropped up, and tied up most of the major railroads and municipalities in exclusive service agreements. This left little room for competition, but it is quite likely that much of the urgency behind the 1888 construction program and the negotiations with the railroads stemmed from the fact that the Bell Telephone Company had reason to fear a much broader assault on its monopoly.

In 1884, Erastus Wiman, the promoter of a Canadian telegraph merger, had tried to enlist Sise's help in protesting a proposed amendment to the Canadian Pacific Railway charter which would allow that company to engage in the telegraph and telephone businesses.[56] Sise did not collaborate with Wiman even though he suspected the motives of the CPR; he was more concerned about possible competition arising from the telegraph company. Rumours abounded that Wiman and his successors in charge of the Great North West Telegraph Company were sufficiently agitated about the loss of business to the long distance telephone that they were about to start up an intercity system of their own. Without local exchanges, however, this remained a hollow threat.[57]

But in 1888 the possibility of a rival network surfaced in Montreal, the very heart of Bell's territory, financed by the most threatening of all groups, the CPR syndicate. As the angry directors of the Bell Telephone Company looked on from the sidelines, the Federal Telephone Company—incorporated by Sir Donald Smith, W. C. Van Horne, R. B. Angus and C. R. Hosmer—received permission from the city of Montreal to plant its poles and string its wires in April, 1888. Federal advertised rates of $35 and $25 for business and residential telephones. Bell had no choice, Sise reported to the president of American Bell, but to meet these prices: "I have talked the matter over with many friends not in the Telephone business, and the general opinion is that we cannot compete with any opposition Co. giving good service unless we put our rates as low or lower than theirs."[58]

The new rates had the effect of attracting more business and requiring more investment than Bell could comfortably handle. "The Montreal situation remains practically unchanged," Sise reported to his head office after a year and a half of open competition with Federal, "except that we are adding [too] many subscribers, and the Federal, having . . . 1200–1350 against our 4500, seem to be taking out as many instruments as they put in." As business stabilized at the new price levels and neither firm seemed to be able to drive out the other, Bell began to gesture toward an accommodation. It feared that the Federal syndicate or another might launch similar raids in some of the other major cities, and that these isolated exchanges might then be linked up by long lines provided by the CPR telegraph service. The threat of Federal's competition in Toronto prompted Sise to settle upon an exclusive contract with the city.[59]

Smith, Van Horne, and Angus indignantly rejected Bell's first offer to purchase majority control of the Federal Company. According to Sise, "Sir Donald stated that he would prefer to double his investment to selling out on our terms and Mr. Angus said the same, while Mr. Van Horne wished Hosmer to take it over and make it part of the CPR telegraph system, opening exchanges at Winnipeg, Hamilton, London and elsewhere." Even though Bell's board of directors considered this a bluff, they concluded that some kind of settlement with the CPR group over the Federal matter was absolutely essential. If control could be purchased, Sise explained to Hudson, then president of American Bell,

> we are assured of the cordial support and cooperation of these people, *who to all lookers-on appear to own Canada.* We would be enabled to advance rates in Montreal to a point which would, in a few years, repay all this outlay. We must shortly go to Parliament for an increase of capital, or must issue new Bonds to replace those now maturing in 3 years, and it would be impossible for us either to sell Stock or issue Bonds if we are engaged in a competition with the Canadian Pacific Railway.[60]

The competition made a counter offer on June 19, 1891, on a take-it-or-leave-it basis that put Sise and his board on the spot. "We had to concede much more than we intended, but Mr. Van Horne & Sir Donald Smith were leaving to-day, and we had to say yes or no. The Board, unanimously, but reluctantly, said yes," Sise scribbled hastily to the head office. Bell bought only 52 percent of the Federal stock for Bell shares with a par value $188,500, and agreed to assume liabilities of $75,000 besides. This costly but calculated move on Bell's part eliminated powerful competition in the heart of its territory; it brought the company a sound physical plant that could accommodate expansion for several years to come; it made possible an exclusive agreement with the CPR much like those being negotiated with the other railroads; and it meant that "we need fear no opposition in Toronto or the North West," Sise proudly reported.

In the emotional letdown after these tense negotiations in Toronto and Montreal, Sise complained to a friend in Boston: "I have not found life in Canada to be all I had hoped for, and we have been engaged in a fight of some kind ever since I came here."[61] So it seemed to the battle-weary man who had successfully made a Canadian telephone monopoly. Yet this very letter goes on to report that the Bell Telephone Company did more than merely survive following the loss of its patent protection; rather, it flourished.

If the Canadian experience was anything to go by, Sise counselled his U.S. correspondents, they had nothing to fear from the termination of their patents in 1893. His experience had led him to agree with the view of Theodore N. Vail: "In this business the possession of the field is of more value than a patent." He comforted another inquirer with the observation "that when our patents were still good, and our Capital $1,000,000, we netted 12%. Now with no patents, and a capital of $2,500,000, we net 16%."[62] Indeed, the earnings of the Bell Telephone Company, even during the height of the contest with the CPR interests in Montreal, reached levels that were simply too embarrassing to reveal in public. When he submitted his draft statement for 1890 to the Boston head office, Sise explained:

> You will note that in order that the statement may not be *too* good, we have for the first time acknowledged an "increased rental liability"; and have reduced our revenue thereby over $88,000. There is also an item of Bond interest charged to Revenue, $6,324, although not due until April, but these Bonds were sold with April coupon attached, and we were paid the accrued interest.[63]

At this point the company recorded average costs per subscriber of $20.12 and average revenues of $30.11. This substantial margin allowed the company to raise a good deal of capital internally, reduce its dependence upon the somewhat erratic capital markets, and build up a surplus fund that amounted to more than a million dollars by 1891. Bell could therefore well afford to absorb the expense of fighting isolated rivals into submission or to pay a premium to gain control over particularly dangerous competitors.

In the 1880s and 1890s there was other equipment that could have connected to Bell lines; the telegraph and railroad companies could have operated rival intercity communication systems; and connectibility between competitive telephone companies could have been required by law. Indeed, as we have seen, some of these alternatives were threatened. But Bell Telephone policy, guided by the U.S. head office and vigorously pursued by adroit local management, effectively precluded all those possibilities.

The telephone monopoly did not just happen. It was created and then protected in a vicious struggle. Stripped of patent protection in 1885, the Bell Telephone Company developed a carefully worked-out strategy to preserve and extend the monopoly it had already established by that time. Rivals could not cope with the company's predatory pricing technique; its investment in long lines "occupied the territory"; and the agreements with the railroads and the municipalities effectively shut out potential competitors from essential markets. Only the promoters of the Canadian Pacific Railway commanded the resources necessary to challenge Bell on a broad front by the late 1880s, and for a time they did attack the company's urban citadel with the threat of further opposition to come. But even they retreated, counting their money, when Bell agreed to buy control from them at an outlandish price. Once again, monopoly was a product of policy vigorously pursued.

Monopoly was a function of that drive on the part of businessmen everywhere and at all times for control over their markets. It could be accomplished, however, only in certain capital-intensive industries. This desire, it should be noted, did not produce the same results everywhere. In London and Tokyo, for example, no single gas, electric, or transit companies emerged during this period, much less huge consolidated enterprises.

As Leslie Hannah and Thomas Hughes have shown in the London case, local and national politics raised insuperable obstacles to consolidation in the electrical industry.[64] Technology and business had to come to terms with politics and culture. In Europe the latter two forces tended to be more powerful than the former. In North America the reverse tended to be the case. At the outset, the fragmented Canadian political system placed few barriers in the way, and in some instances actually abetted the consolidation movement. The highly concentrated Canadian utilities industry that took shape before 1905 represented not so much a triumph of technology alone as it did of business will—and access to other people's money.

Making Money 6

During the summer of 1912 a federal cabinet minister and former Premier of New Brunswick bearded the legendary Canadian utilities magnate, Sir William Mackenzie, on board ship during a transatlantic crossing and attempted to interest him in reorganizing the decrepit Saint John Railway Company. Mackenzie summarily dismissed the invitation, reported a dejected J. D. Hazen upon his arrival in London: "He does not seem to be much impressed with the proposition. He says that the price you ask is too high in view of the figures you have shown, as it is nothing more than a 6% stock. He does not think there is much money to be made out of it."[1] Sir William's gruff assessment of the Saint John situation serves to remind us of one of the primary objects of this whole game. The purpose of making monopolies was making money.

Between 1885 and 1905 a small group of men made and protected local monopolies in the telephone, electric, and public transportation sectors in Canada. The propitious growth of Canada's cities, the contemporaneous flowering of Canadian capitalism, and the elimination of competition in these markets allowed these men—William Mackenzie foremost among them—to succeed beyond the wildest dreams of avarice. Like their U.S. counterparts—Whitney, Elkins, Widener, Forbes—the Canadian utilities entrepreneurs were soon among the richest men in the country. It required boldness and determination to make these monopolies in the first place, and ruthless management to get the most out of them; quite understandably such people expected and contrived to get more than bank interest for their efforts.

If anything tipped the balance toward consolidation during this period, it was something external to the companies themselves—finance. The scale of these enterprises gradually drew them into the concurrently growing and increasingly more institutionalized capital markets. But in the process of capitalization, these enterprises became something other than

115

simply large operating companies with debts; they became utilities—a class of securities to be floated, underwritten, amalgamated, merged, recapitalized, and pyramided (with commissions and bonuses all round) according to the needs and opportunities of this secondary market. Like alchemic engines the utilities impelled that golden cycle of investment, returns, capital gains, and more investment upon which financial intermediaries depended.

Promoters thus found themselves at that gilded nexus of production and investment, where capital was seemingly created and reproduced. Their behaviour was governed by the contingent capacity of their properties to accumulate and multiply capital and to concentrate that process in a few favoured places. Here the lessons of modern capitalism were first learned in Canada, along with the temptations of frenzied finance.

———— Raising the money to establish trunk lines and telephone exchanges, build hydroelectric stations and transmission networks, electrify street railways, and provide these systems with necessary working capital opened a new chapter in Canadian financial history. Even in the 1890s works of this sort required hundreds of thousands of dollars. The scale and technological complexity of the projects later pushed capital requirements up into the tens of millions of dollars and helped coax into being a larger, more articulated Canadian capital market. Certainly such markets had existed before, but these capital-intensive public service companies helped widen them and change their practices. Money was raised in new ways from new sources as a new class of individuals and institutions became attracted to the securities offered for sale.

The statistics compiled in Table 10 are more than usually misleading if taken at face value. They are presented primarily to convey an impression of the magnitude of capital invested in this sector and the relative size of the major firms. The list is far from comprehensive, but together the 23 companies listed here accounted for about 90 percent of the telephones in use at the end of 1905, 80 percent of the installed electrical generating capacity, and 60 percent of the electrified railway mileage.[2] These were the largest companies that regularly went to the market for their capital and produced publicly traded securities.

Much more important omissions from Table 10 are the railway, light, and traction companies in the United States, Mexico, the Caribbean, and South America that were promoted and financed wholly or in part by Canadians. In 1905, 14 of these foreign companies represented a nominal investment of $276 million, compared with $137 million in the domestic utilities sector. Just for purposes of reference, the Canadian Pacific Railway Company was capitalized at $228 million in 1905. Thus, in round numbers, these Canadian and overseas utilities promotions absorbed about as much capital as two transcontinental railroads. Seen from a different

TABLE 10
CAPITAL STRUCTURE OF MAJOR CANADIAN UTILITIES, 1905

Company	Common Stock	Preferred Shares	Bonded Debt	Total Capital
GAS				
Consumers' Gas	2,250,000[a]			2,250,000
TELEPHONE				
Nova Scotia Telephone	572,480			572,480
New Brunswick Telephone	204,050		100,000	304,050
Bell Telephone[b]	8,604,840		2,325,000	10,929,840
British Columbia Telephone	750,000		556,000	1,306,000
STREET RAILWAYS				
Montreal Street Railway	7,000,000		2,509,367	9,509,367
Ottawa Electric Railway	995,700		500,000	1,495,700
Toronto Railway	7,000,000		3,613,373	10,613,373
London Street Railway	460,000		500,000	1,010,000
ELECTRIC LIGHT AND POWER				
Ottawa Electric	1,000,000		500,000	1,500,000
Toronto Electric Light	2,991,910		1,000,000	3,991,910
London Electric	392,500		102,083	494,583
Shawinigan Water & Power[b]	6,600,000		4,000,000	10,600,000
Canadian Niagara Power[b]	500,000		5,000,000	5,500,000
Electrical Development	6,000,000		5,000,000	11,000,000
Ontario Power[b]	6,000,000		6,000,000	12,000,000
COMBINATIONS				
Halifax Tramway	1,350,000		600,000	1,950,000
Saint John Railway	800,000		675,000	1,475,000
Quebec Railway, Light & Power	2,500,000	250,000	2,500,000	5,250,000
Montreal Light, Heat & Power	17,000,000		8,464,000	25,464,000
Hamilton Cataract Power	1,700,000	2,895,700	2,694,000	7,289,700
Winnipeg Electric Railway	4,000,000		3,500,000	7,500,000
British Columbia Electric Railway[b]	1,455,000	2,012,750	2,232,940	5,700,000
TOTALS	80,126,480	4,933,450	52,421,763	137,481,693

Sources: Houston's *Annual Financial Review* (Toronto, 1906); minute books of New Brunswick Telephone,
   British Columbia Telephone MB.
[a] All amounts given in dollars. Pounds sterling converted to Canadian dollars at $4.85, the rate of the BCER in
   its annual report.
[b] Indicates foreign control or significant financing abroad.

perspective, they created obligations which in 1905 approached 63 percent of the outstanding liabilities of all Canadian chartered banks.[3]

But the best explanation of why these numbers, however useful they may be for comparative purposes, do not represent what they purport to show (namely, capital actually invested in the companies) was provided by one of the leading company promoters himself. Speaking in his capacity as senator against a clause in a general incorporation bill that seemed to prevent the issuing of shares below par value, L. J. Forget gave rare firsthand testimony to show that the practice was not only widespread but also impossible to stop—a revealing lecture in corporate finance that is worth quoting at length. Usually, he said,

> when a company is formed, bonds are issued for the cost of the railway or of the boats (if it is a railway company or a navigation company), and afterwards it is capitalized at two or three millions, as the case may be, and generally that stock represents half water, sometimes all water, and sometimes only 10 or 15 per cent of money, and the stock is distributed to a syndicate which has formed the company, called the provisional directors, and those directors divide among themselves the four or five millions of stock which cost ten cents on the dollar, and it is listed on the stock exchange for whatever it brings, and very often it goes at a premium. In Toronto a foreign tramway company was formed and issued five millions of stock for nothing to the syndicate who had organized the company, and that stock, for which never a cent was paid, is selling at a five per cent premium. There was also a syndicate formed in the Toronto Tramway Company, and they invested $600,000. They built a railway and issued bonds to pay for the cost of it and the $600,000 was capitalized at $6,000,000 and that stock is selling today at $121, because the value of the franchise made it worth that. It is a good company and paying a good dividend.[4]

Senator Forget's practical illustrations—both selected from Toronto rather than Montreal, it will be noticed—need to be supplemented with several general observations. First of all, he is too modest. Neither he nor his Toronto associates would let impersonal market forces establish something as important as the price of the common stock of a company in which they were interested. Second, the practices he described in this 1902 debate were not uniformly followed during the entire period under discussion, and did not hold for all utilities companies or even all companies within a subsector. Consumers' Gas and the Bell Telephone Company both studiously avoided this new-style financing—partly out of conservatism and partly because they feared public repercussions, but primarily because they could raise money more cheaply through the old method of selling common stock, in both cases at a substantial premium.

We can say with some certainty that the bonds and preferred shares indicated in Table 10 did represent capital invested, less discounts and commissions. But the figures in the common stock column stand for many things. In some cases the numbers do represent money paid in to company treasuries. Some common stock was issued to acquire property in mergers. But a large and indeterminate proportion of the values listed merely reflects capitalized expectations of future earnings, as Senator Forget explained. The sale of common stock, usually to existing shareholders on a pro rata basis, did bring some money into company treasuries between 1890 and 1905. The minute books of the Montreal Street Railway, Senator Forget's own company, reveal that the $50 par value shares issued in the mid-1890s were fully paid for in regular calls, but at that time these shares were being traded on the open market at more than four times the price.[5] Practices varied between companies and over time. Techniques pioneered in U.S. street railroad promotions seem to have been introduced into Canada by William Mackenzie for his Toronto and Winnipeg companies and then imitated by others, especially in the flotation of the very largest Canadian and foreign utilities promotions.[6] In this new scheme of things, common stock was used as an indirect means of raising money for a corporation and a direct means of spiriting monopoly rents out of it into the hands of the promoters and underwriters. Common stock thus came to represent more or less well-secured hopes.

When old companies were recapitalized during the 1890s and some new companies formed, a syndicate composed of the promoters and a circle of close associates subscribed for the bonds. These principals almost always had accommodation or close ties with one or another of the chartered banks, or trust or insurance companies. This personal interposition in the corporate underwriting process reflected the absence of merchant banking houses; the indirect role of chartered banks in the process of capital formation thus represented the Canadian institutional adjustment to the rise of large-scale finance capitalism. Syndicate members might further subdivide their portions, passing them on to brokers or institutions at less generous discounts with proportionately smaller amounts of bonus stock attached. The virtually certain appreciation in value of this bonus stock made the purchase of bonds all the more desirable, and to that extent it might be said that the stock indirectly helped raise capital.

But the syndicate's responsibilities did not end there, as Senator Forget implied. Usually, one member was designated to manage the stock of the whole group for a specified period, buying and selling from this pool in such a way as to "make a market," or to manipulate the price to entice outsiders to pay real money for the benefit of owning these shares. At this point the stock was deemed to be "going into investment."[7] In the long run, stock values could not be sustained at wholly artificial levels, but they certainly could in the short run in a narrow, unregulated stock market. And over the long run, the promoters enjoyed the unusual advantage with these sorts of companies that monopoly power allowed them (within certain limits) to manage company affairs in such a way as to make these "market" prices a self-fulfilling prophecy. Once a market had been made in a common stock, sustained by a regular dividend, these shares could be quietly sold to realize that capital gain, or pledged at banks as collateral in other underwriting schemes, or held in private or institutional portfolios as investments.[8]

In the meantime, privileged information on earnings gave insiders ample opportunity to buy and sell to their own advantage. Sometimes this insider trading could be astonishingly shortsighted, a case in point being Senator Forget's "bearing" of Montreal Railway stock in 1896, a company in which he held the office of president.[9] Even insiders could make mistakes: James Ross and Charles Porteous, believing their Toronto Railway stock would never live up to their expectations under Mackenzie's management, sold it just before the company finally took off on the strength of sustained growth in Toronto.[10]

In Vancouver, R. M. Horne-Payne followed a different programme, dictated in part by the more advanced institutional development of the London capital market in which he operated. He purposely restricted the amount of common stock, then drove his local manager to distraction by refusing to improve service or spend any money whatever on the physical plant, directing every surplus cent instead into the dividend account. This parsimony, Horne-Payne explained to an impatient Johannes Buntzen, had a long term purpose: "Once we have paid dividends of 4 per cent or upwards on our ordinary, 3 years in succession, we shall be able to raise money more easily, as our stocks will be available for a large number of trustee investment[s]."[11]

Urban utilities depended heavily upon capital markets to finance expansion during these years. The extent of external dependence varied from sector to sector: the gas and telephone companies seem to have relied more heavily upon retained earnings; street railways and hydroelectric companies required more outside capital. C. A. S. Hall estimated that in 1905 the electric and traction companies of Toronto and Hamilton had raised 92.9 percent of their funds from external sources, mainly through the sale of bonds (see Table 11). In his careful calculations, common stock never accounted for more than 22.4 percent of the total before 1914. In gas and telephone companies, however, the proportion of common stock was much higher.[12]

Company promoters could sell bonds of this sort in such large quantities partly because a new class of institutional investor appeared on the scene just as capital requirements began to soar. Before 1899, Canadian life insurance companies had operated under strict rules as to the kinds of securities they could hold. Removal of those restrictions at the turn of the century suddenly freed up millions of dollars of Canadian savings for placement in the relatively secure utilities sector.[13] According to one estimate, utility securities as a percentage of all life insurance company invest-

TABLE 11

SOURCE OF FUNDS, TORONTO AND HAMILTON ELECTRIC AND TRACTION
COMPANIES, 1900–1914

Sources	1900–02	1903–05	1906–08	1909–11	1912–14	1900–14
INTERNAL						
(a) Retained earnings	13.2	7.1	11.1	12.4	17.3	12.4
EXTERNAL	86.8	92.9	88.9	87.6	82.7	87.4
(a) Bank loans and short-term debt	25.2	−2.6	21.5	3.6	15.2	11.0
(b) Bonds	50.3	65.8	40.1	61.7	58.7	56.1
(c) Common stock	10.3	22.4	19.1	22.2	8.8	17.1
(d) Preferred stock	1.0	7.3	8.2	0.1		3.4
TOTAL ALL SOURCES	100.0%	100.0%	100.0%	100.0%	100.0%	100.0%

Source: C. A. S. Hall, "Electrical Utilities in Ontario under Private Ownership, 1890–1914," Ph.D. thesis, University of Toronto, 1968, p. 138. Hall adjusted these figures to take into account bonus stock and bond discounts.

ments increased by 157 percent between 1900 and 1908. Even by 1900, holdings must have been very large. That year, for example, 100 percent of the bonds of the Toronto Electric Light Company were held by only three insurance companies, and 35 percent of the Toronto Railway Company bonds were lodged in the vaults of four insurance companies.[14]

The utilities thus filled a demand for interest-bearing securities on the part of banks, trust companies, private investors, and the rapidly growing life insurance companies.[15] A mutually complementary, almost symmetrical relationship developed between lenders and borrowers. The financial intermediaries gathered in small deposits and premium payments from hundreds of thousands of individuals, building up large liabilities upon which interest had to be earned. The utilities absorbed this capital in large blocks, investing it in tracks, exchanges, transmission lines, and power stations. These capital goods then generated a return flow of small payments from hundreds of thousands of customers—car fares, telephone and lighting bills—which mounted up into very large sums annually in the utilities' treasuries and from which only about 50 percent was needed to meet operating expenses. Such a comfortable margin made for a relatively light burden of debt; it paid the interest, principal, and dividends owed the lenders, leaving a good balance to tuck into depreciation and other reserve accounts that further buoyed up the freely distributed bonus stock or paid-up common stock.

All this capital formation in the utilities sector was made possible, of course, by an extremely favourable general investment climate during the period. Canada experienced extremely high levels of both economic growth and savings; the cities expanded more rapidly than the country as a whole; an intricately ramified system of chartered banks and other financial intermediaries funnelled savings into metropolitan centres for investment, and Canada benefitted from extensive foreign (particularly British) investment as well. Between 1891 and 1910 real gross national product per capita in Canada increased at a compound average annual rate of almost 2.5 percent, making for a total increase of 54 percent in real income over two decades. As income rose, gross capital formation as a percent of GNP reached 17.4 percent between 1900 and 1905. Heavy inflows of British capital after 1901 pushed gross domestic capital formation up to 22.7 percent of the GNP. Much of this growth and investment was concentrated in the cities, which were the markets for these utilities and whose population was growing at approximately twice the rate of the rural population.[16] Most of the utilities met their financial requirements from domestic sources, with the exceptions of the British-owned BCER, the U.S.-controlled Canadian Niagara and Ontario Power Companies, Bell Telephone, and Shawinigan Water and Power. By the end of 1904, utilities accounted for 34.5 percent of all transactions on the Montreal Stock Exchange, the largest single group.[17] Canadian utilities companies had the good fortune, therefore, to come to the market for capital just at a time when unprecedented quantities of domestic and foreign savings became available for investment.

Profits had to be earned. Until World War I, street railways were the main profit centres of utilities combines; income gleaned from car fares helped finance associated electric enterprises. The Bell Telephone Company met a large proportion of its capital requirements from retained earnings. To maximize the rate of return on capital invested, something like the same scientific effort went into improving management procedures as into improving technology.

Effective management depended upon the collection and analysis of routinely generated statistical data. Control over this information was essential also in the process of labour negotiations, the conduct of public relations, and the manipulation of stock markets. Between 1895 and 1905 most of the major street railways in Canada adopted the standardized accounting and operating policies promoted by the American and Canadian Street Railway Associations. Through these organizations the professional managers came to know each other personally; they met regularly and developed something like a collective espirit de corps vis-a-vis their increasingly numerous and vociferous foes.

The American Street Railway Association held its fourteenth annual convention in Montreal in mid-October, 1895. This first meeting of the association outside of the United States was also the occasion for a major change in its scope and nature. The *Canadian Electrical News,* quoting a

St. Louis correspondent, interpreted the proposed creation of a central bureau to act as a clearing house for information on operating methods, patents, legislation, and franchises as an important step in transforming the organization from something like a fraternal order to an industrial lobby. Amidst much back-thumping, self-congratulatory speechifying, and hands-across-the-border rhetoric, the street railwaymen convened to consider such important matters as, in the words of one of the delegates, "the wages paid to employees and how roads could be economically managed to the best advantage."[18] Thereafter, Canadian street railway officials played an active part in the affairs of the association and its affiliated bodies. W. G. Ross, managing director of the Montreal Street Railway, became president of the Street Railway Accountants Association of America and in that capacity introduced standardized accounting procedures and report forms (based on Montreal Street Railway practice, he claimed) that were adopted by all members of the association.[19] Through meetings of this sort and through the main trade journals (the *Street Railway Journal,* the *Street Railway Review,* the *Electrical Railway Gazette,* and in Canada the monthly *Railway and Shipping World,* the *Canadian Electrical News,* and the *Canadian Engineer,* engineers and operating executives shared the latest information on car design, scheduling, labour relations, internal organization, accounting practices, and so forth.

Eventually the Canadian street railwaymen felt the need for an association of their own to address both technical and political issues. The Canadian Street Railway Association met for the first time in Montreal in late December of 1904. The associative urge was sufficiently strong to sustain quarterly meetings throughout 1905; thereafter, the members settled into a pattern of twice-yearly gatherings, at which they heard papers on such subjects as parks and amusements, track maintenance, the discipline of employees, accident prevention, equipment standardization, and the handling of ice and snow.[20] But officials in the industry were drawn together by more than a technical interest in the operation of street railways in a cold climate. Because municipal, provincial, and federal politicians, as well as reform groups, trade unions, and numerous government agencies, had begun to press their demands upon the industry with greater insistence, street railwaymen met to share information on these developments and to establish a common front in the face of politicians and trade unions. Led by A. A. Burrows, secretary-treasurer of the association and business manager of the *Railway and Shipping World,* the organized street railway interests campaigned against interference with "vested rights" wherever it occurred.

The standardization of procedures and accounting practices within the industry did not, however, lead to fuller public disclosure of that information. Over time, published annual reports actually became less informative, especially as street railway data were often lumped with the statements of consolidated enterprises. Standardized accounting classifications and assessment criteria were intended exclusively for internal use as management tools; the less said in public or even to the shareholders about such matters, the better. Information was potentially dangerous and had to be carefully handled.[21]

The street railway companies took special pains to conceal data that offered direct comparative evaluations of company performance. The indices and statistics used by managers and company promoters to assess operating efficiency were not for public consumption. The companies themselves gradually stopped reporting such statistics with their annual reports after the turn of the century. They also mounted a quiet campaign to obscure this sensitive information in data supplied to others. During the 1890s the Department of Railways and Canals began requiring electric railways to submit annual financial and operational returns as the steam railroads had been doing for many years. At first these tabulations contained precise calculations of earnings and expenses per car mile for each street railroad; then gradually the reports became more voluminous but less explicit as individual companies and the Canadian Street Railway Association lobbied successfully to have this information suppressed. Nor should it be assumed that the figures submitted were necessarily accurate.[22]

Profits always concerned the professional managers, but in the late 1890s, profit maximization verged upon an obsession. Charles Porteous's intermittent correspondence with James Ross and William Mackenzie gives a hint of the constant straining, during difficult economic and political times, to wring the utmost surplus from the Toronto Railway Company. In June of 1895, for example, Porteous prepared a comparative statement of earnings and expenses for the previous month for the Montreal, Toronto, and Minneapolis street railroads in which Ross and Mackenzie held a major interest. The most important line (in fact, the second from the bottom line) showed expenses as a percentage of earnings, the ratio that street railroad promoters considered one of the most important indicators of managerial efficiency. During May 1895 the ratios were Montreal 48 percent, Toronto 45 percent, and Minneapolis 41.5 percent. In 1896, Porteous began a major campaign to reduce operating expenses even further in Toronto, and in January of 1897 he planted a professional administrator in the office of the Winnipeg Electric Street Railway to tighten discipline, "re-order the office affairs of the company," and eliminate the habitual "loose and unbusinesslike manner" about the place.[23]

Strict control over the number of miles run, thus increasing earnings per car mile, was one of the keys to maintaining a low operating ratio. "In looking over the May statement I notice that earnings per car mile are down to 14.41¢," Porteous wrote to James Gunn, the superintendent of the Toronto Railway Company, in 1896. "This is very low showing that our present service is too good for the business offering. We must try and cut it down on the least profitable routes," and Porteous added specific instructions as to where to make those reductions. Old horsecar men like James Gunn had difficulty adjusting to the close accounting methods of the new generation of street railroad financiers. In due course he was adjudged "not up to Modern Street Railway management" by Porteous and replaced by F. L. Wanklyn, who plainly did understand the imperatives of the business. He was so good that he quickly moved on to take charge in Montreal, where he also acted as management consultant to a number of the foreign and domestic utilities being organized there.[24]

Wanklyn's successor in Toronto, E. H. Keating, the former city engineer, also had to be tutored by Porteous, who reported that "Keating has allowed the mileage to run up, and the rate per Car Mile to run down. I drew his attention to this and some other matters in the June report." To Keating, Porteous wrote: "You have 6 lines where your earnings per car mile are under 12 cents, these should be looked after first. Compare with Montreal where the average earnings per car mile were 18.37 cents against Toronto 14.92 cents. It is the half cent per Car Mile that makes the difference between the road being run economically or otherwise."[25] Here is the Canadian equivalent to Charles Yerke's famous assertion that "the straphangers pay the dividends."

The Forgets and R. M. Horne-Payne ran their Montreal and Vancouver properties with a similar concern for earnings per car mile and operating costs. In Montreal, company accountants calculated earnings per car mile on each route to two decimal places. The resulting ratios of operating expenses to income, which are not strictly comparable and must be read with some caution, are shown in Table 12. These publicly reported

TABLE 12
OPERATING EXPENSES AS % OF REVENUE

	Montreal	Toronto	BCER
1892	82.7	71.9	
1893	79.0	59.1	
1894	71.2	54.0	
1895	59.2	49.0	
1896	56.6	50.9	
1897	55.0	48.8	
1898	52.1	47.7	68.0
1899	55.2	48.8	60.6
1900	56.3	51.0	56.4

Sources: Montreal Street Railway, *Annual Reports; Canadian Railway and Shipping World.*

figures show Toronto consistently more effective in controlling costs and thus from a financial point of view more efficient than Montreal and Vancouver—a pattern that would hold true for the next decade and a half.

The urgency of squeezing out the maximum revenue after meeting expenses arose not simply from a need to meet interest payments on borrowed money but rather from the slightly unorthodox method of financing. The real money to be made on these properties was to be had from capital gains on common stock that had been acquired for nothing, or next to nothing. Every nickel pared from expenses was available for bond interest, dividends on the common stock, sinking funds, reserve accounts, and depreciation funds, all of which served to enhance materially the value of the equity. In managing a utility of this sort, financed in this way, every action had to be considered in light of how it would affect the price of the shares.[26]

The main reason for the Bell Telephone Company's excellent performance was C. F. Sise's close attention to operating costs. Sise knew how difficult it was to raise outside capital; he also knew the risks of competition resulting from increases in telephone rates. Capital for expansion would have to be generated from within. In 1890 he had a graph drawn up showing a relative increase in revenues of 17.3 percent but in expenses of only 14.5 percent. Over the decade operating costs had been reduced from 36.8 percent to 29.7 percent.[27] Using a standardised accounting system, Sise watched these expense ratios all over his system, keeping a weather eye for anomalies that demanded attention. An 1887 entry in his log, summarizing the increase in company business over the preceding three years, concluded: "It will be seen that an increase of 53% in Capital expenditure caused an increase of 70% in net revenue."[28]

Whether as a result of good management, lower costs in the Canadian market, or both, the Bell Telephone Company apparently performed slightly better than similar systems in the northeastern United States. On average, Sise calculated, his company was able to provide telephone service at $6.38 less per station than its U.S. counterparts, for an advantage of 23 percent.[29] These low average costs contributed to the respectable and improving rates of return on capital invested (Table 13).

The application of modern management practices in a monopoly setting enhanced the demand for the stocks and bonds of these companies in financial markets. The rising demand called forth an ever-increasing supply of paper from this sector and helped generate the capital required to rebuild and expand service. In these secondary financial markets the utilities were notably successful.

———————   Nevertheless at the turn of the century professional utility managers sensed that they were on the verge of crisis. From Vancouver, Johannes Buntzen warned his London directors that their company would

TABLE 13

BELL TELEPHONE RETURN ON CAPITAL

	Capitalization ($)	Net Revenue ($)	Rate of Return (%)
1881	554,960	38,314	7.90
1882	1,072,311	69,590	6.49
1883	1,196,588	112,233	9.38
1884	1,290,720	118,233	9.21
1885	1,635,111	158,000	9.66
1886	1,822,096	190,565	10.46
1887	2,020,981	233,903	11.57
1889	2,490,840	241,710	9.70

Source: BCA, Sise Log Book no. 5, May 6, 1890.

"go to the wall" if they failed to invest in needed improvements immediately: "A Company like ours has four factors to consider: the shareholders, the city councils, the public and the employees, and they must be equally considered or you will have trouble somewhere."[30] In his opinion the legitimate concerns of the last three groups had been sacrificed to satisfy the shareholders.

In Toronto at about the same time, an increasingly dismayed Charles Porteous arrived at a similar conclusion. William Mackenzie's policy of milking the Toronto Railway Company for all it was worth had left it with a worn-out plant and few resources to meet an unexpectedly strong demand. Would it not be a good idea, Porteous suggested, to confess the errors of the past, admit that the company "had been caught napping" by the rapid growth of the city and its return to prosperity, and then do everything possible to build more cars, hire more men, and increase the comfort of the public? "It will not do for the people in Toronto to become imbued with the idea that now so much of the Stock is held in Montreal that the Company is looking for profits only," Porteous counselled, "but they mean to maintain their Railway as one of the best systems in America, and meet the growth of the City. Something in this line, frank in character, properly put before the public, I think will bring them back on our side."[31] W. Y. Soper, who was widely thought to run a model street railway in Ottawa, had stated the problem with down-home brevity in the pages of the *Street Railway Journal:* "Furnish your patrons with a miserable service, not sufficiently equipped in its minor points—in other words, withhold the sprats, and you will soon find that you catch few mackerel."[32]

No sooner had the street railroads of Montreal, Toronto, and Vancouver completed the reconstruction and electrification of existing routes in the central city than an insistent clamour arose for extensions and improved service. Every frantic real estate developer wanted a car line to his subdivision; commuters demanded more frequent, better-equipped cars; municipal authorities sought additional downtown routes to relieve traffic congestion. Journalists, urban reformers, and ambitious municipal politicians rushed to lead these popular crusades for expansion of the wonderfully fast trolley system.

Inevitably, the street railroad owners saw things differently. They greeted the demands for immediate extensions not only with skepticism and a good deal of foot-dragging but also with private alarm. No company could meet all these requests and survive, yet to ignore public pressure completely was also to court disaster. Though it may be difficult to appreciate in retrospect, the street railroad proprietors of the late 1890s considered themselves in an extremely risky situation. They had just committed quite a lot of other people's money to their capital-intensive undertakings; electrification had cost more than expected; and initial earnings proved disappointing. To complicate matters, a deep commercial depression had settled upon Canada in the mid-1890s, and business was sluggish, even the street railroad business. In Toronto, Winnipeg, Halifax, and a few other cities, the companies struggled with the added burden of not being permitted to operate their cars on Sunday. In the United States, several street railroads—some of them in the largest cities—hovered on the brink of bankruptcy as a result of overeager expansion and mergers. Under the circumstances, Canadian traction entrepreneurs believed they needed some time to get their companies established as going concerns, to begin to earn the interest on the borrowed money, and of course to turn a neat capital gain on the speculation for themselves.

Therein lay the conflict between two notions of perceived "rights" that would confound transportation development and poison municipal affairs with fruitless controversy for a generation. The cities believed they had a right, based upon their jurisdiction and their franchises, to regulate street railroads. Entrepreneurs thought they had an equally legitimate claim to maximize income from their property. Some held to this view more firmly than others. The risk in the street railway business arose not so much from any difficulty of meeting operating expenses with earnings as from the necessity of turning these companies into successful stock promotions. Making a profit was relatively easy; making a profit large enough to valorize a mountain of common stock was another matter. At the end of the nineteenth century, then, when mayors came around with wads of city council resolutions demanding extensions, the street railroad men had many other things on their minds: eliminating competition, protecting their territory from incursions by outside roads, forestalling union organizers, establishing profit-generating management procedures, and making a capital gain on the original speculation. The legitimate imperatives of capitalist accumulation were at odds with the politically sanctioned demand for additional service.

From a company perspective, the danger posed by expansion was all too clear. Construction of suburban lines used up capital that might be more profitably applied elsewhere. In the less densely populated outlying districts, cars had to run farther carrying fewer fares than in the urban core; doing so increased operating and maintenance expenses, occupied scarce manpower and equipment in less remunerative service, and lowered the all-important ratio of net receipts per car mile. On the other hand, owners saw some possibility of private gain on the side from real estate speculation. But then there was the general concern about timing in going to the capital markets: would conditions be right to maximize returns from that end of the operation?

To refuse an opportunity or an order to build a line opened up the chance of competition from nuisance companies that would have to be bought out later, from opportunists already poised on the outskirts of the city, or ultimately from the municipal government. Expansion could preempt the most likely routes, foreclose competition, and thus protect and extend monopoly—this might be thought of as the telephone strategy. Over against the indeterminate dangers of fighting city hall the benefits to be gained from negotiated compliance had to be laid. Some managers, taking the long view of the situation, conceived a strategy of forestalling an eventual municipal takeover by perpetuating private ownership through long-term agreements with the suburban governments. Other executives chose to fight and face the possibility of a public takeover when that time came. In short, street railroad companies generally preferred to move slowly, following their own timetables, expanding their systems as population growth, money markets, stock prices, retained earnings, and agreeable opportunities allowed. This was invariably much more slowly than impatient rate-payers, straphangers, real estate drummers, and irate municipal politicians believed necessary.

Confronted by this cold indifference to their needs, real estate promoters and suburban governments (dominated as they were by developers) attempted to entice the street railways with construction subsidies and lenient franchises. Generally speaking, the major companies resisted such temptation during the first decade or more of operations. In Vancouver, for example, when the local management recommended that the company accept the astonishing offer of several land developers to pay for the construction of a line down their street, the London directors turned the proposal down flat.[33]

When the downtown companies refused to build extensions into the suburbs, they naturally ran the risk of competition. During the 1890s the principal street railroads were prepared, or forced, to tolerate a certain amount of controlled competition from the likes of the Montreal Park and Island, the Toronto Suburban, the Metropolitan, and the Toronto and Mimico railways. In the meantime they conducted a determined campaign to neutralize threats from both the municipalities and these outlying rivals.

The main line of defense was the Private Bills Committee of the provincial legislature, where corporate interests always saw to it that they exerted considerable influence. This was the committee that knocked out offensive sections of threatening private bills and pulled the teeth of restrictive municipal legislation. Here the Hamilton Radial Railway lost the authority to run into Toronto, the Metropolitan failed to obtain permission to operate its cars on Toronto Railway Company track, the municipality of Ste. Cunégonde met opposition to its bylaw taxing street railways, and the city of Vancouver discovered it could not go into competition with its utilities without first buying them out.[34]

Gradually, governments began to learn about this new kind of street railroad business and eventually attempted to regulate what they came to regard as its abuses. In 1895 the province of Ontario passed a general statute governing the chartering of all new street railroads. Its provisions, of course, were not retroactive. A bemused Charles Porteous noted: "It might be called an Act to prevent the building of Electric Rys so stringent are its provisions against overcapitalization, for the payment of stock in cash, purchase of materials, etc. Dividends are limited to 8%. Fares are restricted and Sunday running forbidden." Legislation of this sort took all of the fun and most of the profit out of street railroading, and latecomers to the business faced regulations blocking opportunities from which existing companies had already profited. Thus, as governments got tougher with capitalists, their regulations constituted unintended barriers to entry and made the cities unwitting allies of the established enterprises by further reducing the prospect of serious competition. As Porteous wryly observed: "To the Toronto Ry it is beneficial as it makes suburban lines an impossibility."[35]

In small, controlled doses, however, competition had its uses: it muffled the antimonopoly cry, and it meant that unprofitable districts were served—by someone else. The residents of Côte St. Laurent were rebuffed in their petition to the Montreal Street Railway in 1897 and told that the company's agreement with the Park and Island Railway prevented granting them service.[36] When these suburban street railways collapsed, as several did, the urban street railroad proprietors could use such failures to illustrate their case against overambitious expansion. Charles Porteous was positively exultant when the Montreal Park and Island Railway failed in 1898:

> I hear that they ran beyond gross receipts $24,000 in working expenses for the past year, and that every year for the past few years the deficit has been larger than this. They have never made a dollar of interest on their $1,400,000 of bonds. I learn there had been an illegal issue of bonds, over which there is likely to be trouble.
>
> This object lesson before the people of Canada is going to prevent them putting money into suburban roads, and make those who have it there feel

blue. Something like this is what I have been waiting for for some years. It removes all danger at other points. The tale at other points will be the same with variations. There has only been one good done by this profligate building of suburban Railways, namely, to put a barrier around urban properties, with plenty of danger signals both to the investor and the urban roads themselves, as to the danger of premature expansion. *Leave them alone* should be our policy, to die a natural death. There is no danger from them for ten years to come.[37]

Following this disciplined approach to extensions, the Toronto Railway Company increased its track mileage only 7 percent between 1895 and 1900, and by only 4 percent over the next five years.

—————
————— As the cities expanded their boundaries to encompass the spreading population, they expected the street railway companies to service the newly incorporated territories on the same terms as the older parts of the city. When the major companies demonstrated a marked reluctance to expand their operations, the municipal authorities, pressed by angry rate-payers, grew tired of excuses—however politely phrased—and in time began to insist upon extensions.

To a degree that seems astonishing in retrospect, street railroad companies generally preferred to fight the municipalities, often over the smallest matters, rather than give ground. After years of quarrelling, all semblance of civility passed out of the relationship between the companies and the cities, and every negotiation became a test of who was in charge. Companies could, if they chose, be quite brazen in their defiance. The Montreal Street Railway, for example, promised to construct three lines through the suburb of Maisonneuve in order to obtain a strategic franchise, then flatly refused to build two of the three once the agreement had been signed. After grudgingly providing service to Mount Royal Ward, the same company then demanded a premium over the regular fare.[38] Under such circumstances the cities had no choice but to take the companies to court, a riskier business than it might seem. The cities quickly learned that courts tended to construe contracts so narrowly as to favour the companies. And if the court did rule against a railway, the judgement could always be appealed, which at least bought more time and frequently meant vindication for the company.

Toronto offers the most extreme case of bluff intransigence on the part of the company and furious litigation on the part of the city. William Mackenzie's lawyers advised him in 1898 that the city had no right under the 1892 agreement to order the company to build lines in territory annexed subsequently. By that time Mackenzie had begun to surround the city with a ring of suburban railroads—eventually united as the Toronto and York Railway in 1907—none of which paid any franchise fees. Mackenzie preferred to leave suburban service to these roads and to collect another fare from the passengers as they changed at the city limits to his Toronto Railway Company. The unedifying tale of the disputes between the city and the Toronto Railway Company has already been recounted by Michael Doucet and need not be repeated here. However, two things stand out: first, when an out-of-court settlement lay within reach, the company backed out; second, when the city pressed its suit to the ultimate arbiter, the Judicial Committee of the Privy Council, it lost.[39] Usually the courts took a very broad view of the companies' rights over their "property," and adopted a very narrow interpretation of the civic right to interfere in what it deemed to be the public interest. The legal regulatory process thus offered every incentive to company managers to stall, refuse compliance, and let the city bear the costs of a suit.

In truth, entrepreneurs were simply overwhelmed by the sudden growth of the cities after 1898. Years of caution led them to be extremely defensive about the adequacy of their systems to cope with the new conditions. Charles Porteous's advice against being "caught napping" was ignored; instead, the Toronto Railway management chose to deny any difficulties, refuse cooperation, shrug off complaints, and to do the bare minimum to improve service.

In Vancouver, and to a lesser extent in Montreal, the companies took a different tack. Management was disposed to consider meeting the city council part way if in return the city would give the company something it badly needed. In essence, the companies in Vancouver and Montreal chose to barter extensions and service improvements for extended franchises. Invariably, the negotiating took place largely on the companies' terms, and the cities did not distinguish themselves in the bargaining process, but these rare moments of agreement contrasted sharply with the permanent state of seige that paralyzed transit matters in Toronto.[40]

Something like a zero-sum game developed in Toronto, as both the company and the city dug in their heels at a very early date. The persistent refusal of the Toronto Railway Company to build its lines into the new suburbs, its determination to press its rights in the courts, and its unwillingness to enter into serious negotiations with the city created a vacuum that was eventually filled not by private but by much more dangerous public competition. Meanwhile, during all the litigation, the Toronto Railway management continued to pursue with single-minded determination and notable success a policy of profit maximization. The data summarized in Tables 14 and 15 indicate that Mackenzie's Toronto and Winnipeg companies were consistently the most profitable franchises before World War I. These tables also show how quickly the Vancouver company moved after 1901 to improve its market coverage once funds became available in London. But in Toronto the population depended more upon the street railway (Table 15), endured more crowded cars, and suffered the inconvenience and additional expense of not having direct suburban service.[41]

TABLE 14
ELECTRIC RAILWAY NET REVENUE
(in ¢ per car mile)

Year[a]	British Columbia	Montreal[b]	Toronto	Winnipeg
1901	6.8	7.6	8.0	4.8
1902	6.2	8.3	8.3	5.81
1903	7.0	7.9	7.9	9.07
1904	8.0	8.0	8.0	10.0
1905	8.0	8.0	7.0	12.0
1906	9.0	8.0	10.0	12.0
1907	12.4	8.7	11.0	15.2
1908	10.7	10.9	10.9	13.52
1909	11.0	11.0	12.7	11.49
1910	12.5	12.0	13.1	11.89
1911	10.4	12.5	14.0	12.81
1912	10.1	12.5	13.2	13.26
1913	7.7	16.9	13.7	14.27
1914	7.1	15.0	13.3	12.31

Source: Calculated from *Railway Statistics* (Ottawa: Department of Railways and Canals).
[a] Year ends June 30th.
[b] Data submitted for Montreal Tramways after 1911 is spurious.

TABLE 15
DAILY RETURN TRIPS AS % OF LABOUR FORCE

	1901	1911
Montreal	40.6	63.1
Toronto	52.5	83.9
Vancouver/Victoria	29.7	76.6

Sources: *Railway Statistics* (Ottawa: Department of Railways and Canals, 1901, 1911); *Canadian Railway and Marine World,* 1901, 1911; George Nader, *Cities of Canada,* vol. 2 (Toronto: Macmillan, 1976), pp. 126, 203, 381; Patricia Roy, *Vancouver: An Illustrated History* (Toronto: James Lorimer, 1980), p. 168; Frank Denton and Sylvia Ostry, *Historical Estimates of the Canadian Labour Force* (Ottawa: Dominion Bureau of Statistics, 1967), Table 10.

At the outset, the companies in Montreal, Toronto, and Vancouver all followed similar plans. They made profit maximization their first priority in the 1890s and strove toward regional monopoly during the first decade of the twentieth century. But they came to different conclusions in trading off the pros and cons of suburban expansion. The Vancouver and Montreal companies were rather more inclined than their Toronto counterpart to negotiate with their respective cities if desirable objects could be secured in the process. These two companies adopted long-term strategies of franchise proliferation and suburban extensions to secure their property against a partial or a comprehensive municipal takeover. The Toronto Railway Company, on the other hand, pursued profit maximization singlemindedly, placed a higher value upon demonstrating the fullness of its legal rights, resisted negotiation with the city even when such talks might have proved mutually beneficial, and consistently discounted the threat of public ownership.

Unquestionably, the slow growth of Canadian cities in the 1890s (see Figures 1 and 2) helped these companies establish firm control over their territories with a minimum of private competition. Suburban stagnation during this crucial interval blighted the hopes of the struggling independent lines on the outskirts. The stronger companies simply waited for the day when these suburban lines would fall into their hands at distress prices; as soon as vigorous economic growth stimulated a suburban land boom during the first decade of the twentieth century, they moved in on their weak rivals. The Vancouver company already held rights to the territory; it responded with an ambitious program of suburban extensions that had the deeper purpose of securing its franchise against municipal takeover when it expired in 1917. (Transit operators in the large cities in the United States usually faced stiffer competition, partly because suburbanization had begun sooner.)[42]

Just as company strategies differed, so cities too behaved in different ways in the face of the transit crisis; some councils were more capable than others in mounting an effective opposition. In Vancouver the shrewd managers of the British Columbia Electric Railway were generally able to hoodwink an indignant but directionless municipal government. In Montreal the street railway company always managed to maintain enough influence even on reform councils (the general manager of the company was elected to council as a reformer!) to stay out of deep trouble.

Toronto was a different matter. Its civic finances were in better order; it had annexed land early enough to extend beyond its street railway. The city seemed a more fiscally capable, politically aggressive adversary of its utilities than were Vancouver and Montreal. It is thus surprising that the Toronto Railway Company so gravely miscalculated the seriousness of the municipal threat, especially when its general manager throughout this period was himself a former four-term mayor.

Using the conceptual framework employed by T. P. Hughes in his comparative analysis of the establishment of electrical technology in the United States, Great Britain, and Germany makes it clear that technology and business dominated politics during this early period in Canada.[43] Business did not have to seek an accommodation with politics, as in Berlin, and certainly the political process did not dominate utility development, as it

FIGURE 1

SUBURBAN GROWTH IN MONTREAL AND TORONTO

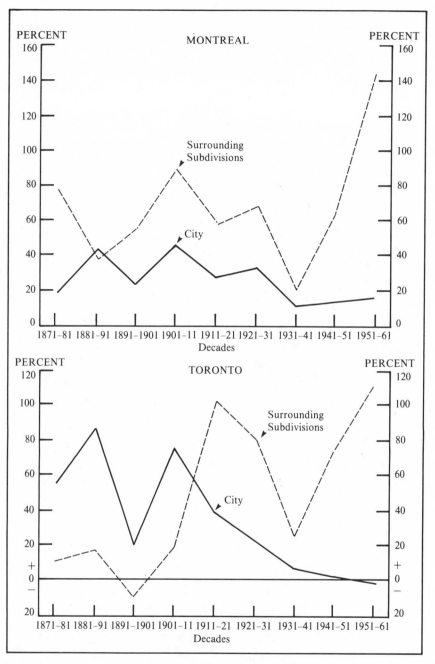

Source: Leroy O. Stone, *Urban Development in Canada* (Ottawa: Dominion Bureau of Statistics, 1968), p. 27. Reproduced by permission of the Minister of Supply and Services Canada.

135

FIGURE 2
URBAN GROWTH IN COMPARATIVE PERSPECTIVE

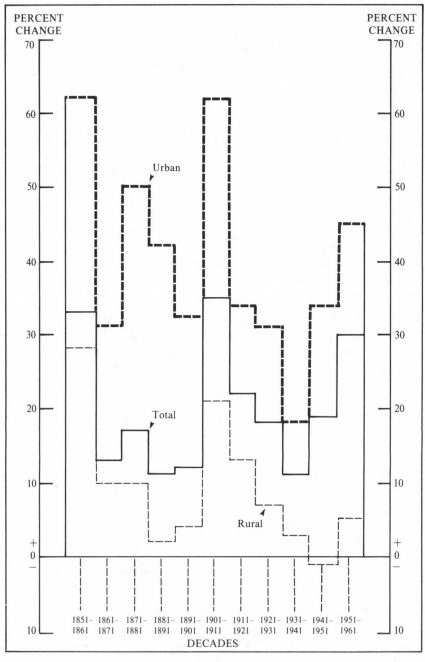

Source: Leroy O. Stone, *Urban Development in Canada* (Ottawa: Dominion Bureau of Statistics, 1968),
    p. 137. Reproduced by permission of the Minister of Supply and Services Canada.

did in London, England. The Canadian owners and their professional managers, by anticipating the direction of technological change and by maximizing self-interest in both capital markets and urban markets for public services, succeeded in building systems of monopoly without much serious political competition. In the process they made a lot of money and a host of enemies.

PART THREE
REGIONS
AND
REGULATION

Civic Populism

Utilities promoters made their world more or less as they pleased in Canada before the turn of the century. Protected by sympathetic judges and their own guile, entrepreneurs were able to devote most of their energies to subduing competition, to making sure that "natural" monopolies stayed that way. The rest of their attention could be applied to coping with costs and the problems created by rapid technological change in a highly capital-intensive industry.

City councils discovered that granting franchises did not give them the upper hand in dealing with the companies. Local politicians rather than members of the federal and provincial parliaments first felt the anger of consumers about poor service and high rates, even as they endured the frustration of interminable and usually futile negotiations. Failure at the bargaining table, defeat in the courts, and rebuffs by higher levels of government added further resentments to the popular indictment of the monopolies. Out of this ferment of individual and collective grievances came the nationwide political movement that we call civic populism. Rooted in similar experiences in towns and cities all across the country, civic populism was a protest against inadequate service by arbitrary, self-serving monopolies from which a small elite grew conspicuously rich.

But it was more than that. Urban populism, like its rural counterpart, also mounted a resistance against the dawning of a new era in which large corporations would dominate economic life. The municipal governments were among the first to sense this change in the social order and to experience its consequences. Civic populism arose in response to a shared concern on the part of urban politicians in Canada that the public corporations they had been elected to command were about to be eclipsed in size, wealth, and authority by a constellation of wholly private corporations— the most obvious and menacing examples being the utilities.

Civic populists had simple solutions: local control, or municipal freedom as it was sometimes called, and public ownership. Ratepayers and aldermen raised hell, just as the farmers were starting to do, against the sway of banks, railroads, and elevator companies. The ensuing crusade also sought to restore the social and economic equilibrium through the revitalization of a nonpartisan democracy. Thus the populist insurgency operated at several interconnected levels: specific objections to the quality of service and entrepreneurial behavior; a search for means to regulate and legitimize a new economic institution, the local monopoly; a struggle for power between the two rival forms of social organization represented by the municipal corporation and the business corporation.

Within a remarkably short period of time the urban populists revolutionized the utilities sector, surrounding some companies with a web of regulation, taking over ownership of others. Some private utilities actually sought regulation as a means to escape a worse fate. But the process varied from city to city and province to province, an untidy fact which requires that attention be paid to particular cases.[1]

A grim prediction from W. D. Lighthall, poet, novelist, historian, lawyer, and mayor of the Montreal suburb of Westmount, called the civic populists to arms: "Unless we municipalities make our stand at present for the principle at stake," he warned in a series of newspaper articles in 1901, "we must submit to a future of most shameful imposition to which no other community in any civilized land would submit." Lighthall's jeremiad, like others of its genre, was at once a lament for the condition of moral and political torpor into which the cities had fallen and a rallying cry for a crusade of redemption.[2] His *cri de coeur* heralded the beginning of a national movement that linked hundreds of urban activists and elected officials in a coordinated campaign against the utilities monopolies.

The occasion for W. D. Lighthall's furious outburst was the incorporation of the Montreal Light, Heat and Power Company in 1901. From his base in the suburbs, Lighthall almost singlehandedly mounted a campaign to resist the consolidation. The newly created monopoly would necessarily raise the price of lighting for merchants, households, and municipalities by ending competition, but far more objectionable was the right of the amalgamated company to enter and use the streets of any municipality within a 100-mile radius of Montreal without municipal consent or competition. By such high-handed means this huge company would obtain perpetual rights in districts where it had no franchise, as well as greatly expanded powers in those towns and cities where it had negotiated agreements. In short, the Montreal Light, Heat and Power Company charter threatened to "open the door to unlimited contravention of municipal rights."[3]

The Montreal city council, however, voted not to fight the consolidation, although some individual aldermen did join a delegation to Quebec City. Premier S. N. Parent was not much concerned by this rather feeble lobby; he promised only that he would amend the charter if the company did anything "inimical to the people." Others apparently took these municipal protests more seriously: Charles Porteous, one of the insiders, reported that the Lieutenant-Governor had threatened to withhold his signature from the bill, normally a formality. But the utility company did not lack influence in high places:

> Our friends in the Ministry stood by the Bill and apparently the Governor, rather than bringing about a Cabinet crisis, has signed the Bill. The agitators against the Bill made wild, foolish statements, and did everything in their power to block us, going even so far as ask [Governor General] Lord Minto to interfere. It will all be over in a day or two, and we have got nothing more than our rights as three other Companies now possess what we have asked.[4]

W. D. Lighthall continued to believe that the premier would indeed intervene if the company misconducted itself. When it subsequently did and he wrote to Parent proposing amendments to be introduced at the next session of the legislature, the truth apparently dawned upon him; Lighthall angrily scribbled across his copy of the letter to the premier: "Parent was crooked."

As he recounted this experience many times during later years, Lighthall drew typically apocalyptic conclusions. First and foremost, he believed, it demonstrated the pervasiveness of political corruption. Monopolies could buy municipal councils and provincial governments if necessary. "The story of guile, folly and greed which brought this about is a disgusting chapter in Canadian public affairs," he told the Canadian Club of Toronto in 1904. "The result has been to saddle Montreal and its large population with a yoke which justifies and necessitates very determined measures of rebellion." Second, the monopolists' financial operations were just as subversive as their political methods. Stock watering and other unscrupulous financial practices levied unjustified tolls upon the entire population, and this tribute provided the means to bend politicians to the will of the corporations. "I believe that if not stayed, this baneful tendency would corrupt all our national and social life," he warned his Toronto audience, "and turn us, both poor and well to do, from a nation with a marvellously free future into servants and victims of a very small and baneful plutocracy." Finally, the passage of the Montreal Light, Heat and Power bill had taught him the importance of organizing municipalities across the country to stop this stream of legislation, break the alliance between corporate power and politicians, restore municipal autonomy, and bring the arrogant utility monopolists to heel.[5]

By the time Lighthall addressed his Toronto audience in 1904, he had already accomplished much. He had immediately realized the futility of organizing within his own region alone, in light of the weight of corporate influence over Montreal's city council. "I see you are having trouble with the Bell Telephone Company claiming control over your streets," he wrote to Mayor Oliver Howland of Toronto on June 10, 1901. "I wish to propose the formation of a league of Canadian Municipalities, like the League of American Municipalities, for mutual protection against such encroachments. Let me know what you think of it." Mayor Howland replied enthusiastically that he, too, had recently been considering the need for an Ontario association. In short order Howland joined forces with Lighthall to call the first meeting of the Union of Canadian Municipalities, to be held in Toronto on August 28, 1901.[6]

Lighthall's letters and articles struck a responsive chord in widely scattered localities, and the slightest organizational effort brought forth a flood of encouraging interest. Similar experiences in dealing with utilities attracted representatives of 52 municipalities to the first meeting in Toronto; two years later the number of members had more than doubled, and by 1907 the response had become so overwhelming that the Union of Canadian Municipalities was able to reconstitute itself as a federation of extremely active provincial organizations.[7]

By holding annual conventions, supporting the publication of a journal, and vigorously lobbying, the organizers of the Union of Canadian Municipalities aimed at increasing public awareness of their problems, attracting new talent to the civic arena, and initiating much-needed political reforms. They also believed that if municipalities acted in concert, they would be better able to secure protection against legislative encroachments and corporate misconduct. When capital conspired with higher levels of government, ex-mayor Howland declared in 1903, "the only remedy, the only means of opposition is the union of the public forces."[8]

Foremost among the abuses the Union vowed to eliminate was the granting of charters by federal and provincial legislatures that permitted companies to trample upon municipal rights. Montreal Light, Heat and Power had received powers from the province relieving it of the necessity to reach agreements with municipalities. Other companies, inspired by the example of the Bell Telephone Company, sought legislation from the federal parliament declaring them to be "works for the general advantage of Canada," which effectively spirited such undertakings out of municipal and provincial reach and placed them under federal control. The Union of Canadian Municipalities denounced this ploy and called attention to other obnoxious applications from railway, telephone, telegraph, traction, and electric companies at both the federal and provincial levels. "A spirit of unblushing defiance of the public, its property and rights breathes through them all," Lighthall informed the lawyers of Canada in 1905. "These schemes are a disgrace to our commercial life."[9]

Lighthall, who occupied the post of honorary secretary of the Union of Canadian Municipalities, spearheaded a remarkably effective counter-campaign to end this wholesale evasion of municipal jurisdiction and the erosion of municipal authority. Particularly flagrant attempts to secure federal charters recruited support for the municipal crusade from powerful provincial governments concerned about the loss of their jurisdiction. Most notably, Lighthall and the union resisted the efforts of William Mackenzie's Toronto and Hamilton Railway Company to obtain a declaration of general advantage from Ottawa in 1903. In this particular case, and as a general rule thereafter, the union managed to have inserted in charters a clause requiring companies to submit to local regulation and to seek municipal consent to use the public streets. Reviewing the Union's satisfying early victories over "the charter-shark, the grasping monopolist, the legal sneak and the venal politician," W. D. Lighthall called for continued efforts "to clean our streets of speculators and grafters."[10]

Lighthall's enumeration of the most frequent complaints against utility monopolies—loss of municipal revenue, unsightly poles and wires, refusal to build underground conduits, obstruction and destruction of the streets, high rates, poor service, indifference to contractual obligations, bribery of public officials, and combinations dangerous to the public interest—led him and other municipal men to the same conclusion: "All these and other evils point to a future in which, if it be permitted to develop, the entire people of the Dominion would inevitably find themselves tied, dictated to and bled by a small group of *trusts* obeying no law but dividends."[11]

The most indelible suspicions and bitter antagonisms arose from the unorthodox financial practices of the monopoly-makers. In his 1907 presidential address to the union, Mayor Emerson Coatsworth of Toronto argued: "The dispute between the municipalities and the corporate owners of the public utilities is that the corporations, becoming rich and powerful, exact from the people too high a price for what they supply and fail to give a fair and proper service for the money paid them." The monopolists were not satisfied with a fair rate of return on capital actually invested—which no one denied them—but schemed instead to secure an illegitimate "rake-off" through buying, selling and amalgamating companies, overcapitalizing them, and then manipulating their stock. "In the effort to maintain a valuation of, and dividends on, $5,000,000 for a $1,000,000 outlay, high rates are charged and poor service given, and the people realize that on this transaction they are just $4,000,000 out of pocket. The public are justly incensed at this kind of thing." Lighthall cast his denunciation of what he termed this "American system of financing" in characteristically moral terms:

Under the transparent assertion that the object is to reduce expenses by combining plants and thus to reduce rates, a few stock manipulators unite existing enterprises into a monopoly, paying extravagant prices which the buying public and the public served are to stand in the end, as well as providing a monster rake-off for the promoters, in bonds and watered stock. With this is combined the most predatory general charter obtainable, all possible sources of production are tied up, all remaining competitors ruined if possible and the whole enterprise is then boomed on the stock market. The result to the public served can only be accurately described as a "hold-up."[12]

Behind this particular phenomenon the civic populists discerned a more worrisome general problem. As Lighthall explained in a confidential letter to the Canadian Prime Minister in 1905: "We municipal men throughout Canada see ourselves thus faced with a new power, that of amalgamated capital, and we have some taste of the evils of permitting such capital to go uncontrolled locally." In his 1904 Canadian Club address Lighthall described this transformation of the economy in terms strikingly similar to the agrarian critique of industrial capitalism:

> It is obvious that the inevitable end of the trust movement arising out of the facilities of share-held capital and stock manipulation will be to place all our national wealth in the power of a few men screened behind their treasury doors. The age of competition, depending on defective transportation and on which the political economy of Adam Smith was based, is passing rapidly away. The small business is everywhere being merged in some universal company. All the railways, all the ships, all the mines, all the necessaries, are moving into one general combination here as elsewhere. Will not all the land go the same way in the end through the power and art of the stock manipulator? The advancing system means our ruin as a free people unless we can prevent it.[13]

The civic populists proposed to reverse this trend and restore a measure of social and economic democracy with an instrument they called "local control" or "municipal freedom." (The American phrase, "home rule," had unpleasant associations with Ireland in a colony loyal to the British Empire and was less frequently heard.) As the terms imply, the objective was to equip the cities with the necessary power to cope with the corporations, and to prevent either their escape to provincial or federal authority or regulatory interference by the higher jurisdictions. Regional markets would be broken up into smaller segments coterminous with municipal political boundaries. Local control would not necessarily prevent the formation of monopolies, but it would put an end to financial malfeasance, ensure conduct responsive to local needs, and thereby remove many of the incentives to large-scale consolidations of capital inimical to the public interest. In practice, local control often implied municipal ownership—for it was widely understood that the proud and predatory utilities promoters would never voluntarily submit to such strict supervision—but many civic populists surrendered only reluctantly to the logic of public ownership and were always willing to consider other avenues of regulation.

Emerson Coatsworth, mayor of Toronto in 1907, was one of these. In his presidential address to the Union of Canadian Municipalities that year, he described public ownership as an expedient, a means to an end: "The people, sweating under the exactions and bad service of the great corporations turn first to governments, and finding no redress then look to the means within their own reach, and the only available one is to own and control the utility themselves." But he warned that inexperience in operating organizations of this magnitude, the lack of continuity in municipal government, and the difficulty of obtaining first-class managers made civic ownership a risky proposition. He personally preferred intermediate solutions short of outright public ownership. Nonetheless, if the utilities monopolies refused to cooperate in the creation of other regulatory regimes, Coatsworth and many others like him considered public ownership the only recourse.[14]

W. D. Lighthall took a similar instrumental approach to the question. He believed that some public services could not be efficiently supplied except by monopolies, and the only method of controlling the "evils of monopoly" was public ownership. He nevertheless confined its "proper field" to "natural monopolies," and explicitly denied the legitimacy of the concept in normal commerce and "the ordinary pursuit of wealth." Indeed, as he explained on many occasions, "the general body of leading municipal authorities, although they agree on the evils mentioned, are exceedingly conservative and anxious not to injure capital and have no sympathy for pure extremists."[15]

Among those who gradually became convinced that public ownership might be necessary in order to control monopolies were the propagandists of Quebec nationalism. Like Lighthall, their experiences with Montreal Light, Heat and Power and the Montreal Street Railway led them to this conviction. In 1903, Olivar Asselin complained to the Prime Minister: "Montréal, entourée de chutes d'eau magnifiques, est tombée aux mains d'une bande de brigands. . . . La force motrice et l'éclairage y coûtent plus cher que presque partout ailleurs." (Montreal, surrounded by magnificent waterfalls, has fallen into the hands of a band of pirates. . . . Power and light cost more there than almost anywhere else.) As the street railway gobbled up its few remaining rivals in 1906, Asselin raged: "Nous sommes d'une ville que la compagnie du Tramway de Montréal est en train d'enfermer dans un cercle de fer." (We are a city that the Montreal Tramway Company is in the process of enclosing in a circle of iron.) And by 1911, Asselin admitted that public ownership seemed essential:

> J'ai cru dans ma jeunesse . . . à la necessité de la concurrence dans tous les services publics. . . . Je suis depuis longtemps convaincu que certains services ne peuvent se faire en concurrence, mais au contraire par leur nature même doivent être exploités en monopole. . . . La seule condition nécessaire, essentielle, indispensable, c'est que le public ait sur l'exploitation, directement ou par ses représentants, un contrôle effectif.[16]

> In my youth I believed . . . in the need for competition in all public services. . . . I have for a long time been convinced that certain services should

not be competitive but on the contrary by their nature ought to be operated by a monopoly. . . . The essential, indispensable, condition of monopoly is that the public have, directly or through their representatives, effective control over management.

Those of more radical bent, the "pure extremists" in Lighthall's terminology, took up the cause of public ownerships with all the zeal of converts as the remedy for civic ills. The Canadian Public Ownership League, founded in 1907, was a body dedicated to the proposition that, "All utilities which are in the nature of a monopolies should be owned and controlled by the people and operated for their advantage, either by municipalities, provinces or the Dominion."[17] For such fundamentalists, public ownership became an end in itself, a positive choice that not only eliminated specific problems but set in train a process of moral reform. Torontonian Frank Spence argued in 1907 that, "there is a social cohesiveness in the cooperation of a community with a common object for the common good. It is thus we attain the ideal. Ours becomes a better city. Ours is a truer Christianity."[18]

The debate between those who saw public ownership as a fundamental end in itself and those who viewed it as an instrument for correcting specific abuses reflected a deep division of opinion on the proper role of the state in economic life. In the early twentieth century, most Canadians were convinced that state enterprise must inevitably be beset with the twin evils of corruption and inefficiency. After Confederation the construction and operation of a railway line linking central Canada to the Maritime provinces had been entrusted to a federally appointed commission. Unfortunately, the Intercolonial Railway became a byword for poor management. As Sir Wilfrid Laurier put it to W. D. Lighthall, "I would not discuss here with you the principle of government ownership and operation of railways as an abstract principle. . . . The Government's operation of railways in this country has not been successful, and, I fear, cannot be made successful except under different conditions which have not yet arisen." And the city of Toronto's lawyer, discussing the possible takeover of the street railway in 1891, wrote, "With the many masters that must of necessity be introduced in the case of civil control, it will be made a dumping ground of incapables, the failures and the needy relatives, who will be hourly applicants for the fat and easy places that must be found for them." Worse even than inefficiency was the corruption many people feared. J. W. Bengough (who ardently supported municipal ownership of Toronto's trams) neatly satirized this point of view in his poem, "The Timid Alderman's Plea":

We know that the benefits ought out to belong
To the citizen; that is quite clear;
A greedy monopoly's had them too long,
And their profits have cost us full dear.
The theory is right that the city should own

The road, not in franchises deal,
But in practice, I guess, we'd best leave it alone.
I'm afraid it might tempt us to steal.[19]

Popular support for public ownership thus gained ground only slowly prior to 1900. True, in 1890 the ratepayers of Toronto voted 5,385 to 427 to approve a takeover of the street railway. But the vast majority of aldermen considered that merely a tactic to ensure that bidders for a new franchise could not use collusion to gain exceptionally favourable terms, and the city quickly handed the system back to private enterprise for 30 more years. A combination of fears about the efficiency of municipal undertakings and the ability of cities to borrow the large sums needed to finance these undertakings in a period of rapid technological change diminished enthusiasm. In 1895, for instance, Toronto ratepayers, by a margin of 4940 to 789, defeated a proposal to spend $277,000 on a municipal lighting scheme; in the same year Vancouver voters rejected the takeover of the unprofitable street railway there.[20]

Within the Union of Canadian Municipalities, the debate between those who regarded public ownership as a fundamental goal and those who looked upon it only as an instrument to be used in certain circumstances was never fully resolved. Neither was the tension between those who sought regulation of utilities by the provinces and those who insisted upon local control, convinced that the cities ought to rule themselves for better or for worse. In Canada, however, this division between provincewide regulators and local advocates did not mark a conservative-radical divide as similar disagreements did in the United States.[21] This was partly because the civic populists in Canada quickly discovered they could accomplish much more by working through the broad jurisdiction of the provincial governments than they could achieve on their own at the municipal level.

In that regard, Canadian municipal reformers differed somewhat from their American counterparts. Canada at this time lacked any sizable group of publicists, intellectuals, and experts like Richard T. Ely, Albert Shaw, Edward W. Bemis, Frank Parsons, Frank Goodnow, Delos F. Wilcox, and Milo R. Maltbie.[22] Instead, the leaders of the Canadian reform movement were almost all elected officials. Only W. D. Lighthall might be classified as one of the type of academics or professionals who took the lead in the United States, but he was a municipal politician before he became an ideologue. The Canadians came to their convictions through direct experience rather than wide reading or deep thinking. On both sides of the border, stress was laid upon the moral value and the practical benefit of municipal regulation, but American advocates were more likely to embed their prescriptions in systematic economic theory.

Collectively, the municipal men were engaged within their cities, their provincial associations, and the Union of Canadian Municipalities in an enterprise similar to that of the rural populists who sought greater public control over transportation, banking, marketing, storage, and communication. The organized farmers aimed to curb concentrated economic power, especially in the service sector, in the interests of primary producers. So, too, the civic populists tried to secure greater control over the municipal infrastructure—the utilities that provided light, power, transportation, and communications—for the producing classes. In both cases the bolder souls saw the possibility of building a new commonwealth based upon public ownership and cooperative principles, though the aims of the majority in both movements stopped well short of such a radical dream.[23] There were other similarities between the two contemporaneous movements. Like the angry farmers the urban populists suspected that the higher levels of government had fallen prey to the "interests" and so emphasized local control and direct democracy. The nonpartisan character of municipal politics in Canada convinced them that theirs was a purer, more public-spirited arena, which might permit a more rigourous cleansing and renewal.

The Union of Canadian Municipalities was born out of a sense of moral outrage. As men like Herbert Holt, Charles Sise, and William Mackenzie constructed their monopolies and carried out their profit-maximizing strategies across the country, bribery and corruption were all-too-common byproducts of the interaction between civic officials and private utilities, and the revelation of scandal reinforced the indignation felt by many municipal leaders at the treatment of their cities. Such concerns fuelled a demand for thoroughgoing reform—to bolster the executive capabilities of municipal government and reduce opportunities for subornation of aldermen—and buoyed up enthusiasm for public ownership.

Among the most spectacular and best-documented of these scandals arose over the letting of the street railway and electric lighting franchises in Toronto during the mid-1890s.[24] The indignation that produced reform there and elsewhere was but one expression of the conviction growing across North America that certain kinds of business interests almost inevitably debased politics and public life, and must be brought under control. Richard McCormick has suggested that this sense dawned upon many Americans around 1905 and helped to power the Progressive movement, one of whose objectives was municipal ownership of public utilities.[25] Alerted by muckrakers in the United States, Canadians too became convinced that they were beset by "rings" and "trusts."

What were the achievements of civic populism? Why in a few places did the campaign for public ownership succeed while in others it was defeated? Why did some utilities fall under tight regulatory control while others were able to preserve a broad sphere of autonomy? One answer, of course, is that Canada's cities exhibited marked differences from one another at any given moment. To take but one example: in 1905, Montreal had perhaps 500,000 citizens, Calgary 10,000, and Saskatoon less than 3,000 (see Tables 1 and 2). The situation in these overgrown frontier towns could hardly be the same as that in the maturing metropolises of eastern Canada. Moreover, the social and political power of proprietors relative to consumers differed markedly from city to city.

Toronto became the first city in Canada to have a board of control, but the drive for reform of the structure of government soon spread to other cities.[26] A stronger executive, often obedient to the interests of the local business elite, was required in order to deal with the problems created by urban services. At the same time, reform could appeal to radicals and trade unionists eager to break the hold of the interests over municipal government. Civic populism, then, was a coalition that could cross class lines and link up those who sought to democratize local government with those who wanted centralized administration performed with businesslike efficiency. And that in turn helps to explain the extent of the movement's success.

The scandals of the 1890s and bitter wrangles with the street railway company convinced many Torontonians that radical steps were required to bring the utilities under control. The first utility to face this threat was the Consumers' Gas Company. Ever since its corporate charter had been revised in 1887, the gas company had been the focus of severe criticism (see Chapter I). Although rates were twice reduced, the company's profits continued to climb; and though reserves piled up, they never quite reached the point where they would trigger further rate cuts. In his campaign for the mayoralty in 1901, Oliver Howland argued that there was "nothing in principle to prevent our acquiring this kind of semi-communal service. They [sic] are as appropriate as highways. They are simply an extension of the ordinary municipal sphere of action." And the citizens agreed: in the same election they endorsed a proposal to build a municipal gasworks.

City council had, however, to face the fact that under existing provincial legislation it must secure the company's consent and buy all its "rights, franchises, privileges and easements." Since Consumers' Gas had a book value of $2,685,000, Howland chose instead to negotiate. He found the company in an unusually receptive mood, owing to the fact that an increase in authorized capital was needed in order to expand the plant; it offered to reduce rates further, limit the size of reserves, and—more important—allow the city to purchase shares. By this means the civic administration could obtain full information about its affairs. City council approved the arrangement in the fall of 1901, only to see the new aldermen reject the plan in 1902.

The seed had been planted, however, and when a renewed challenge to the company through the courts failed, the idea was revived. In 1904 the city was given the right to a seat on the board of directors in return for its purchase of $10,000 (par value) worth of stock. In December the mayor became an *ex officio* director, and relations between city and company altered markedly. When the company's capital stock was increased again in 1909, the city's board of control moved to impose further limits on the size of its reserves. Mayor Joseph Oliver suggested that the company's general manager be invited to meet privately with the controllers to explain why he considered a larger reserve essential. When he did so, the proposal to limit the fund was promptly withdrawn, something unimaginable prior to 1904.[27]

Thus in the case of Toronto's gas company, the civic revolt led initially to a demand for municipal ownership. But when local politicians discovered how strong were the company's defenses, and when appeals to the courts failed to settle the disputes, the city settled for acquiring a share in the equity of the company. Thereafter, Consumers' Gas was left to manage its affairs in comparative peace.[28]

The purchase of shares in private utilities did not become a widely adopted means for exercising municipal control over utilities in Canada, however. Few entrepreneurs were prepared to share their authority in this way, and many citizens felt more comfortable with disciplining the companies through competition. Efforts were made in a number of cities to maintain privately owned rivals, but when these largely failed in the face of determined monopoly-making, many municipalities opted for the establishment of a publicly controlled rival to private interests. This not only curbed the abuses of monopoly but provided a handy yardstick for measuring the efficiency of state enterprise, about which so many Canadians harboured suspicions.

Ottawa, for instance, made persistent efforts to ensure competition in the field of electricity supply. Its offer to purchase a private company having been refused in 1893, the city decided to seek authority from the province to enter the electrical business itself. Permission was granted, but the scheme was effectively blocked by denying the city the right to expropriate any of the privately owned waterpowers in the vicinity. This was done at the instance of the city's own member of the legislature, E. H. Bronson, who was heavily interested in the electrical industry.[29] Having thwarted the city's efforts, he and his friends promptly merged three private companies into one, Ottawa Electric, under a federal charter that they hoped would render them immune from future municipal or provincial regulation.

At the municipal elections in January, 1900, the ratepayers were asked to declare their preference for municipal ownership or for greater competition in the electrical industry, and they endorsed the former by a vote of 3,459 to 2,576. That spring, a disastrous fire swept the vast lumberyards along the Ottawa River and almost totally destroyed Ottawa Electric's plant. As the company struggled to refinance and rebuild, several new private rivals entered the scene, judging that their chances of success were good with the established firm in such disarray. In 1901 the city granted a franchise to Consumers' Electric on condition that its domestic lighting charges would be no more than two-thirds those of Ottawa Electric. The new company constructed a small plant and began to provide some competition.[30]

When the streetlighting franchise came up for renewal in 1905 Ottawa Electric tried to restore its local monopoly.[31] In self-defense the council decided to purchase Consumers' Electric, and the ratepayers approved the purchase in May, 1905.[32] While many citizens still were dubious about this sort of experiment, the conduct of the private company forced the issue beyond competition to public ownership. In this way the notions that the civic populists had been disseminating through the Union of Canadian Municipalities began to capture the public imagination.[33]

Efforts by municipalities to enter the utilities field ran up against serious obstacles, nonetheless. Foremost was the conviction that it was fundamentally unfair for public enterprises to enter into competition with private companies. Some entrepreneurs claimed that the creation of a public undertaking would violate the "vested rights" granted to franchised utilities, upon the strength of which they had secured their capital. Others contended that no company could match the bottomless financial resources of the state underpinned by the power of taxation; losses due to incompetence or predatory rate-cutting could be recouped in such a way as to drive even the best-managed firms into bankruptcy. Even as the angry civic populists gained converts, attempts were made to rule out public-private competition by law, usually by requiring municipalities to offer to buy any existing firms before entering into competition with them.

The successful efforts of the local utilities to insert a "protective" clause, requiring such a buyout, into the Vancouver city charter in 1894 have already been described.[34] When the city sought to have this clause dropped in 1900, the British Columbia Electric Railway joined with the gas and telephone companies to resist. From London, R. M. Payne warned that if the city persisted in this violation of corporate rights, he would do his best to ruin its reputation in the money markets and make it impossible to borrow there. Although the city council, the Trades and Labour Council, and numerous individuals endorsed the charter changes, the BCER was successful in lobbying to have the protective clause retained.

Protection of this sort was granted as a general principle in Ontario in 1899. Utility promoter James Conmee put forward an amendment to the Municipal Act requiring all municipalities to offer to purchase private undertakings, at a price to be fixed by arbitration, before entering into competition.[35] Similar legislation in Manitoba helped to impede the spread of public enterprise in the early years of the century, and the loss of local independence further riled the proponents of civic populism. Even where such blanket protection was lacking, individual entrepreneurs like Herbert Holt of Montreal Light, Heat and Power were able to insist that their firms should be taken over as "going concerns," which meant that the cities must pay for the unexpired franchises and could not take over the parts of a company they desired while leaving the rest in private hands.[36]

In the years prior to 1905, civic leaders tried a number of stratagems to bring private utilities under control. In rare cases like that of the Toronto gas company, they purchased an interest in order to ensure that the city's interests were protected. Elsewhere, as in Ottawa, they tried to promote competition either by private or public undertakings, but these efforts had limited success. Entrepreneurs argued that competition between public and private agencies was inherently unfair, and in a number of jurisdictions they were able to force the cities to offer to buy out existing concerns if they wished to go into the utilities business. These complications convinced many politicians that a simple solution—public ownership of all municipal services—was the only answer, despite lingering doubts about the efficiency of such operations. Early in 1906, for instance, the ratepayers of Vancouver voted by a margin of 4 to 1 to endorse the principle of municipal ownership of utilities.[37] The civic populists were on the march.

The province of Ontario became the major battleground. There the issue of public ownership of electricity supply was fought out during the first decade of the century between the private interests headed by William Mackenzie and the "public power" movement led by Adam Beck from London.[38] Beck's series of surprising victories prior to World War I reveal important reasons why the cause of civic populism was successful in some places and much less so in others.

In 1903 the Liberal government of George W. Ross awarded the last of three franchises to develop the huge hydroelectric potential on the Canadian side of Niagara Falls. Controversy erupted immediately because the syndicate behind the Electrical Development Company consisted of William Mackenzie (who controlled the Toronto street railway) and Henry M. Pellatt and Frederic Nicholls (who ran Toronto Electric Light). Since the other two franchises at Niagara had already been granted to American-controlled companies that expected to do most of their business in New York state, and since the Electrical Development syndicate seemed certain to channel its power to Toronto, municipal leaders elsewhere across southwestern Ontario feared that no cheap energy would be made available to them for industrial development. Most of the province would continue to depend, as it always had, upon high-cost Pennsylvania anthracite. Toronto Mayor Thomas Urquhart hastened to point out to Ross that

> if these parties . . . are granted the privileges of bringing power from Niagara Falls it will be done by the expenditure of a large sum of money, and the Government will thereby prevent itself and also the Municipalities from engaging in similar operations, because it will be argued that to do so will have the effect of destroying the capital which has already been invested in the enterprise.

The time is certainly here, if it has not been here long ago, when public utilities should be owned and operated by the Government of the Province or by the Municipalities.[39]

But Ross merely appointed an investigatory commission to look into the feasibility of a municipal cooperative to distribute electricity.

Meanwhile, the public power movement gained in size and strength. At a meeting at Berlin (now Kitchener), Ontario, in February, 1903, representatives of Toronto and all the other major municipalities in southwestern Ontario met to form a permanent pressure group. The Toronto *World* applauded the populist revolt: "Capitalists get together and create monopolies. The municipal representatives at Berlin yesterday gave practical effect to the belief that the people should get together and create monopolies. . . . Corporate oppression has been possible largely because of the diffusion of the strength of the oppressed. The Berlin Convention is the sign of an awakening." Equally important, Adam Beck and his allies persuaded the provincial Conservative party to adopt the cause. When the party under James P. Whitney won power early in 1905, the stage was set for a decisive advance. The new Premier hastened to declare that the waterpower of Niagara "should be free as air, not only to the monopolist and friend of government as it used to be, but every citizen, under proper conditions, should be free to utilize the powers that the Almighty has given to the Province." Another commission of enquiry reported in favour of a publicly owned system to distribute electricity, and in 1906 legislation was speedily introduced to create the Hydro-Electric Power Commission of Ontario. This was not, however, an all-out commitment to the principle of public ownership of the electrical industry. Whitney insisted that although the HEPC had been granted broad powers to be used as a last resort the government did not intend to generate power itself. But Beck, now chairman of Ontario Hydro, used his influence to conduct a noisy publicity campaign at the municipal level to force the issue. In January, 1907, Toronto and a number of other municipalities voted to build their own distribution systems to take Beck's public power, to be supplied at cost, once it became available.[40]

The provincial government refused Toronto's request for authority to expropriate the Toronto Electric Light Company, but the evident determination of the city to proceed in any event convinced Sir Henry Pellatt, managing director of the private utility, to seek a compromise in the fall of 1907. He suggested that the city buy the company or else acquire an interest and nominate directors, as it had done with the gas company. Council was not, however, prepared to pay his asking price, inflated as it was by the value placed upon the unexpired portion of the franchise stretching till 1919. The majority of aldermen, many of whom had become fanatical fundamentalists during the struggle, were convinced that only public ownership could guarantee cheap, efficient electrical service. The conversion of Torontonians to radical civic populism was complete in January, 1908, when the ratepayers voted by a margin of 15,048 to 4,551 to set up a municipal utility.[41]

Beck proceeded with the construction of Ontario Hydro's transmission line from Niagara Falls, which would bring current to the fourteen municipalities that had signed agreements. City officials negotiating with Toronto Electric Light refused to abandon their plans to take power from the Hydro and assume the existing contract with the Electrical Development Company. Pellatt, Nicholls, and Mackenzie balked at handing over complete control of the largest power market in the province to a deadly rival, Adam Beck. As a result the public and private systems in Toronto competed with one another with the city owned Toronto Hydro Electric System capturing an increasing share of the market. Elsewhere in the province, more and more municipalities signed up to take power from Ontario Hydro's lines.[42]

In Winnipeg, where William Mackenzie and his associates also monopolized the supply of gas, electric, and transportation services, the city's commercial elite—who saw cheap power as a key to economic development—began to press the government for a municipal power plant and gasworks. As Mackenzie's new hydroelectric station at Pinawa on the Winnipeg River neared completion, the "power cranks" stepped up their campaign. In 1906 the city secured the desired amendments to its charter, and the ratepayers approved the construction of a $3,250,000 hydroelectric plant at Pointe du Bois on the Winnipeg River by a vote of over 6 to 1.[43] Once the work was finally under way in 1909, William Mackenzie offered to sell his entire plant to the city, but the council declined to purchase, and in 1911 the city's Winnipeg Hydro entered into competition with the Winnipeg Electric Company.[44]

By 1914, then, civic populists had gained some significant victories in establishing municipal utilities in Canada. On the prairies Regina acquired its private electric company and constructed a municipal plant in 1903; in 1904 Calgarians decided to build a civic lighting system. In traction, too, similar developments occurred. The Calgary Municipal Railway, begun in 1909 and completed in 1911, was the largest publicly owned system in Canada. The voters of Regina also opted for public transit in 1910, by a margin of 410 to 26.[45]

Nowhere was the conflict between a city and its transit company more bitter than in Toronto. Mackenzie's Toronto Railway Company clung stubbornly to its policy of refusing to extend its lines beyond the 1891 boundaries of the city. Infuriated, the aldermen asked the voters in January, 1910, for authority to construct a civic carline in the suburbs; it was approved a majority of nearly 2 to 1. When the city also began to study the idea of building a downtown subway to compete directly with Mackenzie's trolleys, he finally offered to sell the entire system, but the council balked at paying any more than the cost of the actual investment in the plant, and the deal fell through. By 1911 construction was underway on the Toronto Civic Railway, which went into operation soon afterward.[46] Thus Toronto experienced public-private competition in both electricity supply and transportation.

Despite the power of the corporations and the protection afforded to private rights by the courts and the legislatures, civic populists had succeeded in arousing and directing customer antagonism toward private utilities in many parts of the country. Anger and frustration overrode fears about the efficiency of public enterprise. Civic populists also succeeded in cutting off the corporate escape route from local control to friendlier federal jurisdiction. The new federal Conservative government elected in 1911 proved to be even less sympathetic to such schemes than their Liberal predecessors had been. Optimists within the ranks of the Union of Canadian Municipalities might have been forgiven for believing that a new era in the relations between cities and their utilities was dawning.

Civic populism scored its triumphs not solely because of the abuses perpetrated by utility magnates. Had that been so, public ownership would have made far more progress than it did in Montreal or Halifax. Utility managers were not unaware that attacks upon them sold newspapers and won votes. George Kidd of the British Columbia Electric Railway once reported, "Prior to his election I had one or two interviews with Mayor Gale when he told me that his agitation with reference to lighting rates was purely political." But controlling such mischief-makers required adroitness on the part of a private company. Newspaper owners could be granted loans or preferential rates on gas and electricity. Politicians needed even more careful handling; the BCER's Johannes Buntzen never took his lawyers to city hall, because that only made the aldermen suspicious that something was being slipped by them. In fact, company officials rarely attended council meetings at all, though they certainly appeared before committees (and, it seems, kept fuller and more precise records of what transpired than the aldermen); much better to go to a quiet committee meeting and try to work things out behind closed doors.[47]

This concern for detail helped the BCER to resist the civic populists. Aldermen came and went with great frequency at the annual elections, so there was no use trying to create firm, long-standing alliances. Even the mayor had only one vote in the council. And being attacked at election time was nothing to get too excited about; Buntzen and Sperling simply studied the election returns each year with great care in order to single out in advance those who might be particularly friendly or antagonistic in a controversial issue. It did not pay to be too chummy with the company's political friends, however, for fear of destroying their influence with the other aldermen. This approach reaped benefits for the British Columbia Electric Railway, while Mackenzie's flamboyant style played into the hands of the civic populists.

Image, then, was a critical consideration in this political contest. Both management's ability to put a benign face on the company's behaviour and the newspaper cartoonists' daily portrayal of an embattled, virtuous people had much to do with winning over public opinion and determining how the local citizens viewed a utility company.[48] Entrepreneurs and their antagonists had to grapple with that fact in the course of their lengthy struggles.

The most important factors in the success or failure of the campaigns for public ownership organized by the civic populists, however, seem to have been structural.[49] What was the nature of the relationship between different levels of government within a given jurisdiction? To what extent could governments be influenced by companies and pressure groups? And how did the objectives of the civic populists mesh with those of other powerful interest groups within society? Since the answers to these questions varied markedly from province to province, it is hardly surprising that the drive to control urban utilities made much greater headway in some places than in others.

The nature and structure of relations between governments, municipal, provincial, and federal was of critical importance. One of the most useful weapons in the hands of a utility entrepreneur was the ability to divide and conquer. In particular it was desirable to be able to play off the suburbs against the city proper, since the former were often eager to make generous concessions in order to secure service to areas so sparsely populated as to be of little immediate value to a utility. But a street railway or gas, electric, or telephone company might find it worthwhile to extend operations into these regions in order to gain a better franchise or at least to lock the place up against any potential rival. Then when it came to dealing with the city proper over the improvement of the franchise, the company could point out that central city service would be much less valuable without suburban connections.[50]

R. H. Sperling, of the British Columbia Electric Railway, brought this technique to a high art by securing franchises ranging from 40 years to the perpetual in various suburbs of Vancouver. The Montreal Street Railway also succeeded in stitching together a patchwork quilt of franchises for itself.[51] As a result the civic populists sometimes found that there was not very much that could be done because the municipalities had failed to coordinate their earlier dealings with the utilities. This was not such a problem in the smaller cities, but it did have an important effect upon Montreal, Winnipeg and Vancouver.

Toronto was unusual among the big cities because a wave of amalgamations in the 1880s and 1890s had put it in control of almost the entire built-up area as well as the prime land available for subdivision, and the utilities had to deal with city council if they wanted to do business there.[52] Moreover, Toronto was the first city to reform its structure of government, strengthening the executive by the creation of a board of control in 1896. Most other cities did not follow this path until a decade or so later. Even so, as we have seen, the city of Toronto encountered the utmost difficulty in trying to control the traction and electrical enterprises dominated by William Mackenzie; had there been divisions between the city and its suburbs to be exploited, the task might have been more difficult still. As it was, Toronto was able to gain a grip on the gas company and to start up a municipal electric service and street railway prior to World War I.

Not only were the relations between cities and their suburbs crucial in determining the outcome of conflicts with utilities; so, too, were the relations between municipalities and the province. As creatures of the provinces, cities had to look to them for their charter powers. Whatever authority municipal councils possessed depended upon the attention that civic requests received and the degree of influence that utility companies were able to exercise upon provincial governments and legislators. The British Columbia Electric Railway, for instance, was exceptional in the energy it devoted to lobbying and the success it achieved.[53] Whenever legislation important to the company was under consideration, officials, lawyers, and paid lobbyists descended upon the capital in droves, and they seem to have enjoyed extraordinary access to provincial ministers.[54] Sperling arrived in Victoria in 1912 and noted in his diary that he immediately "met with the Attorney General and the Premier and will probably spend most of the week interviewing the Premier." Later he reported to London that

> the Premier, although he was exceedingly busy during the end of the session, was kind enough to give me a number of interviews, and I believe exercised his influence with the Private Bills Committee to throw out legislation objectionable to our Company. Mr. Glover also saw a great deal of him during the time we were in Victoria, and his attitude towards us was one of consistent friendship.[55]

Few other utility companies in Canada seem to have enjoyed quite such close relations with a provincial government, although anguished Montreal reformers sometimes complained that Montreal Light, Heat and Power got special treatment. Another similarity between Quebec and British Columbia was that the largest metropolitan centre was not the provincial capital (which was also true in New Brunswick). What legislators and lobbyists were up to in Quebec City or Victoria was not always so clear to municipal politicians and ratepayers in Montreal or Vancouver as if events had been taking place right across town. In Nova Scotia, Ontario, and Manitoba the citizenry and the press kept their attention firmly focussed upon the legislature, and those who failed to espouse causes dear to the people of Halifax, Toronto, and Winnipeg could expect to find themselves singled out for opprobrium. Naturally, some rural or small-town legislators took pride in ignoring the demands of the big city, but the fact that some cities got undeniably better treatment from their provincial governments than others was a crucial factor in dealing with utilities.

Differing treatment also reflected something of the nature of the pressure groups that civic populists were able to establish in the different provinces. The strongest and most effective by far was the public power movement in Ontario. When the enquiry headed by Adam Beck brought down its recommendation that a publicly owned electrical distribution system be established in 1906, the Municipal Power Union of Western Ontario speedily organized a huge demonstration of support: 1,500 people representing the city of Toronto and 29 other municipalities (with a total population of over a million) as well as Ontario's Boards of Trade and the Canadian Manufacturers' Association descended upon the legislature to express support.[56] Tensions between the metropolis and the hinterland were submerged, because not only Torontonians but the residents of smaller cities and towns wanted to prevent the Mackenzie syndicate from locking up the power of Niagara Falls and denying them cheap power as a means to industrialize. Equally important was the fact that this movement crossed the class divide, including both management and trade unionists. Led by businessmen like Adam Beck, it nonetheless attracted the support of Trades and Labour Councils and a fringe of radicals, single-taxers, and social reformers as well as middle-class ratepayers.

Manitoba provided an instructive contrast. Much of the initial enthusiasm for municipal ownership in Winnipeg also came from the commercial elite and the Board of Trade. While they persuaded their fellow ratepayers to enter the power business in competition with William Mackenzie's monopoly, they could never capture a broad following outside the city. Initially, rural Manitobans could see little benefit to them if the province spent a lot of money to supply cheap power to the cities (although farmers were quickly persuaded of the advantages of securing public telephone service). Moreover, Winnipeg had only four representatives in the 40-seat legislature, even though it contained one-third of the provincial population, so that the wishes of the city did not necessarily command the support of the provincial government.[57]

If the ability to bridge the class and regional divide explains much about the success of the public power movement in Ontario, it also helps to explain the failure of the city of Montreal to secure municipal ownership of its utilities. The reformers who began agitating in the late 1890s were prominent businessmen, but in the working-class wards the old-line aldermen were perceived as more responsive to the needs of their constituents. When the proposal to create a board of commissioners elected at large was put to the voters in 1909, organized labour expressed suspicion of this scheme as an effort by the propertied classes to capture the city. Moreover, municipal politics in Montreal was always complicated by French-English friction; English-speaking reformers offended French-Canadian ward politicians with their assumptions of automatic superiority. Thus, divisions between constituencies upon which the civic populists otherwise might have drawn weakened the movement and limited its achievements.

For all the popular backing that the public power movement commanded in Ontario, it should be noted that its success might have been distinctly less had it not been for the support provided by the provincial government under the aegis of Adam Beck. Respect for vested rights was, after all, as strong in that province as anywhere else in Canada, as the Conmee clause of the Municipal Act demonstrated. But Beck secured an exemption from the clause for municipalities that joined the Ontario Hydro system, so that they did not need to buy out existing electrical companies. And when the Mackenzie interests inspired a series of legal challenges to the contracts between Hydro and its member municipalities, Beck rammed through the legislature a bill validating all the contracts, barring any further litigation.[58] In a province like Quebec or British Columbia, where the influence of the provincial government was quite likely to fall on the side of the private utilities, the supporters of municipal ownership could not have attained their objectives so easily, if at all. Closely coordinated relations between the municipalities and the province proved of crucial importance in the success of civic populism. Local autonomy or "home rule" might be desirable in the abstract, but municipalities found that they needed the wide constitutional powers of the provincial governments to storm the carefully built bastions of the utility entrepreneurs.

Utility owners realized that if municipal or provincial action threatened their interests, they could seek federal legislation declaring their undertakings for the general advantage of Canada. The Bell Telephone Company was one of the first to secure such a charter, but its full significance was not immediately recognized. During the 1890s, however, a number of street railways sought to escape provincial regulation in the same way, which eventually led to strong protests against the practice from the provincial governments. Seeking such a charter was contemplated as a means of defence by a number of electrical utilites in Ontario when the public power movement grew strong, which led the Whitney government to pass legislation nullifying all franchise rights granted to corporations that changed their place of incorporation without permission.[59] The problem so far as civic populists were concerned was that the federal government was too distant from the day-to-day concerns of the municipalities (except the city of Ottawa). Moreover, the federal government, particularly under Sir Wilfrid Laurier from 1896 to 1911, seemed more sympathetic to private entrepreneurs than were the provincial governments.

After 1905 the civic populists stepped up their campaign against private utilities all across Canada, though their efforts were not everywhere crowned with success by any means. Whether they worked through the Union of Canadian Municipalities or through their local governments, what infused these agitators for municipal ownership was the sense that they were dealing with a scarce resource. This sense was particularly strong where the drive for public ownership of electricity made its greatest strides. Comparative abundance seemed to sap the movement of its urgency. Montreal, for instance, was a city so surrounded by water-power awaiting development that despite the determination of local monopolists to swallow up their rivals (in which they were largely successful), competing firms could and occasionally did enter the business. The argument could not be made, as it was in southern Ontario, that without public ownership the advantages of cheap electricity would be irretrievably lost. That fear explains some of the quasi-religious fervour with which Adam Beck's movement was suffused.

In a few places, then, civic populism scored some surprising triumphs in Canada, but in most cities the sheer toughness and skill of entrepreneurs blunted even the strongest efforts of municipalities to break their hold. Nevertheless, even throughout the years of World War I the activists in the public ownership movement were still fighting. A statement of principles adopted by the Union of Canadian Municipalities at its 1918 annual meeting summed up their goals: the power of monopoly must be broken to end the political corruption that had resulted from the actions of utility companies; perpetual franchises should be granted only on carefully calculated terms; citizens must have their rights protected against the power of these private corporations, for their services had now become necessities of modern urban life.[60] This was the distillation of the experience of municipal politicians in a generation of dealing with franchised utilities.

Monopoly's Moment

Under the management of Charles Fleetford Sise, the Bell Telephone Company had attained virtually complete control of Canada by 1900 except for marginal areas where costs seemed disproportionate to returns. Yet such monopolies as his were made to be broken, whether by private entrepreneurship or public enterprise.

The populist insurgency that had such a profound impact upon urban transportation and electric utilities also shook the telecommunications sector. Free markets and contracts had plainly failed, civic populists insisted, first and foremost by producing a national monopoly. Customers became convinced that they were paying too much for Bell service, a conviction shrewdly fostered by the manufacturers of telephone equipment and the promoters of independent telephone companies. Bell's ruthless and largely successful campaign to extirpate its direct competitiors in major markets and its refusal to allow independent companies access to its long distance network sustained the belief that its monopoly had been created by unfair if not illegal means. Bell's contracts with the railroads and the municipalities raised further suspicion. Across Canada, civic populists arrived at the same basic indictment, but they were by no means unanimous about a proper remedy.

In 1902 the Hamilton city council struck a committee to investigate the telephone question. The committee visited 22 cities in the United States where independent companies competed with the Bell system, and returned with a strongly adverse judgement on the value of competition as an appropriate regulator; the nuisance of having two separate telephone systems vastly outweighed any advantages gained from lower-cost service. The councillors concluded: "It is not desirable for any community to have competition in telephones unless it is to regulate some very great evil. Competition in ordinary lines of business may be a good thing, but your committee are of the opinion that in telephony the rates should be regulated by some other means, competition being costly, and, up to the present time, somewhat in the nature of an experiment."[1]

The politics of telephone regulation in Canada revolved around a search for "some other means" or, in modern parlance, the choice of a "governing instrument."[2] At a dangerous moment, with its major markets in peril, the Bell Telephone Company had to confront a coalition of insurgent civic populists in a debate over regulation. What instrument would be chosen to govern the telephone industry if markets were deemed to have failed? In a vital federalism like Canada there was a prior question: What government would do the regulating? In a geographically dispersed polity in different phases of economic development it is perhaps not surprising that these questions—Which government? Which instrument?—received different answers.

Opposition to the Bell Telephone Company arose in several quarters: rural districts denied telephone communication by the company's concentration on the cities; Bell customers suspicious about high prices and variations in rates from place to place; independent companies and equipment manufacturers being driven to the wall by Bell's tactics and its exclusive procurement contracts with Northern and Western Electric; and, finally, municipal governments under popular pressure for lower rates, disgruntled about the terms of their contracts with Bell, and completely frustrated in their efforts to control the placement of poles and wires on city streets. When independent companies commenced operations following the expiration of Bell's major patents, only the marginally profitable rural districts remained to be developed. Once established, these rural independents often discovered that they could not obtain connections with the Bell system in the towns. Customers who expected rates to fall with the development of the technology learned to their dismay that Bell intended increasing rates rather than lowering them.

The trouble seems to have started in Toronto with the unsuccessful effort to renegotiate Bell's exclusive contract with the city when it expired in 1896. The city quite naturally wanted lower rates for telephone users and higher payments for itself in return for an extension of the franchise. Bell Telephone, on the other hand, feeling quite confident of its unassailable position in the Toronto market, refused to negotiate a new agreement on those terms and applied instead to the federal government to increase its Toronto rates.[3] Meanwhile, several independent company promoters made vague offers of service at much lower rates. The conflict ended in a standoff: the federal cabinet refused to approve the rate increase, and the city did not obtain a new contract from the company.[4]

Thwarted in its efforts to raise its rates in Toronto, Bell Telephone simply began charging new subscribers higher prices. When the city protested, it received a laconic reply from the Ministers of Justice and Railways that the 1892 statute "is legally ineffective so far as [new] subscribers are concerned, and that proceedings to restrain the Company . . . would be unsuccessful."[5] The Toronto city council quickly rounded up 140 other municipalities to support its petition to parliament for a more effective scheme of rate regulation.[6]

The city of Toronto tried to use other powers as well to bring pressure to bear upon the company to come to terms. In 1900 the city engineer was ordered to prevent Bell Telephone from erecting poles without a permit. Bell, for its part, claimed the right to locate its poles and wires wherever it might choose. In 1901 the city took Bell to court over the issue. The case hinged on whether Bell's federal charter or provincial legislation took precedence. The Judicial Committee of the Privy Council eventually ruled in 1904 that the charter prevailed, so the company's activities lay beyond municipal jurisdiction. Nor was the company obliged to pay compensation to any municipalities for the use of the streets.[7]

This decision was a dramatic illustration of the sweeping powers conferred upon a private company by a little-noticed piece of legislation in 1882. No longer the frail plant it had been then, Bell Telephone had grown into a huge monopoly which, by virtue of its statute of incorporation, now possessed unprecedented power over public and private property. Moreover, the corporation was safely ensconced beyond the reach of the municipal and provincial governments; only the federal government possessed jurisdiction. Accordingly, the city of Toronto and the recently organized Union of Canadian Municipalities scurried to petition parliament.[8]

Meanwhile, as their lawsuit wended its way up through the courts, Toronto's politicians had begun considering whether to build a telephone system of their own, and the city engineer was instructed to prepare estimates for a 6,000- to 10,000-subscriber service. He reported in September, 1900, that a system using the latest automatic equipment could be built for $675,000 and operated for $12,000 annually (including depreciation).[9] On the basis of this report, a special committee of council laid plans to sign up subscribers at a business rate of not more than $35 and a residential rate of $20 per annum, well below the prevailing Bell schedule. However, support for the plan melted away with the election of a new council in 1901. Instead, a private company offered to build and operate a competitive system itself, and negotiations were well advanced when the decision of the Judicial Committee of the Privy Council wiped out any leverage the city had with Bell. Even if Toronto went ahead with its own system or authorized competition from an independent company, Bell Telephone would still be able to operate its already established network in perpetuity without municipal approval. This, of course, greatly changed the attractiveness of an investment in a competitive Toronto telephone system. Somewhat sheepishly, the city resumed its negotiations with Bell Telephone in 1905.[10]

In Ottawa, dissatisfaction with the Bell Telephone Company prompted the city council to hold a plebiscite on the question of public ownership of the telephone system on January 6, 1902; 4,220 ratepayers voted in favour of a municipal system, 3,058 against. Despite this less than overwhelming mandate, the council set up a telephone committee to work out the details. American cities were visited, independent manufacturers hawked their wares, and several entrepreneurs put in bids. When the Bell Telephone Company eventually took note of this agitation, it summarily refused to consider selling its plant to the city but did offer a new exclusive contract on somewhat better terms. For the next three years a bitterly divided Ottawa city council debated the merits of monopoly vs. competition in the telephone business, public vs. private ownership, independent vs. Bell affiliation. The councillors rejected public ownership, toyed with the idea of an independent system, then finally surrendered to Bell, negotiating a new contract in 1907.[11] At the outset it had been possible to believe that Bell might be forced to sell in the face of municipal pressure, but after the JCPC verdict of 1904, that was no longer a tenable position.

At the Lakehead this debate proceeded well beyond the stage of mere talk. Lingering resentment against Bell Telephone for the manner in which it had crushed local competition in the 1880s prompted the municipal governments of Port Arthur and Fort William (now Thunder Bay) to cooperate in the construction of a publicly owned telephone system at the turn of the century. As competition between Bell and the municipal system intensified in 1902, Bell invoked its exclusive contract with the Canadian Pacific Railway to prevent the publicly owned company from placing a telephone in the railroad station. The municipalities applied to the newly created Board of Railway Commissioners to obtain access to the CPR station and freight sheds. Bell's lawyers argued that the company had a binding contract with the railroad. The Board of Railway Commissioners might order a second phone connection, Bell conceded, but if it did so, compensation must be paid to Bell for the loss of its exclusive privilege.

In one of their very first rulings the commissioners accepted the Bell Telephone Company's contentions in a split decision. Chief Commissioner Hon. A. G. Blair, a former Minister of Railways and president of the Bell-affiliated New Brunswick Telephone Company, concluded that the contract between Bell and the CPR was a valid agreement in law and was not in restraint of trade: the town could put a phone in the station only after paying Bell. M. E. Bernier, largely concurred; however, the third commissioner, Dr. James Mills, vigourously dissented. Taking a broader view of the public interest he reasoned:

> It may be said that an exclusive privilege, such as that in the telephone agreement, does not interfere with the public interest, because the public will be better served by a strong, well-equipped organization such as the Bell Telephone Company, than it would be served if free competition were allowed. That may or may not be so. One thing we do know, viz., that this is the

argument of all monopolists. We also know that, generally speaking, the people are the best judges of their own interests; and on a well-established principle of government in free countries, they should be allowed to decide such questions for themselves—whether to depend wholly on an organization such as the Bell Telephone Company, or to establish a municipal system of telephones for their own use.

Accordingly, he concluded that "the exclusive privilege . . . aims at creating a monopoly, is intended to prevent competition in the telephone business, interferes with the public interest, is against public policy, and as a consequence debars the contracting parties in the agreement from all claims for compensation against the municipality of Port Arthur."[12] The majority finding, handed down in March of 1904, was appealed, but it appeared quite likely that Bell's agreements with the railroads would stand up in court. Even if municipalities went ahead and built telephone systems of their own, they would still have to negotiate with Bell over the all-important matter of telephone connections with the railway station. The judgement of the Board of Railway Commissioners had placed a further obstacle in the way of municipal or independent competition.

Thrown on the defensive, municipal politicians and independent telephone operators began to search for more radical means of wriggling free. In his inaugural address as mayor of Toronto on January 22, 1900, E. A. Macdonald urged the parliament of Canada to take over the long distance telephone and telegraph lines. On March 29 the city council passed a resolution to that effect, a clear indication of the degree of alienation created in Toronto. The city soon headed up a noisy campaign to convince the federal government to operate the long distance lines as a public work and permit municipal governments or locally franchised private companies to operate local exchanges under closer supervision.[13] Under the leadership of W. D. Lighthall, the Union of Canadian Municipalities strongly supported the idea of public ownership of the long distance network.

British experience was much on people's minds and much quoted in public debate. The British Post Office, by virtue of its monopoly over the telegraph, had been active in the regulation of telephone companies and the operation of local exchanges since early in the 1880s. In 1896 the Post Office nationalized all privately owned trunk lines, an action that greatly inspired Canadian critics of the Bell Telephone monopoly.[14] In Great Britain a legitimate alternative to private monopoly seemed to be taking shape.

Francis Dagger, a British telephone engineer, provided more immediate inspiration. After learning the telephone business as an inspector with several British companies, he had emigrated to Canada in 1899 to work for Bell but had resigned after only 11 months with a jaundiced opinion of Bell's operations.[15] Dagger quickly became the leading spokesman in Canada for the idea of independent or cooperative exchanges linked by a publicly owned long distance network. In a stream of articles and hot gospel speeches, he championed the independent telephone movement and damned Bell's high rates, poor service, and outdated equipment. His technical background gave him credibility, and his arguments made a deep impact upon specialized journals like the *Canadian Engineer* and the populist daily press. In 1905 he singlehandedly organized the Canadian Independent Telephone Association, a lobby representing hundreds of small rural cooperatives and municipal ownership enthusiasts.[16]

The maverick Conservative M.P. and newspaperman from Toronto, W. F. "Billy" Maclean, acted as spokesman for this growing movement in the House of Commons. His yellow sheet, the Toronto *World,* had been campaigning on behalf of municipal ownership of utilities for more than a decade. Beginning in 1902 and at every session thereafter, Maclean submitted a private member's bill aimed at regulating the telephone business. Maclean did not have much influence: the Minister of Justice dismissed him as a socialist when he talked about telephones, and the Prime Minister accused him of being a "communist."[17] Nevertheless, Maclean's annual telephone bill served the embarrassing purpose of pointing out how thoroughly inadequate the federal government's regulatory legislation was.

Thus in 1903, when the Liberal government created the Board of Railway Commissioners, Laurier and his Minister of Justice had to surrender to pressure from both sides of the House, led by Maclean, and insert an amendment allowing the municipalities to apply to the board for a ruling on whether or not they could connect public telephone systems to the railroad stations. It was under this provision, wrung from a reluctant Laurier government, that the town of Port Arthur immediately applied— receiving little satisfaction, as we have seen.[18] The adverse decision of the Board of Railway Commissioners early in 1904 and the failure of the city of Toronto's suit against the Bell Telephone Company before the Privy Council later that same year dramatically illustrated the extent to which Bell had managed to manoeuvre itself beyond local control. By the end of 1904 the question "Which government?" had been answered decisively by the courts: the federal government had clear jurisdiction over the Bell Telephone Company. Thus the onus shifted to the most senior level of government to take some kind of action in response to the persistent complaints from the municipalities and other special interest groups.

The notion of public ownership of trunk lines had a particular resonance in the Canadian context. The federal government had just authorized construction of a second—publicly owned—railway, the National Transcontinental. The Conservative opposition had made public ownership of essential services part of its platform. In Ontario, the province already owned a railway, and discussion was well advanced on a plan for a publicly owned hydroelectric distribution system. On the prairies, public ownership had been warmly embraced by both business groups and organized labour; Edmonton had already taken over a failing local telephone company and was operating it in competition with the Bell.[19]

As pressure mounted, the telephone insurgency received powerful and somewhat unexpected encouragement from Sir William Mulock, the Postmaster General and senior cabinet minister for Ontario, where the movement was concentrated. Mulock had always been the most sensitive and progressive member of Laurier's cabinet in social and labour questions, and ever since the British government's takeover of the privately owned trunk lines, the Bell Telephone Company had suspected him of harbouring similar ambitions.[20] During Toronto's troubles with Bell over renewing the franchise and controlling the placing of wires, however, Sir William did not openly declare himself on the question of public ownership of the long lines; sometime in 1903 his proposal to offer some government assistance for the formation of rural cooperative telephone companies had met with fatal opposition in cabinet, most notably from A. G. Blair, who was then still Minister of Railways. After the election of 1904, however, with Blair safely removed to the Board of Railway Commissioners, Mulock tried another tack. In February of 1905 he urged the Prime Minister to take up the telephone question and "give the public something else besides the School Question to talk about." He suggested a full-scale investigation of the telephone industry as a means of informing public opinion, focussing debate, and preparing the ground for subsequent government intervention. "My own opinion is that the proper solution of the question is the expropriation of the whole telephone system of Canada," Mulock wrote to the Prime Minister, "and its being carried on as a public service by some department."[21] He persuaded the Prime Minister to authorize the striking of a Select Committee of the House of Commons to Investigate the Telephone, with himself as its chairman.

Such a parliamentary enquiry was not a powerful instrument; it lacked staff and it automatically expired when the session ended, reflecting the noninterventionist views of many ministers. Nevertheless, formation of the committee brought a flood of appreciative resolutions and immediately raised expectations that at last the government was about to move on the Bell Telephone Company's monopoly.[22]

The committee met for the first time on March 20, 1905, heard witnesses, and gathered evidence until its work was halted by the end of the parliamentary session in July. Mulock himself did not dominate proceedings (he was not even present for the final weeks of testimony), nor did he indicate any strong preference for one system of regulation or another, but his committee gave the municipalities and the representatives of the independent companies ample opportunity to publicize their grievances. Francis Dagger criticized Bell's rate structure and accounting practices; the net result of the Bell monopoly, he claimed, was that Canada had far fewer telephones per capita than it ought to. The exclusive agreements with the railroads were fully examined (and printed), and the situation at the Lakehead rehearsed one more. Thomas Urquhart, the mayor of Toronto, concluded his testimony on the long and futile struggle to regulate the Bell

Telephone Company with the plea that the cities be given back control over their own streets; he also urged the federal government to take over the long distance telephone lines and allow municipalities to purchase or expropriate Bell's local exchanges if they wished. W. D. Lighthall, appearing on behalf of the Union of Canadian Municipalities, communicated a unanimous resolution in favour of public ownership of the trunk lines and unrestricted interconnection between competing telephone systems.[23]

For once the Bell Telephone Company had been taken by surprise. The Speaker of the House of Commons, the Hon. N. A. Belcourt (who received a small annual retainer from Bell Telephone to maintain a watching brief for the company) reported in some distress the day the Select Committee was announced that he had heard nothing from the Prime Minister on the subject. Despite assurances from "the highest governmental authority that nothing serious is intended by the Government," the executives of both Bell Telephone and AT&T regarded the sudden appointment of this committee with the utmost seriousness. In Toronto, Bell's local manager reported that "every paper is committed to Government Ownership in one form or another;"[24] W. F. Maclean seemed to be gathering alarming support from sympathetic members on both sides of the House; and the appearance of a Select Committee, without any of Bell's well-placed friends knowing anything about it, raised unsettling doubts as to whether the Laurier government would withstand a concerted effort by the company's many critics.

C. F. Sise cut short a European holiday to hustle back to Canada. Frederick P. Fish, president of the American Telephone and Telegraph Company, rushed up to Montreal to confer; he was subsequently kept informed on a day-by-day basis of the Select Committee's activities and all political gossip. Bell Telephone was one of the first AT&T operating companies to come under a serious threat of regulation, and the head office therefore took a keen interest in events in Canada. Company strategists expected hostile cross-examination before the committee, and to parry these attacks C. F. Sise chose the able and politically well-connected Allen B. Aylesworth of Toronto to represent Bell. To neutralize the glowing propaganda about government ownership in Britain and Europe, Bell summoned Herbert L. Webb, a British telephone expert who considered government telephone monopolies "a blight." Webb not only appeared before the Select Committee but was also accorded a long interview with the Prime Minister. In the meantime, Bell lobbyists began the delicate business of seeking out sympathetic members of the committee. By early May the Bell management was reassured that six of the fifteen members could be considered "rather friendly" and that a clear majority of friends lay within reach.[25]

When the time came to present the Bell's case, C. F. Sise and Lewis B. MacFarlane testified that the Bell Telephone Company wanted to extend its rural business but that the economics of the situation at least temporarily prevented it. They insisted that their company would make connections with any noncompeting company as long as its equipment measured up to Bell's exacting technical standards. Both men received fairly rough treatment from W. F. Maclean and his allies, but invariably the Quebec members intervened to get Bell witnesses off the hook. Allen Aylesworth adopted a hard line, arguing that Bell's act of incorporation constituted a contract between the company and the people of Canada that could not be interfered with barring compensation. He denied the existence of any telephone monopoly, pointing to the hundreds of independent companies, and rejected the demand for government regulation:

> I am objecting to any compulsory legislation. I am urging that the shareholders of the Bell Telephone Company, whose money has been put into it just as legitimately as any man's money has been put into his farm, want and are entitled to manage their property according to their own best interest. Those interests are identical with the best interests of the public.

After this, Sise and Aylesworth sensed that much of initial fury against the company had been spent and that the "tone" of the committee had significantly changed.[26]

As the mood shifted, the company's expectations began to rise. From fearing imminent government ownership at the outset, Sise considered it within the realm of possibility by June that the committee might be prevented even from issuing any recommendations. Bell lobbyists urged the committee, in light of its inconclusive deliberations, to do nothing more than publish its extensive transcript.[27] When the House of Commons rose in July, thus ending the work of the Select Committee, that is precisely what happened. Not only did the low-powered committee make no report, but it further obscured the telephone question by burying it under three thick volumes of tedious and contradictory technical detail. That in itself represented a clear victory for the Bell Telephone Company and a major defeat for the civic populists.

After deflecting this first regulatory thrust, C. F. Sise assembled the company's four lawyers (Eugene Lafleur, T. C. Casgrain, Lewis Macfarlane, and Allen Aylesworth) on October 7, 1905, to devise a strategy for the next session of parliament. They now discounted the likelihood of public ownership either of the system as a whole or of its trunk lines. Nevertheless, Sise reported to the president of AT&T: "The general opinion expressed at the conference was that some legislation would be attempted, and the main feature of it would be [requiring] physical connection. Under these conditions it seems that the proper course for us to pursue will be to endeavour to steer that legislation, and make it as harmless as possible to us." Sise had concluded that Bell could not hope to control such a vast country in its entirety; independents would have to be tolerated and connected, but not rivals: "It follows that legislation will compel physical connection and it can only be a question as to terms."[28]

The problem was how Bell could open up its system to some independent companies without at the same time being required to give connections to direct competitors. Forced interconnection would most certainly encourage new entrants in the local exchange business. Sise had already confided to the president of AT&T: "The difficulty which I experience personally as a witness [before the Mulock Committee] is in explaining why—except that we propose to maintain our monopoly—we grant physical connection under certain restrictions to certain independent but non-competing Companies but refuse it to competitors?"[29]

To avoid compulsory interconnection C. F. Sise marshalled support in the House of Commons during the fall of 1905. In addition to his usual firm of parliamentary agents, Pringle and Guthrie, he hired two more professional lobbyists. Various lawyers and Members of Parliament received small retainers with promises of more if harmful legislation could be forestalled.[30] The team saw to it that the telephone issue did not become a partisan question, seeking friends on both sides of the House. The fact that the leader of the opposition had formerly been the company's counsel in the Maritimes eased this effort somewhat.

On October 11 the Laurier government signalled that it had decidedly rejected the most extreme forms of regulation. On that day William Mulock resigned as Postmaster General to become a judge, and Sir Wilfrid Laurier appointed none other than Allen Aylesworth to Mulock's old portfolio. Mulock pleaded ill health; Sise attributed the resignation to his own political influence. He congratulated himself on having the company counsel named to the cabinet and exulted to AT&T: "We can have no one in Mulock's place who will be as bitter and unfair an opponent as he was—and if Aylesworth is obliged to continue the enquiry it will be conducted fairly."[31]

Aylesworth's appointment showed that the government had not been swayed by public pressure. Minister of Justice Charles Fitzpatrick had long been skeptical of strong government intervention. In 1903 he had had his officials prepare a long memorandum, shrewdly drawing upon evidence from Great Britain, showing the inadequacies of both competition and, especially, public ownership as governing instruments. As for the telephone, this memorandum argued: "It is in fact a natural monopoly."[32] Fitzpatrick never wavered in that belief, and took particular delight in denouncing W. F. Maclean's "confiscatory" private bills.

The Prime Minister, though less forthright in public about the matter, nonetheless shared Fitzpatrick's opinion. Laurier's friendship with the top officials and lobbyists of Bell Telephone and the company's strong support among the Quebec members insulated him against the enthusiasm for alternative telephone systems emanating primarily from Toronto and western Ontario. Laurier paid particular attention to the advice he received from Thomas Ahearn, an Ottawa utilities entrepreneur, successful businessman, and staunch Liberal. Relying on Ahearn's briefing, Laurier dismissed the analogy of the telephone system with the publicly owned railways. He doubted, too, whether publicly owned trunk lines could be made to pay their own way, judging from recent British experience, and claimed that his government could not afford to acquire and then subsidize a national network.[33]

When the House met in 1906, the government presented its solution to the telephone question by introducing a series of amendments to the Railway Act designed to bring all federally chartered telephone companies fully under the jurisdiction of the Board of Railway Commissioners. From the broad array of governing instruments, the Laurier ministry had selected the regulatory commission—a form, incidentally, that the Bell Telephone Company considered most congenial, although it took exception to some particulars of the draft bill.[34]

Naturally the legislation produced profound disappointment among reformers. An angry W. F. Maclean ridiculed the appointment of Aylesworth, reminded the House of some of his extreme views as expressed before the Mulock Committee the previous year, and concluded by accusing the government of being more attentive to entrenching the vested rights of corporations than protecting the public interest. Charles Fitzpatrick, taking up the gauntlet, made a clear statement of government policy. The telephone had become an essential requisite of civilization, he argued, as necessary as water and light. Accordingly the government had decided that "it is important that we should make provision for as effective control over the telephone companies as we can have consistent with private ownership; and I think myself that private ownership with effective government control is an ideal system."[35]

According to the proposed amendments, the Board of Railway Commissioners would have to review and approve all telephone rates, and it could order railway companies to allow any telephone company to connect with their stations without having to pay compensation to Bell. Telephone companies were required to submit to municipal supervision in the stringing of wires and placing of poles, subject to an understanding that the municipalities could not abuse this power to stand indefinitely in the way of improvements. The draft bill also contained sections making it possible for independent companies, municipal systems, and Bell's direct competitors to connect with its system, but Sise was confident that bill would be amended in committee "that we may not suffer thereby to any great extent"—and lobbying did force the Minister of Railways to restrict competitive connections to the long distance system only. A minor revolt in cabinet, however, prevented Bell Telephone from having its way entirely. The legislation as finally presented to parliament authorized the Board of

Railway Commissioners to hear applications for interconnection and to approve those, subject to suitable compensation, that met standards of technical efficiency and did not entail "undue or unreasonable injury to or interference with the telephone business of such a company."[36]

C. F. Sise did not consider these safeguards satisfactory. He hinted that he would fight to have the legislation amended in the Senate, but an interview with the Prime Minister convinced him that he could live quite comfortably with the regulations. Laurier pointed out that Senate amendments involved certain risks: since the current session was about to end, the amended bill might not pass in time—in which case "a more stringent Bill may be brought up next year." Sise reported to Fish:

> As Sir Wilfrid and the other Ministers stated to me, we were now precisely in the same position as the Railways, subject to the Railway Commission. In case of parties applying for connection with our Lines, which we declined to give, we will go before the Railway Commission, and if possible make good our case. It is then for the Railway Commission to decide whether or not such connection shall be made, and on what terms as to compensation &c.[37]

Above all, the Bell Telephone Company had been able to obtain legislation that provided security. "The Railway Commission," Sise pointed out for the benefit of the president of AT&T, "in whose hands the matter had been placed, is, as I have before explained to you, a non-political and permanent body, and we would far rather go before them than go before Parliament for redress."[38]

The 1906 legislation effectively ended an intense moment of political uncertainty for the Bell Telephone Company. One of its important bulwarks had been sheared off in the controversy—the exclusive contracts with the railroads—and in future it would have to make a case for denying connections to independent companies, but it received much more substantial protection in return: the assurance that its most dangerous potential competitor, the government of Canada, preferred a regulatory commission to public ownership. At the same time, Bell escaped from the hands of parliament to the relatively safe haven afforded by the quasi-judicial procedures of the Board of Railway Commissioners.

The federal government's choice of regulatory instrument preserved private power over the telephone business and did little to disturb the prevailing pattern of industrial organization in that sector. The outcome can be attributed to the success of Bell's lobbying, the company's great strength among the Quebec members on both sides of the House, the ideological bias of the Laurier ministry, and the weakness of the independent telephone movement in Ottawa. C. F. Sise managed to blunt the populist agitation, turn it to his company's advantage, and enhance Bell's long-term security. The company did not want to be regulated, but since something of the sort had to be conceded, Bell Telephone had done its utmost to ensure regulation on its own terms. Thus when Theodore N. Vail returned to take charge of AT&T in 1908 and began to consider the merits of government regulation, he had this altogether heartening Canadian experience before him as a guide.[39]

————— The decision taken in 1906 to regulate the Bell Telephone Company by independent commission did not end the debate; it merely changed the theatre, driving advocates of intervention back to the provincial and municipal levels of government. Western Canadians in particular were not satisfied with the answers given to the questions: "Which government? Which instrument?" On the prairies the preferred means of regulating a "natural monopoly" became provincial public ownership. Circumstances unique to the West shifted public choice further to the left on the regulatory spectrum.

The Bell Telephone monopoly on the prairies was broken in large measure by the extraordinary growth of the region after the turn of the century. During the 1880s and 1890s the company had been able to meet most of the telephone requirements of the area without difficulty. It operated local exchanges in the main urban centres and began to build a limited network of trunk lines. By 1896 there were still only about 2,000 telephones in the company's North West Department, where its investment of roughly $250,000 returned 7 percent.[40] C. F. Sise found that this western business could be easily accommodated with an investment of less than $4,000 annually.

But cyclonic growth, the optimism that attended it, and a heightening of interregional tensions between metropolis and hinterland changed everything. Suddenly the Bell Telephone Company could not keep pace with the demand for telephones in the towns, much less the limitless countryside. In the alchemy of western politics, complaints about faltering service converted the telephone into a symbol of something thought to afflict the entire prairie economy: eastern monopoly. And it was on this level of political metaphor that the ensuing struggle over telephone regulation was waged.

The Bell Telephone Company responded with considerable vigour to this astonishing growth: by July of 1903 it had more than 4,000 telephones installed in the West, mainly in Manitoba. Within two years this number would double, and between 1905 and 1907 it would more than double once again. The North West quickly became the fastest growing of Bell's three operating divisions (see Table 16).

Yet even exponential growth of the system failed to satisfy the demand in the West. The Bell Telephone Company had always encountered stiff resistance to its rates from the Winnipeg business community; and now western communities in general and Winnipeg in particular were filling up with ambitious and impatient migrants who demanded telephone service on terms comparable to those prevailing elsewhere.[41] Bell could supply ade-

TABLE 16

GROWTH OF THE BELL SYSTEM

| | Instruments in Use | | | |
	April 1905	December 1907	Increase	% Increase
Quebec	25,166 (33.2%)	34,368 (28.9%)	9,252	36.8
Ontario	42,116 (56.5%)	64,596 (54.3%)	21,925	51.4
North West	7,760 (10.3%)	19,943 (16.8%)	12,183	157.0

Source: BCA, Sise Log Books nos. 20 and 22, 1905–7.

quate service by its own lights, but it could never hope to meet what it considered the exaggerated expectations of its western customers.

Nor could the company direct all of its energies to meeting western needs. As Table 16 shows, relative growth was strongest in the North West Department, but nominal growth was greater elsewhere. Fully 50 percent of the new telephones connected between 1905 and 1907 were added in Ontario, compared with only 28 percent in the West. Thus the Bell management had to deal with competing demands for the company's scarce resources.

By 1900, western growth had reached a stage where it could not be handled as a relatively minor adjunct of a basically central Canadian business. Each new telephone required an investment of approximately $150 in capital equipment—lines, poles, underground conduits, real estate, buildings, switchboards, stores, and the like. Materials and labour were more expensive in the West than in the East; moreover, the distances to be covered were greater, while population densities were much lower. It took more expensive copper wire and higher-priced labour to do a comparable volume of business. A dollar invested in Ontario unquestionably earned more than a dollar sunk into the wiring of the West. This problem of internal resource allocation became especially acute as the company approached the upper limit of its authorized capital. C. F. Sise kept a close watch over the marginal rate of return on capital invested in each of the company's divisions. He could justify a slight preference to the West to satisfy its growing needs, but there were limits, as he reminded his ambitious special western agent early in 1907: "Told him we had no desire to open small exchanges on the Lethbridge Line, as we had better use of our money."[42]

Sise realized that the demand for telephone service in the West and elsewhere could not long be denied, but he could find no satisfactory way out of this financial dilemma. At first he considered spinning the North West Department off into a separate regional operating company, as he had done with the Nova Scotia and New Brunswick divisions in the late 1880s. In 1899 he addressed a letter to Bell's Winnipeg lawyer, F. H. Phippen, asking whether he could locate some energetic western business-man willing to launch a local telephone company to which Bell could then transfer its western assets for $200,000 in stock and $50,000 in cash. "To carry this out successfully," Sise explained, "the promoter should not be supposed to be interested in or connected with this Company, but it should be ostensibly promoted and put into operation by an outsider; otherwise I would ask you if it would be possible for you to undertake it." Sise recog-nized, however, that given the many splendid opportunities in real estate, services, and commerce, there would be few westerners willing to tie up such a large amount of capital where it would only earn 7 percent; appar-ently he soon thought better of the whole idea, for the letter is marked "Not Sent."[43]

In 1904, when Bell Telephone had almost expanded its full $10,000,000 capitalization, Sise's mind again turned to ways of separating the eastern and western departments. "The Country and the people will not wait for us, nor will they give us any consideration on account of financial troubles if others are willing to step in with new Companies," he informed Frederick P. Fish, president of AT&T. But the Bell Telephone Company did have a small subsidiary in eastern Ontario, the North American Telegraph Com-pany, which it had kept separate because it possessed a charter almost as sweeping as that of Bell Telephone itself. Sise proposed to man this com-pany with a body of nominee directors from western Canada and Ontario, then apply to increase its capital from one to ten million dollars.

The plan was approved by the Bell's board, and parliament readily approved the recapitalization. Then Sise hesitated. Having created such an attractive vehicle, he could not make up his mind what to do with it. "I am somewhat at a loss as to whether we should sell to the North American Telegraph Company the entire North West plant, now representing $800,000 in our books," Sise wrote to Fish in June, "or whether we should turn over to the North American Telegraph Company the entire *Long Dis-tance* property of the Bell Telephone Company, we, of course, taking suffi-cient stock in payment to enable us to control."[44]

There matters stood in 1905 when the appointment of the Select Committee on Telephones took Bell by surprise. The sudden intervention of the government of Manitoba in the telephone question later that same year was a further shock. Competitiors had not flocked to the North West as they had to the U.S. Midwest, perhaps because they were inhibited by the same economic bias that restrained Bell. Independent companies were far more numerous and vociferous in the East, especially Ontario, where the municipal telephone movement seemed also to have taken firmer root (although the towns of Neepawa, Manitoba, and Edmonton has established municipal systems in 1900 and 1904 respectively); the city council of Winnipeg appeared less interested in the telephone question than that of Toronto, for example.[45] And the Telephone Committee of the Union of Manitoba Municipalities did issue a pamphlet in 1905, *Shall the People Own Their Own Telephones or Shall They Contribute to the Octopus?* Still, Bell Telephone's main opposition was concentrated in southwestern Ontario. During this phase of the populist insurgency, the West remained very much on the sidelines—watching, listening, sympathizing, but not participating notably. Perhaps that is why, when trouble did arise, Bell officials tended at first to discount it.

In January of 1905 two independent companies applied to the Manitoba legislature for charters of incorporation. The Private Bills Committee threw out the applications, however, on the grounds that their stated objective, "correcting the abuses of monopoly," would not be accomplished through competition. Instead, the committee recommended that the government should investigate the propriety of either taking over the existing Bell system or building a new one under public ownership.[46] Rodmond P. Roblin's administration seems to have seized upon this suggestion as a means of brightening up an otherwise lacklustre term of office. Besides, in the spring of 1905 the issue acquired a certain salience as a result of the evidence presented to the Mulock inquiry and the rapid progress being made by the public power movement in Ontario.

Relying upon the advice of his well-placed informants, Sise reported to AT&T: "The movement in Manitoba is a purely political matter. Rogers, the Minister of Public Works, is impressed with the idea that it would be to the advantage of his Party to take up the matter, and at present I can only say that the efforts of our friends are directed towards convincing him that the introduction of the System proposed by him would do his Party more harm than good." Nonetheless, Sise sped west at his earliest opportunity to investigate the trouble firsthand. He interviewed Robert Rogers in Winnipeg and came away with the impression that Rogers wrongly believed Bell's property in Manitoba could be expropriated by the provincial government and, more distressing, that the government would proceed with some plan no matter how convincing the arguments to the contrary. Experience in such matters had led Sise to the conclusion that "it is very difficult to block a scheme based upon political measures, and one in which a possible loss of money will have no weight with the promoters, as it is public money, and not their own, which is to be used."[47]

Eminent counsel confirmed C. F. Sise's view that a provincial government could not expropriate property from a company that had been declared "for the general advantage of Canada" by federal statute. What was more, the federal Minister of Justice offered the comforting reassurance that the Canadian government also believed such property to be untouchable.[48] Legally, then, the Bell Telephone Company was secure.

Nevertheless, a political defence had also to be erected. In July, 1905,

C. F. Sise met F. P. Fish at the AT&T head office in Boston to map out a defensive strategy. The two presidents agreed that the plan to divest the company's western plant to the North American Telegraph Company should be revived; that Bell should begin to promote independent companies and farmers' cooperatives, using Bell equipment in places where it was uneconomic for the company itself to operate; and that a major expansion of urban exchanges and trunk lines should be pressed forward immediately in the North West, particularly a line between Brandon, Manitoba, and Moosomin, Saskatchewan. Such a seemingly low-priority line would "carry out the provision of our Charter which declares our works to be for the general advantage of Canada as we connect different provinces. Manitoba, although connected with the United States, is not at present connected with any other provinces." Back in Montreal the board of directors resolved "to proceed with our business precisely as if no competition was threatened." Nevertheless, W. C. Scott, a former newspaperman with excellent contacts, was despatched westward as a special agent to conduct the counterattack. Local managers were briefed, lobbyists retained, and newspapers lined up with advertising contracts (for a company column called "Telephone Talks") and the promise of free telephone service.[49]

But as the situation looked desperate, more drastic measures seemed called for. By October the Roblin government appeared certain to proceed, so C. F. Sise travelled to Boston, where the president of AT&T introduced him to Messrs. Webster and Potter, two Iowa telephone company promoters who were said to be on good terms with the Manitoba government. They claimed to have great influence with Bob Rogers and said they could wean him from a policy of public ownership. Specifically, Webster and Potter promised to convince Manitoba to incorporate an independent company, under their control, that would achieve the government's objectives—lower rates, better service, and elimination of the Bell monopoly—without the risk and expense of government ownership. In reality, they would be acting as cat's-paws for Bell and AT&T. For once such an enterprise had been launched, Bell would sell the new company its western assets and then direct the telephone development of the West from behind this corporate veil. A deal was struck: Sise bought a worthless charter from the promoters for $27,500 and retained their services for $4,000 a year, and they set promptly to work.[50]

Premier Roblin announced his intention of proceeding with a publicly owned telephone system on November 23, 1905, and in January, 1906, appointed a Select Committee of the legislature to gather evidence and investigate ways and means. When Colin Campbell, the Attorney General, took counsel on the question of whether the province could expropriate Bell property, he was stunned to receive a conclusive opinion in the negative.[51] This setback notwithstanding, the government went boldly ahead with two bills: one to tax private telephones, and another authorizing construction of a joint municipal-provincial telephone system subject to the approval of the ratepayers.

Defending this legislation in the assembly, Campbell relied heavily upon passages from the history of AT&T in the United States and the anti-Bell testimony given to parliament's Select Committee concerning high rates, poor service, irregular accounting practices, monopoly tactics, and watered stock. The federal government could not be relied upon to protect the interests of the customers, Campbell insisted, because the Bell Telephone Company had the Laurier ministry firmly in its pocket, as the forced resignation of Mulock and the appointment of a Bell lawyer in his place clearly revealed. And even if the federal government could be persuaded to take over the long distance lines, that would not remedy the major Manitoba grievance of absentee ownership. Control would still lie in the East. Working in cooperation with the municipalities, Campbell claimed, the province would build a telephone system employing the latest automatic equipment. With advanced technology and lower depreciation charges, and relieved of the necessity of paying dividends upon inflated capital, the province would likely be able to cut telephone rates in two despite a rapid expansion of the system, especially in the rural districts. The telephone would help the farmer "by removing his present isolation," reducing his discontent and uneasiness, and thus stem the drift toward the cities. Lobbying by the Bell Telephone Company and the Canadian Pacific Railway pulled the teeth of the tax bill, but the government's telephone legislation was enacted in March.[52]

Up to this point C. F. Sise and his informants had undoubtedly been correct: the telephone issue seemed a political phenomenon without deep social roots. No interest group had clamoured for legislation of this sort; it had no basis in any popular outcry against Bell's service. The organized farmers, in whose name the government claimed to be acting, seemed to be excited about almost everything *but* the telephone monopoly before 1906. The Union of Manitoba Municipalities had to be coaxed to pass an endorsement and then did so by an unimpressive majority. Irked by this obvious indifference, Bob Rogers reportedly said, "when asked how he would get the Municipalities into line in the matter of erecting exchanges, that they would force them to do so."[53]

Such circumstances seemed ripe for intrigue. Webster, Potter, and friends wormed away in the shadows and in February claimed to have a commitment from Rogers that the government would charter their independent company in return for 33 percent of the stock under the table. C. F. Sise bridled at the bribe, but he was more concerned about rumours reaching him that Rogers was secretly negotiating with other parties in Minnesota as well. Accordingly, he called a halt to this discreditable charade—and that, apart from some unpleasant recriminations over the payment of expenses, was the last that was heard from Messrs. Webster and Potter.[54]

The government of Manitoba now had to convince to ratepayers of the province to endorse its policy. Under the terms of the legislation, each municipality was required to hold a plebiscite on whether or not it would own and operate its own telephones after December, 1906. To bring about the desired result, the expatriate English expert Francis Dagger was retained by the province "to begin a Campaign of Education along Telephone Lines," in the words of the Attorney General. This meant writing editorials and letters to the editor, compiling information for the electorate, and holding meetings—all, of course, "absolutely nonpolitical."[55]

Although C. F. Sise was preoccupied in Ottawa during the spring and early summer of 1906 with the crucial business of amending the federal Railway Act, he nevertheless remained confident that this "political" opposition in the West could be contained. He was also encouraged by some early returns in the plebiscite campaign. In April two rural municipalities, one of them in Bob Rogers's own riding, rejected taking part in the proposed public telephone scheme. It was thus with some hope of success that W. C. Scott was equipped with $12,500 to wage a publicity campaign throughout Manitoba in the autumn, emphasizing the great strides Bell had been making in the expansion of its western system and the perils of public ownership.[56] The most troubling development that fall was the announcement by the government of the newly formed province of Alberta that it had set aside $25,000 in its first budget to build long distance lines in regions denied service by Bell.

The Manitoba government could not claim a decisive victory in the municipal plebiscites. When all the returns were in, it appeared that only 55 towns had given the required 60 percent affirmative vote; 67 had rejected participation; and a count of the total popular vote showed only a slight majority (13,688 to 11,567) in favour of the government policy. In the two largest cities, Winnipeg and Brandon, ratepayers endorsed public ownership, but in Portage La Prairie, the third largest town, the proposition failed to carry.[57] Such an ambiguous outcome, however, did not sway the government. The Bell officials had anticipated that if the province received any encouragement whatever, it would press ahead—and it did. Indeed, Premier Roblin's Conservatives made public ownership of telephones the major issue in a general election called for March, 1907.[58] When the government was handily reelected with strong support from the towns but a reduced majority in the countryside, Roblin predictably interpreted the result as a clear mandate to continue; he wrote to the president of the Bell Telephone Company suggesting a trouble-free takeover. C. F. Sise, in a slightly wounded reply, declined to sell.[59]

The subtle electoral magic worked by the telephone issue in Manitoba naturally aroused interest elsewhere. The government of Alberta, having tested the waters with a line from Calgary to Banff, decided to jump in headlong in February, 1907, with a proposal to own all long distance lines, to operate local exchanges wherever desired, and to build an interconnected system of farmers' lines. Discussion of this government initiative in the legislature on February 14 was not so much a debate as an oratorical contest, with speakers competing mainly in the categories of denouncing monopoly and making ever-greater claims for publicly owned telephones. February 14, in the hyperbolic language of the occasion, was proclaimed "Emancipation Day," "People's Day," the day that "manacles had been broken," the "incubus" removed, the "blood sucking corporation" vanquished—the day Napoleon Sise had met his Waterloo in Alberta. In this rhetorical frenzy the telephone was transformed into a healing instrument. Wrested from the grasp of eastern monopoly, it could at last work its wonders, soothing cares, banishing anxiety, ending the "loneliness of womankind toiling in the scattered homes." Commerce would be stimulated, money saved, emergencies alleviated, friendship and sociability bound in cords of copper and steel. In the afterglow of this debate, the ratepayers of the city of Calgary—urged on as well by both the Board of Trade and the Trades and Labour Council—voted heavily in favour of building a municipal telephone system in competition with Bell.[60]

Something was going on in Alberta and Manitoba. If the telephone issue had lacked a social basis before 1906 it most certainly acquired it thereafter. In Alberta as in Manitoba, the telephone had been thrust onto the public agenda by politicians, not by aggrieved customers or angry farmers. The main proponent of the Alberta project, Minister of Public Works W. H. Cushing, admitted as much in an interview with a reporter from the Strathcona *Plain Dealer*.[61] A jaundiced Bob Edwards, the sage proprietor of the Calgary *Eye Opener*, wondered in February, 1907, what the "big hullabaloo" over telephones was all about:

> It is certainly a great measure but people can get along in a pinch without telephones. The Bell trust certainly deserves busting and the Alberta government will bust it all right, but why does the legislature remain silent on matters of more serious import? To wit the grain combine and the lumber combine? The first of which oppresses the farmer and the second drives the new settler back east on the break. The explanation may be that none of the members of the legislature are in the Bell trust. Then again it may not.[62]

In western Canada by early 1907 the telephone had entered a realm of discourse where rational calculation of cost and benefit counted for little. With one eye on the Ontario public power experience, the Manitoba government had discovered a related crusade with a special resonance in a western context. But in the first instance, politicians had to be promoters. As one student of Manitoba politics has observed with measured understatement: "It would perhaps be unfair to say that Roblin manufactured the telephone issue among the farmers, but in truth he was instrumental in bringing the farmers' grievances to their attention."[63] In an aspiring, debt-ridden, grievance-prone hinterland of a metropolitan economy, politicians found something that they *could* do, at an absentee's expense, which they claimed would also address other deep-seated complaints. Soon their words came echoing back from town councils, boards of trade, trade unions, and farm organizations. Soon two prairie governments were vying with each other for leadership of the public ownership movement on the continent. Politicians raised public expectations that neither the Bell Telephone Company nor they themselves could hope to satisfy, but once released, those expectations were political facts that had to be accommodated.

The Bell Telephone Company could only reply to this increasingly fervid rhetoric with wholly ineffective arguments about specific complaints. C. F. Sise and his agent, W. C. Scott, responded that Bell's rates were now regulated by the Board of Railway Commissioners, that up to this point the company had received no complaints to justify such a hostile political outburst, that it was expanding its facilities as fast as humanly possible; in places, they admitted, service had been inadequate in the past—Calgary being one example—but that would soon be dramatically rectified. The company also reminded zealots of the expense and waste of public competition, and the likely consequences of political management.

In the spring of 1907, Bell adopted new tactics in its negotiations, especially with the government of Alberta, which it believed to be more amenable to persuasion. W. C. Scott managed to open up direct lines of communication with W. H. Cushing and the Premier, Alex Rutherford, and he claimed to have made progress in convincing the top men that Bell would cooperate rather than fight. Following instructions from Montreal—cleared first with Boston—he suggested that perhaps the territory in Alberta could be divided between Bell and a government system so as to avoid direct competition. Scott and Sise seemed optimistic that a jointly owned public-private company could be set up which Bell would quietly control and to which it could sell equipment.[64]

The company made similar overtures to Manitoba, but Sise regarded Roblin and Rogers as too committed to their own plan at the moment to consider compromise. There he preferred to fight the public competition: "Were we to sell out in Manitoba, we would be very much at the mercy of the governments of Alberta and Saskatchewan."[65] On into the summer of 1907, then, the Bell Telephone Company stood pat, hoping to work out a face-saving deal with Alberta and Saskatchewan that would solve its problem of raising capital for and controlling western development.

The financial panic of 1907 was followed by a major shake-up at AT&T. Dissatisfied with its management in the face of serious inroads by independent competitors, J. P. Morgan led what amounted to a bankers' coup: Fish was forced to resign the presidency; the head office was moved from Boston to New York; and the organizational genius Theodore N. Vail, back from a self-imposed exile in Argentina, resumed control of the troubled company.[66]

In Canada these events compelled C. F. Sise to reconsider his huge programme of capital expenditure and to rethink his strategy toward the regulatory insurrection going on in the West. He laid the whole situation out before Vail, who was an old friend, and asked for his advice. Bell occupied a position of considerable strength, he believed, and eventually the government of Manitoba would have to come to terms. In Saskatchewan and Alberta he thought deals could be struck. On the other hand, he wondered, "with the financial stringency of today the question arises whether it would not be wise to dispose of our plant in Manitoba?" In round numbers he calculated it to be worth slightly more than $2,500,000. Bell sorely needed $5,000,000 that it could not hope to raise from its shareholders, bankers, AT&T, or on the open market. He thought it possible that in Manitoba "the Government has gone so far in the direction of Government ownership that they may be compelled to go on." Perhaps after taking over the Bell property, the government would discover the folly of its action and sell it back in the future; meanwhile, "we, while very reluctant to consider selling our property in the North West, are met with the question of where we are to obtain money for its proper development, as well as the development of Quebec and Ontario, and it is possible that the capital invested there, if available for Quebec and Ontario, would show far better results." As Sise succinctly summarized the Manitoba situation in his log, his company stood "to lose territory with the money or without it."[67]

Vail examined the correspondence between Bell and the prairie governments, reviewed the company's operating statistics, and on October 4, 1907, recommended selling the Manitoba business for $4,000,000. Sise summed up the decision for a new member of the board: "If we are sure of losing money in Manitoba through competition with the Government, I think that with $4,000,000 or whatever price we may receive, in our pockets, we would be better off than conducting a ruinous competition without the $4,000,000."[68] After making one last stab at a joint venture with the government of Manitoba, Sise got down to haggling with Roblin and Rogers over price. On December 7, 1907, they struck a deal: Bell would receive $3,400,000 in Government of Manitoba 4 percent bonds, and the province would take over all Bell Telephone facilities in the province except its North West Department stores.[69] As anticipated, this Manitoba surrender led to rapid capitulation in the adjacent provinces. Bell sold out to the government of Alberta on similar terms for $650,000 in April, 1908; and after a certain amount of prodding from the company, the government of Saskatchewan agreed in May of 1909 to buy the telephone business within its jurisdiction for $367,500.[70]

The Bell Telephone Company came to the realization about 1907 that it could not own all of the telephone business in Canada and still maximize profits. In its own interest it would have to tolerate a division of ownership and do its best to make money by selling equipment and exchanging traffic. The company had already come to this conclusion about service in rural areas; now it had to face the same prospect on the prairies. Government ownership was certainly not the most desirable outcome from Bell's point of view, but as long as it could be assured fair dealing in the equipment market, this outcome was only marginally less acceptable than organizing a local operating company in the region. Bell was satisfied with its relationship with the British Columbia Telephone Company, for example, to which it sold switchboards and telephones; Bell expressed no interest in acquiring control of that firm even when it had the opportunity to do so.[71]

In effect, Bell traded off territorial dominance for security in its lucrative central Canadian market. Defeat in the West was not inevitable; it was a private choice, the product of a rational decision about the allocation of scarce resources. Bell had better uses for its money than competing with governments that were unlikely to be deterred by losses, especially when their objectives more or less demanded losses. Moreover, Bell could shift some of its capital from West to East, where it would earn a better return. The proceeds from the sale of the Alberta plant, for example, went straight into providing additional switch gear in Toronto and Montreal.[72]

———————   The politics of telephone regulation in Canada produced two outcomes. At the federal level, public choice was guided toward an independent regulatory commission, one of the earliest in North America. But in Western Canada the campaign for telephone regulation ended in provincial public ownership. Canadian constitutional law did not have much to do with this twofold result except in a permissive sense. The western outcome occurred even though the provinces lacked power to expropriate Bell's property. We are dealing here with two quite different political games in which interest groups had quite different access to power.

The telephone movement in the West was a political movement whose main objective was symbolic, the elimination of eastern monopoly. It was a crusade that struck chords of recognition and reverberated in the prairie environment precisely because it seemed consonant with broader patterns of economic domination. Moreover, compared to the federal effort, it was a cheap crusade: for $650,000 and $367,500, Alberta and Saskatchewan purchased a good deal of psychic gratification. Manitoba, in its eagerness, paid rather more.

The Bell Telephone Company did not seek regulation but certainly sought to shape it once public pressure made it inevitable. When faced with what the company considered a near-hysterical opposition movement, Bell determined to obtain whatever regulation would do it the least harm. Bell was closely connected with the power structures at the federal level, and there it obtained a regulatory result in keeping with its own views. An independent commission was acceptable to the company, although it was unable to secure one as tightly restrained on the issue of connections with competitors as it would have liked. In the west, however, where Bell had neither shareholders nor local directors, and where it was thought to be an alien, exploitive presence like the banks, railroads, and elevator companies, political entrepreneurs were able to seize control over the telephone—at a price, of course, and not without advantages to the retreating company.

The two different governing instruments—a regulatory commission and public ownership—also embodied differing goals. But it should not be assumed that the governments first thought up their goals and then sought out appropriate instruments; rather, the two processes unfolded simultaneously. Public ownership had a symbolic mission—regaining control over a portion of the western economy. During the course of discussion it also acquired a social function—rapid dissemination of telephone service at rates lower than those charged by Bell.

The means and ends of federal telephone regulation emerged from the collision of different interest groups; the debate led to the conclusion that both interests were legitimate. In general terms it might be said that the objective of federal telephone regulation was the balancing of consumer and producer interests in a monopolistic industry by means of third-party arbitration. It was assumed that service would be governed by economic criteria: namely, a positive and reasonable rate of return on capital invested, facts that could be elicited by independent examination. Such regulation tacitly accepted the legitimacy of the existing monopoly and its ownership, and for that very reason could not meet the needs of the prairie governments, which did not accept the underlying premise.[73]

The objectives of first-phase of the telephone movement—public ownership of the long lines and municipal control of the local exchanges—depended upon the formation of a majoritarian coalition.[74] The costs of such a programme would be widely spread, as would the supposed benefits. Thus people and parties had to be convinced to pay, to be willing to deprive a company of its property, and to be persuaded by results that such drastic measures were necessary. The telephone movement failed to make such broad inroads; despite impressive early gains, it did not acquire enough support to shift existing alliances. The Bell Telephone Company could thus confound it through influence with both political parties at Ottawa, especially the governing Liberals. In the East, Bell was an established, politically well-connected institution, part of the power structure, fortified by influential shareholders and sustained by the ideological bias of key members of the cabinet.

In the West, during the second phase of the telephone agitation, the company faced a structurally different situation. There the costs of control fell largely upon outsiders, and the benefits were thought to be widely shared. Political entrepreneurs needed only to convince constituents to act at relatively small cost against absent third parties. From different games came different outcomes.

Competition is but one way of controlling business for socially desirable ends. When markets fail and common law offers no acceptable corrective, or when participants want to circumvent markets, recourse may be had to a wide range of regulatory measures from taxes, subsidies, and tariffs to more direct control by statute, commission, and public enterprise. The spectrum of regulation extends from markets on the right to public ownership on the left. It is one of the primary functions of modern government, pushed and pulled by special interests, to select from this continuum the socially optimal instrument of economic regulation, a process that also necessarily embodies goals.

In Canada, of course the targets of regulatory activity were vigourous participants in the process. The utilities entrepreneurs read the political portents and tried to shape an outcome that would maximize their independence. Because regulation came from "outside," they usually fought it before they sought it. The first struggle was over the *kind* of regulation. When businessmen reluctantly conceded the necessity of some form of state control over their enterprises, they nevertheless insisted that the scope of regulation be strictly confined. The choice of a governing instrument was never made in a vacuum: it represented an institutional statement about the balance of power between producers and consumers, businessmen, politicians, and bureaucrats. That balance was not settled once and for all with the birth of a Public Utilities Commission, for example, nor did such bodies always fulfill their creators' expectations.[1]

The historical literature on the subject of regulation has interpreted its evolution in several ways. Older works, some written at the time the new regulatory instruments were first devised, tended to stress a "public interest" interpretation. State intervention would correct the failures of the marketplace, enhance the quality of life, and ensure economic efficiency and minimum rates by bringing a broader conception of public responsibility to bear upon the conduct of private monopoly. In recent years this view has been largely displaced by the much more critical "capture" theory, which holds that regulatory agencies almost invariably become servants rather than masters of the industries over which they preside, and that in the rational pursuit of its long-term security, business actively sought state regulation to escape the travails of the market.[2]

But "capture" does not provide a sufficient explanation of public utility regulation in Canada. There *was* a politics of regulation: it was never simply a derived function of corporate will. Out of the conflict of interests, several different regulatory models evolved: public ownership at the city or provincial level; national commissions of judges and experts with authority over rates, standards, and conditions of service; similar bodies at the state or provincial level; and finally, local "service-at-cost" contracts that established rates on a fixed rate-of-return basis. The whole spectrum of regulation appeared during this period, from public ownership to markets governed only by contract. What was particularly interesting about Canada, therefore, during the first decades of the twentieth century was that utility owners had to contend with large-scale ventures in public competition. Their worst fears were not simply imaginary.

The most commonly adopted form of regulation was the provincial commission, beginning with the Ontario Railway and Municipal Board in 1906 and followed by Public Utilities Commissions in Nova Scotia and Quebec in 1909, New Brunswick in 1910, Manitoba in 1912, and Alberta in 1915. The federal Board of Railway Commissioners, created in 1903, was given jurisdiction over all telephone companies possessing national charters in 1906, as we have seen. That covered the Bell Telephone Company in Ontario and Quebec, and the British Columbia Telephone Company after 1916.[3] In the maritimes the telephone companies remained provincially regulated, while in the prairie provinces regulation was by public ownership.

If businessmen could make regulatory agencies work for them, so much the better, but they would have preferred a world without them. "The ideal state of affairs, if you can secure it," wrote George Kidd of the British Columbia Electric Railway, "is no Commission at all and freedom to run our business as we like."[4] Regulation was always a second choice; as a means of staving off public competition or preventing discrimination by capricious politicians, a commission might have to be tolerated, but if complete freedom lay within their grasp, businessmen pursued that goal with single-minded determination.

—————
————— After 1905 the civic populist agitation all across the country made regulation virtually unavoidable. Railways, for instance, had long been subject to some control by governments because they possessed the same quasi-public character that urban utilities acquired and had aroused

the same stern criticisms. In the mid-1880s the federal government had appointed a Royal Commission to enquire into railroad regulation. After looking at Great Britain and the United States, the commissioners reported that "the public interest requires the great powers and privileges granted to railway corporations be exercised under proper control by the state." They concluded, however, that any regulatory body ought not to be too much removed from the control of parliament and so should be composed of members of the cabinet.[5] The result was the Railway Committee of the Privy Council, chaired by the Minister of Railways.

Around the turn of the century, increasing agitation against high costs, rebates, cartels, and inequitable treatment of shippers led to a further investigation. The government eventually accepted the proposal of a body of nonpolitical experts modelled on the Interstate Commerce Commission and the Board of Railway Commissioners was set up in 1903.[6]

The establishment of this board coincided with important changes in the legal aspect of regulation in the United States, which soon had an impact in Canada. In 1871, Illinois created a Railroad and Warehouse Commission with power to fix maximum charges for services like grain inspection. This authority was challenged in court, but in *Munn v. Illinois* (1877) the U.S. Supreme Court sustained the right of the states to regulate businesses "affected with a public interest" which "held themselves out to serve the public." The courts did not, however, rule on how regulators were to determine "reasonable" charges until *Smyth v. Ames* in 1898, which directed them to consider the original cost of the plant plus additions and depreciation, as well as operating costs, in fixing rates to generate a "fair" return on investment.[7]

These principles carried great but not overriding weight in Canada. The demand for a fair return on investment was a touchstone for entrepreneurs threatened with regulated rates. If regulators proved unwilling to accept management's estimates of capital employed, they were forced to enter lengthy and complex controversy about the proper way to value assets. Such disputes became especially acrimonious during inflationary periods when replacement costs rose markedly higher than original costs, and debates over the rate base largely accounted for the slowness and inefficiency of regulation.

Whatever the defects of regulation, civic populists demanded more of it. In 1905 the National Civic Federation in the United States appointed a blue-ribbon panel to assess the relative merits of public and private ownership of utilities. After studying extensive research by selected experts, the committee issued a report in 1907 endorsed by 19 of its 21 members. (The two dissenters were the only private utility executives, though not the only businessmen, on the panel.) This report, whose signers included labour leaders, municipal experts, and academics, argued that competition failed to provide adequate regulation for utilities. However, noting "the danger here in the United States of turning over these public utilities to the present government of some of our cities," they were "unable to commend municipal ownership as a political panacea"; only where political influence could be excluded was success likely. Otherwise, commission regulation was the solution.[8]

Coalitions favouring regulatory commissions had already formed in many states, sometimes from incongruous elements. On the one hand there were those, like National Civic Federation members, who were suspicious of public ownership; on the other hand there were public ownership enthusiasts who were prepared to accept commissions as a stopgap. Robert M. LaFollette rallied these forces in Wisconsin to extend the power of the state Railroad Commission over public utilities in 1907. Within a few years many other states had followed suit.[9]

In Canada, regulation by public ownership of electricity in Ontario and telephones on the prairies greatly influenced the course of regulatory politics. As we have already seen, the newly elected government of James P. Whitney took the decision in 1906 to establish the Hydro-Electric Power Commission to purchase current at Niagara Falls and transmit it throughout southwestern Ontario for sale to municipalities at cost. Nowhere else did a state or provincial government commit itself to the cause of public control of electricity supply so fully.

From an early date Adam Beck, who became the leading figure in the public power movement, made it clear that he considered state ownership the only truly effective means of regulation. In 1910 he argued that private interests should not be permitted to develop the lower St. Lawrence River, because "rate regulation was useless without ownership of the power."[10] In a 1915 speech he predicted: "I look into the future, and not very far, and what do I see? I see this Ontario, generally speaking, without privately-owned electric plants. Why? Because private interests cannot compete successfully with the people's Hydro."[11]

What particularly rankled with the private interests was the fact that Adam Beck, as chairman of the Hydro, not only regulated the industry in Ontario but was an active and aggressive rival.[12] He did not hesitate to use rate-cutting as a means of seizing their markets in an effort to force them to sell out while at the same time exercising control over them. When the new Toronto Hydro-Electric System commenced operation in 1911, it offered domestic lighting for some 40 percent less than the Toronto Electric Light Company.[13] Each year between 1914 and 1917, Ontario Hydro reduced its wholesale power rates so that the municipalities could do the same.[14] In 1914, in fact, Beck ordered the Toronto system to cut its rates 10 percent; and when the commissioners demurred, arguing that residential rates were already at less than cost, the chairman used his powers under the HEPC legislation to force them to post the cuts—despite complaints from the mayor at this "gross and unwarranted interference" in local affairs.[15]

As Table 17 shows, the impact upon the private company was striking: by 1913 half the city's electricity users had switched to the municipal system, and this total had reached two-thirds by 1917. No wonder that Sir Henry Pellatt, president of Toronto Electric Light, complained bitterly that the

> municipal undertaking of the City of Toronto is inequitable and oppressive; that it is economically unsound as it involves duplication of plant and waste of capital; that it has been entered upon under misapprehension of the facts, and in serious error, for the basic price of power upon which it is founded is illusory and fictitious; that its mechanical methods in the transmission line are crude and dangerous; that the estimates of cost to the consumers must necessarily be largely exceeded, casting a burden of taxation upon those not using electric energy, and who do not in any way share in its promised benefits.[16]

In retrospect the managers of Mackenzie's companies admitted that by fighting as hard as they did against Beck's schemes, they had saddled themselves with a man who was both a competitor and a regulator.[17] When a severe power shortage developed in 1916, as industry was fully mobilized for war, Beck took advantage of it to persuade the provincial cabinet to permit him to purchase the Ontario Power Company, one of the three

TABLE 17
GROWTH OF TORONTO HYDRO-ELECTRIC SYSTEM

Year	Power Sales (KWH)	Average Price (per KWH)	% of Total Consumers Served	Annual Revenues	
				Toronto Hydro	Toronto Electric Light[a] (est.)
1911	6,657,700	2.21¢	18	$ 147,524	$1,550,000
1912	35,176,500	2.07¢	38	$ 726,763	$ 825,000
1913	65,025,951	1.78¢	50	$1,159,339	$ 900,000
1914	82,927,015	1.77¢	56	$1,469,506	$1,275,000
1915	109,501,981	1.43¢	60	$1,570,025	$1,175,000
1916	139,003,756	1.20¢	62	$1,663,103	$1,100,000
1917	171,691,213	1.15¢	66	$1,976,772	$1,175,000
1918	230,413,561	0.99¢	67	$2,288,971	$1,300,000
1919	180,609,938	1.34¢	72	$2,413,540	$1,300,000
1920	214,908,545	1.41¢	72	$3,309,809	$1,350,000
1921	221,384,558	1.59¢	75	$3,521,134	$2,000,000

Source: Toronto Hydro-Electric System, *Annual Reports*, 1911–23.
[a]In April, 1911, the company was taken over by Toronto Power Company and thereafter issued only consolidated earnings data; these estimates are derived from a bar graph in the Toronto Hydro-Electric System's annual report for 1923, p. 19.

private generating stations at Niagara Falls. He also secured permission to begin construction of a huge new generating station down the river at Queenston, which would be the largest hydroelectric plant in the world when it finally opened in 1922.[18]

The evolution of Ontario Hydro toward public monopoly reflected Beck's unshakable conviction that regulation without ownership was an unsatisfactory half-measure. The provincial agency he created marked one pole on the spectrum of regulation. Adam Beck did not hesitate to use his regulatory powers to strengthen his hand against his competitors, and by the time of his death he had reduced the private sector to relative insignificance en route to complete elimination.[19]

Yet Ontario Hydro stood alone; not until after World War II did similar institutions begin to emerge in other Canadian jurisdictions. The contrast between the HEPC and other experiments with regulation is clearly marked by the fact that in 1906, the same year that Hydro was created, the Whitney government also set up a conventional regulatory commission for other utilities. Municipal politicians had long complained that the courts had not proven a satisfactory agency for enforcing commitments made by private utilities under their franchise agreements. Not only were lawsuits expensive and time-consuming, but judges lacked technical and managerial expertise and in any event were not able to exercise day-to-day supervision over operations. The logical body to intercede between cities and companies seemed to be a provincially appointed panel of experts whose decisions would be appealable only on points of law.[20]

The three-man Ontario Railway and Municipal Board was given the task of overseeing relations between street railways and municipalities. In its first year this board's most controversial activities were in the field of labour relations, where it tried to mediate in strikes against street railways in London and Hamilton.[21] Tramway operators discovered that it could also provide useful protection against the municipalities in certain instances.[22] Nor did the ORMB interfere in the question of fares. Virtually all companies had five-cent fares fixed in their franchise agreements, and as most were relatively prosperous at that time, there was no pressure to raise them. Any effort to make cuts, of course, would have been greeted with fierce cries about violation of the sacred rights of contract. Similarly, when the board was also given jurisdiction over provincially incorporated telephone companies in 1910, it took little interest in rates and instead devoted itself to the problems of physical interconnection between the hundreds of small and isolated systems outside the federally regulated Bell Telephone network.[23]

Clearly, the same government that sanctioned the most radical experiment in economic regulation was reluctant to extend the principle even to other utilities. Ontario thus created two kinds of regulatory bodies: a regulator-competitor in the form of the Hydro-Electric Commission, and the more conventional Public Utilities Commission pattern represented by the Ontario Railway and Municipal Board.

—————— Manitoba appeared likely to move toward state ownership of all its utilities. As it turned out, however, regulatory politics in that province led to a surprising containment of the public ownership ideology. Winnipeggers did approve construction of a municipal hydroelectric plant in 1906, and the utility went into production in 1911, but it did not evolve into the same kind of provincewide system as Ontario Hydro. There the private electric utilities not only persisted but expanded, despite the competition. The effect of regulation was to stabilize the rivalry between public and private enterprise.

It was to escape acute embarrassment and conceal the mismanagement of the provincial telephone system that Premier Rodmond P. Roblin created a Public Utilities Commission in 1912. In this case the commission was not required to mediate conflict between private utilities and their angry customers but rather to allow the government to avoid responsibility for raising the rates charged by the provincial telephone system.

At first the takeover of the Bell Telephone network had seemed to work the promised miracles. The new Manitoba Telephone Commission had slashed rates, extended service to rural areas, and still reported substantial surpluses. Roblin and his Public Works Minister, Bob Rogers, viewed the telephone primarily as a political instrument, and the nominally independent commission that ran the system took its orders direct from the Premier. In 1910 the Liberal opposition succeeded in extracting from the commission's chairman, F. C. Paterson, the fact that the dramatic rate reductions in 1909 had been ordered personally by the Premier over the commission's objections.[24] A frantic programme of rural line construction in 1910, which just happened to coincide with a provincial election, heightened the conviction that the government was "fishing for votes with telephone poles."[25]

The following year, however, the losses were too great to hide any longer. The chagrined Telephone Commission decided to force the issue by reporting its first deficit, at the same time proposing to eliminate it with a general rate increase for rural subscribers and the introduction of measured service in Winnipeg.[26] The announcement prompted farm organizations, the Winnipeg Board of Trade, the bankers and businessmen of the city, and of course the Liberal opposition to demand a full-scale public enquiry. Even the Telephone Commissioners supported such a course, believing that they were not responsible for the sorry state of affairs.

In January, 1912, Roblin bowed to pressure and named a Royal Commission. Over the next three months 234 witnesses appeared to supply ample evidence of administrative inexperience, improper supervision of employees, patronage appointments, political interference with purchasing and construction contracts, and accounting irregularities. Telephone engineers and citizens alike testified that rural lines had been heedlessly and extravagantly constructed. Large portions of the system would never earn back their costs and would always require subsidies. Low rates and illusory surpluses could be explained by the fact that the commission had failed to charge proper depreciation or to maintain reserves.[27]

Roblin could not block the investigation, but he was determined to do all he could to minimize its political damage. The Royal Commission obligingly cancelled the rate increases, and its final report cruelly pinned most of the blame on the Telephone Commission. The system, it was argued, was fundamentally sound and had not suffered from undue government interference. With efficient management there would be no need for drastic rate increases.[28] Fully exonerated, the Premier called for the resignation of the Telephone Commissioners, but he still had to face the task of getting the system operating on a proper basis.[29] Since public ownership seemed a liability for the government, F. C. Paterson became convinced that the disillusioned ministers might be persuaded to resell the plant to a private owner; to that end he conspired with American Telephone and Telegraph and Bell Telephone to recapture the Manitoba network.[30] But Roblin realized that such a reversal would be politically disastrous. Another solution had to be found, preferably one which would shield the government. As an interim step management was reorganized to reduce expenses, but sooner or later the problem of how to increase revenues would have to be faced.

When the controversy first arose late in 1911, the Attorney General had begun to make enquiries in the United States concerning the role of Public Utilities Commissions there.[31] The cabinet finally concluded that such a body might be useful to sanction unpopular decisions, and at the opening of the legislature in February, 1912, the government announced that it intended to set up a PUC. That proposal, however, produced a startled response from Winnipeggers who were afraid that it would have a significant impact upon the electrical situation in the city. Winnipeg Hydro had begun competition with the Winnipeg Electric Company in the fall of 1911, charging only 3.5 cents per KWH, reputedly the lowest rate on the continent. The company responded with a 50 percent cut in its own rates. Some Winnipeggers feared that the PUC might be used to force the municipal utility to raise its rates.[32]

The situation was further confused by the sudden introduction of a series of seven private bills in the interest of a promoter named E. B. Reese. A close look at the "Reese bills" (as they quickly came to be known) revealed that they were designed to sew up all the remaining street railway franchises in suburban Winnipeg for a single holding company and to secure a perpetual franchise for the city's transit system. Exactly who Reese represented remains a mystery but once the implications of the Reese bills became clear they were inextricably linked in people's minds with the PUC legislation.[33] The government agreed to let the Reese bills pass only if they were shorn of their more outrageous provisions. In return the city consented to permit Winnipeg Hydro to fall under the jurisdiction of the new Public Utilities Commission, along with the provincial telephone system.[34] To demonstrate the PUC's impartiality—and to place some distance between himself and any unpopular judgements—the Conservative Roblin chose as the sole commissioner Judge H. A. Robson, a prominent and fiercely independent Liberal. Almost his first order of business was to deal with the matter of telephone rates; in July the Telephone Commission asked for and was granted a 29 percent increase in the Winnipeg district, and in August an increase averaging 10 percent for the rest of the province.[35] Robson also ordered the collection of proper reserves for depreciation. Thus the first task for the regulatory commission in Manitoba was to rescue a public enterprise from financial crisis and to insulate the government against the inevitable public backlash.

It turned out that private enterprise could also count upon a sympathetic hearing from Judge Robson. In 1914 rural members of the Manitoba legislature began pressing for a provincewide electric utility modelled upon Ontario Hydro. Premier Roblin appointed Robson as a one-man investigatory commission, and Robson's verdict was decidedly negative:

> It is clear that a general hydroelectric undertaking for the provision of electrical service merely for the use of the agriculturalist could not be accomplished on any satisfactory basis, and that such a scheme would depend upon the growth of towns and villages which would make such a demand for power as to give a foundation for the enterprise. . . . It is too sanguine an expectation that the electrical impulse throughout the province would increase local manufacturing and thereby augment population.

Thus armed, Roblin was able to resist the pressure brought to bear upon him by the rural-dominated legislature.[36]

That the Winnipeg Electric Railway Company need have little concern about regulation became clear in 1915, when Robson's report noted that demands for improved service were

> often made thoughtlessly. Improvements involving substantial capital expenditure are demanded without regard to financial possibilities or the likelihood of operating loss. A Commission is bound to meet and deal with all these matters with a due regard to public service, but at the same time to withstand attempts to oppress a public utility through the medium of the Commission.[37]

Many people were convinced that Winnipeg Hydro was able to offer its extraordinarily low rates only because of hidden subsidies from the municipal government; one federal official noted:

> It is generally accepted among those who have studied the situation at all closely, that the city has been selling its output at a loss, that this loss is borne

by the general taxpayer. This is not only unjust to the general taxpayer, but it is exceedingly unfair to competing companies. I have been creditably informed that the Public Utilities Commissioner for the Province of Manitoba has taken a firm stand in the matter, as a result of which it is quite probable that the unfair and unjust conditions referred to will be gradually corrected.[38]

As a matter of fact, the PUC commissioner in Manitoba did not have the power to force Winnipeg Hydro to raise its rates without the utility's consent; wartime inflation was the excuse taken to bring Winnipeg Hydro's rates up to match those of the private company.

In Manitoba an unusual combination of public and private forces conspired to produce a Public Utilities Commission with broad and sweeping powers. The agency was invented to perform an unenviable task: relieving the government of the embarrassing responsibility of restoring rates on the government telephone system to the levels that had prevailed under private management. By a timely coincidence, the commission also helped resolve a dispute between the city of Winnipeg and its street railway. Moreover, under the PUC, competition between the public and private electrical utilities was stabilized. The structural conditions in Manitoba did not present the same possibilities for a provincial utility—public or private—as did those in Ontario. When the hinterland towns and rural municipalities did begin to evince an interest in cheap public electricity, the regulator intervened decisively in opposition to an expansion of the public sector. Judge Robson was no Adam Beck. His goal was the preservation of the status quo on rational fiscal principles through a balancing of public and private interests. Thus regulation by commission, established in order to rescue the government from its telephone embarrassment, ultimately operated to normalize relations between Winnipeg Hydro and the Winnipeg Electric Railway Company.

──────────
────────── Ontario and Manitoba were not the only Canadian provinces to undertake the regulation of utilities prior to World War I. Quebec and Nova Scotia passed legislation in 1909, and New Brunswick followed suit the next year. Yet their legislation provided proof that the mere act of creating a regulatory body need not greatly hamper entrepreneurs.

Nova Scotia had been among the earliest provinces to introduce controls over utility rates. In 1903 all telephone companies were required to file a schedule of tariffs with the provincial cabinet. Complaints might be registered, and rates were not to be increased without the government's approval. The same rules were extended to electricity supply in 1907. But the ministers did not prove to be very effective regulators; not only did they lack technical expertise, but they were heavily burdened with other duties. Doubtless influenced by the examples in other jurisdictions, the Liberal government of George Murray introduced legislation to establish a PUC, which passed without serious debate in 1909.[39]

At that same session of the legislature, a private bill was introduced to charter the Nova Scotia Power and Pulp Company to develop hydroelectricity on the Gaspereau River about 55 miles from Halifax. The bill would have granted the promoters the right to enter the streets of a municipality to string their wires without permission, a right they hoped to use to crack the Halifax market. But the attempt did not go unnoticed by municipal officials or by the Union of Nova Scotia Municipalities, who demanded that the company be placed under the control of the PUC. Seeing a threat to their plans, the bill's backers agreed to confine their activities to the Gaspereau valley in exchange for an exemption from the commission's regulations.[40]

Control of this company soon passed into the hands of a Montreal utilities man, E. A. Robert. In 1912 he and his syndicate organized a takeover bid for Halifax Electric Tramways, a solidly profitable undertaking. The board of the company fought the raid by offering to sign a service-at-cost contract with the city in exchange for a franchise extension. The Montrealers persuaded the provincial legislature to block the deal in 1913, which provoked angry municipal leaders into using their influence to stop the merger of the tramway with the power development company—a merger upon which plans to issue large amounts of new stock rested. Talk began to be heard that Nova Scotia ought to have a provincial utility modelled upon Ontario Hydro, but Premier Murray opposed the idea:

> To take care of the public interest would be sound policy, but this was very different from going to the treasury and making investments in waterpowers. . . . Personally, he would be glad to see private companies come in and develop waterpowers if the legislature took care that their rights were not exercised in such a way as to be inimical to the public interest.[41]

The Montrealers made a second try to gain approval for the merger in 1914. Public agitation mounted in Halifax as it became clear that the new company, Nova Scotia Tramways and Power, would remain exempt from the jurisdiction of the Public Utilities Commission. Eventually the outcry became so intense that the promoters were forced to surrender the exemption; before Nova Scotia Tramways could issue huge amounts of new securities, the PUC must approve its plans.[42]

Although the Halifax tramway, which was the company's only income-earning asset, was worth less than $3,000,000, the Robert group proposed to issue bonds and common and preferred shares with a par value of $12,250,000. After a year's deliberation the PUC announced in 1916 that the syndicate would be permitted to issue securities with a face value of $8,000,000, priced to realize $5,575,000. Even so the insiders probably netted a profit of at least $1,000,000 and still ended up with control of 82 percent of the shares of Nova Scotia Tramways. When these were sold to American interests in 1919, another substantial profit was realized.[43]

Between 1909 and 1919 the citizens of Halifax learned that it took a very strong and determined body of regulators to deal with an experienced utilities promoter like E. A. Robert. Conservative opposition leader Charles Tanner had warned that Robert and his friends "knew how to dodge a bill through the legislature if any men knew how. They had done it in Quebec and thought they could do it down here."[44] Tanner was right. With the support of influential Liberals like federal Minister of Militia Sir Frederick Borden, the promoters got almost everything that they wanted from the Nova Scotia government. Loud public opposition was ignored, despite an extraordinary series of mass meetings in Halifax and the unanimous resistance of the mayor and the city council. The Board of Trade and the Manufacturers' Association of Nova Scotia also joined in the outcry, but to no avail. Although the PUC eventually reduced the size of the profits earned from this speculation, they did not eliminate them by any means, and Halifax tram riders were left to pay the interest and dividends on a vastly larger issue of securities. As if that were not enough Nova Scotia Tramways ultimately failed to carry out its commitment to develop power on the Gaspereau.[45]

Gradually, utility operators learned that while regulation might seem dangerous in principle, in practice it could have its uses. Reformers put too much stress upon the simple act of creating regulatory tribunals and ignored the fact that the process of regulation evolved according to the commission's personnel and decisions of the courts, as well as the political climate of the moment. Since none of these was fixed in stone, suitably handled, regulation might be made to work in favour of entrepreneurs and deflect criticism by legitimizing unpopular decisions.

That lesson became plain in New Brunswick, where the Conservative government of J. D. Hazen introduced legislation modelled upon the Nova Scotia act in 1910. The Public Utilities Commission was intended as a response to protests from Saint John, the province's largest city, about the New Brunswick Telephone Company. In 1904 the Saint John council had ordered consideration of a municipal system. Nothing came of the suggestion, but by 1906 the council was petitioning the provincial cabinet to introduce some form of rate regulation along the lines of that imposed in Nova Scotia in 1903.[46] Between 1904 and 1906 the company had faced competition from the Central Telephone Company; when a merger was arranged, the civic politicians became particularly concerned about the danger of an unregulated monopoly.[47]

The Saint John council was convinced that New Brunswick Telephone was attempting to disguise its high earnings when it applied to increase its capital stock from $600,000 to $2,000,000 in 1907. The lawyer for the newly founded Union of New Brunswick Municipalities even called for government ownership.[48] The Attorney General admitted that for reasons of efficiency the telephone business would ultimately become a monopoly, and that it might even be necessary at some future date to expropriate the company at a price fixed by arbitration, but meanwhile he promised to consult his cabinet colleagues about the idea of formal regulation. The company's lawyer resisted: "There had been no objection to the several companies acting alone, and what would be the objection to them acting as one company? If all the companies amalgamated it would enable them to carry on the business at less expense." Apparently, the promise by the government to consult with the municipalities about the creation of a formal regulatory body was sufficient to persuade the members of the assembly that the bill should pass without drastic amendment.[49]

The government did not take action on regulation, however, and New Brunswick Telephone set about gobbling up the remaining independent companies. In 1910, Premier Hazen finally acted to still the continuing complaints from Saint John by introducing a PUC act. He claimed that the idea of making the cabinet responsible for regulation had been dropped, because he "felt that such a matter ought to rest with some body more removed from politics than the government."[50] The opposition pointed out that while the proposed act made the commission responsible for regulating companies and municipalities that supplied heating, lighting, water, and telephones, it did not apply to street railways. Eventually, Hazen agreed to amend the bill to cover them. But why not specifically order an investigation to deal with inflated phone rates? The premier blandly replied that any citizen would have the right to file a complaint with the PUC, but that "the charter rights of companies should not be unduly interfered with." Still, to defuse some of the criticism, he accepted an amendment specifying that the board would have power to cut any phone rates it found excessive.[51]

The commissioners immediately went to work on the complaints from Saint John. The lawyer for the city contended that rates had always been far too high and that the company had built up huge reserves to mask its level of earnings. He claimed that a return of 20 percent on invested capital "is being taken out of Saint John subscribers in violation of business principles."[52] The company insisted it had done nothing wrong and welcomed "the intervention of this commission, as it must inevitably prove a protection to the company and its shareholders. It has proved a mutual protection towards caring for the rights of shareholders and the company and guarding the interests of the public."[53]

The confidence of New Brunswick Telephone that the regulatory commission would not harm its interests proved well founded. The commission's decision in the spring of 1912 accepted the tariffs submitted by the company with only a single exception. The board could hardly contain its pleasure in its report to the shareholders:

> Your directors feel that this decision was a very important and salutary one from the standpoint of the company and the public at large. Had the findings of the court [sic] been otherwise, it would have been impossible for the com-

pany to have enlisted fresh capital in its undertaking, and thus to have qualified itself to meet the growing demands of the public for an increased telephone service in the province.[54]

New Brunswick Telephone's experience with regulation was thus not an unhappy one. Because the company had been able to more than triple its authorized capital to $2,000,000 before the commission was set up, it did not even have to approach the PUC for a further increase until 1920, thus escaping the kind of scrutiny of its capital structure that the Nova Scotia Tramways and Power Company underwent as a result of its merger. When the New Brunswick company did seek to double its capital to $4,000,000 in 1920 by issuing new stock, the advantages of regulation had been fully assimilated. In the words of the company's counsel: "It has now given to the stockholder, or practically given to him, the safeguard that he shall have a definite adequate return upon his capital and that the rates in any public utility will be made sufficient to give that return."[55]

The only problem was that the public was slow to grasp the change in the relationship between customers and utilities. As the PUC's chairman put it in opening the hearings in 1920: "The true interests of a public utility and the true interests of the public are identical—adequate service for an adequate rate, and if the service is not properly paid for it will fall off in quantity and quality."[56] When the lawyer for large telephone users suggested that a rate increase could be averted simply by cutting the dividend from 8 to 6 percent, the chairman reproved him: "The public would be injured by that. It is going to deter capital. People will not invest in such schemes and plants. I think that the shareholders ought to be dealt very leniently with, because you do not want to shut out capital from these enterprises." And the increase in the capital stock of New Brunswick Telephone was promptly approved.[57]

Most regulatory commissions in the early years of operation do not seem to have undertaken a thorough analysis of the rate base of the utilities under their control, perhaps because they lacked both the staff and the accumulated know-how. Only in a few cases, like the Nova Scotia Tramways merger, did they even affix separate valuations to the different elements of a company's plant—and then the information at their disposal was often inadequate. Instead, they tended to accept the valuations proposed by management with only minor exceptions, and to approve tariffs proposed by companies without major changes. Whatever the powers contained in regulatory legislation like that in Nova Scotia and New Brunswick, Public Utility Commissions tended to act mainly as insulators against complaints for the companies and guardians for investors.

——————   Protection through regulation was not something only companies falling under provincial commissions enjoyed; it was also the experience of the Bell Telephone Company with the Board of Railway Commissioners. The company was required to submit its entire rate schedule to the BRC within the first year; then a hearing was held to assess its reasonableness. Compared with the publicity attending the parliamentary investigation of 1905, where the company's most strident critics had been heard from, the 1907 deliberations took place in a more subdued atmosphere, removed from the glare of publicity. And the company was able to use this to good advantage to shore up its position.

The three-man BRC was composed of A. C. Killam, chief commissioner, along with M. E. Bernier and Dr. James Mills, deputy commissioners. Lawyers G. D. Shepley and W. S. Buell represented the government of Canada; Aimé Geoffrion, Eugène Lafleur, and Lawrence Macfarlane the company. The issue was the way in which company's tariffs ought to be determined. Charles F. Sise, Bell's president, frankly admitted that there had been no rational basis for the widely varying telephone rates; in fact, he joked that he thought the rates "fixed themselves . . . they are not the result of any study as to revenue because we have never been able to regulate them. If we had been able to fix rates, we would probably study the returns from offices as we are doing now." The new schedule that the company had submitted for approval established a uniform toll charge, equalized rates in towns of roughly equal size, raised rates slightly in the East, and lowered them somewhat in the West.[58]

Having seized this opportunity to rationalize its charges, the company stoutly defended them as necessary to meet its heavy capital requirements while still being fair to its customers. Montreal, it was pointed out, enjoyed much lower telephone rates than any American city of comparable size. Bell Telephone officials were particularly concerned to warn the commissioners against thinking that the telephone industry, like other utilities, enjoyed declining marginal costs. "It is very often suggested to me," Sise testified, "that if we would reduce our rate we would double our business. It is quite evident that we might do that, but we would double our capital very quickly so that we would not be earning anything more than we do today relatively." At another point Sise was asked if he meant to imply that an increase in the number of subscribers hurt the company.

> Sise: It would increase our gross revenues in that respect, but not our net revenues.
> Mills: You mean that the less business you have the better it is for you?
> Sise: It looks that way in a great many cases.
> Geoffrion: Unless of course we are allowed to increase our rates.[59]

Most of the inquiry centred upon the company's policy regarding depreciation and its methods of dividing long distance from local exchange revenues. Company officials claimed that rapidly changing technology demanded heavy deductions for depreciation. But how heavy? Counsel for the government succeeded in demonstrating that notwithstanding its large depreciation account, the company was in the regular habit of charging quite a few replacements to current expenses. Company officials were insistent that no rational basis could be found for allocating expenses between the long distance and local exchange accounts. That strategy, which held up throughout the hearings, prevented the commissioners from dividing up the physical plant for rate-making purposes. Rates would have to be fixed for the system as a whole.

The company's lawyers tried to have it both ways. They argued, for example, that rates should be set on the basis of providing a return on the replacement value of the physical plant, yet they did not ask for such a valuation or pretend that their rates had been calculated from such a base. Rather, Geoffrion, Lafleur, and Macfarlane simply defended the slight increase on the grounds that costs had gone up.

For the government, Shepley asserted that, "real regulation will respect and protect the interests of the company. It will respect and protect the interests of the public." Buell, his colleague, suggested that excessive depreciation allowances had swollen the company's capital, permitting the accumulation of assets worth nearly $4,000,000 more than its liabilities. The two counsel also cautioned the commissioners against relying too heavily upon American precedents. "You cannot legislate away private rights in the United States," Shepley pointed out. "In this country you can. . . . If the language of the statute required it, the fact that private rights are interfered with or taken away, has nothing to do with the matter."[60] Overall, the government simply argued for a vague and unspecified reduction in rates.

After days of testimony and thousands of dollars in lawyers' fees, the case was eventually settled in a most macabre manner: the regulator died. Commissioner Killam, upon whom fell the responsibility for writing the judgement, passed away while working on it. Thus the new rate structure proposed by Bell Telephone was allowed to stand.[61] That in itself represented a significant victory for the telephone company, because at that very moment its public credibility had reached an all-time low with the 1907 strike by its Toronto operators.

The degree to which the private monopoly was sanctioned by the regulatory process was indicated by a 1912 judgement rendered by the Board of Railway Commissioners. An amendment to the Railway Act in 1908 had made the commission responsible for adjudicating disputes between Bell Telephone and the independent companies over long distance connections.[62] Some 378 contracts of this sort had been negotiated, but 11 companies in southern and western Ontario could not agree on terms with Bell, and some were actually denied long distance connections on the grounds that they were competing with the Bell system for local markets. These 11 firms, headed by the Ingersoll Telephone Company, applied to the board for an order requiring Bell to grant them connections, and the case was heard by Chief Commissioner J. P. Mabee on May 10, 1911.

In his decision Mabee concluded that the existing telephone situation "grew up perfectly naturally." Bell had done what any company would do under the circumstances; it developed the urban markets first and linked them with trunk lines, leaving the less populous rural markets to others. Gradually, these small independent companies had gathered enough subscribers to enter into direct competition with Bell. "Many people think competition is desirable," observed Mabee in passing. "It is in most things; but competition in connection with telephones never appealed to me. The exploitation of competing lines in towns and cities is simply a waste of capital and a cause of irritation in municipalities where duplicate lines exist."

The Ingersoll company dominated its local market; Bell Telephone claimed only 250 subscribers there. Mabee believed that if Ingersoll were granted free access to Bell lines, the Bell subscribers would abandon the company in favour of the cheaper, more popular, locally owned service. That being the case, the commission was forced to recognize that it had conflicting responsibilities: "There is capital invested there that it is just as much the duty of this Board to protect as it is to see that the subscribers of the Ingersoll system get long distance communication." The trunk lines, Mabee observed correctly, were the "sheet anchor" of the entire Bell system:

> Now while it is our duty, if we can, to give the subscribers of these rural exchanges long distance connection over the lines of the Bell Telephone Company, and while Parliament by putting this law on the book intended that we should act upon it, the question that is presented to us is under what terms are we able to relieve this tension without being unfair either to the subscribers of the Ingersoll Telephone Company or to the stock-holders of the Bell Telephone Company.

With that in mind, Chief Commissioner Mabee ordered the Bell Telephone Company to provide long distance service to the 11 companies but also authorized it to charge them 15 cents per call, over and above the regular toll charge, for the privilege.[63] Thus Bell was insulated by the Board of Railway Commissioners even from this marginal competition. Believing that the Bell monopoly had evolved "naturally" and deserved protection, the Board of Railway Commissioners placed the interests of shareholders above those of subscribers when fixing rates.

The very existence of a regulatory agency seemed to indicate that some action affecting the operations of private utilities would occur, but that was not necessarily the case. The province of Quebec, for instance, appointed a Public Utilities Commission in 1909, the same year as Nova Scotia. Yet an examination of its performance during its early years of operation suggests that it made no significant impact upon the utilities that fell under it. In part, this was because they vigourously contested its jurisdiction in the courts, though it also reflects deficiencies in the powers granted to the commission.

In Montreal both the street railway and the electric company were the focus of intense controversy after the turn of the century. In 1903, Montreal Light, Heat and Power achieved a virtual monopoly in the local market, which was shrewdly and effectively defended by Herbert Holt through his dealings with the numerous municipalities in the area. Blessed with falling costs from hydroelectricity, he was able to offer rate reductions in exchange for long-term franchises without reducing profitability. The Montreal Street Railway, meanwhile, had ensnared the city and its suburbs in a web of 30 different contracts signed by 14 separate municipalities. While the franchise for the city centre was due to expire in 1922, other parts of Montreal were covered by perpetual franchises or contracts extending as far forward as 1959. Outside the city proper, agreements expiring between 1919 and 1961 were in force.[64]

In establishing a PUC, the government of Lomer Gouin evidently hoped to reduce widespread public discontent with this situation. He did not, however, intend to give the commission very broad powers. On the eve of the debate on the bill in the legislature, the council of the Montreal suburb of Westmount (which had its own power distribution system and was something of a hotbed of civic populism) expressed concern that the commission might not even have the authority to fix rates in the event that a company and a municipality disagreed. Gouin's bill did, in fact, make all disputes over rates subject to the PUC but also provided that the commission's powers should be subject to all existing contracts between utilities and municipalities. It was also empowered to order a municipality to permit a utility to enter its boundaries if an agreement between the two could not be reached—another bonus for the companies. Addressing the Private Bills Committee of the upper house, R. C. Smith of Montreal Light, Heat and Power declared that he positively welcomed the appointment of a PUC, since it would relieve the company of the domination of the aldermen and place it under an independent body. He also suggested that the commission be authorized to fix rates charged by municipally owned utilities so as to place them on the same basis as the companies and rule out "unfair' competition. And just to render such competition all the more improbable, Smith was able to secure an amendment to a bill requested by the city of Montreal giving it authority to spend $2,000,000 on a municipal electric plant: In order to do so, the city would first have to offer to purchase the entire plant of Montreal Light, Heat and Power.[65]

The first important case to be dealt with by the Quebec PUC made it plain that companies would have little to worry about. In 1910, E. A. Robert had acquired a controlling interest in the Montreal Street Railway. The price of the stock advanced from $220 to $250 per share in the bidding war, and it was known thàt the Robert syndicate had borrowed $13,000,000 in order to buy it up—which made it essential to issue large amounts of new securities to repay these loans. Early in 1911, Robert announced plans to reorganize the four tram companies on the island of Montreal to form a new enterprise that would raise this money. Failing to reach agreement with the municipal authorities, Robert went over their heads to seek a new charter for his Montreal Tramways Company from the compliant provincial legislature.[66]

The next order of business was to secure approval from the PUC for an issue of $17,000,000 worth of additional securities (although the Montreal Street Railway had an authorized capital of only $10,000,000), the proceeds to be used to pay off the loans. This also meant that the new company would have to pay out $1,450,000 in annual interest and dividends instead of the current $1,000,000—the additional sum to come from the pockets of tram riders. But the commission refused to intervene, noting that "in any consideration of the public welfare and interest, the lawful demands and vested rights of those who have placed their money in the company's enterprise must be dealt with."

In an effort to avert charges that they were authorizing stock-watering on a grand scale, the commissioners contended that the tramway franchises were so valuable as to justify accepting the company's claim that its assets were now worth $23,000,000: "Whatever, therefore, may be the actual value of the stocks to be issued to the Montreal Street Railway Company shareholders, we are of the opinion that they do not involve such fictitious creations of nominal value as to be objectionable on the grounds of public interest." In any event, they noted, unlike their counterparts in Nova Scotia, they did not possess the authority to fix the issue prices of public utility securities.[67]

Having obtained the commission's sanction for the merger, Montreal Tramways quickly made clear that it had no intention of cooperating further. In 1912 the PUC ordered a study to discover whether the company had sufficient equipment to carry out the terms of its franchises properly. When requested to produce information, the company refused, and the issue went to the courts. Not until 1914 was the commission's jurisdiction upheld, and then the company promptly appealed to the Judicial Committee of the Privy Council, effectively blocking the investigation.[68]

Montreal Light, Heat and Power, too, chose to resist regulation by challenging the commission's authority. When a customer complained to the PUC about his gas rates, the company claimed that the commission could not intervene until the company had formally rejected the demand for lower rates. Using this excuse, the company could presumably have stalled almost indefinitely and reduced the whole exercise to a farce. But the PUC rejected this claim, and when the company launched an appeal, the courts upheld the commission. Perhaps fearful that the company would appeal all the way to the Judicial Committee, thwarting the entire regulatory process for several years, the government brought in new legislation in 1911 giving the commissioners specific authority to investigate any allegation that utility rates exceeded what was "just and reasonable."[69]

Neither then nor later did the commission undertake a thoroughgoing review of Montreal Light, Heat and Power's rates or order significant reductions. This was partly because the company itself announced cuts in either electric or gas rates practically every year in the period prior to 1914—usually just before the annual meeting in order to blunt criticism of its steadily rising earnings. Nor did the PUC interfere with the company's decision to increase its authorized capital from $17,000,000 to $22,000,000 in 1913.[70] Once the war had broken out, the demand for power mounted rapidly, and the company earned ever-higher profits. In 1916, Sir Herbert Holt decided to distribute these to the shareholders by setting up a new company called Civic Investment and Industrial capitalized at $75,000,000. Montreal Light, Heat and Power agreed to lease its plant to Civic Investment for 48 years in exchange for a guaranteed annual dividend of 8 percent. Each shareholder of the old company then received three shares in the new, which also took over the accumulated surplus. This tripling of the share capital, which helped to mask a very high rate of return on investment, was accomplished without any intervention by the PUC.[71]

Regulation by commission in Quebec thus accomplished little beyond providing some legitimacy to the financial manipulations of the biggest companies. Shareholders and investors found their rights treated even more respectfully there than in Nova Scotia. Because the commission lacked the power even to fix the issue price of new securities, it could not do very much to control such speculation. And mindful of the great influence on the Quebec government these companies seemed to enjoy, the regulators were hardly likely to take any bold action. Here was a further rightward shift along the spectrum of regulation: form without any real substance.

―――――――――― Three Canadian provinces did not establish any regulatory mechanism to control utilities before the end of the First World War. Tiny Prince Edward Island had only 93,728 people altogether in 1911. In Saskatchewan the major utilities were municipally owned, so provincial regulation was not needed. In British Columbia, however, one major utility, the British Columbia Electric Railway, supplied electric and transportation services not only in rapidly growing Vancouver but also in the capital of Victoria on Vancouver Island. This company was the subject of frequent complaints but was able to avoid any formal regulation. Its methods were those commonly adopted at an earlier date in the eastern provinces: direct lobbying of the provincial government, and reliance upon the courts to uphold existing franchises and agreements. Such freedom from interference marked the right pole of the spectrum, where regulation came only through direct action by the legislature to alter statutes.

The unpopularity of the BCER stemmed from a number of factors. Its lighting rates were among the highest on the continent; rapid suburban expansion in Vancouver made transit service inadequate. Above all, the company's management had a reputation with municipal leaders of driving a very hard bargain. Most objectionable to them was the perpetual franchise, obtained from the provincial cabinet in 1908, to serve the Hastings Townsite just outside the city limits. So much criticism was levelled at this deal (which had been approved without the knowledge of Premier Richard McBride or Attorney General W. J. Bowser) that in 1912, facing an election, McBride felt compelled to announce his intention to reduce the term to 21 years. Although an Order in Council was prepared, it was not put into force because the company's chairman, R. M. Horne-Payne, persuaded the Premier during a trip to England that the results would be disastrous: if the principle of the sanctity of contract were once breached, Horne-Payne insisted, British financial houses would refuse to lend any more money to be invested in the province.[72]

That same year, 1912, the government appointed a Royal Commission on Municipal Affairs, which held hearings across North America. In their report the following year, the commissioners noted that a number of witnesses had complained about "the arbitrary and unreasonable exercise by public service corporations of powers of entry upon public streets." They recommended that the government appoint some body, either permanent or temporary, "with ample powers to enforce reasonable action in such cases, notwithstanding the powers conferred on these corporations by private acts." The tribunal should also have the authority to compel utilities to provide reasonable service at fair rates.[73]

The London board instructed the local management to lobby as hard as possible against any such move: "We must offer uncompromising resistance to the granting to such a commission of any statutory powers to deprive us of the benefits of our franchises, especially in the matter of fixing rates or charges, unless the government guarantee us a fair minimum return on our money."[74] And R. H. Sperling wrote to the Premier: "My frank opinion is that this is psychologically the wrong time to discuss the creation of a Public Utility Commission. Just at present British Columbia needs capital and the goodwill of the British investing public far more than it does a Public Utility Commission." Once again the company succeeded in frightening McBride out of acting. He said, Sperling recorded, that "he and his colleagues were just as anxious as I was to see that the credit of the province was not impaired in any way."[75]

Nonetheless, the company was convinced that such a proposal was likely to be revived in light of what was going on in other provinces, and management set about collecting as much information as possible so that it could quickly mount an effective lobby if necessary. However, most members of the Canadian Electric Railway Association who responded were convinced that by 1914 it was already too late to hope to be left alone altogether.[76] The general manager of the Saint John street railway argued:

> This is legislation against which it is no use trying to do anything, it having passed in Ontario, Nova Scotia and some of the other provinces. The time to prevent legislation of this kind is when it is first brought up in any province, but once having passed all the others will follow suit, particularly when it is first put through in Ontario.

He added that the Public Utilities Commission in New Brunswick had been used by the telephone company "to assist them to maintain their rates against public agitation to reduce them." The manager of the Cape Breton Electric Company also recommended a PUC:

> It takes the matter of regulation out of the hands of the municipal authorities and places it in those of a central body who cannot but, in time become better entitled to handle such matters. . . . Here in Nova Scotia we have practically succeeded in guarding the rights originally conferred upon the companies with the exception of their issuing of securities.

Other utility men, too, pointed out that if popular feeling had been aroused, a commission could provide a refuge. Writing from London, Ontario, one observed:

> If these public utilities commissions are organized under laws which give them powers above those of city councils and if the commissions are composed of strong men, such commissions may be of great service to railway companies by offsetting biased local opinion and possible action on the part of local councils purely for political effect.

Investigating the situation in Seattle, the British Columbians learned the "great advantage" of regulation:

> It has taken power to do harm out of the hands of the local council. . . . This has been the situation all over the [United] States and the Public Service Commissions have been of great assistance to the companies by acting as a buffer between them and the city corporations and the public.

From Quebec came the opinion that customers would accept unpalatable decisions from a regulatory body, since "the public accept the rulings of the Commission in the same spirit as they would the rulings of any court of justice."

The powers granted to the commission were crucial, a Hamilton, Ontario, respondent warned:

> The greatest objection that can be brought against the appointment of such a commission is the tendency to grant it authority to do unlimited harm, at the

same time withholding the power to make and enforce decisions favourable to the business interests not only of corporations, but ultimately and in a broader sense, of the public at large.

Of particular importance to utility operators was the choice of personnel to staff the commissions. Even those like J. W. Crosby of Halifax, who thought that "with the proper man on the board, the commission will be of great assistance to the companies," would not have disagreed with H. C. Mathews of Quebec City that "the appointment of biased, dishonest or inexperienced persons to a commission could work incalculable harm." What would happen, for instance, if a one-man commission developed ideas detrimental to the companies' interests?

The BCER officials were not convinced that they would be better off in the hands of a commission. They were prepared to surrender autonomy only in exchange for an iron-clad guarantee of 5.5 percent earnings on invested capital.[77] In the spring of 1915, London ordered them to draft a bill creating a PUC, but no hint of this was allowed to escape, not only because it might encourage the government to act but because Attorney General Bowser "would resent having a bill which had been drawn up by the company put into his hands, and he would be more likely, in such a case, to include provisions in his bill that we did not want." The company's bill was modelled on the New Brunswick act, as that seemed most favourable to the interests of companies. The sole virtue of such an act was to make it possible for the PUC to prevent "reckless competition" from municipally owned undertakings. Management worried incessantly about who might be chosen to head such a body. Would it be somebody nonpolitical and independent-minded like the province's chief justice, or would it be some municipal demagogue determined to pay off old scores? Should it be one man who could act decisively, or would a three-man panel prove less likely to be caught up by some passing fancy?[78]

As long as Sir Richard McBride remained Premier, the British Columbia Electric Railway was confident that it could rely upon him to do all in his power to help the company. During McBride's annual visits to Britain, R. M. Horne-Payne used a mixture of threats and flattery to persuade him not to take any action that might adversely affect the BCER. McBride did not introduce legislation to establish a PUC in 1914 or 1915, (even though he pleaded with the BCER owners that "a sane and common sense commission" would place their interests above politics). This protection was extremely effective, but it rested upon an intricate web of personal relationships that could be swept away. In December, 1915, McBride resigned to be replaced by Bowser, his Attorney General; Bowser had never been as friendly toward the company as his leader although he had been helpful from time to time. George Kidd, who was by then heading the local management, was philosophical: "I do not suppose for a moment we shall get as much from Bowser as we would like, but I think we shall get as much from him as we are likely to get from anybody. The best that a public service corporation can hope for is to be left alone."[79]

After 1906, Canadian utilities faced regulation from a variety of newly created tribunals, but the effects varied markedly between jurisdictions. Although superficially similar, these commissions were quite different. As the correspondents replying to the BCER demonstrated, there were many breeds of the regulatory cat, some distinctly to be preferred over others.

The regulators had different views of their responsibilities. Adam Beck of the Ontario Hydro-Electric Power Commission tried to use his authority to drive his rivals out of business. Other officials took a much more benevolent and paternal attitude toward their "clients"; establishing some equilibrium between contending forces was their primary goal. A judicial conception of equity and a healthy respect for property rights led them to protect capital they believed to be legitimately invested and to permit rate of return that would continue to attract private investment. In general, utility regulators like the Board of Railway Commissioners intervened lightly. They tended to accept management's arguments in determining rates, not because they had been captured but because they accepted the legitimacy of both producers' and consumers' interests, and they sought some means of dividing costs and benefits between the two equitably. Then there were the blatantly transparent exercises in public opinion management, such as the Quebec Public Utilities Commission, which scarcely affected the operation of the utilities at all. The chosen instrument in each case reflected the relative balance of corporate and populist power in each jurisdiction.

Most politicians (and all but a few regulators) believed that at least a limited degree of interference with private enterpreneurs was desirable: that some quasi-judicial body should hear complaints and apportion costs and benefits in accordance with principles other than profit maximization. A minority saw this as a step toward nationalization. Fears that state enterprise could never be as efficient as private enterprise—which seemed to be confirmed by the experience in Manitoba—remained widespread. Thus the objective of a Public Utilities Commission was not to preside over the disappearance of the private monopoly but to temper its abuses. For their part, the utilities owners recognized that there was a point at which it was more prudent to concede to the demand for regulation than fight it. The managers of the British Columbia Electric Railway, who thought the problem through with the greatest care, concluded that "those companies which have suffered most from their commissions are those that feared them and resisted their appointment in the first instance."[80] If it was bound to come, then, regulation might have its uses.

PART FOUR
MEDIATION
AND
LEGITIMACY

Class Against Community

Poet Carl Sandburg once paid an uncommon tribute to the highly respected leader of the Amalgamated Association of Street and Electric Railway Employees of America. "When in Detroit sometime, we are going to look up Bill Mahon," wrote Sandburg in 1930. "We haven't seen him since the last streetcar strike in Chicago. He is philosopher, statistician, poet and commander who keeps close to his men amid the civil war of a city transportation tieup."[1] Sandburg's metaphor was apt, for "civil war" was not too strong a term for the tumult and violence that often accompanied a street railway strike in early twentieth century North America.

A strike against the street railway or any utility touched a city much more directly, much more immediately, than a strike in any other line of business. If the lights went out, if the water was turned off, if the gas failed to flow or the telephone operator refused to answer, everyone felt the impact. The public interest latent in every industrial dispute was instantly made manifest.

Thus in one way utility workers possessed unusual power. Because there were no substitutes for the services they supplied, ordinary citizens were bound more tightly to them than to any other group of employees. Moreover, their private employers were monopolists despised for their money-grubbing. When workers did go on strike, local elites, elected officials and newspaper editors frequently sided with them—a far from normal state of affairs in labour disputes at the turn of the century.

Utility strikes prior to World War I also cast a revealing light upon class relations, exposing conflicts which, once revealed, seemed to threaten the existing social order. When crowds took to the streets, they soon provoked a response from the keepers of the established order. As the mob flung rocks and swung lumber at the streetcars and the strike-breakers called in to drive them, and peace officers brandished swords and billy clubs, citizen was set against citizen: it *was* a kind of civil war.

In time the social bond between utility workers and their communities began to dissolve as the relationship between cities and their services altered. When utilities were publicly regulated or even publicly owned, gains for the employees could no longer be extracted from monopoly profits; instead, consumers would pay through higher charges to improve the lot of the workers. That made for a much more complex moral universe in which it was harder to identify friend and foe. Regulation made labour relations in the Canadian utilities sector less dramatic, but it also drained away much of the sympathy that the workforce had once enjoyed, especially if the community itself became the employer.

The millions of dollars in fares, tolls, and rates flowing through the coffers of Canada's utility companies did nothing to guarantee that their workers would earn a living wage. Every advance of a penny an hour in wages had to be fought for against a management determined to keep the operating ratio as low as possible. Whatever labour gained was the product of collective strength and will. When notoriously underpaid workers demanded modest wage increases and the right to organize trade unions, they frequently garnered widespread support from their fellow citizens, not least because their employers were detested monopolists. And the workers wisely took pains to identify themselves with the objectives of the civic populists when advancing their own interests.[2] Conflicts between labour and capital in this sector involved the public in another sense: when negotiations failed, not only did the entire community suffer, but the climax often occurred on city streets for all to see.

A typical street railway strike around the turn of the century would begin with the secret formation of a union local, the preparation of a list of desirable adjustments in working conditions, then the publication of these demands along with a claim for higher wages and a request for formal recognition of the union. If the bargaining committee members had not been fired at this point, their petition would be accorded a frosty reception by the company. The general manager would concede many of the non-monetary changes right away; he would profess his goodwill, undying interest in the welfare of his employees, and an earnest desire to raise wages at the earliest possible opportunity but regret that circumstances would not permit such a large increase as that demanded. Moreover, the historic prerogatives of management absolutely prevented the company from putting itself "under the control of a labour union whose headquarters and managing officers are in the United States,"[3] which is the way the issue of union recognition was presented.

There would then follow an agonizing test of claim and counterclaim. At this stage, union leaders—perhaps even William Mahon himself—might visit the city to confer with the men and urge steadiness, deliberation, and a continuation of the bargaining. Perhaps then a group of self-appointed mediators—the mayor and some councillors, a committee of the Board of Trade, some leading citizens, or the ministerial association—would begin scurrying back and forth between the parties. But the will to negotiate would be weakening under a host of minor irritations as both sides sought and prepared for a decisive showdown.

The public at large looked on with gathering dismay as such a situation deteriorated. Newspapers reported at length upon the course of the negotiations amidst swirling rumours of an impending strike. When the headquarters of the Amalgamated Association finally sanctioned a strike and the men voted, the decision would come almost as a relief after all the uncertainty.

There would be excitement in the air as dreary daily routines were interrupted, and coping with the novel situation consumed everyone's immediate interest. It was at this point that labour usually received its strongest and most tangible expressions of public support. As the cars rolled to a stop, a spirit of camaraderie would spread through the ranks of pedestrians; "We Will Walk" buttons sprouted; organizations donated food and money; mass meetings echoed with declarations of solidarity from other unions and all quarters of the community; crowds in the streets clapped and stamped and shouted their encouragement to parading strikers. Ministers expatiated upon the dignity of labour, the theological justifications of labour's right to organize, and the need for capital to give way to the needs of humanity. Editorialists pronounced secular sermons on the public's right to service, a fair day's pay for a fair day's work, and the deplorable irony that such an advanced civilization must resort to such crude methods of resolving conflict. In these early days the company had few friends: politicians, preachers, editorial writers, union leaders, and even some members of the business elite would denounce it as a model of the heartless modern corporation and rehearsed its numerous transgressions against the city, God, and man.[4]

In the meantime the company grimly prepared for the day of the strike. Agents of the Pinkerton or Thiel detective agencies explained procedures, signed contracts to supply strikebreakers, and took command of the situation. Squads of case-hardened scabs arrived in town and took refuge in local hotels under police protection. Special constables by the score were sworn in to protect the company's property and preserve the peace as the new men prepared to operate. Crowds gathered around the car barns, daring the men to bring the cars out and greeting them with a hail of insults and missiles when they emerged. If the police managed to clear a path for the trams, teamsters would dawdle in front of them, form blockades, and casually obstruct their progress—to the general amusement of the onlookers. Operators and passengers were jeered by pedestrians at every stop.

More stones and bottles were thrown. Judging by newspaper accounts the stone-throwing was almost universally condoned. For a time it was all good sport—innocent, boisterous, good-humoured, and entirely at the expense of the hated company and its imported scabs.

Then some incident would loosen the bonds. In Toronto in 1902 it happened at the very first provocation; in Winnipeg and Hamilton in 1906 it took weeks of demonstrations. An arrest, an assault, a funeral, or the sense perhaps that the company seemed likely to win out—the precipitating cause varied, but almost everywhere it happened eventually. When the real trouble occurred, only rarely were strikers themselves implicated directly. Angry agitators led thousands of curious onlookers through the streets as the violence began in earnest. Newspapers preached calm while their headlines fed the panic: "Three Days of Industrial Warfare"; "Police Are Now Powerless"; "Mob Takes Possession of Streets." Now rioters wrecked cars completely; strikebreakers assaulted their tormentors; strikers sought revenge; and the mob turned on the company, vandalizing its offices, smashing the hotels and rooming-houses of strikebreakers, and threatening company sympathizers. Rioters and special constables slugged it out in the streets.

The mayor, who up to this point had been an impartial, evenhanded conciliator, suddenly came under tremendous pressure from the police, frightened merchants, property owners, the company, and the city council to restore order at all cost. Sadly, hurriedly, he had to read the Riot Act, unleash the police, and call the militia to the aid of the civil power. Troops summoned from their barracks or summer parades, went to work without much enthusiasm. They brandished weapons, fired shots, bashed heads, snapped limbs with clubs and charging horses, and in one instance killed a participant. (Only in Hamilton in 1906 did the soldiers seem to relish their assignment. "Give it to them boys," shouted Lt. Col. Septimus Denison as he led his cavalry, swords flashing, into the bewildered mob. He personally whipped two strikers that night, a thoroughly satisfying experience, he later testified, for it produced "the most pitiful shrieks it has been my pleasure to hear.")[5]

Soon the streets would be empty, and an uneasy calm would descend upon the city as the citizenry assessed the damage and contemplated the visceral rage that had been released by the strike. Resentment would be dampened by shame, sadness, and contrition. Third parties would redouble their mediation efforts. Sometimes entirely new arbiters appeared. In Ontario, where many of these early strikes took place, the Ontario Railway and Municipal Board often intervened at this stage. Typically, the settlement reached granted most of the wage demands, met the grievances concerning working conditions, ordered the reinstatement of the strikers, and forbade discrimination between union and nonunion personnel. Frequently, the terms fell short of formal recognition of the union through the

Amalgamated Association won de facto recognition in most of these disputes, especially from those who really mattered: the employees who had learned how to conduct a successful strike.

After these days or weeks of intense excitement and intermittent rioting, the return of the cars to normal operation was almost an anticlimax. Many charges were dropped; the strikebreakers melted away; grudges nursed for a time gradually died; and the workers went on their rounds with a new-found pride. Here and there, though, thoughtful members of the community shuddered at the brief glimpse of the furious emotions lying just barely concealed beneath the orderly surface of urban life.

This, or something very much like this, took place in cities all across Canada before World War I: in London in 1899 and 1906, in Toronto in 1902, Montreal a year later, Winnipeg in 1906 and again in 1910, Halifax and the Lakehead in 1913, and Saint John in 1914, to name the most notable examples.[6] And there were several other cases—in Toronto in 1906 and Vancouver in 1913, for instance—when at the very last moment mediation succeeded, to the surprise of the battle-ready participants. All of this occurred against the backdrop of much more violent outbursts that galvanized public attention in the United States.[7]

Disputes in other utilities were considerably less traumatic, although the public could become caught up in those as well. A walkout of telephone operators and linemen in Vancouver organized by the International Brotherhood of Electrical Workers late in 1902 disrupted telephone service on the lower mainland for several weeks. Managers attempted to fill the vacant places and continue serivce, but with no great satisfaction to the public. Then a frenzied mediation effort by the Vancouver city council brought enough pressure to bear upon the utility to settle the dispute more or less on union terms. The linemen and the operators won raises in pay (the men much more than the women), an eight-hour day, a grievance committee, and full recognition of their union.[8]

A brief strike of telephone operators in Toronto early in 1907 alarmed the city council and the business community sufficiently to have them summon a Department of Labour mediator even before the walkout occurred; when it did happen, it led to the appointment of a special Royal Commission of Enquiry. Once again public sympathy lay with the "Hello Girls," who were portrayed as the innocent victims of a monstrous corporation. All the newspapers in the city supported the operators, expressing unusual concern about their health, working conditions, and living costs.

The Bell Telephone Company actually provoked the strike by brusquely announcing the end of experimental five-hour shifts and reversion to an eight-hour schedule at seemingly higher rates of pay. But since the operators had customarily stayed on for one or two hours of overtime each day to make the five-hour system work, the net effect of the new arrangement was a cut in pay and a substantial reduction in the company's labour costs. That the latter was the company's primary objective became clear from internal correspondence produced before the Royal Commission. Although the local manager knew that even on their present wages, "operators cannot earn enough to pay for their board and clothing," he nevertheless proceeded to lengthen their hours and reduce their pay.[9]

Meanwhile, the strikers benefitted from the sentimental concepts of maternal feminism. Extensive medical testimony before the Royal Commission coupled with the evidence of the women themselves pointed to the conclusion that the high pressure of this kind of work over long periods was detrimental to the operators' mental and physical health, and likely to impair their mothering capacity. In addition, the operators' deportment and dress received favourable comment in the press, and their evidence that supervisors and managers could listen in on any private conversation caused a sensation.

Giving in just enough to obtain a settlement, the local manager drew up a compromise proposal that maintained the wage schedule but reduced the eight hours of work to seven and spread it over nine hours to accommodate relief breaks. This was enough to satisfy one of the commissioners, William Lyon Mackenzie King, and he was able to persuade his colleague, Judge John Winchester, to accept the offer and terminate the inquiry.[10] Universal public sympathy had not led to a complete victory: the operators did not receive a raise, nor was the International Brotherhood of Electrical Workers able to capitalize upon the discontent to organize a more effective union among the women. Seen from one perspective, the arbitration procedure had allowed the company to carry out its reorganization and get its way on the monetary issues. Nevertheless, the strike and the Royal Commission hearings had provided a curious public with an unsavoury look into the inner workings of a giant corporation where the health and dignity of female employees were quite secondary considerations to profits and dividends.

Strikes in other utilities more closely resembled ordinary industrial disputes because they caused much less disruption. It took very little labour, for example, to operate a large-scale hydroelectric system; over short periods of time, power could be maintained by supervisory personnel with no apparent difference. Strikes by linemen and construction workers delayed expansion of electrical systems but did not affect existing customers. An IBEW local struck the major power companies in Montreal in May, 1903, seeking wage increases and union recognition. Timed to coincide with a street railway strike, this strike caused little public inconvenience over its two months' duration. It ended, characteristically, with a 33 percent wage hike and a 13 percent reduction in working hours, but no union recognition. By contrast, gas workers had no luck whatever informing strong unions or bargaining for higher wages. In an industry in relative decline, which required few skilled workers, most strikes were ruthlessly broken.[11]

Electricians, who worked for power companies, contractors, and manufacturers, experienced above-average success in their contract negotiations. As a rule these skilled tradesmen worked in smaller groups, mainly on construction projects and were tied into bargaining cycle and craft traditions of the closely related building trades. Their strikes, which tended to be brief and effective—as reflected in their relative wages—did not affect the public any more or less than other building trades disputes. These workers approached their strikes with a certain nonchalance; they jealously guarded their craft's jurisdiction and frequently went out in sympathy with other unionized trades. Winnipeg electricians organized by the IBEW went out on strike at the height of the 1909 construction season and stayed out for several months. Some went threshing. Others enjoyed a little holiday. "We have been playing ball and having a good time generally," replied the union president when asked how his men were faring. Eventually the contractors came to terms.[12]

Between 1900 and 1930 the Department of Labour recorded 138 strikes and lockouts in utilities all across Canada. During this period the utilities sector accounted for only 3.5 percent of all strikes; the total number of man-days lost through strikes and lockouts, 538,594, was 2.4 percent of the Canadian total, just under the utility sector's relative weight as an employer. These numbers do indicate, however, that this quasi-public sector was by no means pacific as far as industrial disputes were concerned. As a group these employees did not merely benefit from wage gains achieved by others; they contributed to their own cause and that of all wage earners.[13]

The strike pattern within the utilities sector deviated from the Canadian average in two important respects as can readily be seen from Table 18. During the first decade of the century, utilities strikes occurred with about the same frequency as disputes in the economy as a whole. The first major departure from the industrial norm took place in the second decade, particularly between 1916 and 1920, when the sector experienced 40.6 percent of its strikes and 80.3 percent of its man-days lost compared with 30.3 percent and 27.2 percent respectively for all industries. Utility workers struck with much greater regularity than other industrial workers during the final years of the war and its immediate aftermath. But in the 1920s a reverse trend set in; strikes in the utilities sector fell well below the national average.

Some groups of workers were more strike-prone than others. Table 19 provides a breakdown of all recorded strikes by sector for five-year periods. From these data it can be seen that electric light and power workers were slightly more inclined to strike than street railways workers (30.4 percent versus 29.7 percent of all strikes, respectively), but the far more numerous street railway workers accounted for three times as many lost man-days. The vast majority of both strikes and lost time for the street railwaymen and the electric light and power workers occurred in the second decade.

TABLE 18

UTILITIES STRIKES IN RELATION TO ALL CANADIAN STRIKES

| | *Number of Strikes (%)* | |
	Utilities	*All Industry*
1901–05	12.3	15.5
1906–10	12.3	15.7
1911–15	19.6	14.5
1916–20	40.6	30.3
1921–25	8.7	13.3
1926–30	6.5	10.5
Total	100.0%	100.0%

| | *Man-Days Lost (%)* | |
	Utilities	*All Industry*
1901–05	4.4	9.9
1906–10	6.1	14.1
1911–15	4.6	20.0
1916–20	80.3	27.2
1921–25	4.0	25.1
1926–30	1.0	3.9
Total	100.0%	100.0%

Sources: See note 13, and *Labour Gazette,* Feb., 1931, p. 139.

Electricians and telephone workers occasioned 21.7 percent and 13.8 percent of the disputes; gas workers a miniscule 4.3 percent. These strikes were also much less costly than the others in terms of man-days lost. Here again the wartime aggressiveness of the street railway and electrical workers can be clearly seen, as can the relative quiescence of all employees in this sector during the 1920s. Thus it can be inferred that only through an unprecedented strike effort, beyond that mounted by workers in other sectors, were utility employees able to stay slightly ahead of inflation between 1916 and 1920. Having made small gains in real income and demonstrated enough cohesion to retain most of these, utility workers had less reason to strike during the 1920s when other industrial workers were still struggling to catch up.

By 1931 the 74,000 employees of utilities were vastly outnumbered by more than 1,000,000 Canadian farmers, 500,000 people in the

TABLE 19
STRIKES IN THE UTILITIES SECTOR

	Gas	Street Railway	Telephone	Light and Power	Electricians	Total	%
1901–05							
No. of strikes	0	6	2	4	5	17	12.3
Man days lost	0	5,745	180	9,718	8,190	23,833	4.4
1906–10							
No. of strikes	1	6	5	0	5	17	12.3
Man days lost	375	15,944	7,152	0	9,500	32,971	6.1
1911–15							
No. of strikes	2	3	3	15	4	27	19.6
Man days lost	1,770	3,210	1,500	11,215	7,260	24,955	4.6
1916–20							
No. of strikes	3	21	7	16	9	56	40.6
Man days lost	2,726	329,889	21,615	59,045	19,048	432,323	80.3
1921–25							
No. of strikes	0	4	2	5	1	12	8.7
Man days lost	0	16,423	39	1,244	3,575	21,281	4.0
1926–30							
No. of strikes	0	1	0	2	6	9	6.5
Man days lost	0	36	0	339	2,846	3,221	0.6
TOTALS							
No. of strikes	6	41	19	42	30	138	
Man days lost	4,871	371,247	30,486	81,561	50,419	538,594	
PERCENTAGES							
No. of strikes	4.3	29.7	13.8	30.4	21.7		100.00
Man days lost	1.0	68.9	5.6	15.1	9.4		100.00

Source: See note 13.

retail and wholesale trades, and the 250,000 construction workers. Steam railroads employed two-thirds again as many workers. Considering only those directly engaged by utilities, the workforce was about the same size as the mining and financial sectors in 1931. Adding the 27,000 employees in the related engineering, manufacturing, and construction occupations brought the total number of workers to just over 100,000. Nevertheless, this relatively small group of workers possessed an importance and a power out of all proportion to their numbers.

In labour as in technology, the utilities were thoroughly modern industries. They gave rise, for example, to a host of new machine-tending occupations—motormen, electricians, operators, technicians. Proto-industrial unions attempted to combine all the workers within a single industry. The utilities also exhibited the squat pyramid of employment now common: a few highly paid professionals, skilled workers, and managers at the top; large office staff in the middle; and a mass of unskilled workers responsible for operations at the bottom of the pay scale. Both the office and the operating staff experienced extremely high rates of turnover. This hierarchical pattern of occupations was more or less established by the turn of the century, as the technologies stabilized, and did not change much before the Great Depression, although in later years attempts were made to reduce labour requirements through the introduction of automatic switching equipment in the telephone industry and pay-as-you-enter cars on the street railroads. A worker from the 1890s would have found most of the equipment, operating procedures, occupations, and organizational structures of the 1920s quite familiar.

As Canadian society became more urbanized and interdependent during the late nineteenth and early twentieth centuries, the number of workers in this sector increased both nominally and relatively. In 1881, utilities accounted for only 0.36 percent of all nonagricultural employment in Canada. However, as energy, transportation, and communications assumed greater importance, the workforce of the utilities relative to other occupations reached 2.64 percent of nonagricultural employment in 1931 (see Table 20). The greatest growth occurred during the census decade 1901 to 1911, when sectoral employment increased by a full percentage point.

By 1931, 21 percent of the workers in this sector were women. Most female employees were telephone operators (Table 21), though there were significant numbers at work in gas, electric, and street railroad offices

TABLE 20
EMPLOYMENT IN CANADIAN UTILITIES, 1881–1931

	1881	1891	1901	1911	1921	1931
ELECTRICITY AND GAS WORKS	39	184	570	7,323	7,650	22,482
STREET RAILWAY	350	805	3,158	10,548	12,182	15,976
TELEGRAPH AND TELEPHONE	2,195	3,982	4,867	14,845	24,189	35,679
TOTAL	2,584	4,971	8,595	32,716	44,021	74,137
% NONAGRICULTURAL LABOUR FORCE	0.36	0.57	0.81	1.83	2.06	2.64

Sources: *Census of Canada,* 1921, vol. 4, Table 1; *Census of Canada,* 1931, vol. 8, Table 6.

TABLE 21

FEMALE EMPLOYMENT IN CANADIAN COMMUNICATIONS

Year	Total Female Employees	% of Workers in Communications	% of All Female Employees
1891	821	20.6	0.42
1901	995	20.4	0.42
1911	5,114	34.4	1.40
1921	13,768	56.9	2.80
1931	15,284	58.3	2.29

Sources: *Census of Canada,* 1921, vol. 4, Table 1; *Census of Canada,* 1931, vol. 8, Table 6.

as well. Almost all of the wartime female streetcar conductors had been replaced by men by 1921. The feminization of telephone labour was long-standing. In 1891 when the first figures become available, women already constituted 20.6 percent of all telephone workers. By the close of World War I women formed a majority, and by 1931 they held 58 percent of the jobs. As a percentage of all women workers, the number of female telephone employees rose from 0.42 percent in 1891–1901 to a high of 2.8 percent in 1921, after which it declined slightly to 2.3 percent in 1931.

The workers who collected the fares, drove the cars, answered the telephones, handled the paperwork, and wired the country were fairly representative of the customers they served in 1921. With a few exceptions these employees reflected the ethnic composition of the broader Canadian labour force. As Table 22 indicates, native-born workers predominated among telephone operators and electricians' apprentices; were underrepresented as labourers, motormen and conductors, and electrical equipment factory hands; and were about evenly distributed among telephone linemen, in office employment, and in electrical generation and distribution activities. Immigrants, for the most part British, were more numerous than might be expected—given their national labour force participation—in electricity supply and street railroading. It would not appear from these statistics that Canada had to rely upon the United States, the source of much of the technology, for the labour to assemble and operate it. European immigrants were most numerous as labourers and were greatly underrepresented in all other occupations.

In sum, it might be said that the workers who operated, maintained and built the Canadian utilities were mainly native-born young men, although the street railroads were manned by distinctly older British immigrants. Canadian women under the age of 24 operated the telephone switchboards, while men in their mid-twenties strung the wires and main-

TABLE 22
ORIGINS OF CANADIAN UTILITIES LABOUR FORCE
(selected occupations, 1921)

Occupation	Native Born (%)	Britain (%)	U.S.A. (%)	Europe (%)	Other (%)
CANADIAN LABOUR FORCE, NONAGRICULTURAL	65.2	20.5	4.2	7.3	2.6
ELECTRICAL SECTOR					
Generation and transmission	66.2	26.8	4.3	1.5	1.0
Labourers	43.8	36.6	1.9	16.6	1.5
Electric equipment manufacturing	53.4	39.2	4.4	1.9	—
Electricians, construction	61.1	29.1	6.0	2.5	1.4
Electricians, apprentices	76.9	19.1	0.9	2.0	1.4
STREET RAILWAY SECTOR					
Conductors and motormen	53.5	39.7	2.9	2.7	1.0
Officials	60.1	32.2	4.9	1.3	1.5
Office workers	64.9	28.9	2.4	1.7	2.2
Labourers	44.7	30.8	1.2	22.5	0.9
COMMUNICATIONS SECTOR					
Linemen	67.2	24.7	5.6	1.7	0.9
Operators	70.8	22.3	5.2	0.9	0.8

Source: *Census of Canada,* 1921, vol. 4, Table 6.

tained the equipment. Immigrants were concentrated in the lower-paying unskilled occupations, and European immigrants were restricted almost exclusively to manual labour. Higher-paying, higher-status occupations—engineers, officials, electricians, linemen, and operators—tended to draw more heavily upon the ranks of the native-born. In the Maritimes the native-born predominated; on the burgeoning prairie, immigrants made up more than half the labour force.

According to contemporary testimony, most of these utilities occupations experienced an extremely high rate of labour turnover. Female telephone operators had little hope of promotion beyond supervisor, and most expected to leave their jobs shortly after marriage. Cohort after cohort of teenage women learned how to patch calls through their switchboards, then left after four or five years. Before World War I and to a lesser degree afterward, streetcar conductors and motormen also came and went at a rate disturbing to their employers. The technique of driving a streetcar could be learned in a few days, and the operating rules mastered in a couple of weeks. There were few barriers to entry. Before an arbitration board in 1928, an official of the Toronto Transit Commission explained: "All that is required of an applicant is an ordinary physique and a public school education." Advanced schooling could be a liability for street railwaymen, the official continued: "They must not be too damn smart, not too well educated. No tradesmen are employed because they don't stick."

Apparently, workers did not stay long in these low paying, monotonous jobs if they could avoid it. "Few follow the vocation by choice," the street railway employees journal readily admitted. A survey of U.S. street railways in 1912 revealed annual turnover rates among operating employees of between 28 and 56 percent. In Toronto during 1926 almost half of the street railways employees submitting resignations left for better jobs. Telephone and electric light and power linemen were notoriously mobile; young single men quit work with great regularity.[14] People took these jobs because they were relatively easy to get, easily learned, and paid the bills for the time being, but most hoped to move on to better opportunities or, in the case of the women, left the paid labour force.

Transiency posed a major obstacle to the effective organization of the workers in this sector. Nevertheless, two major organizations—the Amalgamated Association of Street and Electric Railway Employees, and the International Brotherhood of Electrical Workers—succeeded against heavy odds in building strong, centrally controlled, continentwide unions to improve the welfare of these young, volatile, unskilled workers. The early street railway unions organized by the Knights of Labour had collapsed by the late 1880s. Under the initial encouragement of Samuel Gompers and the American Federation of Labour, the Amalgamated Association took shape in 1892 around a core of Michigan and Ohio unions. During the hard times of the mid-1890s, numerous independent local unions spontaneously joined and sought help from this Association. William Mahon became president in 1893, and gradually, amidst the turmoil of a long series of largely disastrous strikes, he and his colleagues built up a disciplined, well-managed union, increasingly successful after 1899. In principle, the Amalgamated Association embraced all the employees in the industry; in practice, it usually consisted only of the operating men. The labourers and office workers remained unorganized; the shopmen sometimes belonged to craft unions of their own. The street railwaymen in Toronto revived their union in 1893 and affiliated with the Amalgamated Association when it began organizing in Canada at the turn of the century. The Vancouver local was one of the first Amalgamated-inspired unions to be formed in Canada and, in due course, the first to gain recognition. As an indication of the tremendous flow of workers through this business, the Amalgamated Association enrolled more than half a million North American workers between 1911 and 1930 but never had more than 100,000 members at any one time.[15]

The heterogeneous and geographically dispersed electrical workers were an even harder group to organize. The International Brotherhood of Electrical Workers, founded in 1876, gathered strength as the industry expanded during the 1890s. The ambitious leaders of this organization aimed at nothing less than uniting all electrical workers on the continent— linemen, generating station operators, isolated plant personnel, electricians in the construction sector, electrical equipment factory employees, technicians, telephone linemen and operators—into one vast industrial union. Their very success in joining inside and outside workers, men and women, electric light and telephone employees, tradesmen in widely separated lines of work in the same union led inevitably to conflict and a long series of secession movements that weakened the Brotherhood. Nevertheless, in its prime—after 1901 and again during and immediately after World War I—it was a powerful and extremely aggressive body. Periodic shortages of electricians and a close link to the house-building trade cycle alternately helped and hindered the organizational drive. Essentially, the IBEW was a union of linemen and electricians to which other occupational groups in the sector opportunistically allied themselves. Locals of the Brotherhood appeared in rapid succession after 1901 on the Niagara peninsula; in Hamilton, Toronto, Montreal, and Winnipeg; across the prairies; and on the west coast. Without a central strike fund but supported by an excellent benefit programme, the IBEW built up its membership through a strategy of short, well-timed strikes.[16]

At every stage the going was tough, for most employers fought these organization efforts tooth and nail. Everywhere the tactics were the same. Professional union-breakers, usually detective agencies, supplied operatives to spy on workers and report organizing drives before they could make much headway.[17] Ringleaders would be summarily dismissed for some trumped-up infraction. In the event of a strike, these same detective agencies would provide a corps of experienced strikebreakers to maintain operations. After a strike, if the company had had to promise not to discriminate against union members or had agreed to recognize the union, the employer would bide his time until labour conditions were ripe. Then the leaders of the union would be fired, often after having been lured by *agents provocateurs* into some petty violation of company rules: for instance, in 1910 secret agents enticed two Winnipeg unionists into a tavern while they were in uniform.[18] More subtly, key figures would be promoted into minor managerial jobs that were outside union jurisdiction.

At an early date the companies realized the advantages of welfare capitalism as a means of stabilizing the highly fluid labour force and discouraging trade unionism. It was no coincidence that the Montreal Street Railway announced the formation of its Employees' Mutual Benefit Association during a union organizing campaign in 1903.[19] The American Electric Railway Association and its Canadian counterpart endorsed "humanitarian" schemes of this sort as "sound business" (the accumulated funds often being invested in company stock) and as a means of avoiding state-sponsored welfare along European lines.[20]

Montreal Light, Heat and Power and Bell Telephone were among the earliest utilities to establish pension plans to help control labour turnover, while Ontario Hydro set up one of the first contributory schemes in 1919. The advantages of such a plan from management's point of view were that it attracted a desirable breed of employee who intended to stay with the utility, and prevented the bureaucracy from becoming overloaded with older workers who could not afford to retire. Such paternalistic motives induced the Hydro to agree to contribute 5 percent of the salary budget toward the programme, to be added to a 2 percent contribution from the workers. Contributions, noted the Hydro's consulting actuary, not only gave the employee a clearer sense of the benefits he was gaining but also reduced the amount the employer had to contribute, allowing it to pay wages more in line with those of firms that lacked such programmes.[21]

Canadian utility magnates ruthlessly attacked and persistently undermined the union movement during the early twentieth century. Nowhere were unions greeted by employers with enthusiasm or even equanimity, though at the British Columbia Electric Railway the unionists encountered something like fair dealing at the beginning. The BCER recognized the Amalgamated Association in 1899 and signed a contract with the IBEW shortly afterward. The executives of the company took pains to maintain good relations with local labour leaders, especially with William Mahon, head of the Amalgamated Association, who personally took charge of negotiations on several occasions. Mahon was consulted by the company in his Detroit headquarters during delicate moments; his opinions were highly valued; and the banquet the company held in his honour during a visit to

British Columbia in 1902 was a genuine display of respect. In that year the company launched a profit-sharing scheme with union approval. Whenever possible the BCER attempted to distance itself from the virulently anti-union policy of the street railroad and electrical associations.[22]

Separated by mountains and British-based management from the utilities in the rest of the country, BCER officials could not comprehend the visceral hostility to trade unions and the shortsightedness of their eastern Canadian colleagues. In 1902, when the BCER negotiated a mutually satisfactory contract with the Amalgamated Association, the street railways in Toronto and Montreal entered a period of stormy labour relations ending in devastating strikes—which, in effect, they lost.[23] As Johannes Buntzen of the BCER shrewdly observed in reporting the Toronto strike to the company's president, R. M. Horne-Payne: "After raising wages 20% Mackenzie stands in the same relation to his men as before the strike. There is a bitter feeling of emnity, and the public is with the men. They could not get a jury in Toronto to convict the conductors who were caught stealing in the act while we were in Toronto, simply because they stole from Mackenzie." The stubborn refusal of Mackenzie to recognize the union formally while actually negotiating with it could only mean more trouble: "Really, is not his distinction childish, and will he really have another strike before he recognizes the shadow of the substance he has already recognized?" Buntzen calculated that in the long run his more generous and realistic approach would redound to the advantage of the industry:

> I am confident we shall do better than ever before under our profit-sharing arrangement, and if I had Mackenzie's ear I should advise him to follow our lead now, instead of waiting till he is forced to do so, and save himself much heartburning and much needless expense to strikebreakers and track fighters and Pinkerton's Agents Provocateurs.[24]

But Mackenzie and some of the others were barroom brawlers themselves; they actually preferred the low road.

Despite the antagonism—even treachery—of the employers, and in spite of the formidable disadvantages presented by a youthful, transient, and in large part female labour force, union organization made more headway in the utilities sector than it did in many other parts of the economy. In 1921, when utilities provided 2.6 percent of all nonagricultural employment, these two unions accounted for some 4.9 percent of the unionized workers in the country.[25] As indicated by Table 23, the Amalgamated Association experienced greater success in organizing the workers in the street railway industry than the IBEW did in the more difficult and dispersed telephone and electrical industries. Membership in the two unions ebbed and flowed with the business cycle, with labour supply conditions, and the success of unions in winning wage increases, improvements in working conditions, and greater benefits. Over time, the Amalgamated

TABLE 23

UNION MEMBERS IN RELATION TO TOTAL WORKERS IN UTILITIES

Year	Amalgamated Association Members as % of Street Railway Employees	IBEW Members as % of Telephone and Electrical Employees
1911	37.0	8.6
1921	92.7[a]	13.5
1931	53.2	5.3

Sources: H. A. Logan, *Trade Unions in Canada* (Toronto: Macmillan, 1948), pp. 601–14; Table 18 above.
[a] The 1921 data for street railways is spurious, a function of either a mistaken recording of union membership or an undercounting of street railway workers in the census.

Association also enjoyed greater success in retaining its membership and holding its own as a proportion of total membership within the international union.

Wages paid to the predominantly unskilled workers in the utilities sector were determined largely by national trends operating within regional labour markets. From an index of industrial wages compiled by the Department of Labour (Table 24), it can be seen that changes in electric railway wages closely paralleled increases in the national average up to 1915. In 1901, for example, motormen and conductors with three years' service earned 18 cents an hour on the Toronto street railway and worked a 58½-hour week. By 1913 the maximum rate for this category had risen to 27½ cents. Over the same period similar workers in Halifax also won a 10-cent-an-hour raise.

While wages rose everywhere at about the same rate, the starting points were not the same. In a country the size of Canada, any national index obscures significant regional variations. Some wages were ordered on a fairly steep gradient running upward from east to west. Data gathered by the Department of Labour on the maximum rates paid electricians and street railwaymen (Tables 25 and 26) indicate that wages were lowest in Halifax and only barely higher in the city of Montreal. Toronto workers occupied a midpoint on this east-west slope. Utility workers in Winnipeg commanded a premium over Toronto, and wages were consistently the highest on the west coast before World War I. In 1901, for example, experienced electricians in Halifax earned less than half the hourly rate of their counterparts in Vancouver. The gap between the coasts narrowed only slightly before 1915. Over this entire prewar period, Vancouver electricians and street railwaymen earned hourly maximum wages an average of 50 and 30 percent, respectively, above Toronto levels.

TABLE 24

DEPARTMENT OF LABOUR WAGE INDEX
(1913 = 100)

	Building Trades	Electric Railways	Steam Railways	Average
1901	60.3	64.0	68.8	67.4
1902	64.2	68.0	72.0	70.0
1903	67.4	71.1	75.1	72.5
1904	69.7	73.1	76.9	74.5
1905	73.0	73.5	74.5	75.7
1906	76.9	75.7	79.3	78.6
1907	80.2	81.4	81.0	82.8
1908	81.5	81.8	86.1	84.9
1909	83.1	81.1	86.3	85.9
1910	96.9	85.7	90.1	88.9
1911	90.2	88.1	95.7	92.3
1912	96.0	92.3	97.9	96.0
1913	100.0	100.0	100.0	100.0
1914	100.8	101.0	101.4	101.3
1915	101.5	97.8	101.7	101.4
1916	102.4	102.2	105.9	105.8
1917	109.9	114.6	124.6	119.0
1918	125.9	142.9	158.0	142.6
1919	148.2	163.2	183.9	165.3
1920	180.9	194.2	221.0	197.8
1921	170.5	192.1	195.9	191.2
1922	162.5	184.4	184.4	182.4
1923	166.4	186.2	186.4	183.3
1924	169.7	186.4	186.4	183.7
1925	170.4	187.8	186.4	179.7
1926	172.1	188.4	186.4	180.5
1927	179.3	189.9	198.4	184.3
1928	185.6	194.1	198.4	187.4
1929	197.5	198.6	204.3	192.7
1930	203.2	199.4	204.3	194.4

Source: Department of Labour, *Wages and Hours of Labour in Canada* (Ottawa, 1931), pp. 3–5.

At the same time, workers within the sector were ranked on a skill gradient skewed by sex. Female telephone operators earned the lowest wages, less than 13 cents an hour during the first decade of the twentieth century. Street railway track layers occupied the next rung on the wage ladder, at the bottom of the male pay schedule. The upper end of the scale for construction labourers merged with the starting pay for street railway operating trainees. After three years on the job, men in this category reached the top of a scale that had only a 4- or 5-cent-an-hour spread. Next

TABLE 25

INDEX OF ELECTRICIANS' NOMINAL WAGES
(1913, Toronto, 40¢ per hour = 100)

	Halifax	Montreal	Toronto	Winnipeg	Vancouver
1901	35	43	58	58	83
1902	48	50	63	58	98
1903	50	50	63	70	98
1904	48	55	63	75	110
1905	50	55	63	75	110
1906	48	55	83	88	110
1907	50	63	83	88	110
1908	63	70	83	88	125
1909	63	70	83	100	125
1910	65	70	88	100	125
1911	65	70	100	100	125
1912	75	75	100	113	158
1913	88	88	100	113	158
1914	88	100	100	113	158
1915	95	100	100	163	158
1916	95	100	120	163	155
1917	95	108	138	163	158
1918	125	112	170	175	188
1919	175	175	188	188	188
1920	175	183	220	232	250
1921	175	158	220	225	208
1922	150	145	200	203	208
1923	150	170	200	203	220
1924	150	170	200	213	220
1925	150	163	200	213	220
1926	150	163	200	250	238
1927	150	175	225	250	250
1928	175	175	250	250	250
1929	200	188	288	275	275
1930	225	208	313	275	273

Source: F. H. Leacy, M. C. Urquhart, and K. A. H. Buckley, eds., *Historical Statistics of Canada,* 2nd. ed. (Ottawa: Statistics Canada, 1984), Series E 248–267.

in rank and pay came the semiskilled employees, mechanics, shopmen, installers, repair crews, linemen, and cable splicers. Skilled workers—highly specialized mechanics, outside electricians, and trouble shooters of various sorts—commanded the highest wages at the peak of the nonmanagerial labour hierarchy. When senior streetcar conductors were earning 18 cents an hour at the turn of the century in Toronto, experienced electricians were

TABLE 26

INDEX OF STREET RAILWAY CONDUCTORS' AND MOTORMEN'S
MAXIMUM WAGES

(1913, Toronto, 27.5¢ per hour = 100)

	Halifax	Montreal	Toronto	Winnipeg	Vancouver
1901	60	58	65	69	80
1902	62	60	73	76	91
1903	62	69	73	87	91
1904	62	69	78	87	98
1905	62	69	78	87	98
1906	65	69	78	95	98
1907	65	73	85	95	115
1908	70	73	85	95	115
1909	70	73	85	95	115
1910	70	73	91	98	127
1911	73	89	91	105	127
1912	85	91	91	116	127
1913	91	91	100	125	127
1914	91	91	100	125	127
1915	91	91	100	125	116
1916	91	98	100	125	127
1917	105	105	135	131	145
1918	118	134	135	138	185
1919	158	174	200	200	203
1920	189	200	218	218	218
1921[a]	189	175	218	218	236
1922	171	175	218	204	213
1923	164	175	218	204	225
1924	164	185	218	204	225
1925	164	185	218	204	225
1926	164	185	218	207	225
1927	182	185	218	211	229
1928	200	185	218	215	229
1929	211	185	218	215	229
1930	211	200	218	218	229

Sources: Department of Labour, *Wages and Hours of Labour in Canada* (Ottawa, 1921), p. 18; (Ottawa, 1931), pp. 12–13.

[a]During the 1920's operators of one-man cars in these cities received a premium of 5 to 6 cents an hour above this schedule.

paid 23 cents. By 1913, electricians at the maximum hourly rate received 40 cents, compared with $27\frac{1}{2}$ cents for conductors with three years' seniority.[26] With the exception of these skilled workmen and electricians, who in any event were more closely tied to the building trades, employees in the utilities sector were generally considered to be among the lowest-paid workers in their cities, although they did enjoy somewhat steadier employment than most.

The meagre increases before the First World War came as a result of fierce struggles across a broad industrial front, notable episodes of which took place within the utilities sector. Raises had to be wrung out of grudging employers acutely sensitive to the supply of unskilled labour in their localities. If the experience of the British Columbia Electric Railway is an accurate guide, management seems to have been most concerned about starting wages. As Johannes Buntzen explained to his British board of directors concerning the 1902 union negotiations: "My principal endeavour was to hold the 1st year men down to 20¢ because their pay actually decides the pay of all unskilled labour." A tight labour supply situation early in 1907 forced Buntzen's successor to grant a hefty wage increase because the experienced men were leaving in droves, and the younger men forming the bulk of the union had grown "restive."[27] The boom collapsed shortly afterward, and R. H. Sperling had to suffer a good deal of abuse (some of it from Buntzen himself, by then a director in England) for making such a bad bargain. Certainly during the next round of negotiations in 1910, the company proved much more obdurate.[28] Again in 1913, amidst serious strike preparations on both sides, the company managed to hold the line on wages in an overstocked labour market, despite the fact that the city of Vancouver, under the influence of the trade unions, paid its day-labourers more than the street railwaymen earned.[29]

Union efforts to improve wages were constrained at least before 1914 because unskilled workers could be easily replaced—indeed were being replaced on a daily basis as a result of constant turnover. As a rule the Amalgamated Association of Electric and Street Railway Employees experienced greater success in bargaining for recognition, proper grievance procedures, overtime, better working conditions (heated cars, closed platforms, etc.), free uniforms, and scheduling according to seniority. The work week was shortened only slightly from the 60-hour norm at the turn of the century. In Canada the 48-hour week on the street railway became common only after 1918. Electricians, on the other hand, whose skills were in shorter supply during the periodic building booms, pushed their wages up somewhat more quickly, along with the other building trades. Higher wages compensated in their case for much more erratic employment.

Money wages virtually doubled during the First World War, in sharp contrast to the glacial movement during the first decade and half of the twentieth century. Initially, however, the uncertainty of war put downward pressure on some wages by increasing unemployment. In 1915 the British Columbia Electric Railway actually inserted a "Notice To Unmarried Men" in the workers' pay envelopes: "Your King and Country Needs You. We Can Spare You."[30] But a sudden inflationary surge in 1916, coupled with a general labour shortage, launched an upward spiral. At first, price increases outdistanced wage gains, but as a result of a period of intense social unrest and unprecedented labour militancy in all sectors—utilities included—the wage gains of organized workers eventually caught up with and surpassed the rise in the cost of living. Table 27 compares the wage indices of three groups of utility workers to movements in the national price index between 1913 and 1921. The skilled electricians fared best in this fierce contest, followed by the highly unionized street railwaymen. The wages of the largely female telephone labour force responded more sluggishly to the crisis. In this less-organized industry, wage gains did not fully compensate for general price increases until the middle of 1921.

Figures 3 and 4, drawn from a Bell Telephone rate submission, chart the impact of wartime inflation upon different groups of employees within a major utility. Workers in the company's telephone manufacturing plant won the largest percentage increases, followed by the operators in the traffic division, though the latter started from a much lower base rate. The better-paid engineering, commercial, and accounting personnel received

TABLE 27
WAGE AND PRICE INDICES
(1913 = 100)

	National Price Index	Street Railway Workers' Wages	Electrical Workers' Wages	Telephone Workers' Wages
1913	100.0	100.0	100.0	100.0
1914	98.0	101.0	100.0	100.0
1915	102.6	97.8	100.0	95.1
1916	120.3	102.2	120.0	96.3
1917	142.7	114.6	138.0	105.5
1918	155.8	142.9	170.0	112.7
1919	169.3	163.2	188.0	141.3
1920	187.2	194.2	220.0	183.0
1921	157.3	192.1	220.0	180.8

Sources: National price index is the Bertram and Percy index from Eleanor Bartlett, "Real Wages and The Standard of Living in Vancouver, 1901-1929," *BC Studies* 51 (1981): pp. 3-62; street railway index from Table 27; electrical wages from Table 26, using the Toronto index as a surrogate national average; telephone wages from a Bell Telephone Company index located in PAC, RG 46 A, vol. 529.

FIGURE 3

CHANGES IN BELL EMPLOYEE EARNINGS VIS-À-VIS COST OF LIVING

Changes in Cost of Living ━━━━━
Changes in Average Earnings ━ ━ ━ ━ ━

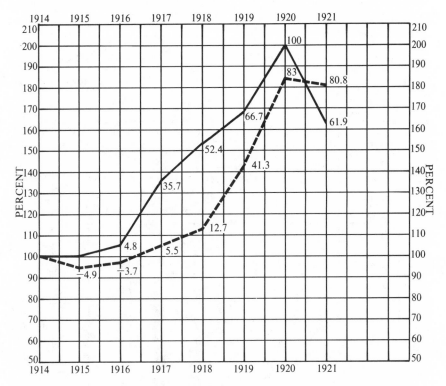

Source: PAC, RG 46, volume 529, case 955, Exhibit 3.
NOTE: Earnings are based on average wages and average number of employees for June of each year. Cost of living figures use average family budget shown in *Labour Gazette*; June, 1914 = 100.

lower than average increases, while the small group of general office workers suffered a severe reduction in real income.

After 1914 the Amalgamated Association seems to have largely succeeded in reducing the intercity wage gap among street railway workers. This was not the case for the IBEW, however; electricians' wages were still largely determined by conditions in the different urban labour markets. The street railway union managed to bargain wages up to roughly the same level across the country by 1918, and fought to preserve the standard during the postwar recession when other unskilled workers' wages were falling. This remarkable union achievement—the elevation of all street railway wages to a national scale during the war and then resistance to cutbacks during the 1920s—probably explains both the aging of the street railway

FIGURE 4
RELATIVE INCREASE IN EARNINGS OF BELL EMPLOYEES

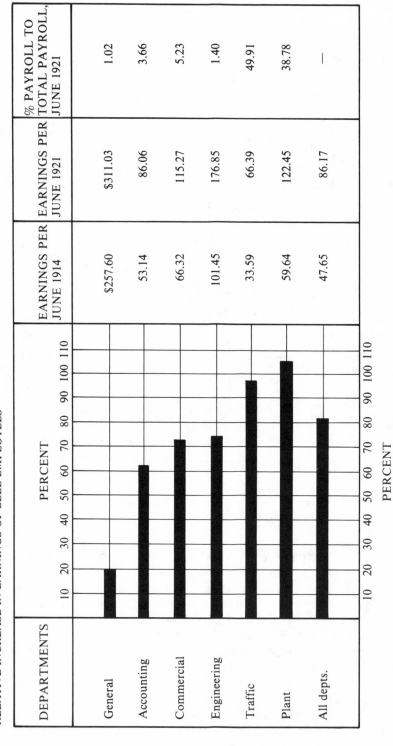

DEPARTMENTS	PERCENT	EARNINGS PER JUNE 1914	EARNINGS PER JUNE 1921	% PAYROLL TO TOTAL PAYROLL, JUNE 1921
General		$257.60	$311.03	1.02
Accounting		53.14	86.06	3.66
Commercial		66.32	115.27	5.23
Engineering		101.45	176.85	1.40
Traffic		33.59	66.39	49.91
Plant		59.64	122.45	38.78
All depts.		47.65	86.17	—

Source: PAC, RG 46, Volume 529, Case 955, Exhibit 3.

labour force and the comparatively high degree of adherence to the international union.

What can be said about trends in real wages during these turbulent decades? Several studies of individual communities have reported that the slight real wage gains of the prewar era were wiped out by wartime inflation.[31] But as we have just seen, most workers in the utilities sector were able to make up these losses by the end of the war or soon after. Moreover, many unionized workers maintained their wages during the short interval of postwar deflation and thereafter managed to keep pace with price changes over the rest of the decade. The published data concerning employees in the utilities and related sectors suggest that the workers who held these jobs in the early 1920s received marginally higher real wages than their counterparts in 1913, and over the next decade they either held their own or improved their position slightly.

It would be a mistake to read these indices too literally as the career wage records of individuals, especially in view of the high degree of labour turnover. The wage indices measure only the remuneration of the categories; they cannot take into account career changes, promotions, military service, short time, overtime, unemployment, or the impact of technological change. For example, the hotly contested introduction of one-man streetcars at the end of the war reduced the total amount of labour required to operate the street railway system; at the same time the remaining workers received significant bonuses, which are not captured in the Department of Labour index, to compensate for the increased responsibilities of running these cars. The index numbers, based as they are upon the easily compared top wage classifications and an unstated assumption of continuous employment (though not wholly unrealistic in this sector), also present too optimistic a view of the labour situation.

Prices and wages for the city of Vancouver have been well studied for this period, and a fairly comprehensive schedule of wages has survived for many of the categories of labour that concern us here. Table 28 uses Vancouver data to record the pattern of nominal wages and to estimate the path of real wages for various occupations in the three main utilities industries. Again, caution is advised: Vancouver, it will be recalled, had the highest wages in Canada—also the highest prices. The columns of estimated real wages have been derived from two statistical manipulations of the nominal data and are therefore doubly suspect. At a bare minimum, what these tables suggest is that the money wages of most workers in the utilities sector stopped rising early in the 1920s; some wages fell back to a somewhat lower level to be raised again at the end of the decade. In the light of other price changes, however, the real wages of all these workers improved—but just barely, in some cases. As usual the electricians won the largest nominal and real increases. At the other end of the pay scale, telephone operators' and labourers' real incomes crept up ever so slightly.

TABLE 28
NOMINAL AND REAL WEEKLY WAGES, VANCOUVER

| | ELECTRICAL WORKERS (44 hr.) | | STREET RAILWAY WORKERS | | | |
| | | | CONDUCTORS (48 hr.) | | LABOURERS (44 hr.) | |
	Nominal	Real	Nominal	Real	Nominal	Real
1920	$44.00	22.31	28.80	15.58	25.95	14.04
1921	39.60	20.22	31.20	19.27	26.40	16.31
1922	39.60	22.85	28.08	18.85	23.76	15.96
1923	39.60	22.50	29.76	19.80	23.76	15.81
1924	39.60	25.16	29.76	20.15	24.64	16.68
1925	39.60	24.63	29.76	19.81	23.32	15.52
1926	44.00	28.61	29.76	19.43	23.32	15.23
1927	44.00	29.48	30.24	20.00	23.32	15.43
1928	44.00	29.10	30.24	19.93	25.96	16.25
1929	49.50	30.80	30.24	19.62	25.96	16.83

| | TELEPHONE WORKERS | | | | ELECTRIC LIGHT & POWER WORKERS | | | |
| | Linemen (44 hr.) | | Operators (48 hr.) | | Linemen (44 hr.) | | Switchboard (48 hr.) | |
	Nominal	Real	Nominal	Real	Nominal	Real	Nominal	Real
1920	$35.20	19.05	19.00	10.28	40.70	22.02	37.20	20.12
1921	35.20	21.74	19.00	11.73	44.40	27.43	37.20	22.98
1922	35.20	23.64	19.00	12.75	39.16	26.30	37.20	24.99
1923	35.20	23.41	19.00	12.65	39.16	26.07	37.20	24.77
1924	35.20	23.84	19.00	12.86	39.16	26.52	37.20	25.19
1925	30.80	20.51	19.00	12.65	37.20	26.17	37.20	24.77
1926	30.80	20.11	19.00	11.76	37.20	25.58	37.20	24.29
1927	33.00	21.82	18.00	12.57	37.20	25.91	37.20	24.61
1928	33.50	22.02	19.00	12.53	37.20	26.83	37.20	24.52
1929	33.50	21.73	19.00	12.32	37.20	26.40	37.20	24.13

Sources: Nominal wages drawn from schedules published in Department of Labour, *Wages and Hours of Labour in Canada* (Ottawa, 1931); real wages estimated by reducing nominal wages to 1913 equivalents and adjusting to real wage index for Vancouver in Eleanor Bartlett, "Real Wages and the Standard of Living in Vancouver, 1901–1929," *BC Studies* 51 (1981):3–62.

Street railway workers kept their wartime gains and in real terms improved their lot significantly. If Vancouver can be taken as a hint of what was happening in other places, it would appear that while nominal wages stabilized in the 1920s, real income in most categories of utilities employment rose marginally.

This same question concerning the relative gains of labour can be pursued in a different fashion by asking what percentage of total industrial income was paid out to labour. Did labour's share of gross income rise, fall, or remain stable over this period? The statistics brought together in Table 29 show that labour's relative income share in the street railway

TABLE 29
LABOUR'S SHARE OF GROSS INCOME

	Street Railway	Telephone[a]	Electric Light and Power
1905	33.4		
1910	28.1		
1911			
1912			
1913		24.4	
1914		25.3	
1915	36.4	27.5	
1916		28.8	
1917		31.7	
1918	48.7	35.5	
1919	49.7	35.4	19.8
1920	51.5	40.9	22.3
1921	53.8	37.4	20.8
1922	50.3	43.7	17.6
1923	49.9	43.1	16.2
1924	50.5	41.3	18.9
1925	49.5	40.5	18.3
1926	47.7	49.9	22.4
1927	48.4	46.1	22.1
1928	47.6	46.1	20.6
1929	46.3	48.6	20.2
1930	49.3	46.2	21.7

Sources: Calculated from data in Department of Railways and Canals, *Railway Statistics;* Dominion Bureau of Statistics, *Statistics of Electric Railways of Canada;* PAC, RG 46, Board of Railway Commissioners Papers, vol. 140, 144, 145; Dominion Bureau of Statistics, *Telephone Statistics,* and *Historical Statistics of Canada,* 2nd ed., series Q 197–13, 126–30.

[a]Data for 1913–21 are for Bell Telephone only; all other percentages refer to industry totals.

industry increased from an average of about 30 percent before the war to over 50 percent by the early 1920s, where it stabilized. Returns to labour in the telephone industry increased steadily from about 25 percent before the war to 40 percent by the end of it, then continued to climb to a high of 49 percent in 1929. At the same time, labour productivity in this industry rose sharply as a result of increasing returns to scale.[32] Thus in this industry the returns to labour remained low and constant at about 20 percent, less than half the level of the other two industries. Capital, materials, and supplies received less as labour took more in all but the electrical industry. However small the gains to individual workers, the total claims of labour relative to other factors of production increased substantially during and after the war in the public transportation and telephone industries.

Over the course of 30 years, then, workers in this sector won significant improvements in both their nominal and real wages. By the early 1920s they were no longer the lowest-paid employees in their communities; they had demanded and achieved wages to more than compensate them for their wartime losses and, in doing so, pushed up labour's relative share to consume almost 50 percent of gross income in the two industries where most of the employees were concentrated. The nominal, real, and relative increases to labour began at that point to drive up the price of service—which all members of the community had to pay.

—————————— The threat to the social order posed by strikes against utilities helped to bring about state regulation of the relations between capital and labour. The most important piece of national labour legislation in Canada during this period, the Industrial Disputes Investigation Act of 1907, arose in the first instance in response to industrial warfare raging in the western coalfields. But it should be observed that the experience of labour disputes in the utilities sector brought the need for such intervention home to more citizens with greater directness than the disorders in the coal mines. And the framer of the act, the young Deputy Minister of Labour, Mackenzie King, learned the extent of public interest in the settlement of disputes as a result of his experience with a telephone strike.

Much has been written about the Industrial Disputes Investigation Act and its principal author, if only because King became Prime Minister of Canada in 1921 and remained so with only brief interludes until 1948. We need not reexamine his ideas in detail except to point out that they hinged upon the conviction that there were always three parties to any industrial dispute: labour, capital, and the community. To compose such a dispute, all three parties—not merely the first two—ought to be represented. King had great faith in using publicity as a means to bring the parties to an agreement. A calm, impartial examination of all the facts before the court of public opinion would not only create pressure upon workers and management to arrive at a settlement but also ensure that it was fair to all sides.

Public utilities, as the most obvious examples of businesses in which the public at large had a direct interest, were set apart for special treatment in the legislation.

Such treatment was justified by King on two grounds: "In the first place, inasmuch as monopolies are creatures of public policy, public policy has a right to a say in their operation. In the second place, since the community is dependent upon the operation of these monopolies, the government, representing the community, has the duty to intervene in favour of continuous operation."[33] Therefore, for this class of businesses, conciliation would be automatic, not voluntary.

Mackenzie King had an opportunity to try out some of these ideas when he had to drop work on drafting his bill to attend to the 1907 telephone operators' strike in Toronto. The Royal Commission, which he and Judge John Winchester chaired, was a prototype conciliation board. Publicity proved its effectiveness in this case by bringing the previously hostile and intractable company to the point of compromise, as described already. And the commission's report, drafted by King, made a case for the legitimacy of third-party interests in the industrial relations of this sector. Under competitive conditions, customers could shift their business away from firms that mistreated their employees, but patrons had no such choice with publicly sanctioned monopolies. These firms also earned unusual profits, which fair-minded investors needed to be assured had not been exacted from the health of the employees.[34] The ideas of the special duty of the state in the monopoly sector, a public interest in uninterrupted service, and the inherent fairness of public opinion, flowed directly into the debate on the Industrial Disputes Investigation Act later that year.[35]

It is doubtful that the Industrial Disputes Investigation Act greatly altered the history of labour relations in the utility sector. It would appear that the conciliation procedures were most effective during the first few years;[36] certainly the most intense period of strike activity occurred long after the passage of this legislation. But other, more subtle forces probably had a greater bearing upon the changing pattern of industrial conflict. Gradually, as workers achieved many of their primary objectives and as utilities came under more direct public regulation, the mutual identification between workers and their communities—so notable during these early strikes—began to break down.

The unions had always been among the most ardent advocates of public ownership of public utilities. Only complete replacement of private control, they argued, would ensure fair treatment of the public users as well as proper justice to the public servants.[37] They were not alone in this, as we have seen: a belief in the public ownership of natural monopolies was one of the shared objectives that linked organized labour to other groups in the community. It was assumed that such a dramatic change in owners would eliminate most of the conflict that had surrounded these utility franchises, labour-management disputes included. The city council of Calgary set itself the goal of being an exemplary employer when it opened a municipal street railway, and for the first few years, at least, it largely succeeded.[38] When the Toronto Civic Railway commenced operations, its workers received higher wages than their counterparts toiling for William Mackenzie's Toronto Railway Company.[39] But this romantic attachment to public enterprise did not last for long.

In May of 1913 the employees of the municipally owned Port Arthur street railway went out on strike. The dispute began when management fired several of the employees who had been instrumental in forming a local of the Amalgamated Association of Street and Electric Railway Employees Union. During the strike the municipal Transportation Committee behaved in much the same way as a private employer. It contracted with the Thiel Detective Agency to supply operators and armed guards from Winnipeg. Its attempt to run the cars despite the walkout precipitated a riot, and when the mob attacked the police station to free a Hungarian who had been arrested, one man was killed and several wounded in the ensuing melee. But the anticipated public support for the strike failed to materialize. The cars run by strikebreakers were well patronized, and only two unions answered the call for a general strike in sympathy with the street railwaymen. The Department of Labour correspondent reported: "No public sympathy at all for the striking trainmen owing to their unjust demands." And in less than a month both the strike and the union were broken.[40]

Cotton's Weekly, a socialist magazine, drew an important lesson from the incident. The primary objective of public ownership was low fares and, it followed, low wages: "At Port Arthur the workers found that under capitalism there is no difference between municipal ownership and private ownership." The new regime, the magazine concluded, mainly benefited the employing class. The defeated members of the street railwaymen's union would likely have concurred with this assessment. Jean Morrison, in her sensitive analysis of developing class relations at the Lakehead, argues that this strike polarized the community in a way that previous strikes had not. Key portions of the middle class, which had previously lent support to workers striking against large, externally controlled corporations, refrained from identifying with the strikers in this case.[41] Municipal ownership made it appear that the workers were striking against the city and its citizens.

It might be said, then, that the street railway strike at the Lakehead in 1913 marked the dawning of a new era of industrial relations in the utilities sector. No longer could it be easily assumed that the community interest and the workers' interests were identical. The change in viewpoint would not occur at exactly the same moment in all cities; even as the bond between class and community was disintegrating at the Lakehead, it was still being forged in the Halifax and Saint John street railway strikes of

1913 and 1914. But in time, all across the country, this social transformation took place.

Wartime inflation and a heightening of social conflict greatly accelerated the process. When workers' real wages began to decline drastically in 1917, the Amalgamated Association and to a lesser extent the IBEW authorized a series of massive strikes in various cities across Canada to raise the pay and shorten the hours of their members. The previously strike-free British Columbia Electric Railway experienced two strikes, in 1917 and in 1918. Toronto suffered three disruptions in streetcar service in as many years; so did the city of London. With a determination never before seen, street railway employees all across the country seemed resolved to halt work until their wage demands were met. Similarly, operators and linemen insisted upon substantial raises, especially from the provincially owned telephone systems in the West, and they struck often to demonstrate that they were serious. Employees downed tools everywhere, even against that much-vaunted instrument of the public will, the Ontario Hydro-Electric Power Commission.

The sheer frequency of such walkouts and the seemingly huge increases demanded by the workers—all against a backdrop of war in Europe—gave these strikes a significantly different complexion. In the first place, all employers, whether public or private, made it clear that higher wages for their employees necessarily involved increases in the price of service. Private companies developed a strategy of bartering wage increases for their workers in return for the surrender of concessions by the city: regulation of jitneys in Vancouver, higher fares and altered franchises elsewhere. Nonpartisan mediators and arbitrators in different regulatory jurisdictions all came to the same conclusion at about the same time; that greater income would be needed to meet the increased wage bill, and that the users must pay. This was the judgement of Dr. Adam Shortt's enquiry in Vancouver, the Montreal Tramways Commission, Public Utilities Commissions in the Maritimes, the Ontario Railway and Municipal Board (which ordered fare increases in several cities), and the federal Board of Railway Commissioners in the 1919 Bell Telephone rate case. Only the city of Toronto held out against the obvious. There, the private traction and lighting franchises were due to expire in 1921, and because of hard feeling and lingering suspicion, no one could countenance granting the company any quarter even in its final hours. But that was simply spite. Everywhere else city councils and riders eventually had to confess that a five-cent ticket would no longer cover costs.[42]

A closer look at these strikes reveals a subtle shift in the public perception of the conflict, and certainly in the newspaper reporting of the events. The three streetcar strikes in Toronto after 1917 did not lead to a repetition of the violence of 1902, or that of 1910, when a riot over working rules damaged 360 cars. The fact that the company made no attempt to run its cars during the later strikes removed the most serious threat to the public peace. Conciliation under the Industrial Disputes Investigation Act did not prove satisfactory, however. In one instance the board bungled the settlement, and in another the union struck before the board could report.

What is conspicuous in the news stories reporting these walkouts is how detached the public appeared to be through it all. "Toronto Carless But Not Unhappy," reported the Toronto *World* during the 1917 disruption. "The street railway, generally typified as an octopus, was not treated with invective, and the striking men were not regarded by capital as outlaws and objects of contumely." During the 1920 strike the involuntary pedestrians cheered the arrival of the jitney drivers who offered to carry them to work, for a price. The *Mail and Empire* railed against "Our Street Railway Masters," the employees. Only the *Star* and the *World,* both of which courted a working-class readership, showed much sympathy for the strikers. The *Globe,* the *Mail and Empire,* and the *Telegram* accepted the circumstances with varying degrees of resignation and exasperation. But they were quite prepared, in the words of the *Globe,* to stand aside, making the best of a bad situation, as the men and the company fought it out. Newspapers in Hamilton, Brantford, Ottawa, Montreal, and Halifax observed that by 1920 the aggressive street railwaymen in Toronto could no longer command the automatic support of the citizens in their disputes.

In other places the same distancing occurred. During the second Vancouver street railway strike in 1918, the papers reported that many women volunteered to replace the striking motormen and conductors. In Halifax earlier the same year, street railway workers who had received such overwhelming public encouragement during their 1913 strike forfeited that support when they walked out in the midst of a snowstorm after giving only an hour's notice. As a result, the Department of Labour correspondent wrote, "feeling against the employees is very bitter." A two-week strike of street railwaymen in Ottawa in 1919 failed utterly and in the process "alienated public sympathy."

Perhaps the clearest indication of a changed relationship between the utilities workers and their communities showed up in Winnipeg in 1918 and Saint John in 1921. When the telephone operators employed by the provincial utility walked out in May of 1918 in sympathy with striking Winnipeg civic workers, the Manitoba government not only delivered an ultimatum to the women to return to work but began training strikebreakers to replace them if they didn't. At the same time an organization of soldiers' wives published a statement deploring the unjustified strike by the telephone girls: in the name of the men overseas, these women implored the operators, who had no grievances of their own, to return immediately to their jobs. In other words, as workers responded more vigorously and collectively to their class interests, public support gradually melted away.

This was obvious as well when the introduction of one-man cars precipitated a walkout of Saint John street railwaymen that started in 1921 and lasted two years. Some scenes from the 1914 strike were repeated, but on this occasion the wholesale stoning of company cars being driven by strikebreakers was not widely condoned. Instead, pedestrians cheered the jitneys; when the strikers paraded through the streets, no one clapped; and when a striker smashed the window of a car, the newspaper headline emphasized that a little girl had been injured. The Union Bus Company, organized by the men in competition with the streetcars, failed after only a month. Denied the public support necessary to sustain a long struggle, the union gradually disintegrated. The strikers were readily replaced; public transportation quickly returned to normal; and the dispute continued only because there was no one left to declare it over.[43]

Where once utility workers had been able to count upon broad public sympathy, they now found their demands viewed with suspicion, particularly during the latter years of the war, when they were seen as obstructing the Allied cause. The chief engineer in charge of Ontario Hydro's huge Queenston project could complain bitterly in 1919 that "the attitude of labour has been to make these great public works an agency for enriching themselves at the expense of their fellow citizens and not out of the pockets of private capitalists as is ordinarily the case." Regulation—up to and, in this case, including public ownership—had subtly altered the perception of the role of labour. To give in to the men's demand for their current ten-hours' pay for an eight-hour day would be fatal to the principles of public ownership, the same engineer argued.

> If there is any increase allowed in the present rates or if the work is organized on any basis other than the ten-hour day, the Niagara development scheme will undoubtedly be an economic failure and enemies of public ownership will advertise this fact throughout the world. Two incidental consequences of this failure would be the destruction of public confidence in the radial railway and the St. Lawrence [power] development schemes to such an extent that both would probably have to be abandoned to the great detriment of the working classes, both from the employment and the cost of living standpoint.[44]

Union leaders plainly sensed the change in the public temper. John Flett, an important official of the American Federation of Labor, tried to persuade Ontario Hydro to grant the men's demands by contending that "the government should be a model to other employers." George Pay, secretary of the Niagara District Trades Federation, reminded Sir Adam Beck how much the largest publicly owned utility in North America owed to the support of organized labour. To date, however, Pay observed gloomily, "the Hydro-Electric Power [Commission's] canal [project] has proven anything but satisfactory from a workingman's point of view."[45]

Such an appeal fell upon deaf ears. Sir Adam Beck was already scheming to free Ontario Hydro from the jurisdiction of the Industrial Disputes

Investigation Act. He felt that the commission, as an arm of government, was fully able to express the popular will. Beck even ignored the pleas of the Premier of Ontario, who pointed out that this stand made it difficult for him to convince union leaders that the Hydro was fully independent of the government and thus need not have "fair wage" clauses written into its labour agreements, as was being done with government contractors during the war.[46] Beck insisted that the Hydro had none of the selfish interests of a private company but was merely a trustee for its member municipalities. How could it submit to binding arbitration without sacrificing those interests if the board were to find for the unions?[47]

This defiant attitude undoubtedly percolated through to the municipal electrical utilities in Ontario. Toronto's Hydro-Electric System, which began operation just prior to the war, experienced its first strike by the International Brotherhood of Electrical Workers in the spring of 1914. In an effort to dampen growing discontent, Toronto Hydro granted a 5 percent raise in 1917, along with a special wartime bonus of the same amount to help employees cope with inflation. In 1918 the company agreed to raise its wages to the level of the private company, but in 1919 resisted demands to cut the work week and convert the wartime bonus into part of the regular pay scale. The following year the employees again demanded arbitration under the federal act, calculating that their chances of a further raise were good in the light of continued inflation. This proved correct, and Toronto Hydro eventually conceded the 15 percent increment recommended by the board.[48]

In its first decade the Toronto Hydro-Electric System was taken to arbitration under the Industrial Disputes Investigation Act on five different occasions. The finding of these boards helped to nearly triple linemen's wages, from $27\frac{7}{9}$ cents to 78 cents per hour. When the men demanded a further increase to 85 cents per hour in 1921, however, and again applied to the federal Labour Department for arbitration, the patience of the Toronto Electric Commissioners was exhausted. Having arranged to purchase their private rival, thus ending all competition, they were now determined to cut wage levels in line with the falling cost of living. To avoid another arbitration, the commission's lawyers argued that it was not subject to the jurisdiction of the act, because a municipal body was created by the province, which controlled matters such as wages and hours of labour.[49] Eventually the issue went to the courts, and in 1925 the Judicial Committee of the Privy Council in a landmark decision held that Mackenzie King's cherished Industrial Disputes Investigation Act was *ultra vires* because it overrode the constitutional authority of the provinces.[50]

The Judicial Committee's decision in *Toronto Electric Commissioners v. Snider* might stand as a symbol of the direction in which the relations between utilities and their employees were evolving. Originally the Industrial Disputes Investigation Act had singled out utilities as a class of undertakings in which the community at large possessed a special interest. Labour disputes were to be dealt with by boards of arbitrators who would reflect the interests of the public as well as those of capital and labour. But the growing power of trade unions and their militant stance in the face of wartime inflation worked to convince many Canadians that the objectives of the workers and the community were no longer identical. Perhaps predictably, it fell to a publicly owned undertaking to mount the final assault upon the constitutionality of the legislation. The commissioners who managed the Toronto Hydro-Electric System and the telephones in Manitoba now believed that *they* embodied the public will, and even privately owned utilities, who were increasingly subject to control by various regulatory bodies took the same view.

Using the strike weapon without restraint, utilities workers were able to improve their economic position. No longer were they considered poor cousins in the Canadian labour movement. But in the process this group of workers also acquired a new set of masters: instead of demanding raises from cartoon caricature monopolists, they had to contend with boards, tribunals, commissions of one sort or another, and even public owners—all of whom claimed to represent the broader public who would ultimately have to pay. As a result of the changed regulatory environment, the community through its new governing instruments had taken on some if not all of the responsibilities of ownership. Because this group of relatively well-off workers could improve its position only at the expense of the community, and could not do so in the absence of broad public sympathy, strikes in the utilities sector virtually ceased during the 1920s.

The Utility of Regulation

The attitude of utility operators toward regulation changed in the course of time. Prior to 1914, when profits flowed in smoothly, management's time-honoured strategy had been to insist upon the sanctity of contract. But wartime inflation brought profound changes. Labour-intensive street railways discovered that the five-cent fare no longer generated sufficient revenue to cover steeply rising costs.[1] Telephone companies faced new wage demands as well as the need to invest large sums in capital equipment. After 1917, transit and telecommunications utilities across North America were plunged into desperate financial crisis, and their survival depended upon *changing* the terms of existing franchises so as to raise rates. Only electricity suppliers escaped this squeeze—economies of scale from large hydroelectric stations permitted them to maintain profit levels even if they had to cut rates—but many of these utilities formed part of larger integrated enterprises that now had money-losing divisions. Faced with this unhappy situation, utility managers and their financial backers and employees came to appreciate that regulation had its uses.

When the fiscal crisis broke over the utilities, both the political and the technological environment in which the industry operated were undergoing important changes. First of all, under pressure from civic populists many governments were wavering in their determination to protect private corporations from competition by public enterprises. Most of the provinces had enacted some sort of shield at the behest of monopoly-makers, such as the Conmee clause of the Ontario Municipal Act. But this self-denying ordinance had been swept away in Ontario by the public power movement, and the success of Ontario Hydro inspired people in other provinces to call for the repeal of such statutory limitations upon competitive public enterprises. At this point the regulatory commission assumed a new importance.

Nor were the cities, their populistic politicians, and public entrepreneurs the only dangers that private utilities faced. Particularly in the street railway sector, technological change brought new challenges. Could antagonistic city councils be persuaded to moderate the competition from jitneys and motor buses? Enhancing the need for mediation was the fact that many early franchises were due to expire in the 1920s. This forced the "recontracting" problem upon companies and cities as the World War I drew to a close. Would franchises be renewed, rewritten—or perhaps recaptured from their owners by the municipalities?

The recontracting issue led to paralysis in Montreal. As the inconclusive negotiations between the city and its street railway entered their sixth year in 1917, the Quebec government was prevailed upon to override local jurisdiction in order to end the impasse. A new institution was interposed between the company, the city, and a discredited provincial Public Utilities Commission, and this new body employed an entirely new method of reconciling the competing interests of labour, capital, the larger community, and the regular passengers.

The Montreal Tramways Company reorganized by E. A. Robert and J. W. McConnell in 1911 operated in the city and its suburbs under 30 different contracts signed with 14 separate municipal corporations, each of which contained different terms, conditions, and expiry dates. The franchise for the all-important city core would terminate in 1922; other parts of the company's territory were covered by perpetual contracts or by agreements lasting until 1959. The legislation creating the consolidated Montreal Tramways Company, which was passed over the strenuous objections of the Montreal city council in 1911, contained a clause granting the company a 42-year extension to its franchise for the entire region, provided that it could reach an agreement with the interested municipalities. Thus as soon as E. A. Robert got hold of the street railway situation in Montreal he had a powerful incentive to strike a new bargain with the city.

For their part the city councillors were eager to renegotiate the franchise. Heretofore they had been powerless to satisfy ratepayers' requests for extensions to the lines or to reduce overcrowding on certain routes. The trade unions wanted new clauses inserted into the franchise setting forth minimum wages, maximum hours, and the right to form a union. The city itself was determined to recoup its due portion of the undistributed profits of the street railway that had been capitalized so audaciously by Robert and his associates.

Yet mutual suspicion and a lingering sense of grievance on both sides inhibited fruitful discussion, and a confusing separation of powers between the city council and its executive Board of Commissioners further hampered the process. Bargains made by the commissioners were thrown out by an unhappy council; in the light of previous negotiations with utilities in Montreal, the council suspected the worst of any such agreement. For its part the company complicated proceedings with its own form of intransigence and obstructionism as the council upped the ante. In the bad old days, bribery had helped point the way out of such difficulties, but in the post-reform era such methods were not only in disrepute but less likely to prove effective.

Talks between the company and the city had commenced in April of 1911, only to be disrupted by the controversy surrounding the amalgamation of all the street railways on the island into the Montreal Tramways Company. Angered by the promoters' ability to appeal over the head of the city to the provincial government, the city council in turn invited the provincial Public Utilities Commission to determine whether Montreal Tramways was in violation of the terms of its franchise, owing to the poor service being offered. This body, it will be recalled, had served Robert's purposes earlier by authorizing a huge stock issue. That job done, Robert effectively prevented the PUC from taking up the Montreal complaint by challenging its jurisdiction in the courts.[2] With its authority on trial, the PUC could do nothing, and the legal mills ground exceedingly slow.

Prevented from seeking redress through normal regulatory channels, the city resorted to a publicity campaign in an effort to shame the company into adding more cars and more stops, and building more lines. The major newspapers sponsored an informal "Commission on Transportation" to recommend ways of improving service. At length this unorthodox strategy bore fruit: E. A. Robert resumed negotiations with the city in April, 1913, submitting a detailed proposal to reduce congestion. But the possibility of agreement on the narrow question of immediate improvements ran afoul of the city council's determination to renegotiate the entire franchise before authorizing any changes. Public hearings were arranged to establish priorities, and the City Engineer was ordered to draw up a comprehensive plan. By January of 1915 it appeared likely that the city and the company would at long last come to terms.[3]

Mayor Médéric Martin and his team of negotiators actually hammered out a new contract with the company—only to have the capricious city council reject it. Again the councillors blamed the company for the debacle; a temporary reduction in service during the recession of 1914 and especially after the outbreak of war was interpreted as an insult. Angered by this and by the fact that the company was $603,911 in arrears on its payments to the city, the council raised awkward objections to the draft agreement. Various outside bodies such as the Trades and Labour Council, the Board of Trade, and la Chambre de Commerce also balked, doubting the ability of Martin to work out an honest, straightforward agreement in the public interest with such a notorious manipulator as Robert.[4]

In June of 1915 the city council made a counteroffer, proposing to pay Robert a fixed rate of return on the capital actually invested in the company with the provision that the city would have the right to take it over at this valuation plus additions at any time. Robert took umbrage: "The whole tenor of your proposal of June 9th from the commencement of the preamble to the last of its conclusions is a proposition to municipalize the system in an indirect way before the city is entitled to do so."[5] Soon he would have occasion to reconsider this position, but in the meantime, negotiations collapsed amidst mutual recriminations.

It was this deplorable state of affairs that set the stage for outside intervention. The provincial Public Utilities Commission, created to regulate the industry, had been rendered powerless by Robert's legal challenge to its jurisdiction, which he insisted upon carrying all the way to the Judicial Committee of the Privy Council. As public discontent at interruptions in service mounted and direct bargaining between the city and the company broke down yet again, private citizens and business organizations appealed to the provincial government to do something to end the stalemate. In 1916 the provincial government authorized a five-man commission to conclude a binding agreement on behalf of the city with the tramway company. Replacing all other contracts, the agreement was to last for 36 years, after which the city could expropriate the company on six months' notice. At long last the provincial level of government had decisively intervened to settle a dispute that had frustrated improvements in Montreal's public transit system for more than six years.

When the Montreal Tramways Commission began its investigations, the street railway system in Canada's largest city was on the verge of collapse. Business had recovered under the stimulus of wartime production. Trams were once more packed to overflowing with munitions workers bound for suburban arms plants (some of which were owned by the tram company itself), as well as offices, shops, and factories in the urban core. The sudden economic revival led to power shortages, brownouts, and frequent interruptions in street railway operations as a result.[6] As the demands upon the system soared, costs rose even more rapidly. The company's income was relatively fixed at a simple multiple of the five-cent fare, and it was difficult to hold down expenses, especially labour costs, in a period of inflation. (see Figure 5). Thus the appointment of the commission coincided with the impending bankruptcy of the company. In 1917 both the company and the city were financially weak, so the mediator possessed unusual strength.

The commission spent a year studying the Montreal situation, aided by investigations of public transit problems in Detroit, Chicago, Cleveland, Indianapolis, Boston, Baltimore, and Philadelphia (there was no point visiting Toronto where relations between the city and the company were, if anything, even worse than in Montreal). At length the commission agreed that massive new investment would be needed to extend and completely refurbish the street railway, but that some means had first to be found to harmonize the three separate interests involved, the company, the city and the public. Should a new contract much like the old one be drawn up,

FIGURE 5

THE MONTREAL TRAMWAYS COMPANY

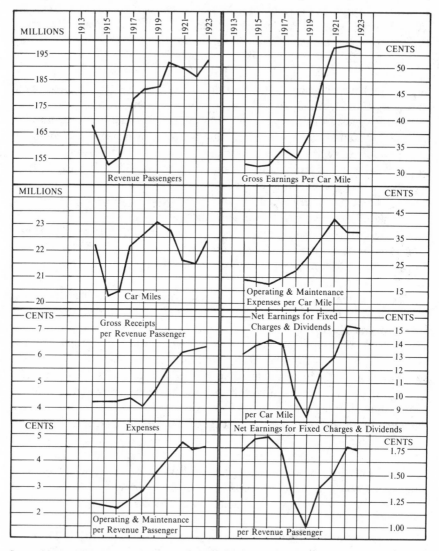

Source: Montreal Tramways Commission, Fifth Annual Report, 1922–23.

giving the company the widest measure of independence to serve the public as it saw fit after paying a percentage of its receipts to the city? Or should the street railway be taken over by the city and operated as a public work? Neither of these alternatives satisfied the Tramways Commission. Contracts were not flexible enough to meet all contingencies, and companies could not be relied upon to respond promptly to public needs, especially when such needs conflicted with private imperatives. On the other hand, municipal ownership, in the view of the commission, had failed to demonstrate any innate superiority where it had been tried, certainly none sufficient to justify such a massive increase in the public debt. The Toronto Civic Railway, for example, operated at a perennial deficit which the property taxpayers were forced to cover. Besides, as the commissioners pointed out, Montreal's lamentable financial condition precluded the city from acquiring the whole system, and there was no point in taking over only part of it.[7]

The commission therefore proposed a third option, a new idea that had just begun to circulate in the United States: a service-at-cost contract. Under this scheme the physical plant of the street railway would be valued, and the company would be allowed to earn a 6 percent rate of return on its capital investment. With this security the company would be able to raise new money for extensions and improvements, these additions being included in the rate base. Fares could be adjusted from time to time to accommodate additions to capital or rising costs. The city would be assured efficient, low-cost service free of the financial shenanigans of the past without having to shoulder a burdensome debt itself. The public would receive desperately needed transit improvements with the assurance that slightly higher fares would be applied directly to the business, not be diverted to promoters' pockets. Such a scheme had much to recommend it: a service-at-cost contract would preserve private enterprise, establish a new climate of mutual confidence, allow for any fare increases justified by changing circumstances, and contain enough internal checks and balances to ensure that the interests of the city as a corporation, the users, and the ratepayers would be protected. The system would not work automatically, however; a permanent Tramways Commission would be needed to audit the company's financial statements and oversee its day-to-day operations.[8]

As a starting point the Tramways Commission conducted a detailed valuation of the Montreal Tramways Company. The book value of the company's outstanding securities amounted to $39,013,296. Consultants hired by the commission established an actual value of $36,286,295, excluding the franchise itself from the valuation. This estimate closely approximated a similar valuation of $36.3 million prepared by Stone and Webster for a group of underwriters in 1916. The commission recommended that the company henceforth be assured sufficient income from the paying passengers to meet its legitimate operating expenses, provide a $500,000 annual rental to the city, and earn 6 percent on its capital (including any future investment).

In earlier times the company would have haughtily refused to don such a financial straitjacket, but by late 1917 a service-at-cost contract was looked upon as a godsend. Before the war, street railway entrepreneurs had expected a good deal more than a mere 6 percent rate of return; as we have seen, they had managed to wring a substantial surplus out of their properties *and* valorize their stock from the five-cent fare. However, wartime inflation had completely eroded the earning power of the nickel, and capitalists with millions at risk were more than willing to accept a guaranteed 6 percent return rather than see their assets wither. Labour, too, realized that some way would have to be found to meet its demands which had, after all, only barely kept pace with the rate of inflation. And so the Montreal Tramways Company accepted these terms, even jumped at the chance of winning one of the first service-at-cost contracts on the continent.

At the next session of the legislature, the provincial government ratified the contract arrived at by the commission on behalf of the city and established a permanent Montreal Tramways Commission to supervise it. Public transportation decision-making was thus removed from both the company and the city and placed in the hands of a provincially appointed body, paving the way for dramatic improvement in both the financial health of the company (see Figure 5) and the quality of transportation in the city—but at the cost of a loss of local, democratic control. Commission arbitration replaced direct negotiations, accountants supplanted politicians, and a rigid financial formula balanced competing notions of equity. Nevertheless, the province of Quebec had found a way out of the dilemma of inflationary times for Montreal's public transit. Despite a good deal of complaining on all sides, the settlement imposed upon the city and the company proved surprisingly durable and lasted more or less unchanged for another generation. Compulsory recontracting in Montreal provided a trial of what would become the U.S. utility owners' preferred solution to the fiscal crisis of the street railroads. As Delos F. Wilcox wryly observed: "The People of Montreal and its suburbs can have exactly the kind of service that two commissions [PUC, MTC] think is good for them and are willing to make them pay for."[9]

When the British Columbia Electric Railway eventually got into the same kind of serious trouble in 1917, it had neither a Public Utilities Commission nor a friendly provincial government to fall back upon. As we have seen, the company had stubbornly resisted the establishment of a PUC; the BCER management preferred to be "left alone" to conduct its business as it saw fit, confident that intimate personal relations with the premier and leading members of his government would provide adequate protection against any harmful municipal measures. Such a reliance upon personal connections rather than a formal regulatory procedure had its advantages, but it also entailed certain risks.

The company's problems had begun in 1915 with the sudden appearance of jitneys on city streets; these were a Los Angeles invention that swept up the west coast and eventually across the continent. Motorists, some of them unemployed workmen who rented idle automobiles, cruised the main thoroughfares, usually just ahead of the streetcars, picking up passengers at crowded stops and delivering them to their destinations. By March, 1915, more than 100 jitney drivers in Vancouver had already organized themselves into business associations and at least one large incorporated company. Riders in Vancouver, angered by the BCER's poor service and a recent fare increase to five cents, eagerly welcomed the innovation. Service might be a bit erratic and the driving a little harrowing at times, but the jitneys were a blessing to people in a hurry. At the very least they broke the numbing routine.[10]

Jitneys made their deepest impression upon the earnings of the British Columbia Electric Railway. Company officials privately calculated that the rapidly multiplying automobiles were costing the company more than $2,000 a day in lost revenue after only a month of operation[11]—at a time when the BCER's street railway division was only a break-even proposition at best. Discomfited by this unprecedented intrusion into its monopoly over public transportation, the company opened a quiet campaign to drive the competition off the city streets. The Vancouver Trades and Labour Council, alert to the fact that competition would in the long run threaten the jobs of unionized workers on the street railway, took the unusual step of supporting the company's petition to the municipalities and the provincial government.[12] The publicity campaign against the jitneys went nowhere at first. "The citizens ignore that we run a good but unremunerative railway system and consider that the jitney competition is responsible for lower fares and better service," general manager George Kidd explained to his London board of directors, "and we must admit there is a certain element of truth in their view."[13]

As long as the company could make up for street railway losses with unusually high profits from its electric light and power business, the situation could be tolerated for a while. Thus the BCER advanced upon the Vancouver city council in a mood of concern but not desperation over the delicate matter of regulating the jitneys.[14] For more than a year the company explored ways of gaining the cooperation of the deeply suspicious council, and eventually offered to lower its lighting rates if the city would promise to crack down on the jitneys. Here was an old ploy—give up something the other side wants which will cost little in order to get something urgently needed. This time the city refused to play, preferring instead to deal separately with each matter on its merits. The approaching expiry of the company's main franchise in 1919 stiffened the council's resolve to make up for previous mistakes. In 1916 the Ratepayers' Association also began agitating for cheaper domestic electric light and power service. George Kidd knew that the BCER's rate schedule was not constructed "on the most up-to-date basis" and could not be readily defended in informed discussion, but he nevertheless held out, waiting for the city to do something about the pesky jitneys.[15] Exasperation with this situation prompted some ambitious aldermen to advocate a municipal electric utility. To that end the city called for the repeal of the "protective clause," inserted into the city charter in 1895 at the behest of the utilities, which effectively prevented the city from going into competition against private companies.[16]

In other days the BCER might simply have been amused by this threat, but times had changed. The ouster of the Conservative government and its replacement by the Liberals late in 1916 ended more than a decade of close and confidential relations between the company and the provincial government. In other provinces, legislation similar to the protective clause had been repealed, and municipalities had begun to compete with private utilities; the Vancouver city council's petition could point to these precedents. Moreover, both Premier H. C. Brewster and his Attorney General held Vancouver seats, had risen to prominence in part through the agitation against the company, and were thus particularly susceptible to civic populist influence. Finally, the debate on the clause occurred in a political environment excited by a major scandal involving the provincially owned steam railway, which blackened the reputation of all business interests momentarily.

The instinctive response of the BCER's London directors to this crisis was to sell. Why not unload the property now when its earnings still sustained the value of its securities rather than face a long and wearing fight? R. M. Horne-Payne snorted that "the robbery of Public Utilities Companies is now popular and is becoming a vote catching plank in every political platform"; he insisted that as a matter of "simple justice" the provincial government should purchase the BCER rather than repeal the protective clause.[17] In an act of transparent generosity, he offered to assist the province to raise the funds by placing the necessary bonds in New York. Sir William Mackenzie, a director who was busy trying to unload his own railroads and utilities onto various governments, also strongly advised this course and used his good offices with the new premier to that end.[18] Tentatively, the company suggested that the province should set up a hydroelectric power commission, like the one in Ontario, to buy the whole property and then divest itself of the street railroad operations to the respective municipalities. The problem was that Brewster's government did not think it could afford to finance the mammoth transaction, and the company refused to divide its assets.

A calm reassessment of the situation in late January, 1917, convinced Kidd and Horne-Payne that they would have to fight rather than run; it was just possible that the company might emerge from the fray better off. So another of those ritualistic struggles between a city and its principal utility unfolded on the west coast during the spring of 1917. Mayor McBeath and aldermen Kirck, Gale, and Clark championed Vancouver's crusade "to be freed of the shackles of the B. C. Electric Railway Company." Gale personally negotiated an option on the Bridge River hydroelectric site, some 150 miles away. The city council proposed to develop this waterpower, connect it to a modern municipal distribution system, and deliver cheap hydroelectricity at long last. Many illuminating comparisons of electricity rates in Vancouver, Winnipeg, and Toronto clinched the point that the BCER had been denying Vancouverites their birthright. Appealing to incurable boosterism, the council claimed that if Vancouver hoped to take its place among the great cities of the world, "she must be placed in a position to offer inducements to manufacturers."[19]

For its part the company rang the changes on the themes of the sanctity of contract and the dangers of a flight of capital. Millions of pounds sterling had been raised and invested in British Columbia, with only a modest return thus far, on the strength of a commitment that municipalities would not be allowed to compete against private utilities. Having made this promise, the provincial government was honour-bound to stand by it; if it repudiated this pledge, the wrath of the entire British financial community would most certainly descend upon all provincial securities, making it impossible to borrow money for public or private purposes at prime interest rates. At the appropriate moment a chorus of 11 merchant banking houses chimed in by telegram to lend credence to this campaign of intimidation.[20]

An air of unreality surrounded the whole dispute. The company knew it could get along perfectly well without the clause; it had only symbolic importance. What was more, the Vancouver hydroelectric project was a pipe dream, and so too was the city's threat to recover the street railway in 1919. Direct talks between Mayor McBeath and George Kidd during the hearings before the Private Bills Committee confirmed Kidd's belief that the whole campaign was a bluff on the part of the city to pressure the company into lowering its electricity rates. Thus the most likely outcome of this dispute, seen from both sides, was a negotiated settlement of some sort.[21]

Still, the good fight had to be fought. Delegations of earnest aldermen visited Victoria. As usual the BCER massaged the Private Bills Committee, this time with new lobbyists, and consulted endlessly with the Premier and members of his cabinet. George Kidd reported with some pride that the mayor had accused the company's representatives of "infesting the corridors of the House." Company lobbyists discovered to their surprise a good deal of closet sympathy for the plight of the BCER. Even the Premier expressed embarrassment at the situation, gave private assurances that no harm would come to the company, and promised to use his influence with some members, even though he could not come out openly against the Vancouver petition, sitting as he did for a city riding. The Private Bills Committee once again did its duty and reported a bill more favourable to the company than to the city. But a revolt on the floor of the legislature undid all of this private persuasion. Although the city had come to realize the overall weakness of its plan, it nevertheless could summon up enough political influence with the new Liberal members to reverse the decision of the committee. It was pointed out, to the acute embarrassment of the BCER, that the company's claim that money had been raised on the strength of the protective clause could not be demonstrated by any precise statement in a prospectus. Nor were the members much impressed by threats from London, knowing that in the future they would be looking to New York for their borrowing requirements. So the city prevailed, and the legislature voted late in the spring of 1917 to remove the protective clause from the city charter.[22]

R. M. Horne-Payne, fulminating against this "act of brigandage and robbery," ordered Kidd to have the clause reinserted at the next session of the legislature or have the new act disallowed by the federal government; in London he set about making good on his promise to punish the province. George Kidd tried to calm down his excitable chairman, recognizing that the BCER had actually emerged in a much stronger position than before. Vancouver's hollow victory would prove suicidal if the council actually tried to follow through with action. Lower lighting rates would probably benefit the company, which had a huge surplus of power at its disposal. The city had exhausted its political capital in a pointless crusade, and the BCER had unexpected reserves of this precious commodity already banked in Victoria. The only real problem was how to put the struggling street railway division back on a sound financial footing.[23]

Here organized labour inadvertently came to the rescue. After months of futile negotiations, the street railwaymen's union struck for higher wages on June 13, 1917, to compensate for the soaring cost of living.[24] The BCER had precipitated the walkout by refusing to consider the possibility of any significant wage increase, arguing that jitney competition, rising costs, stable revenues, and the impossibility of raising fares made a higher wage bill intolerable; the employees and the city, it said, could no longer expect the company to subsidize public transit from its electric lighting revenues. At the height of the war effort, the city could not endure a lengthy transit shutdown, and having made no progress in its own protracted talks with the company over electrical matters, it appealed once more to the provincial government for help. Premier Brewster complied by appointing a Royal Commission of Enquiry into the Vancouver utilities question on the clear understanding that its recommendations would be binding upon both parties.[25] Since the whole issue of financing public transit would be taken up by the commission, the BCER put an end to the strike by conceding an interim wage increase on an emergency basis, pending the final report. In Vancouver, as in Montreal, outside intervention broke the recontracting deadlock.

The Solon selected for this task, Dr. Adam Shortt, one of two federal civil service commissioners since 1908, was eminently acceptable to both sides and the provincial government. Shortt had devoted most of his professional life to broadening the middle range of established facts—in historical studies, in industrial relations, and in public policy—upon which contending interest groups might agree. For a former moral philosopher, Carl Berger has observed, "the most striking feature of Shortt's outlook was his empiricism." S. E. D. Shortt echoed this judgement: "For Shortt, then, knowledge could not be equated with intuitively held beliefs, but rather rested upon facts empirically observed."[26] Adam Shortt had no time for demagogues or dogma. His relentless pursuit of the facts made him a frequent labour conciliator and an obvious candidate to sort out this vexing dispute with its much wider ramifications. Besides, he was an old friend of George Kidd, the manager of the BCER.[27] The company had no qualms about making a full disclosure of its affairs to such a man.

With characteristic efficiency Shortt examined the company books, heard all the testimony from representatives of the numerous interests involved, and wound up his on-site inspection by mid-August, 1917. As he retired to write his report, Shortt gave George Kidd a précis of his tentative conclusions—an indiscretion which assured company officials that their confidence had not been misplaced. Shortt said that he considered competition between public and private agencies in the utility sector utterly "iniquitous"; he dismissed aldermanic demands for enormous cuts in light and power rates as "stump oratory"; and he several times referred to the "immorality" of repudiating the protective clause, an act he thought would have much greater impact on financiers in New York than in London. Streetcar fares would simply have to be increased, Shortt intimated, and the troublesome jitneys outlawed. Over the long term, he believed, a Public Utilities Commission was the only way of preventing destructive collisions of the sort he had come to investigate. Shortt ended his comforting revelation, Kidd reported, by explaining that he was "alive to the somewhat predatory tendencies of the municipalities, and he said that from our point of view he thought we should not show any great anxiety to sell the company, as this would naturally create the impression that we were anxious to get rid of a bad bargain, neither should we throw any obstacle in the way of any offer we may have."[28]

The formal *Report of the Commissioner Appointed to Investigate the Economic Conditions and Operations of the British Columbia Electric Railway and Subsidiary Companies,* presented in November, 1917, fleshed out and justified these conclusions. It contained just enough criticism of company policy to satisfy the city, and supported the council's contention that light and power rates were too high and ought to be reduced. The company could accept this criticism with equanimity and agree to the electricity rate reductions, because the report also settled the street railway problem and in effect insured the company's long-term security. The jitneys could not replace the street railway system, Shortt argued, but they had the power to destroy it; therefore, the jitneys should be strictly regulated by the city to provide supplementary but not competitive public transportation. Moreover, transit operations must be put on a self-sustaining basis and the cross-subsidization from light and power revenues ended. If circumstances required a reduction in light and power rates, they also required an increase in streetcar fares to six cents to permit the company sufficient income to meet its legitimate expenses and allow for a small return on its investment. (Shortt dealt with the BCER as a single entity when he considered the question of its relations with government but divided it into its operating divisions for rate-making purposes.) The report effectively scotched the notion of competition between the city and the company, legitimized company views on public utility financial questions, and obliged the provincial government to create a permanent Public Utilities Commission to remove BCER affairs from politics—though much would depend upon the scope and personnel of such a commission.[29]

It would be gratifying to report that the outcome closely followed these recommendations and that Adam Shortt's intervention settled the Vancouver utilities dispute for a generation, but history is rarely so tidy. It took another strike by the street railwaymen to force the city to accept the authorized street railway fare increase, and then it did so only on a temporary basis. On the other hand, the city did act promptly to curb the jitneys, once it realized its own revenues were at stake. At length the province drafted a Public Utilities Commission bill, but the BCER had to lobby furiously to amend this legislation in such a way that the commission would be required to allow companies a fair rate of return on their capital, and its scope would be expanded to embrace publicly as well as privately owned utilities. Then the BCER only escaped having its old nemesis, Mayor R. H. Gale of Vancouver, named commissioner by the timely appeal of the Great War Veterans Association, who insisted upon a returned soldier for the job.[30]

So far, so good. But as the BCER prepared itself for a detailed valuation of its property by the new PUC, in order to arrive at a permanent street railway rate base, a bizarre legislative oversight in Ottawa accidentally swept the company into the federal regulatory arena. A 1919 amendment to the national Railway Act stipulated that any local railway or telephone company whose lines crossed those of a federally chartered company fell under the jurisdiction of the Board of Railway Commissioners.[31] Pragmatic as ever, the BCER then set about extracting permission from the distant Board of Railway Commissioners to charge a permanent six-cent streetcar fare and to bring its light and power business under federal jurisdiction as well. The company weighed the alternatives and came down in favour of federal regulation.[32] The provincial government responded to the confusion by abolishing the PUC, which had suddenly lost its functions, after less than a year of operations. Besides, the commissioner had turned out to be something of a nuisance and the cabinet was quite happy to see the whole mess of utility regulation landed in someone else's lap.[33]

But Mayor R. H. Gale of Vancouver was not prepared to see the British Columbia Electric Railway escape to far-off Ottawa without a fight. He had, after all, built his entire political career around attacking the company. Vancouver's argument received a sympathetic hearing from members of parliament: the federal Minister of Railways introduced legislation in 1920 correcting the original oversight and returning local street railways to provincial jurisdiction, where it was generally conceded they belonged. Since the provincial PUC had been abolished, the BCER struggled to stay within the federal fold, knowing that if it reverted to provincial control, the five-cent maximum fare specified under the 1901 franchise agreement would come back into effect. All the company could succeed in winning from parliament, however, was one more year of grace under federal regulation.[34]

In desperation the BCER launched a three-front campaign in 1920 to entrench itself. At Ottawa the company lobbied furiously to obtain a federal charter declaring it to be a work for the general advantage of Canada, which would bring its entire works under the benign care of the Board of Railway Commissioners. At Victoria the company urged the provincial government *not* to create another Public Utilities Commission should it revert to provincial jurisdiction: such a body would only invite frivolous complaints; the whole idea had gone out of favour in recent years in the East; and there were no objections to light and gas rates—only the street railway fares needed attention. And at Vancouver the company reopened direct negotiations with the city to obtain a new street railway franchise allowing a permanent six-cent fare.[35] Using the stick of possible federal incorporation and the carrot of lower streetlighting rates, the BCER eventually persuaded the city council to amend the 1901 franchise to permit a fare increase and to provide for arbitration procedures regarding the fare structure at three-year intervals.[36] Everything else remained the same, and that suited the BCER. The provincial government considered this an entirely satisfactory outcome, eliminating the embarrassing necessity of recreating a PUC; it confirmed the settlement in the BCER Passenger Rates Act passed just before Christmas in 1922.[37]

Everything changed, but in the end nothing changed. After a bewildering peregrination through three regulatory regimes—the Shortt commission, the Public Utilities Commission, and the Board of Railway Commissioners—the BCER ended up back where it started: under contract with the city, but with all of its basic objectives secured. The city had at last come to accept the necessity of raising car fares to compensate for higher labour costs and wartime inflation. The weight of independent, professional judgement had repeatedly come down against public competition with a private utility, and since the city did not really want the trouble of running the street railway itself and could ill afford an electrical utility of its own, it had to negotiate the best deal possible with private management. The competition from jitneys had been effectively contained. The operations of the company had been divided for the purpose of calculating a return on investment, but the property remained united under exclusively private control and was likely to remain so for the foreseeable future. The company had never been eager to have its affairs controlled by a provincial regulatory agency—though it had wavered during a particularly dangerous moment—and in the end it succeeded in retaining control over its gas, light and power business while negotiating a new agreement with the city to adjust street railway revenues to cover costs.

The route to this corporate triumph had by no means been easy and certainly not direct. Company officials muddled through, making the best of each sudden turn. When the company reviewed its position in 1921–22, it concluded that it had arrived at the best of all possible outcomes: the jitneys abolished, the city neutralized, a six-cent fare obtained, and no regulation of its light and power business. It had secured an unusual degree of freedom from government supervision, but state intervention, however fitful and transitory, had plainly done much to legitimize and stabilize private ownership in rapidly shifting political and economic circumstances.

The street railways in smaller cities like Regina, Saskatoon, Calgary, and Edmonton faced the same problems of rising costs and competition from jitneys. There, however, public ownership converted these issues into an internal political debate, which eased the brokerage problem by placing full responsibility upon the city councils. They might squirm under pressure from competing interest groups, but they could not avoid the issue. As the street railway deficits mounted, costs had to be met either out of the fare boxes or from municipal taxes. Everywhere the outcome was the same: the jitneys came under tight regulation, and car fares were steeply increased to cover costs. Indeed, because of the relatively small scale and higher cost schedules of these utilities, by 1922 their fares were the highest in the country.[38] This fact did nothing to burnish the reputation of public ownership for efficiency.

In Winnipeg the problem of regulating automobile competition, balancing revenues and expenditures, and recontracting the street railway franchise had to be fought out not only in the familiar divided terrain of public-private conflict but also in the highly polarized class relations of a city after a traumatic general strike in 1919.[39] To handle these delicate matters, the company recruited the much-travelled and widely experienced A. W. McLimont. His task was made somewhat easier in 1919 when, with the retirement of Sir William Mackenzie from the board, the Winnipeg Electric Railway Company came under local ownership and control. At long last it had become the property of the Winnipeg commercial elite. The city was persuaded with relative ease to crack down on the jitneys in 1918, but it fought tooth and nail the company's applications to the Manitoba Public Utilities Commission for fare increases. Nonetheless, in 1919, after a thorough valuation of the company, the PUC granted one fare increase and another a year later.[40]

The aggressive McLimont then decided to press his advantage by asking the city to extend the company's street railway franchise for another ten years beyond its expiry in 1927. In the aftermath of the general strike, an anti-Labour coalition commanded a majority at city hall, and McLimont hoped to seize this opportunity to lengthen the street railway franchise, thereby securing the long-term demand for power needed to finance a major hydroelectric project on the Winnipeg River. J. W. Dafoe, editor of the *Free Press,* observed that the "able, resourceful and not very scrupulous" general manager of the Winnipeg Electric Railway Company, by forcing this issue, was certain to deliver the city council over to the Labour faction at the next general election.[41] And that is exactly what happened.

Instead of extending the street railway franchise, the hostile city council elected in 1923 immediately set about investigating the possibility of taking over the transit operations of the utility when its franchise expired in 1927. A Special Committee of council looked into the matter and at length recommended paying $13 million for a physical plant with a $15 million replacement value.[42] In addition, the city would also be required to finance expansion of its hydroelectric generating capacity to handle the street railway load. This was rather a lot to swallow for a city council with many other pressing matters on its agenda. Would the huge new debt be worth it? Would it prevent the city from raising money for other purposes? At this point the Labour majority began to splinter. To some councillors the disadvantages of a takeover vastly outweighed the gains. On the far left of the political spectrum, Alderman A. A. Heaps argued that it made no sense to pay out $13 million for a system of transportation that was rapidly being made obsolete by motor buses: let the private capitalists keep their depreciating assets. The left and the right agreed; thus in 1925 the Winnipeg city council rejected public ownership by voting to do nothing. When the franchise came up for renewal in 1927, it would be automatically extended for another five years.[43]

It is altogether possible that by 1925 the Winnipeg Electric Railway Company might have wanted to unload its street railway system on the city, especially since it had just managed to strike a gentleman's agreement with the city-owned electrical utility to divide the power market and stabilize rates. By the mid-1920s the real money to be made in the utilities business was in the electrical sector. The street railway was a partial liability, representing a large quantity of sunk capital which, if liquidated, could be put to more profitable uses. But if it could absorb a large base load of power and be made to earn enough income to cover costs and provide a minimum guaranteed rate of return, and if it could be kept free of competition to negotiate the transition from street railroad technology to motor buses on its own, then it was still worth having. Such was the security that the regulatory regime in Manitoba delivered.

As we have seen, regulation, however fitful and unsystematic, helped protect capital and preserved the private ownership in Montreal, Vancouver, and Winnipeg. It lifted the ceiling on fares, controlled competition from jitneys, and smoothed the recontracting process. The same thing did not happen in Toronto for two reasons: first, there was the elemental intransigence of the city council; second, the most likely mediator—the provincial government—was itself a partisan in the dispute by virtue of its promotion of the interests of the Ontario Hydro-Electric Power Commission. Private control would not be renewed when the province was an active competitor.

As early as 1913 the Toronto city council had determined to take over the private street railroad and electric company; the question was when, and at what price? Indeed, in that year the mayor had actually negotiated a conditional purchase of Sir William Mackenzie's properties, only to have the deal rejected by the council—at the urging of the chairman of the Ontario Hydro-Electric Commission—as too expensive. The city already operated its own electrical system, distributing Niagara power delivered "at cost" by Adam Beck's provincially financed Hydro-Electric Commission, and the Civic Railway had just begun filling the gaps resulting from the Toronto Railway Company's refusal to serve suburbs beyond the 1891 city limits. By the end of 1913 the rapidly growing Toronto Hydro-Electric System could claim 50 per cent of all electrical accounts in the city, and for the first time its revenues surpassed those of the private Toronto Electric Light Company. The battle for the control of the Toronto electrical market was being won by the aggressive public authority. Adam Beck and his city council supporters argued that acquisition of the unnecessary duplicate distribution network for $8 million would serve only to drive up electric rates. This same group insisted that the street railroad could be recovered for considerably less, when its franchise expired in 1921, than the $22 million agreed to by Mayor Horatio Hocken.[44] The outbreak of war in the fall of 1914, which dried up municipal credit for the duration, and the election the leader of the *guerre à outrance* faction. Tommy Church, as mayor from 1915 to 1920 effectively ended all possibility of a negotiated settlement.

During the remaining time of the street railroad franchise, the city demonstrated an irrational willingness to cut off its nose to spite its face. On June 25, 1915, for example—Mayor Church led a band of municipal vigilantes on a midnight mission to tear up the 1,320 feet of track linking Mackenzie's suburban Toronto and York Radial Railway with his Toronto Railway Company at the city's northern boundary when, the franchise on this small portion having lapsed by a technicality relating to annexation. As a result of this triumph of civic populism, hundreds of commuters had to trudge that windy quarter of a mile twice a day, their mood not appreciably improved by beckoning jitney drivers.[45] The Toronto city council's stubborn and at times unreasonable attitude actually prevented a solution to the transportation problems it complained of. The strikes after 1917 did nothing to improve matters, and of course the city, while sympathizing with the employees, would not countenance any suggestion of a fare increase.[46]

The owners of the system responded by reducing operations to a minimum and stripping the company's assets. Cars and track were neglected, and as several city inquiries confirmed, service fell well below adequate standards.[47] To the mounting clamour against overcrowding, the hardbitten general manager replied: "Take the next car." From 1907 to 1913 the Toronto Railway Company had paid an average 57 percent of its net revenues as dividends, retaining the remainder for investment in the system and contingency funds of various sorts. During the four years after 1913, it increased the dividend payout to an average of 78 percent, thus further endangering the financial health of the enterprise as inflation took hold.[48] These actions were simply added to the lengthy bill of indictment. *In extremis,* the company pleaded for a service-at-cost contract like that imposed in Montreal. But the Ontario Railway and Municipal Board lacked the authority to grant it, the provincial government lacked the will, and the city positively sought an impasse, believing that the temporary inconvenience would be more than compensated for after 1921 when, under civic auspices, riders would finally receive the service they had been owed all along. There matters stood until midnight of August 31, 1921, when the city took possession of the company and a new era of public transportation commenced.[49]

In other cases the provincial government had overridden municipal intransigence of this sort; why did the province of Ontario not intervene in Toronto's recontracting process? First and foremost, the province was itself an interested bystander. The provincial government took guidance on utility questions from Sir Adam Beck, chairman of the Ontario Hydro-Electric Power Commission, whose vast and fiercely loyal extra parliamentary pressure group had the power to make or break governments. During the World War I and immediately after, Beck was intent upon his own drive toward monopoly in the hydroelectric field. Certainly Ontario might have imposed a settlement of the transit dispute upon Toronto, much as Quebec did in the Montreal case, or it might have established a commission of investigation. It did not take these steps because the progress toward public ownership of transit in Toronto was thought to be directly linked to the long-term success of the provincial electrical system. The owners of capital did not have the same access to the provincial government in Ontario that they had elsewhere, and even if they had tried to plead their case for mediation, they would not have been accorded a very sympathetic hearing around a cabinet table dominated by the figure of Adam Beck. At that very moment he was battling these very people for control of the regional electrical market, and a municipal takeover in Toronto helped swing the struggle in his favour.[50] Nor could anyone in the provincial government doubt the determination of the city to carry through its plans, or underestimate the consequences of standing in the way, after observing municipal politicians vying with one another for a decade and a half to be seen as the staunchest defenders of public ownership.

As the arbitration proceedings to determine the price to be paid for the Toronto Railway Company, now in municipal hands, got underway, Beck also began negotiating for the remaining hydroelectric assets of Sir William Mackenzie's utilities empire. Mackenzie had been willing to sell for some time, but his price, Beck's pride, and the war had stood in the way. But by 1922, Adam Beck had a powerful inducement to buy, quite apart from the satisfaction of capping his victory over an old adversary. Beck needed Mackenzie's water rights at Niagara Falls to run the world's largest hydroelectric generating station, which was nearing completion at Queenston. On this basis of mutual need a grand "Clean-Up Deal" was consummated whereby the provincial Hydro-Electric Commission took over Mackenzie's generating, transmission, and radial railway properties, and the city of Toronto acquired the Toronto Electric Light Company's rival distribution system, at a price to be settled by arbitration.[51] In this way the city obtained a monopoly of public transportation and electricity distribution within its boundaries, and the publicly owned Hydro-Electric Power Commission was in a position to create a provincewide power grid.

What influence did ownership or type of regulation have upon fares? The federal Department of Railways and Canals began collecting systematic figures on tram fares from street railroads across Canada in 1913. In the 1920s the fledgling Dominion Bureau of Statistics (DBS) reworked this data, compiling tables of nominal fares and index numbers for each province. Unfortunately, this method of aggregating the data at the provincial level partially obscures the situation in the cities we have been observing. Nevertheless, since DBS used a weighted average biased by the number of riders at each fare level, the data do reflect changing fare patterns in the major cities.

A Dominion Bureau of Statistics *Occasional Paper* in 1927 showed that in most provinces fares remained fairly stable until 1919, when steep upward revisions began. Ontario is an exception to this generalization because average fares did not shoot up until 1922, following the takeover of the Toronto Railway Company by the city in that year. Up to that point Toronto's insistence that the company stick to the letter of its contract served to keep fares lower than the national average. Once the street railway came under public control, however, the fares rose more rapidly in Ontario than in most other jurisdictions. The other exceptions to this trend were the largely publicly owned systems in Alberta and Saskatchewan, where fares started to mount as early as 1915.

The data presented in Table 30 compare all street railway fares to the Canadian average of 1913. As a result of this recalculation of the DBS figures, it is possible to compare fares between provinces as well as within provinces over time. Fares increased most in Nova Scotia; at almost the same rate in Quebec, Ontario, and the prairie provinces; and least in New Brunswick and British Columbia. The differences are too small to place much weight upon; nevertheless, the data suggest that whatever the other virtues of public ownership, it did not have much bearing upon fares—except to facilitate more rapid increases to keep pace with rising costs as can be seen from the Alberta, Saskatchewan, and Ontario information. British Columbia fares remained well above the national average throughout the period, but having started at an initially higher level, fares did not then increase at the same rate as in other provinces. In short, the somewhat chaotic regulatory situation in British Columbia may have resulted in fares rising sooner and higher than most other provinces, though the overall increase was lower. The service-at-cost contract in effect in Montreal, which can be seen operating upon the Quebec average and index numbers, seems to have held fares near the national average for the whole period but helped to increase them more sharply during the crisis of 1919. The most

TABLE 30
COMPARATIVE STREET RAILWAY FARES, 1913–26
(Canada 1913 = 100)

	1913	1917	1919	1920	1921	1922	1924	1926	Increase
CANADA	100	100	111	119	121	140	142	142	+ 42
PROVINCES									
Nova Scotia	104	102	102	126	145	142	164	176	+ 72
New Brunswick	111	109	140	145	166	140	130	140	+ 29
Quebec	104	104	119	140	145	145	145	147	+ 43
Ontario	95	95	97	92	92	135	138	138	+ 43
Manitoba	97	92	119	133	142	140	140	140	+ 43
Saskatchewan	102	107	116	133	145	147	147	147	+ 45
Alberta	97	104	126	130	138	138	135	138	+ 41
British Columbia	121	123	152	152	154	152	152	150	+ 29

Source: Dominion Bureau of Statistics, Internal Trade Branch, *Street Car Fares and Index Numbers* (Ottawa: King's Printer, 1927), 62-D-96.

significant price changes occurred in Nova Scotia, where rate-of-return regulation was administered by a Public Utilities Commission. After 1923 utilities were permitted an 8 percent return on capital invested, and it is likely that the substantially higher fares after 1922 are a reflection of the operation of this extremely generous policy.

Everywhere fares increased, usually at about the same rate, and to about the same levels. Public ownership did not necessarily hold fares lower than private operation, and there is a slight suggestion that absolute public control facilitated closer adjustment of fares to rising costs. In all provinces but Nova Scotia, fares stabilized after 1922 and remained more or less constant for the remainder of the decade.[52] Thus the type of regulation was probably a less influential factor in rate-making than such matters as city size (scale), local costs, and perhaps the extent of radial railway development. Here again Ontario before 1922 (thanks to Toronto's refusal to recontract) and Nova Scotia after 1922 (with rate-of-return regulation) would be polar exceptions.

_____
_____ Regulatory politics in Ontario followed a course different from that of Quebec, Manitoba, or British Columbia. Whereas conflict between cities and their utilities usually led to provincial intervention and resolution by third-party arbitration, in Ontario the province stood aside and let the dispute between Toronto and its street railway wind to its bitter conclusion. Then, driven by a determined public entrepreneur, the province supplied the credit necessary to swallow up the remaining pieces of the private system into Hydro's monopoly.

Elsewhere, as we have seen, provincial mediation helped protect private enterprise during a dangerous moment. It would be overstating the case, however, to label this a "capture" of the regulatory process by the owners of capital. Legislatures were not bought and governments were not overtly "cliental," nor were regulators unduly influenced by the companies. Rather, there was something about the choice of regulatory instrument itself that helped determine the outcome. The boundaries of a likely settlement were laid down by the province in interposing a new professional class of commissioners between the combatants. Regulators, employing bureaucratic accounting procedures, began by accepting the legitimacy of the contending interests and set about trying to find a rational basis to accommodate rival claims. Regulators accorded companies legitimacy, and that was more than half the battle. The doctrine of "fairness" embodied this principle. Capital did not have to control directly, or try to suborn, regulatory commissions staffed or supported by professional bureaucrats, whose view of the world already admitted of the possibility that private capital could be made to serve public interests.

In Ontario, on the other hand, it was the legitimacy of private capital in this sector itself which was at stake in a protracted political struggle.

Something like a zero-sum game developed at *both* the municipal and provincial levels. No professional arbitrator could negotiate a compromise as long as the province, through the Hydro-Electric Power Commission, had an interest in the outcome.

The route to accommodation passed through different regulatory forms in the cases we have examined, but in most places the outcome was the same—the preservation of private capital and a renewal of the contract. The important exception was Ontario, where capital was denied provincial mediation, and a grim dialectic gave rise to an alternative regulatory regime: public monopoly.

Rates and Regulation

The telephone industry in Canada experienced cost pressures similar, though not identical, to those that affected street railways during World War I. In an interesting contrast to the United States, the telephone system was not commandeered by the federal government to further the war effort, as happened on orders from the Wilson administration between August 1, 1918, and July 31, 1919. Thus the direct impact of the war was confined to a loss of skilled manpower to the armed forces and the steeply rising cost of labour and materials. Both public and private telephone systems were acutely affected by these dramatic cost increases, which coincided with the need to raise new capital for expansion and modernization. The only escape from this difficulty lay in increasing revenue which, of course, required the approval of the industry's regulators.

The Bell Telephone Company, serving Ontario and Quebec, took its case to the federal Board of Railway Commissioners, while the other systems, public and private, were dealt with by provincial authorities. This round of applications and hearings made clear the legitimizing effects of regulation: tribunals granted most of the increases requested, despite strong protests from municipal leaders. Regulators argued that subscribers should pay rates that would fully cover costs and generate enough surplus to permit renewal and expansion.

Both public and private undertakings were subject to certain inescapable constraints: rural service was bound to be expensive; large systems could operate more efficiently than small ones and so charge lower rates. While regulation and public ownership had their effects, these were neither so simple nor so striking as some of their early-day proponents had expected.

Federal regulation most certainly worked to protect the interests of the Bell Telephone Company and its shareholders. Since the first rate case in 1907 the Board of Railway Commissioners had consistently found in favour of the company. In 1911, as we have seen, the board had approved an interconnection fee for independents in the Ingersoll case. In 1911, 1912, and again in 1915, the board approved Bell Telephone's rates in hearings prompted by complaints from the cities of Toronto and Montreal.[1] On the strength of a steadily growing demand, in the absence of serious competition, and with the congenial protection (and noninterference) afforded by federal regulators, the Bell Telephone Company greatly increased both its business and its profitability in the years before 1914. Large surpluses were reinvested and reserve accounts expanded to keep the dividend down to 8 percent. Share prices nevertheless reflected the appreciation of assets and earning power. New Bell Telephone stock issued at $100 in 1911 traded between $148 and $153, and a further flotation in 1913 fetched from $152 to $172 a share on the open market.[2]

During the war the Board of Railway Commissioners relented somewhat on the matter of compensation for interconnection with independent companies. Parliament eventually amended the federal Railway Act to authorize the board to order such connections and to determine suitable charges, *if any*.[3] But by this time a loss of legislative protection against marginal competition was largely irrelevant, and was so regarded by the company. Bell had already established unshakable hegemony in the major urban markets of central Canada.

Until this time the Bell Telephone Company had appeared at the hearings to defend itself against criticism and complaints about its high charges from customers, competitors, or aggrieved municipalities. A looming financial crisis in 1918, however, brought the company before the board for the first time in the unaccustomed role of petitioner, asking for a general rate increase. Over the next few years this would become a habit.

From 1914 through to the end of 1917 the Bell Telephone Company had been able to absorb the rather modest increases in costs that it encountered. Rising revenues meant that the company was able to maintain an operating ratio (expenses as a percentage of revenues) that changed little through 1917 (see Table 31). In the last year of the war, however, inflation finally caught up with the company as expenses shot up to consume 86.2 percent of revenue. Over the summer of 1918, as the directors nervously observed growing union activity among their employees in Toronto and Hamilton and voted raises totalling $1,270,000 in September to prevent work stoppages, they decided that the time was ripe to apply to the Board of Railway Commissioners for a general rate increase of 20 percent.[4]

Thus on January 8, 1919, Chief Commissioner H. L. Drayton and the full board opened hearings in Ottawa on the Bell application. AT&T executives in New York and Boston, who had had considerable experience with state public utilities commissions in the U.S., had suggested asking for simple percentage increase on all rates to cope with an emergency rather than

TABLE 31

BELL TELEPHONE PERFORMANCE, 1913–18

	Operating Ratio	Net Income / Revenue
1913	79.1%	21.9%
1914	80.5	19.5
1915	78.3	21.7
1916	77.5	22.5
1917	78.1	21.2
1918	86.2	13.8

Source: Board of Railway Commissioners, *Judgments, Orders, Regulations and Rulings* (Ottawa: King's Printer, 1922), vol. 11, p. 69.

undergoing the contentious and time-consuming process of valuing assets to derive a "scientific" rate of return. In short, Bell wanted it both ways: it sought a generous return on its capital, but it did not want to be tied down to a rigid formula.[5]

Lawrence Macfarlane and Glyn Osler were retained to make the plea that sharply rising costs, wages, taxes, and interest rates had suddenly combined to compel the company to seek emergency relief. Their difficulty was that the company's data through 1917 failed to demonstrate the existence of serious financial difficulties, and the more ominous 1918 results were not complete when the lawyers had to marshal their evidence before the board. Osler and Macfarlane had to strain mightily to persuade the commissioners that even a small difference in the ratio of earnings to assets required a large change in the rates. In the end Bell argued that rising labour and materials costs had forced price increases in almost every sector of the economy; surely, therefore, the telephone company deserved some consideration too. C. F. Sise made much of the fact that he knew of no other industry where prices had remained fixed for over 30 years. If the figures did not prove that the company required higher revenues, surely common sense and business judgement did. In his summation, Glyn Osler attempted to address this fundamental weakness of the Bell argument:

> Taking the whole case, I submit that the company has demonstrated that while there is not perhaps an emergency in the sense that the company is likely to go into liquidation tomorrow if this increase is not granted, there is an emergency in the sense contemplated by the authorities in the United States, that is to say, the service has reached a point where it will require money for extensions, and if that new money is not provided the service will be starved.[6]

Thus the Bell Telephone Company asked the Board of Railway Commissioners to share its apprehensions about a fiscal crisis.

Toronto and Montreal both retained telephone experts who submitted complicated briefs refuting or qualifying Bell's contentions.[7] Throughout the hearings the municipal intervenors stressed three essential points: first, there was no emergency; second, even if there should be one, the company had ample financial reserves to handle it; third, Bell could get along quite nicely with the existing rates if it simply lowered its excessive depreciation charges. "They are crying before they are hurt," I. S. Fairty claimed on behalf of the city of Toronto. "In 1918 after paying the bond interest, after paying an eight percent dividend, and after maintaining all these reserves, the company will have an undivided profit of about a quarter of a million dollars." Did that mean that Bell must wait until it was ruined before it applied for a rate increase, asked Macfarlane? Whereupon Chief Commissioner Drayton unexpectedly interjected:

> Drayton: No. When you boil the whole thing down it comes to this, that you show a surplus account of $3,200,000 against which at present there is no charge . . . and that surplus account might well be used, unapplied as it is to any purpose, in discharging your interest and dividend liability until the situation is further developed. That is practically Mr. Fairty's position? Is that right?
> Fairty: Yes.
> Drayton: That is the whole thing.[8]

Over the years Bell had built up various huge reserve funds, supposedly to cope with contingencies of this sort. Why not use them, asked a lay observer from Montreal:

> As a common citizen and not as an engineer, it does seem strange that a company which has lived in opulence in regard to its dividends on its stock issues, a company which has put aside $10,000,000 on Reserves, that has built up a plant which exceeds its book value, cannot for a short time during a strenuous period such as we have had get along without an increase. They should take the bitter with the sweet.

The Bell lawyers argued that while surplus accounts had been accumulated, the actual money itself had been reinvested in the business rather than in easily liquidated assets. This was a perfectly proper business practice from which telephone users had benefited in the form of a more rapidly growing service than would otherwise have been the case.[9]

Depreciation was the crux of the matter for the municipal critics. Francis Dagger, appearing for Toronto, insisted like others that Bell Telephone's 6.573 percent average annual depreciation rate across its entire plant was about 50 percent higher than need be. E. W. Bemis, the renowned U.S. utilities expert, weighed in to testify that independent companies in the Midwest charged much lower rates and had accumulated reserves about half those of Bell. Besides, he argued, the only scientific means of determining an appropriate revenue requirement was through an appraisal of the company—precisely what Bell Telephone was earnestly hoping to avoid.[10] For days, the hearing degenerated into a discussion of abstruse theories of depreciation, the rates allowed by other regulatory bodies, and the propriety of Bell's deductions compared with those of other systems in Canada and the United States. The cities insisted that if Bell lowered these unusual expenses it would have more than enough income to meet its obligations without increasing its rates.

Several noteworthy events broke the monotony. The commissioners were completely unmoved, and sometimes even hostile to anything verging upon a "political" argument. To T. G. Meredith's assertion that there would be "a great howl" from the public if the commission allowed the rate increase, Drayton shot back: "That would be unfortunate, it might be almost as bad as the situation in Manitoba"; he meant the complete government monopoly there, not popular discontent. F. R. Waddell, appearing for the city of Hamilton, fared no better with an implied threat that labour would not tolerate a ruling favourable to Bell and in his city would likely insist upon municipal ownership for better, or more likely for worse: "People down here do not know the labour people as well as I do. . . . It is a critical time with labour, and we should try and keep people in ordinary circumstances from kicking over the traces." The commissioners also heard W. D. Lighthall's testimony on behalf of the Union of Canadian Municipalities with ill-disguised impatience. When he rambled on about the regulation of near-monopolies, Commissioner S. J. McLean cut him short; that line of argument belonged in another forum. When he warned the commission against applying precedents from the United States developed under a legal system where the confiscation of private property was prohibited while in a Canadian situation such judicial injunctions did not apply, the commissioners unkindly pointed out that his own argument relied rather heavily upon U.S. authorities.[11] By 1919 W. D. Lighthall was an anachronism. In quasi-judicial proceedings of this sort there was no place for populists or idealists—only for accountants, engineers, and lawyers.

The most surprising testimony came from a quite unexpected quarter. W. H. Butler submitted, without first reading it, a detailed brief drawn up for the city of Montreal by the noted consulting firm of Hagenah & Erickson of Chicago. Close scrutiny showed that it made a better case for a rate increase than the Bell application. W. G. Hagenah himself collapsed under the nervous strain of cross-examination, and thereafter the municipalities—including Montreal, which had paid for the report—totally disassociated themselves from his findings. Bell, on the other hand, capitalized upon this embarrassment and quoted from the document with great effect.[12]

Before the hearings ended, the commissioners gave at least one clue as to the direction of their thinking. During I. S. Fairty's concluding argument, as he reviewed the way in which the word "emergency" had been narrowly construed in 20 recent cases before U.S. courts and public utilities commissions, Commissioner McLean interrupted him to ask: "Would it be a fair summary of the decisions you have read if we say that where an emergency exists as defined by you, division [of the burden] is a fair principle?" To which Fairty conceded: "Yes, to a certain extent."[13]

As it turned out, McLean wrote the principal judgement in a unanimous ruling awarding Bell Telephone a 10 percent rather than 20 percent rate increase. Once the full 1918 statement became available, it could readily be seen that Bell's revenues had increased by 9.38 percent over 1917, but since its expenses were up 16.8 percent, net earnings were down 21.85 percent. And during the first two months of 1919, Bell reported, its operating ratio rose slightly above 90 percent. In short, McLean concluded: "There is such an emergency as justifies aid by way of increased returns being allowed so that the company may be able to meet increased operating costs, meet its service requirements, and be in such a position as will enable the necessary reconstruction and extensions to be made." The commission calculated, allowing for a 5.7 percent depreciation rate, that the company needed an additional $1,550,000—half of what Bell had applied for. Moreover, under the circumstances such an outcome had the additional virtue of fairness: "The burden of the emergency should be divided between the Bell Company and the public."

Commissioner A. C. Boyce's supporting judgement went furthest toward convoluted admission that it was the board's duty to ensure Bell sufficient revenue to guarantee its long-term financial security:

> The functions of this Board are, as I take it, upon an application of this kind, first to endeavour to protect the public interests. Concern for the welfare and profit of the shareholders of the private corporation operating that utility is an incident only so far as it is necessary to safeguard the public interests, having regard to the palpable truth of the proposition, which cannot be questioned, that if the rates and tolls charged for the service given by that public utility do not provide as well for all operating and other expenses, and a safe reserve to provide against depreciation, and to insure the efficient maintenance of its plant, a fair margin of profit on the money invested by its shareholders, the rates and tolls are inadequate for the service of the public by such utility, and a revision should be made after careful scrutiny of the position of the company. That provision should be made, not in the interests of the shareholders, except incidentally, as above, but of the public, whose interests are to suffer by the weakening of the company by the adverse conditions mentioned, endangering the breaking down or impairment of the service in which the public is interested. The interests of the public are not distantly related in this respect to those of the shareholders.

Boyce followed up this strong statement of identity between the public interest and profitable private operation with a defence of the depreciation rates charged by Bell, the absolute size of its reserve accounts, and the policy of reinvesting those funds in the business.[14]

Thus in 1919 the Bell Telephone Company succeeded in its primary goal of obtaining a rate increase without having to undergo a complete valuation of its property. It also received strong moral support from its regulator in a time of uncertainty. But to do so it had to argue for relief on the basis of a temporary emergency. The Board of Railway Commissioners was prepared to accept that argument, but as a matter of equity it insisted upon dividing the burden of the emergency between the company and its customers, with the result that Bell obtained only half of the increase it had requested.[15]

While the municipalities appealed what they considered an overly generous decision to the federal cabinet, the directors of the Bell Telephone Company gathered in Montreal to consider preliminary data that forecast a deficit of $223,762 for the current year, even with the 10 percent increase. The company's problems were compounded by the fact that a $4.5 million stock offering in 1919 also exhausted the limit of its share issue. To raise new money, it would have to obtain the permission of parliament, something it had not had to do since 1906. Beyond that, if Bell hoped to sell any additional shares, something would have to be done to improve its net earnings.[16]

Once more the officers of the Canadian company repaired to New York to consult AT&T about strategy. The heads of several AT&T operating companies lent experts who descended upon Montreal to investigate the possibility of a quick analysis of the company's assets to arrive at a temporary valuation for rate-making purposes. This was not the most desirable course as far as Bell was concerned, and these plans were dropped following an informal meeting between the company's lawyer and two members of the Board of Railway Commissioners. Following Lawrence Macfarlane's explanation of the cost and the necessary delay involved in conducting a satisfactory valuation, the Chief Commissioner, he reported, "intimated that our case, which might be heard in January, could be presented without a prior investigation." Bell's directors then resolved to petition parliament to increase the company's capitalization to $75,000,000 and "immediately after our bill is assented to we will go to the Board of Railway Commissioners for a hearing in the matter of an increase in our rates." A private member's bill was introduced late in the spring of 1920, passed with surprisingly little debate, and received Royal Assent on June 16, 1920. At the next Board of Railway Commissioner meeting in July, the directors made formal application for a hearing.[17] Thus even before the Privy Council had disposed of the appeals arising from the last case, Bell was boldly asking for additional income.

The second round of hearings commenced in September, 1920, and the Commissioners rendered their unanimous judgement on April 1, 1921. Bell asked for permission to introduce installation charges, long distance toll increases, and measured service in the larger urban markets. Counsel for the Bell Telephone Company sought to demonstrate that the 1919 increase had not been sufficient to meet the company's requirements. Glyn Osler laid great emphasis upon the need for earnings sufficient to raise new capital, as suggested by the drift of the 1919 judgement. The recent earnings of the company, he pointed out, made it impossible to raise the vast quantities of new investment required, a sum estimated to be in the range of $30,000,000 over the next three years. The division of the burden of inflation in 1919 had effectively discouraged investors, who would not put their money into a company that had not fully earned its 8% dividend in 1920.[18]

Critics contended once again that the company could overcome most of its temporary difficulties by reducing its excessive depreciation rate and drawing down its contingency reserves. Heretofore, the company had experienced little difficulty in disposing of its stock which still traded above par. Of course the cities raised a chorus of alarm about measured rates. If customers were required to pay for each call, counsel for the city of Toronto calculated, some business rates would rise to over $5,000 per month.[19]

The Board of Railway Commissioners' ruling, again written by S. J. McLean, gave Bell Telephone most, but not all, of what it had requested. The company received permission to raise its local rates an average of 10 percent and its long distance tolls by 20 percent, and to impose service charges for installations and repairs. On the other hand, the commission rejected the proposal to introduce measured telephone service in the major cities, and it reduced the permissible depreciation rate to 4 percent for ratemaking purposes. As the municipalities again made preparations to appeal the decision to the federal cabinet, Bell executives calculated that these changes would bring in an additional $2,100,000 annually, on the strength of which the board of directors authorized a huge stock issue.[20]

Less than six months later, Bell Telephone was back before the Board of Railway Commissioners asking for a third rate increase. Since the appeal on the last application had yet to be heard, the municipalities raised a tremendous hue and cry, but Bell pressed ahead. The stock issue had not gone well over the summer of 1921. Apart from AT&T, only 28 percent of the company's registered shareholders had taken up their allotment. Underwriters reported resistance to Bell shares because the regulatory agency had not provided the company with sufficient income to guarantee a proper rate of return. With the cities and customers clamouring for extensions to the service on the one hand and investors withholding their capital on the other, the Bell Telephone Company decided it had no choice but to proceed with another unpopular application.[21]

The third rate case was distinguished from the two preceding ones mainly by the fury of the intervenors, their evident hostility toward the company and even toward the commission itself. The cities were firmly convinced that the commission had been too compliant in the past, too willing to see the Bell Telephone point of view. The lawyer representing the province of Ontario, R. A. Reid, began by charging the chairman of the hearing, F. B. Carvell, a former director of the New Brunswick Telephone Company, with a conflict of interest: surely it was "highly improper" for someone who until recently had shared decision-making responsibility with C. F. Sise and Lawrence Macfarlane now to sit in judgement on their rate application. Carvell, his pride wounded, indignantly refused to step down, but in defending himself and in his conduct of the proceedings he did nothing to allay suspicions about his impartiality. This running feud, charged with a good deal of personal animus, introduced some electricity into the ritualistic regulatory discourse. On October 11, for example, Reid claimed "that the general opinion abroad in the country, and my own personal opinion, is that the Chairman, either consciously or unconsciously, is obsessed with pro-corporation ideas and anti-public ideas, and ideas that pertain to bloated monopolies such as the Bell Telephone Company, that I am afraid he cannot see our side of the case at all."[22] After a day of this sort of allegation and charges that "you are sleeping with them (Bell Telephone) and one and indivisible with them," Carvell grumbled openly about young men who make "violent attacks in public places" for their own "self-gratification." On December 21, as Reid read out a long list of information which had not been supplied and without which the commissioners could not possibly arrive at a proper verdict, Carvell interjected: "You do not need anything, Mr. Reid, to complete your education except about five years trying to finance a public utility corporation which is now struggling along, trying to give good service on insufficient funds." Reid had in effect put the commission on trial.[23]

Otherwise it was business as usual. The cities complained of the indecent haste of the application, manipulated the figures to their advantage, demanded more information about the financial relations of Bell and Northern Electric, argued that the long-admitted irrationality of the company's rate structure should be addressed before another ad hoc increase worsened the situation, and mocked Bell's apparent reluctance to face the rate question squarely. Counsel for the city of Toronto observed in a review of Bell's tactics in previous rate cases that the company preferred "to get one little patch on here; come back to you again and again, just so long as they think they can get a few hundred thousand or $1,400,000 out of you." Nevertheless, neither side strongly argued for a valuation of the corporate assets to determine a precise rate base. Glyn Osler simply insisted that the last rate increase had not delivered enough income for Bell, that there were 16,000 households waiting for service the company could not supply, that the recent stock issue had been a failure, and that the company would continue to experience difficulty raising new capital for expansion until it received additional revenue.[24]

Close observers of the hearings might have expected that Commissioners Carvell and McLean would conclude that the evidence demonstrated a $600,000 shortfall in Bell Telephone Company receipts, which the Board of Railway Commissioners was duty-bound to alleviate. The surprise came when the three other commissioners disagreed. Commissioner Boyce, who drafted the majority ruling rejecting the Bell application for an across-the-board increase, contended that this modest deficiency ought to be repaired by internal operating economies rather than rate increases. "The conclusion I arrive at on the above facts," Boyce wrote, "is that the telephone company did not, before launching this application, so readjust its business, and institute proper and reasonable economies as would in their result have shown that the temporary increase granted in April was sufficient to enable it to carry on without any further increase until a stable rate schedule could be prepared for approval of the Board." Boyce went on to chastise Bell for its less than candid presentation of the evidence and for pursuing the "temporary emergency" strategy to the point of "pure fiction."

> The telephone company . . . has not produced any satisfactory evidence to this Board that the proposed tariffs are such as would be suitable, just, and reasonable . . . in the various areas referred to. The same inequalities and discriminations appearing in the former tariffs in the same places (with the exception of Montreal and Toronto), and commented upon in the judgement of this Board, and admitted by the company, appear in these tariffs. There seems to have been no effort . . . to adjust the rates in any scientific way to the value of the telephone service to the subscriber, having regard to the population of the telephone area, the number of stations, or the cost of service therein. The proposed rate increases, over the present rates in those places, serve to accentuate the inequitable and obsolescent features of the existing rate.

This curt rejection ended the regular pilgrimages of the Bell Telephone Company to Ottawa for rate increases. A revival of business, a stabilization of wages, and unexpectedly buoyant revenues from existing rates removed that necessity. Bell now realized that it could not cry "emergency" indefinitely but would henceforth be expected to defend its rates both by comparison with other service and commodity charges and with reference to the "reasonableness" of its rates "as a tax upon the people who ultimately pay."[25]

Nevertheless, the essential task had been accomplished. Bell's rates had already been jacked up 20 percent in all, and income had risen sufficiently to bring the operating ratio back into line. And the company had not been required to submit to a costly valuation procedure or tie itself down to a rigid revenue-producing formula. The Board of Railway Commissioners had proved cooperative at a critical juncture.

—————— Of course, a significant portion of the Canadian telephone industry remained provincially regulated. In Nova Scotia and New Brunswick, commissions supervised the affairs of privately owned Bell affiliates. On the prairies the provincial governments regulated the telephone business through ownership. These quite different regulatory regimes all had to cope with inflation after 1917.

Prewar regulatory agencies had done little to modify private rates or limit the earnings of the companies. Even on the prairies the Bell Telephone rate schedule survived the transition from private to public management. When asked by a Toronto lawyer for a comparison of telephone rates before and after the government takeover, the Premier of Saskatchewan replied: "I may state that the telephone rates now prevailing in Saskatchewan are the same as when the system was operated by the Bell Telephone Company."[26] This was largely true in Alberta as well. Manitoba flirted briefly with lower rates, only to suffer the embarrassment of having to raise them close to previous levels in 1912.

Among the regulatory commissions, only Nova Scotia instituted what had become the standard practice in the United States following *Smyth v. Ames.* There the first commissioners took as their starting point the observation that both courts and community sanctioned a policy of fixing telephone company revenues so as to provide a fair return on investment. That being the case, the commissioners first had to establish the extent of investment for rate-making purposes. Finding out just how much money had actually been put into the business was, the commissioners concluded, far too difficult: "Under the circumstances the only safe ground from which rate-making can start is the existing value of the property employed with the addition of such intangible capital as may be properly considered." Instead of historical cost, the commissioners would first establish the replacement cost of the principal telephone utility, Maritime Telephone and Telegraph. The fact that this simpler method of determining the value of the company took four years tended on balance to discourage this practice in Canada.[27]

〜 Neighbouring New Brunswick created a Board of Commissioners of Public Utilities at the same time as Nova Scotia but tried a different regulatory procedure. The New Brunswick commissioners began in 1911 by attempting to determine whether existing rates were "reasonable." In this the board followed the practice of the federal Board of Railway Commissioners by applying a modified adversarial procedure, calling critics of the New Brunswick Telephone Company's rates to make a case for reductions, while the company defended its tolls. H. A. Powell, representing the city of Saint John, argued that any regulatory body intent upon simulating the effect of competition upon a natural monopoly would insist that the company reduce its reserve funds, which served only "to conceal excess profits." The company lawyer began his defence with a frank statement of the underlying purpose of regulation: "The company welcomes the intervention of this Commission as it must inevitably prove a protection to the company and its shareholders. This has been the opinion of corporations wherever public utility commissions have been established."[28] He went on to defend the company's depreciation reserves, its accounting procedures, the quality of its service, and the fairness of its rates. As a result of these hearings, the board subsequently upheld the company's rate structure in all but one minor instance.[29]

Public and private companies both encountered the same cost spiral after 1917, and in each case the regulatory process acted to bring income into line with expenditures. The Nova Scotia Board of Public Utility Commissioners recalculated the Maritime Telephone and Telegraph Company's rate base and then authorized revenues designed to produce an 8 percent dividend, a level which the legislature subsequently enshrined for all provincial utilities by statute.[30] An adversarial rate hearing in New Brunswick concluded in 1920 with the observation by the chairman of the Board of Commissioners: "While there is no better asset a utility can have than a contented public, the converse is true, that the public cannot expect good service unless it pays adequate rates." With that the New Brunswick Telephone Company received permission to raise its rates and tolls to provide what was deemed to be a reasonable return on its investment.[31]

In Manitoba and Saskatchewan the publicly owned systems, too, wrung rate increases out of their respective provincial governments. The Alberta Government Telephone system, by contrast, kept its rates down by persuading the provincial government to vote it an annual $170,000 subsidy.[32] In 1916, British Columbia Telephone escaped from the unpredictable environment of control by the provincial government to the jurisdiction of the Board of Railway Commissioners by acquiring a federal charter. Thus when the company encountered difficulties in 1921 it was from Ottawa that it received authorization to increase its rates to meet its substantially higher costs.[33]

Everywhere, and at about the same time, telephone companies used the regulatory process to increase their incomes over costs by a sufficient margin to raise new capital. Clearly the Bell Telephone Company's success before the Board of Railway Commissioners served to justify and legitimize similar increases in other jurisdictions. Moreover, the regulatory process "worked" at another level: private companies negotiated a potentially dangerous confrontation with consumers, municipalities, and politicians sensitive to pressure without being seriously threatened by an expansion of public ownership.

In different ways and in different places, regulators strove for "fairness" in attempting to find the minimum rates at which the interests of consumers, companies, and investors most closely coincided. Consumers might complain of the result, but it was incumbent upon their representatives to present a case in language appropriate to the regulatory forum, to acknowledge the validity of the interests on the other side, and to frame counterproposals that could also be justified as equitable to capital. These procedural requirements of regulation helped shield private capital and provided it with the kind of moral leverage it would not otherwise have had in an open political arena. That would be regulation's lasting legacy.

In only one jurisdiction, Nova Scotia, did a regulatory agency first conduct a thoroughgoing analysis of the assets to be counted into the rate base before proceeding to a determination of revenue requirements. Elsewhere, both regulators and regulatees seemed to prefer the alternative method of establishing reasonableness and fairness through quasi-judicial adversarial hearings. Everyone shied away from the four-square rate-of-return regulation that was becoming standard practice in the United States. Instead of systematic appraisals and rationally constructed rate structures, Canadian participants chose more pragmatic, speedier, incremental arrangements to deal with what they preferred to think of as a temporary "emergency."

However messy or intellectually unsatisfying the procedure, the private telephone companies obtained what they desperately needed, higher earnings and long-term security. That they did so without acquiring open control over the regulatory process conferred that highly valuable intangible, legitimacy. It was perhaps just as well for Bell Telephone's longer-term interests that it lost the third rate case. Such demonstrations of independent judgement on relatively minor matters helped maintain public confidence in the impartiality of regulation, even though in fact, institutions ostensibly created to protect the public against monopolies had been converted into agencies to protect monopolies.

But it would be a mistake to conclude that the regulators had been captured by their clients. The very notions of equity and fairness that regulators brought to their mediating tasks required the survival, continuation, and if necessary the protection of private interests in the furtherance of the broader public interest. This was what set the regulatory process apart from the demands of the radical proponents of public ownership.

———————— It remains to examine the manner in which rates changed under different regulatory regimes. Did the kind of regulation have much apparent bearing upon charges? Did it matter whether a telephone system was publicly or privately owned, whether it was regulated by a federal or provincial commission, under tight or loose control?

Federal officials did not begin to collect comparative data on telephone use until 1919 and on telephone rates until 1925.[34] However, some isolated data for 1913 permit a limited comparison between average rates before the war and during the mid-1920s. In 1913 domestic telephone rates were highest in Manitoba, Quebec, and Saskatchewan and lowest in

Alberta. Ontario also enjoyed rates considerably below the national average. Thus both public and private systems were among the cheapest and the most expensive (i.e., high in Manitoba and Quebec, low in Alberta and Ontario). As can be seen from changes in the index numbers in Table 32, telephone rates rose from 1913 levels most steeply in Alberta, Manitoba, and Ontario. Quebec rates, which were among the highest at the beginning, rose least of all, followed by those in British Columbia. The index numbers in Table 33 have been calculated by using the Dominion Bureau of Statistics (DBS) data on a base of the 1913 national average as 100. This allows interprovincial comparisons during the interval: the variation in weighted averages by province in 1913 and 1926 can be seen more clearly, as can the pattern of relative change over the 13-year period. Average nominal rates increased by 20 points for the country as a whole but by only 6 and 9 points in Quebec and British Columbia respectively. The highest absolute rates were to be found in Manitoba, as well as one of the sharpest average rate increases; only the Alberta rate of change (from a much lower base) exceeded it. The privately owned systems in eastern Canada as a rule charged lower nominal rates in 1926 and received relatively smaller rate increases during this period.

On the prairies, where publicly owned systems pursued the expensive business of rural service—following, of course, their political mandate— customers had to pay at higher than average rates, and rate increases were generally largest. Alberta briefly charged lower than average rates before the war, but subscribers in that province had to make up for it with much higher rates in the 1920s. In effect, the commitment of the publicly owned systems to the provision of high-cost rural telephone service helped to make the rates charged by private companies in more urbanized provinces seem modest by comparison. Thus, in a quite unanticipated way, public ownership inadvertently contributed to the security of private enterprise elsewhere, for the heretofore hated monopolies did not charge the highest rates; to the regret of their managers, that distinction belonged to the publicly owned systems.

If the regulators made only a slight impact upon the rate-making process, what then did they control, if anything? This question might be rephrased to ask to what extent were regulators able to compensate for natural impediments to service created by geography and by regional, social, and economic differences as well as widely varying per capita incomes. Did public and private companies provide similar service everywhere, or were there differences?

As might be expected, telephone ownership was highly income-sensitive. Table 34 provides information on personal income by province, the number of domestic telephones per capita, and average monthy telephone bills per household for seven years following 1926, the first year for which reliable income statistics by province are available. Casual inspection

TABLE 32
DOMESTIC TELEPHONE RATES IN CANADA

	Number of Localities	RANGE OF MONTHLY RATES				AVERAGE RATES WEIGHTED BY NUMBER OF TELEPHONES				INDEX NUMBERS			
		1913	1925	1926	1927	1913	1925	1926	1927	1913	1925	1926	1927
Canada	74	1.25–2.50	1.50–3.17	1.50–3.17	1.50–3.17	2.01	2.40	2.42	2.59	100	119.4	120.2	128.8
Prince Edward Island	1	1.66	2.25	2.25	2.25	1.66	2.25	2.25	2.25	100	135.5	135.5	135.5
Nova Scotia	6	1.67–2.17	2.25–2.50	2.25–2.50	2.25–2.50	2.00	2.43	2.43	2.43	100	121.5	121.5	121.5
New Brunswick	3	1.67–2.50	2.25–3.00	2.25–3.00	2.25–3.00	2.16	2.75	2.75	2.75	100	127.3	127.3	127.3
Quebec	14	1.50–2.40[a]	1.85–2.46	1.85–2.46	1.85–2.75	2.31	2.42	2.42	2.67	100	104.8	104.9	116.0
Ontario	32	1.25–2.08	1.50–2.57	1.50–2.57	1.50–3.10	1.84	2.31	2.31	2.56	100	125.5	125.5	139.1
Manitoba	3	1.66–2.50	2.25–3.17	2.25–3.17	2.25–3.17	2.46	3.12	3.12	3.12	100	126.8	126.8	126.8
Saskatchewan	4	2.25	2.33 2.58	2.33–2.68	2.33–2.58	2.25	2.56	2.56	2.56	100	113.8	113.8	113.8
Alberta	5	1.25–1.67	2.00–2.50	2.50–3.00	2.50–3.00	1.67	2.50	2.81	2.81	100	149.7	169.4	169.4
British Columbia	6	1.50–2.00	1.65–2.00	1.65–2.00	1.65–2.20	1.98	2.17	2.17	2.17	100	109.5	109.5	109.5

Source: Department of Trade and Commerce, Dominion Bureau of Statistics, *Telephone Rates and Index Numbers in Canada* (Ottawa: King's Printer, 1927), 62-D-99.
[a] Approximate.

TABLE 33

INDEX NUMBERS OF WEIGHTED AVERAGE DOMESTIC TELEPHONE RATES
(Canada 1913 = 100)

	1913	1926	Increase
Canada	100	120	+ 20
Nova Scotia	99	120	+ 21
New Brunswick	107	136	+ 29
Quebec	114	120	+ 6
Ontario	91	114	+ 23
Manitoba	122	155	+ 33
Saskatchewan	111	127	+ 16
Alberta	83	139	+ 56
British Columbia	98	107	+ 9

Source: Department of Trade and Commerce, Dominion Bureau of Statistics, *Telephone Rates and Index Numbers in Canada* (Ottawa: King's Printer, 1927), 62-D-99.

suggests that overall telephone ownership increased and decreased (with a slight lag affecting the latter) with per capita income in all provinces. Much more rigorous statistical analysis confirms this first impression. Fully 98.7 percent of the variation in telephone ownership in Canada during these years can be accounted for by changes in income, time, and province. Of these three factors, income was by far the most important. Price, which remained more or less constant over the period, was accordingly of no significance in explaining variations.

Domestic telephones per capita were most numerous in British Columbia and Ontario, least numerous in Nova Scotia, New Brunswick, and Quebec (in ascending order); the three prairie provinces lay between these poles. In the West the number of domestic telephones per capita was highest in Saskatchewan and Alberta, lowest in Manitoba. Closer analysis of this data holding income, price, and time constant indicates that the provinces recorded the following number of telephones per capita above or below the Ontario level:

Nova Scotia	−0.064
New Brunswick	−0.059
Quebec	−0.053
Manitoba	−0.054
Saskatchewan	−0.038
Alberta	−0.053
Ontario	−0.000
British Columbia	+0.013

TABLE 34

INCOMES, TELEPHONES, AND PRICES IN CANADA

IPC=Personal Income Per Capita in $
TPC=Domestic Telephones Per Capita
RATE=Average Monthly Bill in $

| | NOVA SCOTIA | | | NEW BRUNSWICK | | | QUEBEC | | | ONTARIO | | | |
Year	IPC^a	TPC^b	$Rate^c$	IPC	TPC	Rate	IPC	TPC	Rate	IPC	TPC	Rate	Year
1926	291	0.075	2.43	278	0.074	2.75	363	0.094	2.42	491	0.169	2.31	1926
1927	299	na	2.43	276	na	2.75	377	na	2.67	512	0.175	2.56	1927
1928	324	0.078	2.43	294	0.079	2.75	402	0.104	2.67	540	0.183	2.56	1928
1929	334	na	2.43	300	na	2.75	424	na	2.67	569	0.189	2.56	1929
1930	318	0.084	2.43	280	0.082	2.75	394	0.111	2.67	532	0.190	2.56	1930
1931	269	0.091	2.43	238	0.083	2.75	336	0.105	2.67	453	0.181	2.56	1931
1932	217	0.064	2.43	286	0.076	2.75	272	0.095	2.67	366	0.166	2.56	1932

Year	MANITOBA			SASKATCHEWAN			ALBERTA			BRITISH COLUMBIA			Year
	IPC	TPC	Rate	IPC	TPC	Rate	IPC	TPC	Rate	IPC	TPC	Rate	
1926	464	0.111	3.12	438	0.125	2.56	489	0.117	2.81	535	0.188	2.17	1926
1927	419	na	3.12	448	0.129	2.56	559	0.119	2.81	549	0.197	2.17	1927
1928	486	0.118	3.12	468	0.132	2.56	500	0.123	2.81	585	0.208	2.17	1928
1929	307	0.119	3.12	309	0.134	2.56	424	0.124	2.81	611	0.212	2.17	1929
1930	423	0.116	3.12	263	0.107	2.56	387	0.119	2.81	557	0.216	2.17	1930
1931	321	0.105	3.12	159	0.090	2.56	276	0.096	2.81	468	0.185	2.17	1931
1932	279	0.096	3.12	161	0.079	2.56	234	0.085	2.81	386	0.171	2.17	1932

Source: Income data from *Historical Statistics of Canada* 2nd ed. (Ottawa: Statistics Canada, 1983), Series F 91-102; population estimates from *Population, 1921–1971, Revised Annual Estimates* (Ottawa: Statistics Canada, 1973), 91–512; telephones and rates from *Telephone Statistics* (Ottawa: Dominion Bureau of Statistics, annual), 56–202, and *Telephone Rates and Index Numbers in Canada* (Ottawa: Dominion Bureau of Statistics, 1927, 1931, 1933), 62-D-99.

[a]IPC = annual personal income per capita in $.
[b]TPC = domestic telephones per capita.
[c]Rate = average monthly bill in $.

British Columbia according to this standard comparison had 0.013 more telephones per capita than Ontario, and Nova Scotia 0.064 less. Perhaps the only surprising result of these calculations is the performance of Saskatchewan, where telephone ownership verges more closely upon the Ontario level than that of the prairie or eastern provinces. Something was obviously happening unrelated to income or rates charged which made telephone ownership more common in that province than in any others except Ontario and British Columbia.

The exceptional performance of the Saskatchewan telephone system in reaching a widely dispersed population can be seen as well in Table 35, which averages income, telephone, and rate data from the four pre-Depression years. In this table provincial per capita income, the number of telephones per capita, and telephone rates are expressed as a percentage of Ontario figures. Such a standard of comparison can be justified on the grounds that the public telephone movement in the West rested upon a desire to obtain telephone service as good as or better than that in central Canada. Once again the data reveal substantially lower incomes per capita east of Ontario and much lower per capita telephone use at roughly comparable monthly rates. Per capita income in the prairie provinces 21 and 7 percent lower than Ontario's generated a demand for telephone service between 35 and 28 percent of the Ontario standard. In British Columbia, higher incomes and significantly lower rates produced an effective demand for telephones 12 percent above Ontario levels. What is noticeable in this

TABLE 35

COMPARATIVE PERSPECTIVE ON INCOMES AND TELEPHONES IN CANADA, 1926–29

	Income per capita as % of Ontario	Telephones per capita as % of Ontario	Rate as % of Ontario
Canada	86.0	74.5	101.6
Nova Scotia	59.1	44.4	97.2
New Brunswick	54.5	43.6	110.0
Quebec	74.1	57.3	104.4
Ontario	100.0	100.0	100.0
Manitoba	86.3	64.8	124.8
Saskatchewan	78.7	72.2	102.4
Alberta	93.4	67.5	112.4
British Columbia	108.0	112.5	86.8

Source: See Table 34.

table too is that telephones were more numerous in Saskatchewan than might be expected on the basis of income alone. By contrast, telephone use was much lower in Alberta despite a much higher per capita income. Table 34 shows that telephone use remained abnormally high in Saskatchewan despite rapidly falling income during the first years of the Depression. Once people had their phones, they were reluctant to face the necessity of giving them up.[35]

On the strength of these statistics it might be argued that neither regulators nor private companies provided service in the three eastern provinces at rates commensurate with income. The same might be said of Alberta and Manitoba. The two public systems in those provinces did not penetrate their markets at levels more broadly than relative income levels dictated; in Alberta, performance was considerably below what might have been expected. Nevertheless, public ownership did succeed better in Saskatchewan than in the neighbouring provinces—and much better than the private systems in the East—in overcoming barriers to telephone use of geography, low density, and relatively low per capita incomes. To that extent, then, regulation did—or could, matter. Ownership and rates charged were of less importance than the effectiveness of the delivery system. Clearly, the Saskatchewan method of government control over major exchanges and trunk lines, linked to a network of government-aided rural cooperative companies, worked more effectively as an instrument of telephone diffusion than the centralized, wholly government-owned systems in Alberta and Manitoba or the lightly regulated private systems in the Maritimes and Quebec. Neither public nor private ownership necessarily maximized telephone utilization, however; that remained a matter of policy.

All telephone enterprises found the cost of rural service very heavy during the 1920s and were forced to modify their corporate strategies in order to cope with the problem. Bell Telephone had consented to sell its prairie system to the three governments in the first place because the cost of rural service prevented the company from realizing a satisfactory return on its investment. Bell preferred to concentrate upon the more compact eastern market and its lucrative long lines. While serving Quebec and Ontario, Bell retained a minority interest in Maritime Telephone and Telegraph and New Brunswick Telephone, leaving the far West to another private company.

The telephone industry demonstrated that a variety of organizational forms lay between the polar opposites of public enterprise. Having suffered defeat in the campaign for national public ownership of telephones around 1905, the municipal populists switched their sights to the provincial level. In 1912 the Ontario government revised its telephone legislation to permit the formation of so-called "municipal" systems. Devised by the redoubtable telephone "expert" Francis Dagger, these were not simply owned by the municipalities they served but were the property of local landowners. Dagger's plan made it possible for rural areas and small towns to establish over 100 such systems, overcoming the shortage of capital by having the municipalities borrow the money on the security of the subscribers' real estate.[36]

The proliferation of publicly owned systems in a province where Ontario Hydro was so successful seriously alarmed the management of the Bell Telephone Company, who feared that the provincial government might go further. And, indeed, municipal politicians repeatedly pressed Adam Beck to enter the telephone business. Uncharacteristically, he declined, perhaps recognizing that he already had enough to occupy him. After carefully studying the situation Bell's board decided upon a policy of cautious expansion, and in 1915 set aside a small fund for the acquisition of rural companies. The company's minute books for some years thereafter are quite regularly punctuated with announcements of purchases.[37]

In fact, though, the company had little to fear from the independents, because Bell's federal charter made it largely immune to provincial regulation or expropriation, and the Board of Railway Commissioners proved so sympathetic. As time went on, it dawned upon Bell's management that the independent telephone movement's promotion of cooperative and municipal ventures was actually benefitting the company by freeing it from pressure to serve marginal and unprofitable markets. In 1912, for instance, New Brunswick Telephone resolved "that an endeavour be made, where possible, to get farmers to erect their own lines and supply their own telephone instruments, and that an agreement be made with them to connect with the company's switchboard. This was deemed more profitable than a continuance of the Company doing the constructing."[38] By the mid-1920s, as a result, Nova Scotia and New Brunswick had significantly fewer telephones per capita than the national average.

After purchasing a number of companies, Bell reverted to a nonexpansionary policy in 1922. Having been turned down by the Board of Railway Commissioners for a third rate increase, the directors immediately approved the sale of a long list of rural lines and small exchanges. Again, the minute books reflect the change, recording the sale of scores of such marginal properties to independent companies or cooperatives. Now that the Railway Commissioners could order connections between independent companies and Bell's long lines and urban systems, the likelihood of agitation for a takeover of the company was much smaller.[39]

Public or private, all telephone systems had to face the fact the rural lines were not only expensive to build and maintain but once built generated little revenue. The private companies responded by shedding this load wherever possible. More surprisingly, the provincial systems on the prairies, where the problems were even more acute, followed suit during the 1920s—even though cheap rural service had been the *raison d'être* of public enterprise. As costs mounted, so did the pressure for economies, which were all the more difficult without the urban base and the long lines that sustained Bell Telephone.

Each of the western systems coped with the problem in a different way. Manitoba had created a centralized system, but rural expansion soon led to a financial crisis. Thereafter, the Manitoba Telephone Commission charged higher than average rates and relied a good deal upon subsidization of rural subscribers by city dwellers. In Alberta, too, rural construction costs provoked a financial crisis, an investigation, and during the 1920s the voting of an annual subsidy to hold down rates. Saskatchewan, the most cautious of the three, avoided what one scholar has described as "the suicidal policy" of having the province supply each farmer directly with telephone service. Instead, the government encouraged the farmers to serve themselves through the formation of locally owned and managed cooperatives, somewhat like Dagger's "municipals" in Ontario.[40]

Manitoba's effort to keep rural and urban phone charges on a par produced a crisis in 1930, by which time rural subscribers were covering less than half the cost of their service. Alberta found itself with the same problem as long distance revenues for Alberta Government Telephones fell off with the onset of the Depression, and its deficit mounted. With $8,000,000 tied up in rural service, either rates would have to be raised or unprofitable lines shuffled off. Finally, the government bit the bullet in 1934. Arguing that good roads, more travel, and the radio had reduced the farm telephone "to little more than a social convenience," the province began to promote the formation of rural mutual companies to take on the lines, which AGT sold at a substantial loss.[41]

The similar constraints under which both private and public enterprises operated brought them roughly into alignment on the issue of rural telephone service by 1930. Bell Telephone realized that it had little to fear from independents or even public enterprises that served only fringe areas and so could afford to sell off marginal properties at some advantage. Saskatchewan and Ontario pioneered in encouraging local mutuals and cooperatives in the country, and in due course this pattern was widely imitated elsewhere. Thus the telephone industry became a mixture of public and private enterprises, a mixture that endures to the present day. At the same time, the physical interconnection of farmer cooperatives and rural municipals with large urban-based systems like Bell to some degree rendered the issue of ownership irrelevant. More important was the fact that all telephone businesses found themselves operating under the same economic contraints and tended to behave in similar ways.

⸻⸻⸻   During the 1920s there occurred a kind of normalization of relations between public and private enterprises supplying the same services, and the antagonism that had marked the earlier dealings between the two segments of the industry declined. By 1930 this process, which affected not only technological but financial and organizational aspects, was well advanced in the telephone industry, because both technological and market forces seemed to demand it. By the time of the First World War it had become technically possible to transmit voice signals across the North American continent;[42] callers showed an increasing interest in such service, and supplying it required linking up regional networks so that signals could be interchanged. The first call between Montreal and Vancouver was made with much fanfare in 1916, but it used American long lines; there were no direct links even between the Maritimes and Quebec, between Ontario and Manitoba, or between Alberta and British Columbia at that time.

As interest in the idea grew, the newly formed Telephone Association of Canada began investigating an "all-Red" route on Canadian soil in 1921. By the mid-1920s the various provinces were linked together, but the quality of the lines was not such as to permit calls across Canada, so transcontinental long distance was still routed through the United States. A national telephone hookup was finally created for the diamond jubilee of Confederation on July 1, 1927, and the popular enthusiasm it engendered prompted the Telephone Association to commission Bell Telephone in 1928 to study the feasibility and cost of a coast-to-coast hookup. All the regional systems approved Bell's report in 1930, and work was begun on a $5,000,000 line. In 1931 the participators set up the TransCanada Telephone System as a cooperative venture to manage the traffic and divide the toll revenues amongst them when the line opened for business early in 1932.[43]

By that time one could reach almost any other telephone subscriber in the country, whether one paid one's bills to a farm cooperative, a provincially owned system, Bell, or some other private company like British Columbia Telephone (which in 1927 passed into the hands of Kansas City interests). With Bell as the benchmark and standard-bearer, all the instruments were becoming technically compatible with one another. The Trans-Canada Telephone System was the formal embodiment of this growing integration.

A clear sign that public enterprises were coming to view their activities in the same light as private companies was the grudging and gradual acceptance by the three prairie systems of accounting standards that included adequate provision for depreciation. By the 1930s all telephone systems were valuing their assets in roughly the same way, sharing the revenues they collected through the TransCanada Telephone system, and approaching technical and service problems from the same point of view. Over time, suspicion abated; vocabulary and equipment became more compatible; and a significant degree of functional integration between systems commenced, bridging different organizational styles.

By the 1920s the utilities of Canada had evolved into a form that would persist for several decades thereafter. Both technologically and organizationally, the industry had matured; change during the 1930s and 1940s would be steady and cumulative, unlike the rapid transformations that marked the first half-century of growth.

International transfers had rendered Canadian utilities technologically uniform with the United States. Nonetheless, as Thomas P. Hughes has observed of regional electricity supply networks elsewhere, differing "styles" emerged to distinguish the organizations from one another.[1] In Canada the key stylistic difference proved to be the shifts in the balance between public and private enterprise. In electricity supply, in street railways, and in telephones there were both private companies and public agencies of significant size by the 1920s. In some places they competed for business; elsewhere they carved up the market between them, formally or informally. By 1930 public and private undertakings had begun to link up in semiintegrated provincewide systems.

The economic impact of these service industries may be gauged by noting the very large sums of capital invested. Electricity supply was particularly capital-intensive: by the beginning of 1918, when accurate statistics were first collected, equipment with a rated generating capacity of 2,300,000 horsepower had been installed at a cost of $356,000,000. By 1932, when the first detailed consumption figures became available, capacity had increased to over 8,000,000 horsepower and investment had almost quadrupled to $1,335,000,000 (see Table 36). The industry had become second only to railways in size of investment. By 1913 there were 500,000 telephones in service; the number reached 1,000,000 in 1923 and hit a pre-World War II peak of 1,400,000 in 1930 (see Table 37). The value of property and equipment employed had mounted from $34,700,000 in 1911 to

TABLE 36

ELECTRICAL GENERATING CAPACITY IN CANADA, 1918, 1933

	HORSEPOWER INSTALLED, JAN. 1, 1918[a]			HORSEPOWER INSTALLED JAN. 1, 1933[b]
	Central Stations	*Other*	*Total*	*Central Stations*[c]
PROVINCE				
P.E.I.	170	1,559	1,729	2,439
Nova Scotia	3,354	22,670	26,024	112,167
New Brunswick	6,878	7,991	14,869	133,681
Quebec	597,601	245,160	842,761	3,357,320
Ontario	791,163	193,897	985,060	2,208,105
Manitoba	64,100	12,072	71,172	390,925
Saskatchewan[d]	—	—	—	42,035
Alberta	32,580	300	32,880	71,597
British Columbia and Yukon	231,625	94,190	325,815	726,991
CANADA	1,727,471	577,839[e]	2,300,310	7,045,260

[a] The Dominion Bureau of Statistics began annual publication of *Central Electric Stations* (Ottawa: King's Printer) in 1918, providing the first national figures.

[b] *Central Electric Stations in Canada,* 1932, was the first to differentiate between residential, commercial, streetlighting, and large and small power users.

[c] *Central Electric Stations,* 1932, gives no figures for other electricity producers but notes that central stations produce 86% of all power so that total capacity was about 8,000,000 horsepower, with pulp and paper companies generating 6.5% of power and purchasing 35% of the output of central stations.

[d] Since there were utilities in the major Saskatchewan cities in 1918, the omission of that province is an obvious error although total production cannot have been very high.

[e] In 1917, pulp and paper companies produced 352,214 horsepower and purchased 100,000 horsepower from central stations.

$320,000,000 by 1930 when the largest firm, Bell Telephone, had assets of over $200,000,000.

Only the street railway segment of the industry experienced no real growth during the 1920s. The development of the trolley car was essentially complete by the time of the World War I. During the 1920s, competition from automobiles and motor buses ended the growth of ridership and system extension, although the decline was less severe in Canada than in the United States, owing to the smaller size of the cities and the slower adoption of the automobile. Nevertheless, from a peak of 800,000,000 riders in 1920, numbers slid to 725,000,000 in 1925. Despite a recovery to previous levels by 1928, the Depression of the 1930s prevented any further expansion of the industry. The greatest opportunities for growth lay in the con-

TABLE 37
TELEPHONE SERVICE IN CANADA, 1920–30

Year	Total Telephones	Business Telephones	Residential Telephones	Pole Line Mileage	Cost of Property & Equipment
1920	856,000	266,000	590,000	161,270	$144,560,969
1921	902,000	280,000	622,000	178,093	158,678,229
1922	944,000	289,000	655,000	184,147	167,332,932
1923	1,009,000	311,000	698,000	188,408	179,002,152
1924	1,972,000	305,000	767,000	193,399	193,884,378
1925	1,143,000	325,000	818,000	194,370	210,535,795
1926	1,201,000	341,000	860,000	201,604	227,155,900
1927	1,260,000	355,000	905,000	204,245	243,999,135
1928	1,335,000	377,000	958,000	207,566	263,201,651
1929	1,383,000	398,000	985,000	220,525	291,589,148
1930	1,403,000	406,000	997,000	222,113	319,101,191

Source: *Canada Year Book* (Ottawa: King's Printer, 1932), p. 614; M. C. Urquhart and K. A. H. Buckley, eds., *Historical Statistics of Canada* (Toronto: Macmillan, 1965), Table S323–331, p. 559.

struction of interurban railways, but the mileage in service reached a high point in Canada in 1917 and then began a steady decline that continued over the next 40 years before such lines disappeared altogether.[2] Sir Adam Beck's failure to persuade the government of Ontario to approve an ambitious system of radial lines fanning out from Toronto under the management of Ontario Hydro marked a serious setback for interurbans. Whether publicly owned—as in Edmonton, Calgary, Saskatoon, Regina, and Toronto—or under private control, street railways basically marked time. Capitalization grew slowly from $170,000,000 in 1920 to $220,000,000 by 1925, but thereafter the industry stagnated (see Table 38). By 1930, Bell Telephone alone was almost as large in investment terms as all street railways combined.

Public transit, a key element on the demand side of the electricity supply industry in its early days, thus dwindled into relative insignificance as a power consumer. By the 1920s, such industrial consumers as pulp and paper mills, mines, and electro-chemical plants had usurped that role. Street railways, which had once produced the cash flow needed to finance large-scale integrated utility companies, now became liabilities. Taken together, however, the electrical utilities had become in a surprisingly short time very big businesses by Canadian standards. As an employer of labour, a generator of income, and an absorber of investment funds, this sector became a major growth centre of the Canadian economy in the 1920s.[3]

TABLE 38

ELECTRIC RAILWAYS IN CANADA, 1920–30

Year	Passengers Carried	Total Car Miles[a]	Gross Earnings	% Expenses	Surplus (Deficit)	Capitalization[b]
1920	804,711,333	114,481,406	$47,147,245	79.16	$(2,421,286)	$170,826,404
1921	781,175,654	111,576,949	44,536,832	80.71	(2,472,634)	177,187,436
1922	738,908,949	116,711,189	49,660,485	72.47	89,557	188,258,974
1923	737,282,038	119,374,416	50,191,387	72.07	(545,637)	199,069,870
1924	726,497,729	119,803,072	49,439,599	73.07	(943,535)	213,767,660
1925	725,491,101	119,684,151	49,626,231	71.39	(1,294,519)	221,769,220
1926	748,710,836	122,935,055	51,723,199	70.48	(285,260)	215,808,620
1927	781,398,194	131,583,717	53,506,401	70.30	398,526	222,552,727
1928	808,023,615	133,689,589	55,632,761	69.71	30,278	221,302,236
1929	833,496,866	139,199,634	58,268,980	68.79	(1,310,780)	222,422,815
1930	792,701,493	140,014,000	54,719,258	71.50	(55,034)	224,089,539

Source: Dominion Bureau of Statistics, *Electric Railways of Canada,* 1922, 1926, 1931 (Ottawa: King's Printer, 1923, 1927, 1932).

Note: These totals include some interurbans.

[a] Includes mileage run for freight service.

[b] Stocks issued and funded debt.

Regions

ont.

During the 1920s, the regional electricity supply networks in Canada's two largest, most urbanized provinces displayed radically different organizational styles, one completely dominated by private enterprise and the other by a public monopoly. Each was a product of a carefully conceived corporate strategy that fit well with local conditions. The Ontario Hydro-Electric Power Commission was unique among North America utilities as the only regional electrical system under public ownership in the 1920s. The Hydro was very much the creation of one man, Sir Adam Beck, who remained its chairman until his death in 1925; its distinctive style was a partial reflection of his personality. A hard-driving "public entrepreneur,"[4] he left no doubt about his ambitions: in 1918, Beck told an American congressional committee, "We want to create a real monopoly."[5] By that date he had already acquired one of the three private generating stations at Niagara Falls and secured permission to commence construction of a huge new generating plant at nearby Queenston. After this opened in 1922, Beck devoted himself to rapidly expanding his system; by 1925, Ontario Hydro was producing 950,000 horsepower annually.

Beck proved phenomenally successful as demand for power grew—at the rate of 10 percent anually during the boom of the 1920s. Like other publicly owned systems, Ontario Hydro subsidized its voter-shareholders at the expense of other consumers.[6] Domestic customers were granted very low rates, probably below cost on certain classes of service. From an average of 2.1¢ per kilowatt hour in 1921, rates were steadily reduced to 1.5¢. Long before it was common elsewhere in North America, Beck began to promote rural electrification by paying half the cost of primary and secondary distribution lines to serve farm customers. At the same time industrial power rates were also kept comparatively low.[7] By 1932 almost 70 percent of all current from central stations in Ontario was used by large power consumers (see Table 39). Ontario Hydro supplied 75 percent of the electricity consumed in the province and was well on the way to eliminating its private rivals entirely.

The biggest problem that faced Beck and his successors, in fact, was securing enough power to meet demand.[8] The shortage reached such an acute stage after Beck's death in 1925 that the Hydro, with the approval of the provincial cabinet, signed power supply contracts with four private Quebec companies during the late 1920s. Altogether, the utility bound itself to take nearly 800,000 horsepower annually by 1936. Despite its traditional hostility to private utilities, Ontario Hydro's very success in marketing power bound it closely to the fortunes of these companies by 1930.

Beck had realized from the outset that his strength depended upon skilfully courting public opinion. That, in turn, demanded low domestic rates and extended rural service, even though this required cross-subsidization from other customers, a frequent cause of criticism. As a result, industrial power was not as cheap in Ontario as in Quebec (though it was still below levels in most other parts of North America), but by following this strategy faithfully, Hydro's management created by far the largest public enterprise in electricity supply in North America.[9]

In the neighbouring province of Quebec, Sir Herbert Holt displayed equal drive and determination in system-building with two great differences: his undertaking was privately owned, and he did not gain complete control of the provincial market. Rather a loose alliance of separate but interconnected companies supplied power in Quebec. Beginning with Montreal Light, Heat and Power, Holt forged a series of corporate interlocks with other companies, particularly Shawinigan Water and Power; in 1924 the two firms joined to purchase the Montreal Tramways Company. Shawinigan had already secured control of the troubled Quebec Railway, Light, Heat and Power Company, which served the provincial capital. Southern Canada Power, operating south of the St. Lawrence, purchased current from both Shawinigan and the Montreal company. In the late 1920s the Beauharnois Power Company was set up to construct a huge development on the St. Lawrence west of Montreal. Holt first secured an agreement that the new firm would not retail power in the city and ultimately procured a controlling interest when the company ran into financial difficulties.

Although electricity supply in Quebec thus came to be dominated by a

TABLE 39
ELECTRICITY CONSUMPTION IN CANADA, 1932
(in millions KWH, central stations only)

	KWH Available[a]	Domestic Service	Commercial Lighting	Small Power Users	Large Power Users	Streetlighting
PROVINCE						
P.E.I.	4,662	1,498	920	639	614	224
Nova Scotia	279,854	21,213	14,054	14,660	205,171	4,118
New Brunswick	421,142	19,230	12,364	5,898	355,687	2,882
Quebec	6,845,565	239,032	173,727	91,849	4,609,533	40,514
Ontario	5,250,962	912,169	362,300	239,000[b]	3,618,000[b]	119,000[b]
Manitoba	1,087,167	270,272	88,362	52,249	494,588	17,260
Saskatchewan	135,898	36,142	18,649	18,920	33,729	7,556
Alberta	197,395	29,792	24,137	30,418	61,563	7,520
British Columbia/ Yukon	1,170,273	110,150	72,809	5,520	748,847	19,180
CANADA	15,392,918	1,639,498	767,313	459,153[b]	10,127,732[b]	218,254[b]

Source: Dominion Bureau of Statistics, *Central Electric Stations*, 1932 (Ottawa: King's Printer, 1933).

[a]Some power was suppplied free and some lost in transmission so that the total of the five categories provided is less than the power available.

[b]Ontario failed to disaggregate the 3,976,493 million KWH supplied to small and large power users and for streetlighting in 1932; these estimates are arrived at by using the 1933 percentages: 6%, 91%, 3% respectively.

privately controlled monopoly, its internal organization differed significantly from that of Ontario Hydro. Where Beck created an integrated electrical system that generated most of its own electricity, transmitted it across country, and delivered it to local distribution systems or even directly to the farm gate, the organization over which Holt presided reflected greater specialization. Some firms like Shawinigan concentrated heavily upon primary production and wholesaled power to distribution companies like Montreal Light, Heat and Power. The latter, which had a reputation for being rather conservative and unadventurous technically, preferred to concentrate mainly upon retailing and rely upon Shawinigan, Cedar Rapids (a joint venture with Shawinigan), and Beauharnois to supply most of its bulk power. Thus while it operated as a system with provincewide scope, Quebec's power industry was less unified organizationally than Ontario's.

The availability of huge quantities of cheap hydroelectricity at ever-diminishing costs underlay Herbert Holt's corporate strategy. Domestic rates were reduced from 9¢ per kilowatt hour in 1910 to 3¢ by 1930, but costs fell so much more rapidly that this service remained immensely lucrative, and average domestic rates in Quebec remained twice as high as in Ontario (see Table 40). Less than 5 percent of power in Quebec was sold for nonindustrial purposes but produced between 30 and 35 percent of revenues. (In Ontario, by contrast, over 17 percent of power was used outside of industry and generated about 50 percent of total revenues.)[10]

TABLE 40

DOMESTIC ELECTRICITY SUPPLIES IN CANADA, 1932

	Average Consumption (KWH per capita)	Average Cost (per KWH)	Customers per 100 Population	Domestic Service as % of Provincial Consumption
PROVINCE				
P.E.I.	17	8.67¢	4.52	32.1%
Nova Scotia	41	5.66	9.05	7.6
New Brunswick	47	5.05	8.69	4.6
Quebec	82	3.43	13.26	3.5
Ontario	262	1.77	16.92	17.4
Manitoba	381	1.06	10.21	24.9
Saskatchewan	39	4.99	4.63	26.6
Alberta	40	5.75	7.76	25.1
British Columbia	156	3.04	17.88	9.4
Yukon				
CANADA	156	2.22	12.92	10.7

Source: Dominion Bureau of Statistics, *Central Electric Stations,* 1932 (Ottawa: King's Printer, 1933).

In response to the activities of Montreal Light, Heat and Power and its allies, a Quebec City dentist, Dr. Phillippe Hamel, launched an attack upon the "electricity trust" in the late 1920s and demanded public ownership. He secured some support from professionals, journalists, and politicians, but the only concrete result was the appointment of a provincial Royal Commission. Its report, issued in 1935, concluded that while the private utilities had been guilty of certain abuses, the remedy lay merely in tighter regulation by the Public Utilities Commission, a notoriously lenient body, rather than in public ownership. In Quebec the utility owners effectively managed the political process for private rather than public ends. By 1930, then, the regional electricity supply networks in the two major power markets, Ontario and Quebec, displayed radically different organizational styles, one completely dominated by interconnected private enterprises, the other by an integrated public monopoly.

The other province besides Quebec where private monopoly reigned almost unchallenged in electricity supply was British Columbia. The British Columbia Electric Railway Company succeeded not only in fending off all formal regulation in the early 1920s but in eliminating serious competition by acquiring both the Western Canada Power Company and the Bridge River Power Company. With lighting rates amongst the highest on the continent, the BCER achieved remarkable profitability. By the middle of the decade, returns on its various classes of shares ranged between 11 and 13 percent annually attracting the attention of a kind of industrial organization new to Canada: the utility holding company.

Power Corporation of Canada was organized in 1925 by Montreal stockbroker A. J. Nesbitt. Like other astute financiers Nesbitt recognized that holding companies offered economies of scale in the provision of technical, managerial, and financial services to a number of operating subsidiaries. The Royal Securities Corporation and its subsidiary, the Montreal Engineering Company, had pioneered such activities in Canada but in a much looser, less structured fashion than such American giants as the Electric Bond and Share Company or Stone and Webster, on which Power Corporation was more closely modelled. Moreover, the stock market boom of the 1920s had created an apparently insatiable appetite for new utility stocks, on which Nesbitt capitalized by acquiring substantial holdings in a number of electricity producers. In 1928 he entered into a bidding war for control of the BCER, and eventually Power Corporation won out. Because of his late entry into the game, however, Nesbitt was not able to profit as fully as his American counterparts did by pyramiding. The loose holding company, more closely resembling British corporate practice than U.S. or German experience, was as far as private entrepreneurs went in Canada in the organizational restructuring of the utilities sector.[11]

Regional electrical systems also evolved in other parts of Canada during the 1920s, but none was exclusively public or exclusively private. Instead, a series of hybrids often linked the two organizational forms together in a single network. Manitoba had a long tradition of support for public ownership, dating from the establishment of Winnipeg Hydro in 1906. When pressure from farm organizations led the provincial government to rush into construction of a long distance transmission line from the capital to the southwest in 1919, public power enthusiasts anticipated that a system like Ontario Hydro's would soon evolve. In fact, however, the private Winnipeg Electric Company continued to coexist alongside the public Winnipeg Hydro, and a kind of equilibrium developed that persisted for years.

The high cost of the transmission line dismayed the provincial government so much that by 1923, Premier John Bracken was contemplating its sale to private interests. To the chagrin of public ownership zealots, Bracken proved to be an instrumentalist: the state would perform certain functions only if private interests failed to act. When the public utility found itself short of power in 1925, it agreed to purchase current from the private company rather than construct a new generating station. At the same time a "power zoning" arrangement was worked out whereby the company exchanged its retail distribution system inside Winnipeg proper for the suburban lines of the municipal utility. By then the general strike of 1919 had rent the fabric of the city's political life asunder on class lines and left the business community much less enthusiastic than before about experiments with public ownership.

The existence of a new equilibrium was confirmed in 1928 when Bracken suddenly announced that the Winnipeg Electric Company would undertake the next major development at the Seven Sisters Falls on the Winnipeg River and supply the province with a large block of extremely low-cost power, which could be used to promote rural electrification. The public power forces reacted with surprise and dismay, including charges that bribery and corruption had been involved. In the end Bracken was compelled to appoint a Royal Commission in order to vindicate himself. The Premier clung to his conviction that the deal was "good business but bad politics. . . . If [the] people want poor business administration and [the] Gov't to play politics [they should] put someone else in power." Winnipeg Hydro had to be content with the much smaller Slave Falls site on the Winnipeg River for future expansion, while the private company went ahead with the much larger Seven Sisters development, which would likely meet provincial needs for a long time to come.[12]

After World War I, both Nova Scotia and New Brunswick created provincial electrical utilities modelled upon Ontario Hydro. These further examples of political entrepreneurship cultivated the popular feeling that cheap power would help to promote lagging industrial development. Despite this political intervention in the regional power markets, private utilities in Halifax and Saint John not only maintained but strengthened their positions.

Loaded up with debt by a group of Montreal speculators, Nova Scotia

Tramways and Power Company first secured a postponement of its highly speculative hydroelectric venture from the legislature in 1917, then was passed into the hands of some Bostonians who abandoned the plan altogether in 1919. A group of local businessmen had begun to promote the development of another site, but finding great difficulty in raising the money in wartime, the promoters asked the city to put up $400,000 in exchange for 51 percent of the common stock. The ratepayers eventually approved this move in April, 1918, but before an agreement could be signed, the syndicate abandoned its plans.

Faced with the failure of two private efforts to develop cheaper power and encouraged by the success of Ontario Hydro, the Nova Scotia government was persuaded to create a provincial electricity commission in 1919. The commissioners had begun construction of a generating station and transmission line to Halifax when, ironically, the city balked at the expense of duplicating the private company's distribution system, fearful that hydroelectricity might not prove significantly cheaper. With a nearly completed power station and no customers, the provincial government found itself in an embarrassing predicament. Eventually, an agreement was worked out to sell the public hydroelectricity to Nova Scotia Tramways and Power. Extending over a 30-year period from 1922, this contract prohibited the city from entering into competition and permitted Nova Scotia Tramways and Power to charge whatever rates were necessary to earn an 8 percent return on its investment. Public enterprise thus came to the rescue of the private utility at a time when it needed additional power but lacked sufficient earnings to underwrite the necessary borrowing.[13]

Across the Bay of Fundy in New Brunswick, another politically inspired experiment in public ownership was underway. The private utility serving Saint John had also become the focus of much controversy during World War I as speculators loaded it up with a heavy burden of debt. Sternly criticized by municipal leaders, Premier W. E. Foster attempted to regain popularity in 1920 by creating a provincial hydroelectric commission. C. O. Foss, the chief engineer, was convinced that cheap hydroelectricity would do much to develop New Brunswick, and the legislation was modelled closely upon Ontario's. The New Brunswick Electric Power Commission promptly began construction of its first generating station, even though it had no customers.

With provincial power soon to be available, a group of young men in Saint John sparked a vigourous debate on whether or not the city should have its own municipal electric system. Under the banner of the United Organization, the pro–public ownership forces captured control of the city government in the spring of 1922. When the mayor reneged on his commitment to build a city system, the electors promptly recalled and replaced him. Within a few weeks contracts had been let for a public system.

Yet the appearance of a public competition in the province's largest power market did not spell the demise of the private company in New Brunswick, any more than it did in Manitoba. As in other cities, the ready availability of cheaper power induced a sharp rise in demand; the private company lost some domestic customers but was able to retain many large power users. Within three years, moreover, when the New Brunswick Electric Power Commission found itself short of power, it chose to purchase from the private company rather than develop another river; by 1929 the private utility was supplying 30 percent of the commission's total load. Ironically, the commission was committed to sell power to Saint John for 1.2¢ per kilowatt hour, which forced it to take a loss of about 3¢ per kilowatt hour on these purchases.[14]

In both Maritime provinces, therefore, public and private enterprises became closely intertwined in the regional electricity network. Electric supply became a mixed enterprise, with the state financing risky and capital-intensive hydroelectric development to the great benefit of the urban distribution companies and their shareholders.

The prairie provinces of Alberta and Saskatchewan had only been carved out of federal territory in 1905 and remained heavily rural and agricultural. By 1931 the four largest cities contained fewer than 260,000 residents out of a population of 1,650,000. Towns and cities had small thermal stations, some municipally owned and some private; the only sizable hydroelectric development was the Calgary Power Company's plants on the Bow River. Almost all the current generated was used for domestic and commercial lighting; by 1932 the two provinces together consumed less than one-fiftieth of Quebec's total (see Table 39). Although efforts were made, both provinces found the costs of establishing regional systems prohibitively high during the 1920s.

Calgary Power, controlled by Royal Securities in Montreal, cherished ambitions of establishing a private network that would cover southern Alberta and western Saskatchewan, using the technical expertise of Royal's subsidiary, the Montreal Engineering Company. But one serious problem plagued these plans: the plants on the Bow River could only generate about one-sixth of their installed capacity during the winter peak because of low flow after the freezeup. The obvious solution was more water storage in the Rocky Mountains to feed high-head plants, which could be operated in combination with the existing run-of-the-river installations. Unfortunately for the company, all the possible sites for storage reservoirs lay inside Banff National Park, and whenever the company approached the federal Department of the Interior for permission to build dams, they ran head-on into an angry coalition of naturalists and conservationists. Despite pleading its case throughout the 1920s, always with strong backing from the city, Calgary Power failed to persuade the department.

During the late 1920s the government of Alberta considered creating a provincial utility to promote rural electrification, an idea promoted by the ambitious engineers at Alberta Government Telephones. Studies revealed, however, that to buy up the private company, expand the Bow River plants, and build the necessary high-voltage transmission line to link Calgary to Edmonton's municipally owned steam plant would cost at least $18,000,000, perhaps ultimately $25,000,000. Despite growing demands for electrification from the powerful United Farmers of Alberta, the cabinet shied away from the size of this commitment—probably made wary by the growing cost of rural telephone service—and the idea was dropped.[15]

Saskatchewan, which had no convenient sites for hydroelectric development, commissioned a study of a central thermal station on the southern coalfields near Estevan in 1913, but the war put an end to that project. By the late 1920s the government was convinced that lack of cheap power was retarding industrial development and ordered another study. Meanwhile, several private holding companies had begun buying up local systems. The Saskatchewan Power Resources Commission concluded that a thermal plant on the coalfields would produce power most efficiently. Saskatoon, which needed additional power, readily accepted the idea, but Regina angrily rejected the province's offer to purchase its municipal system. Instead, the Regina plant was expanded, and Moose Jaw promptly sold its civic system to a private company. The government went ahead and created a Saskatchewan Power Commission nonetheless, but it ended up with little more than the Saskatoon system under its control. Publicly, the ministers affirmed a commitment to a provincewide public system; privately, they let it be known that they did not intend to take over any of the existing companies. As the one private utility executive noted, "Their policy is apparently one of conforming to the sentiment which they believe to be strongly in favour of public ownership, and at the same time not plunging the province into the large expenditure which would be necessary in case of wholesale expropriation of private holdings."[16]

Saskatchewan and Alberta did not acquire regional power systems like those in more urbanized and industrialized sections of the country during the 1920s. The Saskatchewan Power Commission existed only in name; in Alberta the obstacles to securing water storage thwarted ambitions to expand. Small public and private companies in these sparsely settled markets had yet to be integrated into regional systems.

By 1930, then, the electricity supply industry in Canada exhibited three quite distinct organizational styles. Private monoplies dominated completely in Quebec and British Columbia, directing the pace and focus of network development along lines that were familiar in the United States. State enterprise controlled most of the market in Ontario, the largest and most prosperous province, a pattern increasingly familiar to Europeans. What seems to have been a distinctively Canadian style was the mixed public-private systems that evolved in several provinces.

What impact did the development of these systems with their varying organizational styles have upon the crucial matter of rates? First of all it must be emphasized how difficult it is to give a concise answer to this question. Those charged with preparing the Dominion Bureau of Statistics *Index Numbers of Rates for Electricity for Residence Lighting and Tables of Monthly Bills for Domestic Service* noted in 1930:

> The "cost of electricity" is one of the most controversial topics in Canada and in the United States and, quite probably, in many other countries. Also it is seldom that a satisfactory explanation is given of the many differences in rates that exist. This is due chiefly to the fact that there is no "cost of electricity" in the same sense as the cost of flour, sugar, milk and such like which enter into the budget of the housewife where the cost of ten pounds is approximately ten times the cost of one pound.

What the harried statisticians tactfully forbore to mention was that this kind of confusion was fostered and maintained by utilities, both public and private, precisely to prevent comparisons. In addition, large blocks of industrial power were sold at much lower rates than domestic energy, usually under schedules that specified further reductions for interruptibility and for off-peak periods. Thus the average revenue received by a utility for each kilowatt hour of its output could conceal as much as was revealed.

Nonetheless, since rates for domestic electricity chiefly interested consumers and underlay the agitation drummed up by civic populists against private utilities, the effect of the spread of public enterprise after 1910 requires analysis. Only in 1925 did the Dominion Bureau of Statistics begin to collect systematic figures on domestic rates, gathering data for the years 1913 and 1923–25 from municipalities in which 75 percent of all Canadian electricity users resided. Since most rate schedules featured a sliding scale that fell as consumption rose, these estimates were presented separately, based upon the use of 15, 20, 40, 60 or 180 kilowatt hours per month.

Table 41 summarizes this information for the 14 largest cities. There were marked variations in the consumption: Montreal, Toronto, and (surprisingly) Regina led the way with an average of 60 kilowatt hours monthly; Saint John, Quebec City, Saskatoon, and Calgary residents took but a third of that. Why Regina with relatively expensive thermal power from its municipal plant should have attracted so much more custom than Quebec with its relatively cheap current admits of no simple answer. Table 42 compares the cost of 40 kilowatt hours in each of these 14 cities, that being the average consumption in half of them. For 1925, this shows a typical customer paying an electricity bill ranging from $1.15 per month in Toronto, Ottawa, and Hamilton up to $3.20 in Saskatoon, the nationwide big city average being $2.04. Since many of the municipalities from which statistics were collected were tiny by comparison with Montreal or

TABLE 41

COST OF DOMESTIC ELECTRICITY IN MAJOR CANADIAN CITIES

City	Average Monthly Consumption (KWH)	Average Monthly Bills				Index Numbers (1913 = 100)		
		1913	1923	1924	1925	1923	1924	1925
Halifax	40	$4.20	$3.00	$2.48	$2.48	71.4	59.0	59.0
Saint John	20	3.00	1.80	.99	.99	60.0	33.0	33.0
Montreal	60	3.99	2.70	2.55	2.25	67.7	63.9	56.4
Quebec City	20	1.40	1.40	1.40	1.30	100.0	100.0	92.9
Toronto	60	2.20	1.40	1.40	1.40	63.6	63.6	63.6
Ottawa	40	1.66	1.15	1.15	1.15	69.3	69.3	69.3
Hamilton	40	1.66	1.15	1.15	1.15	69.3	69.3	69.3
Winnipeg	40	1.20	1.20	1.20	1.20	100.0	100.0	100.0
Saskatoon	20	1.62	1.60	1.60	1.60	98.8	98.8	98.8
Regina	60	5.09	3.87	3.87	3.33	76.0	76.0	65.4
Calgary	20	2.25	1.08	1.08	1.08	48.0	48.0	48.0
Edmonton	40	3.04	2.66	3.04	3.04	87.5	100.0	100.0
Vancouver	40	3.64	2.68	2.00	2.00	73.6	54.9	54.9
Victoria	40	3.68	3.00	3.00	3.00	81.5	81.5	81.5

Source: Dominion Bureau of Statistics, *Index Numbers of Rates for Electricity for Residence Lighting and Tables of Monthly Bills,* 1925 (Ottawa: King's Printer, 1926).

Toronto, the Dominion Bureau of Statistics also prepared a set of weighted provincial index numbers on residential electricity rates, province by province, showing changes since 1913 (see Table 43).

Taken together these various measures indicate that the spread of public enterprise had a significant effect upon the cost of domestic electricity. Ontario was the province where rates declined most steeply, by almost 40 percent, while the stability of rates in Manitoba reflected the extremely low charges instituted by the civic utility in Winnipeg before the war and maintained unchanged during the 1920s. The effect of competition was to lower rates substantially. The impact of rivalry from public enterprise is particularly evident in Saint John, where charges declined sharply when the provincial commission began to supply the municipal utility in 1923.

Taking Montreal's 1913 rates as a benchmark (since its rates were not far from that year's national average of $3.04 for 40 kilowatt hours), one can see from Table 44 that by 1925 rates had declined almost everywhere except Saskatoon, Edmonton, and Winnipeg. Even those consumers who paid almost the same amount for power in 1925 as in 1913 put up considerably less in comparative terms, since the cost-of-living index had risen by more than 40 percent during that period. The most marked declines

TABLE 42

MONTHLY COST OF DOMESTIC ELECTRICITY IN MAJOR CANADIAN CITIES

City	MONTHLY BILLS (40 KWH)[a]				INDEX NUMBERS (1913 = 100)		
	1913	1923	1924	1925	1923	1924	1925
Halifax	$4.20	$3.00	$2.48	$2.48	71.4	59.0	59.0
Saint John	6.00	3.45	1.44	1.44	57.5	24.0	24.0
Montreal	2.71	1.85	1.75	1.55	68.3	64.6	57.2
Quebec City	2.80	2.80	2.80	2.61	100.0	100.0	93.2
Toronto	1.66	1.15	1.15	1.15	69.3	69.3	69.3
Ottawa	1.66	1.15	1.15	1.15	69.3	69.3	69.3
Hamilton	1.66	1.15	1.15	1.15	69.3	69.3	69.3
Winnipeg	1.20	1.20	1.20	1.20	100.0	100.0	100.0
Saskatoon	3.24	3.20	3.20	3.20	98.8	98.8	98.8
Regina	3.47	2.79	2.79	2.43	80.4	80.4	70.0
Calgary	3.60	2.16	2.16	2.16	60.0	60.0	60.0
Edmonton	3.04	2.66	3.04	3.04	87.5	100.0	100.0
Vancouver	3.64	2.68	2.00	2.00	73.6	54.9	54.9
Victoria	3.68	3.00	3.00	3.00	81.5	81.5	81.5

Source: Dominion Bureau of Statistics, *Index Numbers of Rates for Electricity for Residence Lighting and Tables of Monthly Bills,* 1925 (Ottawa: King's Printer, 1926).
[a] Table 42 shows that 40 KWH per month was the average household consumption in the largest number of Canadian cities, so this was chosen for comparison even though Montrealers and Torontonians used an average of 60 kilowatt hours monthly.

TABLE 43

WEIGHTED INDEX NUMBERS OF RESIDENTIAL ELECTRICITY RATES (1913 = 100)

	1923	1924	1925
PROVINCE			
Prince Edward Island	119.8	119.8	119.8
Nova Scotia	89.6	83.6	83.6
New Brunswick	88.2	79.3	70.5
Quebec	73.6	71.0	64.4
Ontario	63.7	62.0	61.6
Manitoba	99.9	99.9	99.9
Saskatchewan	99.0	100.6	97.6
Alberta	78.1	83.0	82.9
British Columbia	79.3	70.6	70.4
CANADA	74.4	72.2	69.9

Source: Dominion Bureau of Statistics, *Index Numbers of Rates for Electricity for Residence Lighting and Tables of Monthly Bills,* 1925 (Ottawa: King's Printer, 1926).

TABLE 44

INDEX NUMBERS OF URBAN RESIDENTIAL ELECTRICITY RATES RELATIVE
TO MONTREAL

City	1913	1923 (Montreal, 1913 (40 KWH) = 100)	1925
Halifax	154	110	91
Saint John	221	127	53
Montreal	100	68	57
Quebec City	103	103	96
Toronto	61	42	42
Ottawa	61	42	42
Hamilton	61	42	42
Winnipeg	44	44	44
Saskatoon	119	118	118
Regina	128	102	89
Calgary	132	79	79
Edmonton	112	98	112
Vancouver	134	98	73
Victoria	135	110	110

Source: Table 43.

came in Saint John, Halifax, and Vancouver—not surprising, since these cities had had the highest prewar rates, and by the mid-1920s were starting to benefit from the availability of cheap hydroelectricity.

How did Canadian consumers fare by comparison with American users of electricity? International comparisons are even more fraught with complications than intercity ones, but in 1913 a survey of 30 cities ranging in population from 25,000 to over 1,000,000 showed that the average small residential consumer in the United States bought 27 kilowatt hours monthly at an average cost of 9.4¢. Assuming that users could obtain 40 kilowatt hours at that same unit price (by no means a certainty), the average bill would have been $3.76—certainly in line with Canadian rates if we ignore those cities like Toronto, Ottawa, and Winnipeg where public enterprise was already in existence. By 1927 the average U.S. domestic electricity user consumed about 37 kilowatt hours a month at an average price of 6.8¢, bringing charges to about $2.50 monthly.[17] Although the figures for 1913 and 1927 are not strictly comparable—the former omit some relatively high-cost rural consumers, while the latter include them—an overall decline of roughly one-third in domestic electricity rates is not out of line with the Canadian experience in a similar period, as shown by the weighted index numbers in Table 43.

Several generalizations seem to emerge from these comparisons. The absence of public enterprise did not necessarily condemn domestic electricity consumers to paying extortionate charges. Quebec and British Columbia, where private companies reigned supreme, enjoyed the largest overall decline in rates after Ontario and New Brunswick, according to the index numbers. Sir Herbert Holt had the advantage of low-cost hydroelectricity, while the British Columbia Electric Railway acquired a number of hydraulic sites and plants to meet rapidly growing demand. Calgary Power, by contrast, was unable to achieve such dramatic cost reductions, owing to its failure to establish a grid fully utilizing waterpower from the eastern slopes of the Rocky Mountains. But Holt and his counterparts could offer dramatic reductions because of their relatively high rates; the average Montrealer still paid 60 percent more for power in 1925 than the average Torontonian, while a Vancouverite's bill for 40 kilowatts was 75 percent higher (see Tables 41 and 42).

Rate reductions were also possible where system-building linked larger and larger generating stations to a wider area by high-voltage transmission lines. Urban centres, once isolated from one another, became part of regional networks that could lower peaks and improve load factors. Thus the crucial issue was often not public or private ownership but the nature of resource endowment and the level of regional economic development. Rates stayed highest in Regina, Saskatoon, and Edmonton because these communities depended upon isolated thermal stations; the cost of an integrated provincial grid did not yet seem justified in Saskatchewan and Alberta.

The two largest public enterprises, Ontario Hydro and Winnipeg Hydro, were also in a position to benefit from economies of scale. Though businessmen had headed up the movement for public power in both Ontario and Manitoba, they were not always its largest beneficiaries. Ontario Hydro used earnings from industrial power to subsidize domestic service. Bulk power users got lower rates in Quebec than in Ontario because Sir Herbert Holt followed standard private utility rate schedules and perhaps because he also wanted to block any business-led agitation. Thus the benefits from public ownership were not distributed exactly as some of its leading proponents had anticipated.

In general, it might be observed that the drop in domestic power rates between the beginning of World War I and the mid-1920s, while in part the product of technological change, was also an indication that regulation was working. Electrical utilities had earned generous profits before the war, sufficient in most cases to valorize their common stock handsomely. When regulatory bodies began to limit earnings—sometimes to a fixed rate of return, as in Nova Scotia—that, too, helped place downward pressure on domestic rates, which had created most of the political controversy surrounding electricity supply. The process was most evident where public enterprise competed directly with private undertakings, but the same effect was felt in all Canadian jurisdictions—even in British Columbia, where rates were altered not through formal adjudication but by direct negotiation between the municipalities and the company.

Various styles

How can one account for this variety of organizational styles in Canadian electricity supply? T. P. Hughes has argued for the interaction of a whole series of factors: "The style of each system was found to be based upon entrepreneurial drive and decisions, economic principles, legislative contraints or supports, institutional structures, historical contingencies and geographical factors, both natural and human."[18] The difficulty with such an answer is that it seems so broad as to encompass almost everything. Can one be more precise about the key factors that shaped the balance between public and private enterprise in Canada?

Four considerations seem to merit close examination. First of all, Canada was (and is) a country with clear regional disparities in resource endowment, in economic development, and in income levels. Both the more favoured areas and the have-not provinces were imbued with the conviction that cheap energy, particularly cheap electricity, was vital to future economic growth; therefore, the relative abundance or scarcity of such low-cost energy in a particular region was very important in shaping attitudes. In addition, there was Canada's heavy commitment to hydroelectric developments rather than to thermal power. Finally, the diversity of Canadian society was reflected politically in its decentralized federal system, which left important authority in the hands of provincial governments and opened the way for conflicts between national and local priorities. The three main system styles were a function of these variables.

By the 1920s the level of economic development in Canada varied markedly from region to region. Factories and cities were heavily concentrated in Quebec, Ontario, and British Columbia, which were doubly fortunate to have prosperous resource sectors and abundant hydroelectricity (see Table 45). The Maritime provinces were enduring a long period of secular decline, relative to the rest of the country, as their traditional resource sectors and staple trades encountered increasing competition. The fragile prosperity of the prairie provinces was almost completely dependent upon the fortunes of agriculture, even in the boom of the late 1920s. Canadians were well aware of the extent of these disparities, which gave birth to regional movements of political protest in both East and West during this period. By 1926 the average per capita income had reached $491 in Ontario and $535 in British Columbia, but was just $278 in New Brunswick. Each region therefore looked upon electricity supply from a different perspective.

While economists may debate the precise relationship between energy costs and economic development, Canadian politicians of that time had no doubts, especially those in the less well-endowed provinces: "Cheap power attracts industries," Premier W. E. Foster told the New Brunswick assem-

TABLE 45

ELECTRIC POWER EMPLOYED IN MANUFACTURING 1930

	Total Power[a] (HP)	ELECTRICAL POWER		Electricity as % of Total Power
		Purchased	Self-Generated	
PROVINCE				
P.E.I	3,869	631	400	27
Nova Scotia	168,693	62,924	37,873	60
New Brunswick	127,337	47,248	33,456	63
Quebec	1,498,637	1,026,413	56,151	72
Ontario	1,613,214	1,025,354	254,714	80
Manitoba	115,524	101,267	582	88
Saskatchewan	28,815	16,453	89	57
Alberta	65,733	41,884	3,523	69
British Columbia and Yukon	439,922	196,679	91,760	67
CANADA	4,051,744	2,518,853	478,548	74

Source: Dominion Bureau of Statistics, *Production and Use of Electric Energy in Canada,* 1931 (Ottawa: King's Printer: 1932).

[a]Excludes mining; see Table 37.

bly in 1920 when introducing the act to create a power commission modelled upon Ontario Hydro. "The only way for New Brunswick to secure a place in industrial progress is to develop its water power." To critics of state involvement in electrical development, the Premier replied, "The supplying of power . . . might be regarded as a public necessity. Light and power has [*sic*] come to be regarded as a necessity of life the same [as] your water supply, and the supplying of electrical energy becomes, therefore, more or less a natural function of government."[19]

A similar view prevailed in Saskatchewan. In 1925, Premier Charles Dunning told the voters that his government had considered the problem of industrial development and concluded "that the absence of cheap power is the greatest handicap. . . . The results of this preliminary investigation justify the Government in proposing to engage a small body of experts to examine the sources of power within the Province . . . with a view to involving a Provincial power scheme to supply cheap power to our communities for industrial and agricultural purposes."[20] As a result of that investigation Dunning's successor, James Gardiner, brought in legislation in 1929 creating the Saskatchewan Power Commission.

In the same year engineer A. G. Christie, commissioned to examine the power situation in Alberta, reported enthusiastically in favour of a publicly owned system. After reading his report, the provincial treasurer observed to the Premier that this was the most important issue facing the cabinet: "I asked [consulting engineer H. G.] Acres' opinion as to whether or not it would be advisable for the province to go into a Provincial scheme after he had studied Christie's analysis. . . . He replied that . . . it was simply a question of whether or not we had a vision of growth and development in the Province. . . . If we were convinced that development was going to take place, and from everything he could see it was going to take place, then in his opinion there would be no question we should take hold of it." But the high cost of the project deterred the government from acting.[21]

Not only the less-developed provinces looked to electricity for their future prosperity. By the late 1920s three-quarters of all Canadian industries already depended upon electrical energy, most of it consumed in Quebec, Ontario, and British Columbia (see Table 45). One observer noted, "the development of industry is more and more resolving itself into a question of power, improved transportation facilities having made the assembling of raw materials for manufacture progressively easier. Under modern conditions the general tendency of manufacturing is to seek the power and assemble its raw material where the latter is most abundant." As Premier Howard Ferguson put it to the chairman of Ontario Hydro in 1930: "I am intensely interested in seeing that we have ample power to take care of the future expanding needs of the Province. I think the public generally want to be assured that our development will not be delayed or retarded by the shortage of power."[22]

Since electrical energy was accorded such a critical role in economic development, one might ask why the industry did not pass entirely into state hands, as occurred in several European countries. By 1919 publicly owned central stations were already generating 30 percent of all power, a figure that increased to 60 percent in 1923 when Ontario Hydro's large Queenston plant came on line. Thereafter, however, the percentage of production from state enterprises stabilized for several years before beginning a swift decline to only 30 percent again in 1932 (see Table 46).[23] If the power generated by industrial establishments for their own consumption is included in the Canadian totals, then little more than one-quarter of power consumed in the early 1930s was from public undertakings.

That this was so seems related to the second crucial influence upon organizational style: the relative abundance or scarcity of electricity in the different regions of the country. The contrast between Quebec and Ontario is particularly instructive: public enterprise was a negligible factor in one; Ontario Hydro produced 75 percent of power in the other by 1930. Despite the broad similarities in level of development, in resource endowment, and in political organization, there was one significant difference: in Ontario Adam Beck was able to forge a public power movement from the concern that the power of Niagara Falls would be entirely consumed by Americans

TABLE 46

NET GENERATION OF ELECTRICAL ENERGY BY TYPE AND OWNERSHIP
(in millions KWH)

Year	Hydro Plants	Thermal Plants	Publicly Operated	Privately Operated	Total Utilities[a]	Industrial Establishments	Total Output
1919	5,353	144	1,221	4,132	5,497	—	—
1920	5,730	165	1,438	4,456	5,895	—	—
1921	5,448	167	1,298	4,316	5,614	—	—
1922	6,570	171	1,621	5,120	6,741	—	—
1923	7,936	163	3,025	5,074	8,099	—	—
1924	9,159	156	3,291	6,024	9,315	—	—
1925	9,942	169	3,583	6,527	10,110	—	—
1926	11,911	182	4,296	7,797	12,093	—	—
1927	14,346	203	4,605	9,444	14,549	828	15,377
1928	16,106	232	4,877	11,461	16,338	1,173	17,509
1929	17,604	359	5,188	12,774	17,963	1,343	19,306
1930	17,749	345	5,157	12,937	18,094	1,374	19,468
1931	16,025	306	4,140	12,191	16,331	1,289	17,620
1932	15,724	328	3,714	12,338	16,052	1,401	17,453

Source: M. C. Urquart and K. A. Buckley, eds., *Historical Statistics of Canada* (Toronto: Macmillan,
1965), Table 7-13, p. 448.
[a]Central stations only.

or by a group of Toronto monopolists. Without cheap power, ran the rea-
soning, Ontario must fail in the Darwinian struggle for industrial development, particularly by comparison with the United States. Thus province-
building nationalism helped to legitimize nationalization.

In Quebec, hydroelectric potential was superabundant. That was why
Herbert Holt was so vigilant in defending the monopoly he gradually established in the Montreal region. By selling industrial power very cheaply,
Holt isolated the business community and prevented it from mobilizing a
public power movement as it had in Ontario. Lacking business support for
such a step, the provincial government did not move against the private
utilities, despite the complaints about high domestic rates and the financial
manipulation of securities in the 1920s and 1930s.[24] On the west coast the
British Columbia Electric Railway was able to follow a similar strategy of
eliminating competitors and developing sufficient hydroelectricity to
dampen serious threats of a takeover. In Manitoba the large undeveloped
potential of the Winnipeg River made it possible for public and private
enterprise to coexist rather than devouring one another.

The third critical factor in determining the balance between public and
private enterprise in Canada seems to have been the very heavy commit-

ment to hydroelectricity rather than thermal power. From a postwar high of 3.1 percent of central station production, the proportion of thermal power declined to 1.4 percent in 1927–28 before again increasing slightly to 2.1 percent in 1932. By that date information had also begun to be collected on power produced by industrial establishments for their own consumption; of the 1.4 billion kilowatt hours produced in 1932, the overwhelming proportion turned out by mines and paper mills was also hydraulic power (see Table 46). Canada relied heavily upon hydroelectricity because its coal reserves are located in the Maritimes and the three westernmost provinces, away from the centres of population and industry, making transportation costs very high. Hydroelectric stations, however, absorbed very large sums of capital, which private investors often proved reluctant to advance, particularly in the less-developed regions of the country; public enterprise then became the only alternative.

The risk of investing in hydroelectric projects was increased when local monopolies using thermal power were well established and the capacity to absorb additional energy was somewhat doubtful. Halifax was a case in point. When the speculators who controlled the local tramway failed to carry out their promise to develop waterpower, the provincial government decided to acquire their property and develop the power itself. Far from viewing public enterprise as a threat, the private company's directors were delighted to purchase public power; it freed them from the need to raise at least $700,000 to expand capacity at a time when the company was not earning enough to pay the dividends on its stock. "If these large sums could be raised at all, in addition to those required for other purposes, which is doubtful," management was advised, "it would be at very high rates, causing serious harm to the shareholders and undoubtedly compelling the company to increase its rates in order to live." Instead, the taxpayers of Nova Scotia underwrote the capital costs of a new generating station, because the government considered it necessary to supply the infrastructure in the hope of promoting economic development.[25]

Where demand for power was strong, private interests were ready to invest in hydroelectric stations during the 1920s, but in marginal markets such as Nova Scotia and New Brunswick, the state was required to undertake this task. The successful example of Ontario Hydro was particularly important here; the provincial commissions in the Maritimes were closely modelled upon the Ontario agency in the hopes of duplicating its achievements. Moreover, public financing for development of the infrastructure was politically legitimized by Canada's long history of state involvement in transportation and communication, starting with canal construction in the 1840s.

Finally, the fact that Canada was a decentralized federation had an important impact upon the organizational form of the industry. Except for the three prairie provinces, the ownership of lands and natural resources upon which hydraulic rights rested lay with the provincial governments. At the same time, the federal government, through its power of disallowance, could nullify any provincial law completely within one year of its passage. Moreover, Ottawa was responsible both for navigation and international relations, which gave it significant authority over major rivers such as the St. Lawrence. And parliament could declare any undertaking for "the general advantage of Canada," thus bringing it exclusively under federal jurisdiction and regulation. These constitutional arrangements laid the groundwork for a whole series of conflicts between the two levels of government over electricity supply.

The possibility of escaping provincial control through a declaration of "general advantage" was particularly attractive to private utility promoters in Ontario.[26] These efforts to outwit their nemesis, Adam Beck, were largely unsuccessful, but other entrepreneurs did possess federal charters, which had an important effect upon their relations with the provincial governments. For instance, when Premier John Bracken of Manitoba entered into negotiations concerning the development of the Seven Sisters Falls in 1928, his lawyers advised him that his government lacked the authority to expropriate the Winnipeg Electric Company's works; Bracken had to come to terms with the company and permit it to undertake the development. In 1920 the British Columbia Electric Railway tried to place itself under the permanent authority of the Board of Railway Commissioners. As we have seen, despite an intense lobbying effort, the BCER failed in this attempt, but the extent of its exertions was a measure of the benefits it hoped to derive through a flight from provincial control.[27]

Federal control over navigation and international relations created problems for the province of Ontario during the 1920s, when Ontario Hydro sought to develop the Ottawa and the St. Lawrence.[28] The three prairie provinces did not control their own lands and natural resources prior to 1930, jurisdiction being retained by Ottawa in order to manage national development. Until then the federal Department of the Interior controlled the leasing of waterpower, and the very definite ideas of its officials affected the balance between public and private enterprise[29]—as the Alberta government discovered when its application for control of storage sites in the upper watershed of the Bow was summarily dismissed.[30]

Regional disparities, the desire for industrial development, the relative abundance of energy supplies, and the workings of Canadian federalism all affected the balance between public and private enterprise in electricity supply and provided the framework within which the campaign for state ownership took shape. The outcomes differed greatly from province to province not only because these elements interacted differently, but because the intangible leaven of ideology and personality also varied sharply. Manitoba's public power movement lacked a dynamic leader like Adam Beck, and eventually its thrust began to falter. Lack of commitment to the cause by business leaders in Quebec, the utilities' influence with the government, and the ideological hostility of the Roman Catholic church to statism weakened the movement there. More evenly balanced public and private forces arrived at different kinds of accommodation in other provinces. By 1930 the electricity supply industry had attained the organizational shape it would retain until after World War II: public enterprise played a much more significant role than in the United States, yet the private sector continued to dominate in most regions.

 While cooperation and physical interconnection did not advance as rapidly in electricity supply as in the telephone industry, there was nevertheless a steady advance in the links between various undertakings. Producers rapidly converged upon the North American standard of three-phase alternating current generated at 60 cycles per second and transmitted long distances at increasingly high voltages. Large scale hydroelectric development in Canada reduced rates under both public and private ownership. Domestic rates charged by comparable systems tended to be lower under public regimes. Integrated systems were built by both public and private enterprises. Ontario achieved system scale at an early date under public ownership, but lost some of the advantages by dividing its territory into two different frequencies. When Sir Adam Beck began construction of the Queenston plant during World War I, he adopted 25-cycle power, already in use there, because many of his customers had equipment designed for it. Since frequency converters were both expensive and unreliable, the entire Niagara system (which produced 80 percent of Ontario Hydro's output in the mid-1920s) remained on that standard, like the Niagara-Hudson system across the river in New York state. Thus Ontario Hydro was something less than the monolithic superpower system it appeared to be, since it could not supply its Niagara power to markets near Toronto where 60-cycle power was in use.[31]

Because of the highly regionalized character of the Canadian economy and polity, provincial boundaries were initially assumed to be the proper limits for electrical networks. To a considerable extent this was still true in 1930, if only because the distances involved were so great as to make most long distance transmission lines uneconomical. But even then, the first elements of a nationwide power grid were beginning to be put in place. As we have seen, Ontario Hydro began importing large quantities of power from private producers in Quebec in the late 1920s. (The Quebec companies installed special 25-cycle equipment in their powerhouses.) At the same time, power exports across the American border continued, causing some Canadians to become fearful that vital energy would be unavailable when needed at home. Several large schemes to develop the Ottawa River were so severely criticized for this reason that they were ultimately abandoned.[32]

Nevertheless, Adam Beck's Ontario Hydro and Herbert Holt's private Quebec system gradually came to be linked, and both were connected to networks in the U.S., a portent of things to come. Elsewhere across Canada, long distance transmission lines snaked over the landscape, tying generators to consumers.

The two styles of ownership, public and private, did not prevent substantial convergence on matters such as technical standards, power interchanges or accounting methods. This emerging consensus permitted that ultimate form of cooperation, joint public-private systems. Business bureaucracies—whether they operated municipal undertakings, provincial crown corporations, or private companies—increasingly spoke the same language and confided in one another concerning their common problems.

CONCLUSION
MARKETS
OF
THE
MIND

Markets of the Mind

In 1914 an anguished Nova Scotia politician struggled to explain to his legislative colleagues the dilemmas raised by utility monopolies. Relying upon industrial examples familiar to the region, W. L. Hall observed that "it was all right to talk about merging piano companies and underwear companies, because there were lots of other ways men could buy suits of underwear or a piano without buying from a merger, but from the very nature of public utilities they were necessities of life." If the legislature allowed businessmen to monopolize the heat and light of a city, it also owed something to the community; "the citizens had a special right to be protected."[1]

In the mid-nineteenth century gas and water companies had provided early intimations of the tendencies toward monopoly of a new class of public service industries. They also demonstrated the polar opposites—public vs. private enterprise—through which utilities could be controlled. The street railway, telephone, and electric power technologies that followed produced monopolies of much more menacing proportions. This was an altogether novel and bewildering phenomenon in a liberal society and in a competitive economy with profound antimonopolist convictions.[2]

Monopoly control of community property created social and political instability. Angry, suspicious, confused consumers demanded a substitute for the controls normally provided by markets. Managers, owners, and shareholders, united by a determination to preserve what they considered to be *their* property, also sought some measure of security. In politics, however, monopolists had to compete against other interest groups for power. Protection could not be purchased—at least not openly.

The challenge to public policy was to clothe these enterprises with a legitimacy commensurate with their obvious utility. As James Willard Hurst has observed: "An institution which wields practical power—which compels men's wills or behaviour—must be accountable for its purposes and its performance by criteria not wholly in the control of the institution itself." The struggle we have observed in the preceding pages was essentially a contest between corporations and clients over legitimacy, which the corporations alone could not impart to themselves. Regulation was the means whereby powerful economic institutions participated in a legitimizing process and rendered themselves accountable to some judgement other than that of their owners.[3]

Something like a distinctively Canadian style of regulation emerged in the utility sector between 1880 and 1930. The technology transferred to Canada was undeniably American, but the pattern of regulation that evolved might be thought of as mid-Atlantic; it relied more than the United States but less than Europe upon public ownership. This was not so much the result of any clearly stated ideological preference on the part of Canadians but rather the complex sum of many separate interactions of technologies in a distinctive economic and political setting. What evolved in Canada had some parallels in Australia, another parliamentary federation closely bound by the British judicial tradition; there, for example, the electricity supply industry was also divided between the public and private sectors by 1930.[4]

Far from being the product of a strong ideological commitment to public enterprise, the emergence of state-owned utilities in Canada occurred despite profound suspicions about their efficiency. "Colonial socialism," the phrase used in Australia to describe public enterprise, would have had all the wrong associations for most people in Canada, where promoters of state enterprises were always at pains to stress the importance of "business-like management."[5]

A larger public sector than in the United States was possible in part because the legal process was different in Canada. Parliamentary sovereignty plainly permitted control of any and all undertakings without demanding that due process be observed. Legally, then, the corporation possessed a considerably weaker bargaining position in Canada than in the United States; nonetheless, it operated in a political culture in which seizures of private property were generally deplored and, what was more, had grave economic consequences.

Nor did Canadian business have recourse to law alone for protection; the Canadian legal tradition forced business back into the legislatures to seek political solutions to its problems. The great documents in Canadian regulatory history are not judicial decisions—except in regard to questions of jurisdiction—but rather statutes.[6] Law permitted public ownership; other factors created it.

There are markets in men's minds, images of institutions and norms, which determine what is fitting, just, and acceptable in transactions. First, there is the imprint of the exchange economy, where goods and services are traded with varying degrees of efficiency. There is also a political market, where collectively permissible behaviour is defined through the competition of interest groups and parties in the electoral, legal, and administrative theatres. Finally there is a moral economy, a less well understood realm of just price, trust, equity, and legitimacy, where religious and secular ethics reign. Each of these economies has institutional and behavioural norms that demarcate the shifting bounds of expected and acceptable conduct. Perfect harmony between these separate spheres is never wholly attainable, but in a bourgeois liberal democratic society a high degree of consonance normally prevails.

The introduction of new technology created dissonance within and between the exchange, the political, and the moral markets. The monopolistic nature of the new electrical utilities defied all the ordinary rules of the competitive market. Quite apart from giving rise to frightening concentrations of financial—and by implication political—power, the monopolies were also legal entities dependent upon public bodies for their rights and privileges. They could not exist without legislatures. Whether by inadvertence or by conspiracy, business and politics had sired a powerful and threatening creature. Moreover, neither the creation of monopoly nor its well-documented abuses could be morally justified. The ruthlessness and corruption associated with these enterprises were sufficient to condemn them.

The bearers of the new technology—the monopoly-makers—necessarily created confusion and disorder in the markets of the mind. Obviously, they had as much interest as anyone in restoring harmony between the three economies, consistent with their own notions of independence. But blinkered by their own preoccupations and a narrow conception of private property, they required time to understand the disturbance they had created. As a result they did not initiate the process of accommodation through regulation; they procrastinated, and thus in due course they had to react to various forms of social control proposed by others. At the outset the utility owners were not the ones who demanded regulation, as some historians would have it; once it was proposed by others, however, they had definite views about the kind of regulation they preferred.

Regulation was a means of restoring equilibrium in such an unstable situation. It was not one thing but many things; it was not a once-and-for-all act of reconciliation but a continuous process of seeking accommodation. Above all, it was a negotiated settlement arrived at within particular local settings with different resource endowments, power relationships, and political traditions.

The theatre of science helped make a market for new services. In one exhilarating decade aggressive entrepreneurs spread the telephone, electric lighting, and mass transit across urban North America. For purposes of analyzing technological diffusion, the Canadian-American border scarcely existed; Canada was part of the United States. Technological systems had been transferred to a region of rising per capita income by equipment salesmen and migrant technicians and had been eagerly taken up by local capitalists, manufacturers, and consumers. Canada was not merely a passive recipient of foreign technology, but rather a region of active innovation where the state of the art was altered, especially in the case of electrical transmission. Canadian achievements fed back into the common North American technical pool, but in equipment manufacturing Canada was but a miniature replica of U.S. industry, technologically and organizationally. Imports of both producer and consumer goods came overwhelmingly from the United States. British and German heavy equipment penetrated the Canadian market on a small scale, but European standards did not. Foreign equipment was linked into integrated systems of North American design.[7]

The firms that applied the new technologies in Canada also behaved very much like their U.S. counterparts. The industries developed contemporaneously, without much time lag. A compliant political system initially opened the public thoroughfares to this new form of commerce with a minimum of constraint, and the promoters sought monopoly without serious political interference before the turn of the century. Canadian proprietors anticipated the economic characteristics of the firms they organized, achieved effective monopoly at a fairly early date, and by comparison with their American counterparts were able to protect their turf against private rivals. Only in Montreal did there develop something like a U.S. pattern of recurrent private competition, which ended in an expensive amalgamation.

Bell Telephone obtained a charter with sweeping powers from parliament at a time when no one really understood the nature of the telephone business and no one but the company's lawyers fully grasped the implications of declaring a private company "for the general advantage of Canada." Duly empowered and adequately capitalized, the company then cleared the telegraph operators from the field, occupied the territory, and neutralized its most threatening rival, the Canadian Pacific Railway, even without comprehensive patent protection.

Bell Telephone had a national monopoly by 1891; by the turn of the century the street railways had established unassailable control of their respective cities, and the electric light and power industry had shaken down into a mosaic of regional private monopolies. In several cities the light, power, gas, and street railway companies were amalgamated during the 1890s because of imperatives more financial than organizational. This was monopoly's moment.

Yet every corporate action gave rise to an opposite but not necessarily equal political reaction. As the entrenched monopolists set about maximizing the return on their investment, a loosely federated national movement organized a response. Civic populists combined the suspicions of victimized consumers with the grievances of angry municipal corporations in a sweeping programme of social and political reform. Specifically, they demanded that the political process, which had facilitated the rise of the monopolies, now render these creatures of the state responsible to the community at large rather than merely to their shareholders. The civic populists clearly articulated the community's objections to the emerging pattern of industrial organization at the municipal, provincial, and federal levels; they moved the utilities issue near the top of the political agenda and at the same time proposed a number of remedies.

The social and political disequilibrium created by the new monopolies was not eliminated by a single political act or by a single set of institutional arrangements. Rather, a wide variety of regulatory instruments was chosen in different jurisdictions. In a relatively decentralized federation where jurisdiction over property and civil rights was a provincial responsibility, national regulation was not possible, not even within those areas that fell exclusively under federal jurisdiction. The Bell Telephone Company, for example, had by 1904 been assigned by the courts to federal jurisdiction, but that did not prevent five provinces from creating their own provincially owned or regulated telephone systems. The legislatures of the nine provinces—each with its different configuration of social, economic, and political power—became the principal theatres of the regulatory struggle, militating against any uniform outcome.

Even when the monopolists realized that some measure of state supervision might be necessary to protect property—which was vulnerable both politically and legally—they resisted rather than submitting to the logic of the situation. Property owners could no more easily surrender their ideological justification for freedom of action than customers could dispense with their antimonopolist convictions.

In some jurisdictions this dialectical chemistry produced an explosion—public ownership. We have pointed to specific circumstances in each location that either advanced or inhibited the root-and-branch solution of the civic populists. In Ontario the scarcity of hydroelectric resources, the developmental anxieties of hinterland manufacturing towns over energy costs, and inspired political leadership that fused metropolis and hinterland in a united movement overrode the ill-prepared defences of tactless owners. In Manitoba the metropolis went ahead on its own; Winnipeg businessmen and manufacturers pushed the city into the electricity supply business to promote industrial development in competition with an absentee-owned monopoly, without support from the surrounding towns in the comparatively weak urban system of a predominantly agricultural region. Political entrepreneurship at the provincial level stimulated the demand for an alternative to eastern monopoly in the telephone business; as this preference spread across the prairies, Bell Telephone prudently decided to retreat from fruitless competition with the state in the interests of maximizing the rate

of return on its major investment. The new cities of the West started out
with their own water, lighting, and public transportation services. Thus for
different reasons public ownership sprang up at the municipal and provincial levels in the telephone, electric, and transit sectors, posing a concrete
and popular alternative to private enterprise as a form of industrial
organization.

Canadian utility owners, then, entered the regulatory debate determined to protect their property against a public takeover. This was not a
fate they had to imagine; they need only to observe the actual experience of
colleagues in Ontario and on the prairies, and the seeming irreversibility of
radical experiments with public ownership. In province after province, sector after sector, utility owners worked quietly behind the scenes to steer the
current of public opinion—deep with indignation but rather narrow when
it came to specifics—toward "acceptable" forms of regulation. The outcomes in the various jurisdictions reflected the relative influence of the contending interests. In most places the industry sought security through
 regulation—normally a weak Public Utilities Commission—though in British Columbia the industry managed to negotiate security without formal
regulation.

By 1914 this socioeconomic conflict, mediated in the political arena,
had generated a broad spectrum of governing instruments, ranging from no
formal regulation at one extreme, through several varieties of Public Utilities Commission, to public ownership at the other extreme. During World
War I and immediately afterward the regulatory process effectively protected capital (public as well as private) from the ravages of inflation,
assisted delicate recontracting negotiations, and contained the drive for
public ownership. At the same time the spectrum of regulation, by nominally subordinating capital, also necessarily changed the relationship
between labour, the community, and the employers.

During the 1920s, as the elements within each region were integrated
into large-scale systems, the distinct styles that emerged were conditioned
by this regulatory history. Effective regional telephone and electrical systems were constructed under *both* public and private management. Meanwhile, political mimesis combined with an eagerness for economic development prompted the appearance of hybrid public-private electrical
systems in the Maritimes and the West. Rarely did the form of ownership
or system dramatically alter rates or conditions of service, nor did it prevent practical integration and interconnection at the technical level. Price
was probably less important in the final analysis than the certainty
provided by the local system of regulation that it could not be radically
altered.

It might be observed parenthetically that the pluralist, or at least dual-
ist, approach to regulation in the utilities sector seems to hold true in other

other industries

regulated industries as well. Whether in railroads, airlines, broadcasting, or nuclear systems, Canada arrived at a form of mixed public-private organization. Regulation has not simply been entrusted to a regulatory commission and the courts; it has been reinforced by the quasi-competition of public and private agencies.

Canadians are an unsystematic, unreflective people who eschew doctrinal clarity, perhaps owing to the dangers it entails in a culturally and regionally divided polity. A decentralized federalism and a sharply skewed pattern of economic development weighted heavily toward central Canada have forced political settlements to a host of economic questions. The politicization of regulation at the federal and provincial levels thus gives rise to a variety of outcomes. Ideological barriers to public enterprise have become comparatively weak, especially at the margins of economic development, and weaker still through repeated use. In law the barriers are nonexistent.

In Canada both politicians and businessmen diffused technology. The ambit of state action extended beyond mere brokerage, particularly when powerful business interests differed (as in the case of electricity supply in Ontario) or where the costs of intervention fell upon absentee owners (as in the case of prairie telephones). But the state did not have unlimited license to regulate, nor did it always respond to the pleadings of the powerful. When the state overrode the narrow business interests of the corporations directly involved, its actions necessarily rested upon a broad social base, which included the preponderant weight of the business class through appeals to the higher good of general economic development.

For the most part the accomplishment of regulation was the reconciliation of the interests of producers and consumers; in this process, business had certain innate advantages that could be enhanced by the kind of regulatory process chosen. The desire for regulation was essentially protective, as several scholars of the question have observed.[8] Consumers wanted protection against the real and imagined abuses of private monopoly; cities sought collective and corporate access to management of the crucial urban infrastructure; and at length the utilities sought protection against public ownership and political opportunism. It could not be said of Canada that progressives sought protection from urban political machines, because Canadian voters and businessmen tended to trust the public service even if they might doubt its efficiency. But in regulation, efficiency was not necessarily a primary objective: confidence and security were more important goals. Creating some kind of equilibrium between the markets of the mind was more important than seeking optimum output. A balance between the various opposing forces could be struck at any number of points along the spectrum of regulation.

The late 1920s, by which time the Canadian public utilities sector had arrived at an organizational and regulatory equilibrium that would last for two more decades, provide us a convenient stopping point. The producers and consumers of public services were bound in a web of regulations that each had spun around the other. What survived from this period was a conviction that community property could be managed with equal satisfaction and legitimacy by both public and private agencies. It was a political and intellectual legacy that Canadians would never shake off.

Abbreviations

BCA	Bell Canada Archives, Montreal
BCER	British Columbia Electric Railway Company Records, University of British Columbia Library
CGA	Consumers' Gas Company Archives, Toronto
CGC	Consumers' Gas Company Records, York University Archives
CPR	City Passenger Railway Company, Montreal
CTA	City of Toronto Archives
HQA	Hydro-Québec Archives, Montreal
MB	Minute Book
MCA	Montreal City Archives
MCM	Montreal City Council Minutes (microfilm), Montreal City Archives
MSR	Montreal Street Railway Company
MUCTCA	Montreal Urban Community Transportation Commission Archives
OCM	Ottawa City Council Minutes
OHA	Ontario Hydro-Electric Power Commission Archives
PAC	Public Archives of Canada
PAM	Provincial Archives of Manitoba
PANB	Provincial Archives of New Brunswick
PAO	Provincial Archives of Ontario
REC	Royal Electric Company, Montreal
TCM	Toronto City Council Minutes
TCP	Toronto City Council Papers, City of Toronto Archives
VCA	Vancouver City Archives
WESR	Winnipeg Electric Street Railway Company Records, Manitoba Hydro-Electric Commission Archives

Notes

INTRODUCTION

1. *The Financial Post 500* (Toronto: Maclean Hunter, 1984), p. 70; *Report on Business 1000* (Toronto: Globe and Mail, 1984), pp. 64, 92, 225.

2. On this point, see C. Armstrong and H. V. Nelles, "A Curious Capital Flow: Canadian Investment in Mexico, 1902-1910," *Business History Review* 58 (1984): 178-203.

3. See, e.g., George Grant, *Lament for a Nation* (Toronto: McClelland & Stewart, 1965); and Hershel Hardin, *A Nation Unaware* (Vancouver: J. J. Douglas, 1974).

4. Marsha Gordon, *Government in Business* (Montreal: C. D. Howe Institute, 1981); J. R. S. Prichard, ed., *Crown Corporations in Canada: The Calculus of Instrument Choice* (Toronto: Butterworth, 1983); Allan Tupper and Bruce Doern, eds., *Public Corporations and Public Policy in Canada* (Montreal: Institute for Policy Analysis, 1981); Ron Hirshhorn, ed., *Government Enterprise: Roles and Rationale* (Ottawa: Economic Council of Canada, 1985).

5. Most notably, Alfred E. Kahn, *The Economics of Regulation,* 2 vols. (New York: John Wiley, 1970); Richard Schmalensee, *The Control of Natural Monopolies* (Lexington, Mass.: D. C. Heath, 1979); George Stigler, *The Citizen and the State: Essays on Regulation* (Chicago: University of Chicago Press, 1975); Richard Gordon, *Reforming the Regulation of Electric Utilities,* (Lexington, Mass.: D. C. Heath, 1982); James Q. Wilson, ed., *The Politics of Regulation* (New York: Basic Books, 1980); Douglas D. Anderson, *Regulatory Politics and Electric Utilities* (Boston: Auburn House, 1981); Bruce Owen and Ronald Braeutigam, *The Regulation Game* (Cambridge, Mass.: Ballinger, 1978); and in Canada, John Baldwin, *The Regulatory Agency and the Public Corporation* (Cambridge: Ballinger, 1975).

6. See Thomas McCraw, "Regulation in America: A Review Article," *Business History Review* 49 (1975): 159-83; Thomas McCraw, ed., *Regulation in Perspective* (Cambridge, Mass.: Harvard University Press, 1981); Thomas McCraw, *Prophets of Regulation* (Cambridge, Mass.: Harvard University Press, 1984).

7. Thomas P. Hughes, *Networks of Power* (Baltimore, Md.: Johns Hopkins University Press, 1982); Leslie Hannah, *Electricity before Nationalization* (Balti-

more, Md.: Johns Hopkins University Press, 1979), and *Engineers, Managers and Politicians* (Baltimore, Md.: Johns Hopkins University Press, 1982); I. C. R. Byatt, *The British Electrical Industry, 1875–1914* (Oxford: Clarendon Press, 1979); John P. McKay, *Tramways and Trolleys: The Rise of Mass Urban Transport in Europe* (Princeton, N.J.: Princeton University Press, 1976); Charles W. Cheape, *Moving the Masses: Urban Public Transit in New York, Boston, and Philadelphia, 1880–1912* (Cambridge, Mass.: Harvard University Press, 1980); Paul Barrett, *The Automobile and Urban Transit: The Formation of Public Policy in Chicago, 1900–1930* (Philadelphia: Temple University Press, 1984); Robert V. Bruce, *Bell: Alexander Graham Bell and the Conquest of Silence* (New York: Little, Brown, 1973); and John Brooks, *Telephone* (New York: Harper & Row, 1975).

8. Thomas P. Hughes, "The Order of the Technological World," in A. R. Hall and N. Smith, eds., *History of Technology* vol. 5 (London: Mansell Publishing, 1980), p. 2.

9. W. L. Marr and D. G. Paterson, *Canada: An Economic History* (Toronto: Macmillan, 1980); L. D. McCann, ed., *Heartland and Hinterland,* (Toronto: Prentice-Hall, 1982).

CHAPTER 1

1. *Statutes of Lower Canada,* 1801, 41 Geo. III, c. 10, An Act for Supplying the City of Montreal and Parts Thereof with Water; John Kennedy, "The Montreal Waterworks," *Canadian Engineer,* July, 1896, pp. 268–72; W. H. Atherton, *Montreal* (Montreal: S. J. Clarke, 1914), vol. 2, pp. 407–12.

2. Nelson M. Blake, *Water for the Cities* (Syracuse, N.Y.: Syracuse University Press, 1956), pp. 78–99; S. B. Warner, Jr., *The Private City* (Philadelphia: University of Pennsylvania Press, 1968), pp. 102–11.

3. F. Clifford Smith, *The Montreal Water Works: Its History Compiled from the Year 1800 to 1912* (n.p., the author, 1913), p. 14; the quotation is from Newton Bosworth, *Hochelaga Depicta: The Early History and Present State of the City and Island of Montreal* (Montreal: William Greig, 1839), p. 163.

4. On the early history of the gas industry, see Dean Chandler and A. D. Lacey, *The Rise of the Gas Industry in Britain* (London: British Gas Council, 1949); Louis Stotz and Alexander Jamison, *History of the Gas Industry* (New York: Stettiner Bros., 1939); and M. W. H. Peebles, *Evolution of the Gas Industry* (New York: New York University Press, 1980). For the adoption of the technology in Montreal, see Bosworth, *Hochelaga Depicta,* p. 193; Atherton, *Montreal,* vol. 2, pp. 403–5; and Albert Furniss, *Reasons Why the Montreal Gas Light Company Should Be Protected by the Legislature* (Montreal, 1846).

5. TCP, J. Joseph to Mayor T. D. Morrison, March 3, 1836; Albert Furniss to Clarke Gamble, Oct. 3, 1840, Feb. 26, 1841; TCM 1841, item 78, April 19, Report of the Standing Committee on Gas and Water; ibid., item 148; *Statutes of Canada,* 1841, 4 & 5 Vic., c. 65; TCM, 1842, item 300, Aug. 22; *Montreal Gazette,* June 14, 1843; TCM, 1846, items 102, 105, 145, June 15, July 16. See also Elwood Jones and Douglas McCalla, "Toronto Waterworks 1840–77: Continuity and Change in Nineteenth Century Toronto Politics," *Canadian Historical Review* 60 (1979): 300–323.

6. TCP, Albert Furniss to Charles Daly, Sept, 13, 16, 1844; Furniss to Mayor W. H. Boulton, Sept. 22, 1845; TCM, 1845, items 270, 275, 286, Nov. 17, Dec. 1;

John Mathewson, *Remarks on the Present Insufficient Lighting of the City of Montreal and the Necessity for an Application to the Legislature by the Citizens, for Power to Establish a New Montreal Gas-Light Company to be Entitled The Montreal Consumers' Company* (Montreal: Herald, 1846), pp. 8–9.

7. Kennedy, "Montreal Waterworks," p. 268; *Montreal Gazette,* Jan. 14, 28, Feb. 4, 1843; *Montreal Courier,* Jan. 27, 1843. Biographical information on Holmes is from the *Dictionary of Canadian Biography,* vol. 9 (Toronto: University of Toronto Press, 1976), pp. 396–97, and Merrill Denison, *Canada's First Bank,* vol. 1 (Toronto: McClelland & Stewart, 1966), p. 393.

8. *Montreal Gazette,* June 14, 1843; *Montreal Courier,* June 15, 1843.

9. *Montreal Gazette,* July 7, 28, Aug. 4, 17, Sept. 13, 1843; *Montreal Courier,* Aug. 4, 31, 1843; *La Minerve* (Montreal), July 24, Aug. 4, 1843. The crucial meeting at which the council changed its mind by voting 7 to 6 in favour of making the offer occurred Sept. 11; see *Montreal Gazette,* Sept. 13, 14, 1843.

10. Canada, Legislative Assembly, *Journals,* 1843 (where the Bill can be followed from Petition to Royal Assent); E. Nish, ed., *Debates of the Legislative Assembly of United Canada, 1841–1867,* vol. 3 (Montreal: Presses de l'école des hautes études commerciales, 1972), pp. 489–91; Province *Statutes of Canada,* 1843, 7 Vic., c. 44.

11. J. C. Lamothe, *Histoire de la corporation de la Cité de Montréal* (Montreal: Montreal Publishing and Printing, 1903), pp. 27–30; Atherton, *Montreal,* vol. 2, p. 181ff., and J. I. Cooper, *Montreal: A Brief History* (Montreal: McGill-Queen's University Press, 1969), p. 27ff. give only a hint of these events.

12. *Montreal Gazette,* Dec. 3, 5, 1844; *Montreal Pilot,* Dec. 2, 4, 1843; *La Minerve,* Dec. 2, 5, 1844. Elinor K. Senior, *British Regulars in Montreal* (Montreal: McGill-Queen's University Press, 1981), pp. 57–76, surveys these events from a military perspective.

13. See *Report of the Water Committee Submitting Reports of the Engineers on the New Water Works of Montreal* (Montreal: John Lovell, 1854) for Keefer's report and commentary on the consultants' opinions. The quotation is from pp. 36–37.

14. Ibid., p. 16; Geoffrey Bilson, *A Darkened House* (Toronto: University of Toronto Press, 1980), pp. 131–33; Kennedy, "Montreal Waterworks," pp. 268–69.

15. TCM, 1847, item 78, April 12; Jones and McCalla, "Toronto Waterworks," pp. 304–6.

16. *Statutes of Canada,* 1853, 16 Vic., c. 250. The promoters were F. C. Capreol, J. C. Morrison, and Samuel Zimmerman. At the insistence of the Consumers' Gas Company, the Metropolitan's charter limited profits to 10% of invested capital: *Proceedings of the Standing Committee on Fire, Water and Gas, the City of Toronto in Connection with the Supply of Water to the City* (Toronto: Maclear & Thomas, 1854).

17. *Statutes of Canada,* 1857, 20 Vic., c. 81; T. C. Keefer, *Report on a Water Supply for the City of Toronto* (Toronto: Maclear, Thomas, 1857); Jones and McCalla, "Toronto Waterworks," pp. 306–20; Ontario, *Statutes,* 1872, 35 Vic., c. 78, confirmed the Furniss estate's title to the works; c. 79 authorized Toronto to build a waterworks but not to charge a general water rate until the former company was purchased.

18. *Montreal in 1856: A Sketch Prepared for the Celebration of the Opening of the Grand Trunk Railway of Canada* (Montreal: John Lovell, 1856), pp. 14–18;

Kennedy, "Montreal Waterworks, " p. 269. For a brief recital of the problems encountered, see Louis Lesage, *Rapport sur l'agrandissement proposé de l'aqueduc de Montréal suivi de l'histoire de l'aqueduc d'après l'ordre du comité de l'eau* (Montréal: J. Starke, 1873), pp. 5–10.

19. William Rodden, *Montreal Water Works: The Reports of Walter Shanly, esq., T. C. Keefer, esq., and James B. Francis, esq., of Lowell, Mass.* (Montreal: Montreal Printing, 1869); Lesage, *Rapport sur l'agrandissement,* pp. 20–21; Kennedy, "Montreal Waterworks," pp. 269–70.

20. Thomas F. Miller, *The Water Supply and the Hydraulic Question* (Montreal: John Lovell, 1868); Kennedy, "Montreal Waterworks," pp. 271–72; F. H. Pitcher, "Works of the Montreal Water & Power Company," *Canadian Engineer* 39 (July 1920): 116–18.

21. For details and a photograph of a watercart doing a roaring trade on the streets of Toronto in 1895, see C. Armstrong and H. V. Nelles, *The Revenge of the Methodist Bicycle Company* (Toronto: Peter Martin, 1977), pp. 85–103.

22. D. R. Carter-Edwards, "Toronto in the 1890's: A Decade of Challenge and Response," M.A. thesis, University of British Columbia, 1973, pp. 155–56. The city council committee investigating the plans of the Toronto Aqueduct Company, altered in 1894 to the Georgian Bay Ship Canal and Power Aqueduct Company, was aptly named the Gravitation Committee. For additional detail see Armstrong and Nelles, *Revenge,* pp. 137–38. James Mansergh punctured the balloon with *The Water Supply of the City of Toronto, Canada* (Westminster, 1896). For the Aqueductors' impassioned reply, see *The Water Question: Facts for All the People* (Toronto, 1896).

23. "Montreal: A Hygienic Disgrace to Civilization," *Canadian Engineer* 16 (April, 1909): 527–30; ibid., 17 (July, 1909): 31; Paul Bator, "Saving Lives on the Wholesale Plan: Public Health Reform in the City of Toronto, 1900–1930," Ph.D. thesis, University of Toronto, 1979, pp. 89–92.

24. Atherton, *Montreal,* vol. 2, p. 403.

25. *Montreal Gazette,* April 10, 12, 1845; Mathewson, *Remarks,* p. 17.

26. Mathewson, *Remarks,* pp. 1, 8, 11, 18. See also the *Montreal Transcript,* March 18, 1845.

27. Canada, Legislative Assembly, *Journals,* 1847; *Statutes of Canada,* 1847, 10 & 11 Vic., c. 79; Furniss, *Reasons,* pp. 1–4.

28. *Statutes of Canada,* 1847, 10 & 11 Vic. c. 80; *Montreal Directory,* 1852–53, p. 353.

29. *Montreal in 1856,* pp. 18–19. In the preceding year the company was capitalized at £75,000 ($300,000), operated 34 miles of pipe, 455 streetlamps, and consumed 4,084 tons of coal to produce 28,292 MCF of gas.

30. *Statutes of Canada,* 1848, 11 Vic., c. 14; TCP, W. B. Jarvis to George Gurnett, May 14, 1841, Sept. 17, 23, Oct. 20, Nov. 19, 1847, June 5, 1848; TCP, petition of officers and directors of Consumers' Gas Company, Feb. 17, 1848.

31. The number of customers is listed in the company's Annual Reports, a complete set of which may be found in CGA; CGC, MB, Nov. 30, 1848.

32. CGA, Correspondence and Reports, 1853, G. C. Horwood, James Beaty, F. C. Capreol and ten others to the Directors, April 4.

33. Ibid., Henry Sherwood to John Arnold, May 17.

34. Ibid., Samuel Alcorn to Charles Berczy, May 26, 28, 30; CGC, MB, May 25, 1853; *Statutes of Canada,* 1853, 16 Vic., c. 250.

35. CGA, 1861, Steele to Thompson, March 18; CGC, MB, June 12, July 10, 11, 1857.

36. CGA, 1861, Steele to Thompson, March 18.

37. CGC, MB, Oct. 18, 1854; CGA, Draft Clauses of Municipal Corporations Act of Upper Canada given second reading, Oct. 26, 1854.

38. TCM, Report of the Standing Committee on Fire, Water and Gas, Nov. 12, 1860, Jan. 13, 1861; CGC, MB, Nov. 15, 26, 30, 1860, Jan. 19, Feb. 27, March 1, 8, 15, 30, Oct. 28, 1861; CGA, 1861, letters between Stephen Radcliff, Assistant City Clerk, and Henry Thompson, General Manager of the company, Feb.–March.

39. CGA, 1873, Littlehales to Thompson, Aug. 27.

40. CGA, 1865–66, Chief Constable W. S. Prince to Thompson, Sept. 12, 1866; CGA, 1873, Cathels to Thompson, Sept. 2.

41. TCM, 1874, Appendix, Report of the Fire, Water and Gas Committee, Feb. 9.

42. CGA, 1874, Petition of Consumers' Gas Company to Toronto Corporation, n.d., presumably February.

43. TCM, 1874, item 185, Feb. 23; ibid., Appendix, Report of Fire, Water and Gas Committee, April 27; CGC, MB, April 6, May 21, 1874; CGA, 1874, Littlehales to Thompson, June 13.

44. TCM, 1876, Items 1399, 1410, 1423, 1432, Nov. 27, Dec. 4; ibid., Appendix, Report of the Fire, Water and Gas Committee, Dec. 22; ibid., 1877, Item No. 95, Jan. 22; CGC, MB, Jan. 2, 13, Feb. 15, 19, Oct. 29, 1877.

45. See, e.g., CGA, 1869–70, George Yarker to E. H. Rutherford, Aug. 23, 1870; CGA, 1874, C. P. Sheard to Consumers' Gas, Jan. 15.

46. CGA, 1860, 1861, 1862 contain correspondence about the proposed inspection legislation. Report of Messrs. Harris and Thompson to the Finance Committee, April 26, 1860 is quoted; see also Richard Yates to Thompson, April 14, 1860.

47. CGA, 1873, telegrams to E. H. Rutherford from "Presidents of Principal Gas Co.'s of Ontario," April; the quotation is from the Annual Report for 1873. *Statutes of Canada*, 1873, 36 Vic., c. 48, The Inspection of Gas and Gas Meters Act. There being no House of Commons *Hansard* that year, there is no recorded debate on this matter. In the Senate, there were jokes about the relative darkness to be permitted by these regulations in various cities: see Canada, Senate, *Debates*, May 21, 1873. For standards adopted and methods of measurement, see Canada, House of Commons, *Sessional Papers*, 1874, vol. 5, no. 6, First Report of the Commissioner of Inland Revenue on the Inspection of Weights, Measures and Gas, pp. 9–10; see ibid., 1875, vol. 2, no. 2, Second Report, pp. 70–75, for illustrations of the equipment used.

48. Peebles, *Gas Industry*, pp. 11–15; Leslie T. Minchin, *The Gas Industry: Today and Tomorrow* (London: Harrap, 1966), pp. 12–19. Coal gas was produced in a retort, then fortified with petroleum vapour.

49. CGC, MB, April 21, 1879; CGA, 1879, Oiler to Toronto Gas Company, n.d., probably Dec. This file and the one for the following year are filled with complaints from, among others, the Chief Constable.

50. CGA, 1881, John Kerr to W. H. Pearson, June 13; CGA, 1880, J. H. Drought to Pearson, May 25; CGC, MB, Oct. 31, 1881.

51. CGA, 1880, Arthur S. Hardy to W. H. Pearson, Dec. 2.

52. Public Archives of Nova Scotia, Halifax *Annual Report*, 1872–73, Report of E. H. Keating, City Engineer; ibid., 1906–7, City Engineer's Report.

53. Alan F. J. Artibise, *Winnipeg: A Social History of Urban Growth, 1874–1914* (Montreal: McGill-Queen's University Press, 1975), ch. 12, "The Commercial Elite and the Water Supply", pp. 207–22.

54. Glenbow Foundation, Calgary MB, Oct. 6, 27, Nov. 16, 26, Dec. 7, 1887, May 23, July 11, Aug. 29, Sept. 19, 1888, April 16, 19, Sept. 17, Oct. 15, 1889. W. F. Orr, chairman of the Public Works Committee, negotiated this contract with the private company and acted as agent in the sale of its bonds: see Glenbow Foundation, Wesley F. Orr Papers, Letterbook I, especially letters to Hammond & Nanton in 1888–90.

55. VCA, Vancouver Water Works Papers, memorandum, n.d.; Vancouver Water Works Company Papers, Stock Book, Plans, Prospectus, and list of rates; Standing Committee MB, Water Works Committee, Oct. 21, 1890. See also Patricia Roy, *Vancouver: An Illustrated History* (Toronto: James Lorimer, 1980), p. 36.

56. Artibise, *Winnipeg*, pp. 214–22; Ruben C. Bellan, "The Development of Winnipeg as a Metropolitan Centre," Ph.D. thesis, Columbia University, 1958, pp. 210–12; H. Carl Goldenberg, *Report of the Royal Commission on the Municipal Finances and Administration of the City of Winnipeg* (Winnipeg: Government of Manitoba, 1939), pp. 177–84: *Canadian Engineer* 36 (May, 1919): 430.

57. *Montreal Gazette,* March 25, 1845; George R. Baldwin, *Report on the Supplying of the City of Quebec with Pure Water* (Boston, 1848); T. C. Keefer, *Report on the Supply of Water to the City of Hamilton* (Montreal: John Lovell, 1856). See also John Weaver, *Hamilton: An Illustrated History* (Toronto: James Lorimer, 1982), p. 68; T. C. Keefer, *Report on Water Supply for the City of Ottawa* (Ottawa: Bell & Woodburn, 1869); and T. C. Keefer, *Ottawa Water Works: Final Report* (Ottawa: A. S. Woodburn, 1876).

58. Archives of Saskatchewan, Regina MB, July 14, 1903.

59. Public Archives of Nova Scotia, Nova Scotia Light and Power Company Papers, Scrapbook no. 1; Halifax Gas Light Company Papers, MB, July 2, 1881, and a typical annual statement, Sept. 1, 1882.

60. Glenbow Foundation, Calgary MB, July 10, 13, 1905; Calgary Council Papers, Box 19, file 122, Gas; Calgary Trades and Labour Council Papers, MB, May 14, 1915; *Canadian Engineer* 23 (Nov. 14, 1912): 747. See also Max Foran, *Calgary: An Illustrated History* (Toronto: James Lorimer, 1978), pp. 104–5.

61. In 1877 the Toronto waterworks was worth over $2,000,000 and served 4,518 householders; Consumers' Gas, with assets of approximately $750,000 served 2,945 establishments.

CHAPTER 2

1. S. B. Warner, Jr., *Streetcar Suburbs* (Cambridge, Mass.: Harvard University Press, 1962); Peter Goheen, *Victorian Toronto, 1850 to 1900* (Chicago: University of Chicago, Department of Geography, 1970). For subtle qualification, see Theodore Hershberg, Harold Cox, Dale Light, and Richard Greenfield, "The Journey to Work: An Empirical Investigation of Work, Residence and Transportation, Philadelphia, 1850 and 1880," in Theodore Hershberg, ed., *Philadelphia* (New York: Oxford University Press, 1981), pp. 128–73.

2. MCM, Dec. 13, 20, 1859, Jan. 9, 11, 1860; *Toronto Globe,* Oct. 10, 22, 23, 29, Nov. 1, 1860; *Montreal Gazette,* Aug. 3, 1860.

3. Quoted in *Toronto Globe,* Oct, 30, 1860.

4. Jodoin quoted in *Montreal Gazette,* Sept. 14, 1860; other debates were reported on Aug. 3, Sept. 13, and 20; MCM, Aug. 1, Sept. 11, 12, 1860.

5. *Toronto Globe,* Nov. 1, 6, 1860; TCM, Oct. 2, 10, 22, 1860.

6. Michael Frisch, *Town into City* (Cambridge, Mass.: Harvard University Press, 1972); see also Jon C. Teaford, *The Municipal Revolution* (Chicago: University of Chicago Press, 1975).

7. MCM, April 4, 1860, Report of the Road Committee; see also TCM, 1860, Appendix, Report of the Select Committee on Street Railways, Oct. 22; *Statutes of Canada,* 1861, 24 Vic., c. 84, An Act to Incorporate the Montreal City Passenger Railway Company, and c. 83, An Act to Incorporate the Toronto Street Railway Company; MCA, By-laws, vol. 7½, no. 265, To Authorize the Establishment of a Passenger Railway in the City; TCM, Appendix, By-law no. 353, 1861. For the debate, see *Toronto Globe,* March 19, 1861.

8. MUCTCA, CPR, MB no. 1, Aug. 9, 17, Sept. 5, 1861.

9. C. Armstrong and H. V. Nelles, *The Revenge of the Methodist Bicycle Company* (Toronto: Peter Martin, 1977), pp. 27–28.

10. *Montreal Gazette,* Nov. 27, 1861; *La Minerve,* Nov. 28, 1861; *Montreal Witness,* Nov. 30, 1861.

11. MUCTCA, CPR, MB no. 1, Annual Meetings, Nov. 5, 1862; Nov. 4, 1863; Nov. 2, 1864.

12. MUCTCA, CPR, Annual Reports; president's remarks in MB no. 2, Feb. 20, 1866. For a brief introduction to street railway economics, see Clay McShane, *Technology and Reform: Street Railways and the Growth of Milwaukee, 1887–1900* (Madison: State Historical Society of Wisconsin, 1974); and Charles W. Cheape, *Moving the Masses: Urban Public Transit in New York, Boston and Philadelphia, 1880–1912* (Cambridge, Mass.: Harvard University Press, 1980).

13. MUCTCA, CPR, MB no. 2, Annual Meeting, Nov. 7, 1866.

14. For biographical information, see Gerald Tulchinsky, *The River Barons* (Toronto: University of Toronto Press, 1977).

15. MUCTCA, CPR, MB no. 2, Nov. 7, Dec. 5, 1865, Jan. 16, 23, Feb. 20, 1866.

16. Ibid., no. 1, Feb. 15, March 15, 1862, Feb. 21, March 7, 1863, Jan. 9, 1864, Jan. 10, 17, 31, Feb. 28, April 11, 1865. See MB no. 2, Feb. 24, March 2, 1868, for specific discussions of the care and feeding of company livestock. Typically, a pair of horses hauled a car about 20 miles each day. In the late 1860s a horse was valued in the company inventories at $70.

17. Ibid., no. 2, Nov. 7, 1865, Oct. 23, 30, 1866.

18. Ibid., no. 1, June 23, July 29, 1864; no. 2, Aug. 8, Sept. 25, 1865, April 24, 1866; no. 4, June 27, 1872; no. 5, Dec. 5, 1878.

19. Ibid., no. 2, Aug. 11, 1866; Jan. 14, 1867.

20. Ibid., no. 2, Aug. 11, 1868. In 1874 the president of Consumers' Gas in Toronto was in the habit of borrowing company funds for personal use without permission, running up large cab bills, padding his expense account, buying cases of champagne for the office and taking bottles home with him. When an investigation by the board revealed this discreditable behavior the president was asked not only to resign but to reimburse the company: CGC, MB, July 28 to Oct. 15, 1874.

21. MUCTCA, CPR, MB no. 2, May 15, 16, 22, 1866.

22. Ibid., no. 4, May 8, 15, 1873.

23. Ibid., no. 5, April 29, 1880; no. 6, May 7, 1885, June 4, 1885.

24. Ibid., no. 3, Nov. 2, 1870, Oct. 19, 25, Dec. 21, 1871, Jan. 18, Feb. 16, April 11, June 3, Aug. 8, 1872.

25. Ibid., no. 1, Feb. 7, 14, 21, 1865; Letterbook, John Glass to Thos. Ryan at Quebec, Feb. 8, 27, Aug. 17, 25, 1865; MB no. 2, Jan. 18, Feb. 4, 1869, Nov. 17, 24, Dec. 8, 1870; Dec. 30, 1867, Feb. 8, Mar. 1, 29, April 4, July 19, 1869; MB no. 3, Nov. 24, Dec. 8, 22, 1870.

26. Ibid., MB no. 4, Dec. 11, 20, 1873, Jan. 7, June 4, July 31, Aug. 6, Dec. 3, 17, 1874, Jan. 14, Feb. 24, April 22, May 20, 21, 27, July 2, Nov. 3, 9, 11, 13, 16, 17, 20, 26, Dec. 13, 16, 1875, Mar. 2, 1876.

27. Armstrong and Nelles, *Revenge,* pp. 27–34. For a technical description of operations, see L. H. Pursley, *Street Railways of Toronto, 1861–1921* (Los Angeles: Electric Railways Publications, 1958).

28. Not all firms were as fortunate. The Halifax street railway, chartered in 1863 to connect the Intercolonial Railroad station with the city, went bankrupt in the early 1870s and was abandoned. Revived in the 1880s, it fell into receivership again in 1893. See the Provincial Archives of Nova Scotia, Halifax Street Railway Company Stock Register, Ledger and Journal; also Vertical Mss. File, Halifax Transit.

29. MUCTCA, CPR Letterbook, 1861–67, T. Morland to City Road Committee, Mar. 30, 1864; MB no. 1, May 2, 1863, Jan. 30, 1864, Jan. 4, 1869; MB no. 3, June 15, 1871.

30. Ibid., MB no. 4, Nov. 29, 1873.

31. Ibid., July 2, 1875, Memorandum for Councillor David; July 22, 29, Nov. 1, 3, 1875; Feb. 3, 1876.

32. For details of this upheaval, see verbatim report of 1877 annual meeting in the *Montreal Herald,* Nov. 8, 1877. A resumé of each step in the process is printed with the minutes of the company in MB no. 5, Jan. 1877–April 1878, pp. 11–14.

33. MCM, Mar. 8, May 17, 31, 1880, Jan. 10, Feb. 21, Aug. 15, 29, Sept. 5, Oct. 24, 1881; MUCTCA, CPR, MB no. 5, Sept. 8, 1881.

34. MUCTCA, CPR, MB No. 5, April 19, 23, 26, May 4, 10, 1883.

35. For a splendid account of Senecal's career, see *Dictionary of Canadian Biography,* vol. 11 (Toronto: University of Toronto Press, 1983), pp. 806–16.

36. MCM, Jan. 19, 1885, and numerous meetings Feb. and Nov. 1885. The substance of this bylaw had in fact been approved the previous year. It was finally voted on Dec. 21, 1885 and passed 19 to 5.

37. MCA, By-laws, No. 148, Dec. 21, 1885.

38. For details, see Armstrong and Nelles, *Revenge,* pp. 27–34.

39. The events of the 1886 street railway strikes are familiar from at least three recent accounts: Desmond Morton, *Mayor Howland* (Toronto: Hakkert, 1973), pp. 99–104; Gregory Kealey, *Toronto Workers Respond to Industrial Capitalism, 1867–1892* (Toronto: University of Toronto Press, 1980), pp. 199–212; Gregory Kealey and Bryan Palmer, *Dreaming of What Might Be: The Knights of Labor in Ontario, 1880–1900* (Cambridge: Cambridge University Press, 1982), pp. 116–26. That same month the Knights of Labor organized the street railway workers in Philadelphia and led a strike of transit employees in New York City.

40. *Toronto News,* Mar. 5, 6, 8, 10, 11, 12, 13, 1886; *Street Railway Gazette,*

March, 1886. For a compendium of disagreement between the city and the company, see *Toronto Street Railway: Charter, By-laws, and Agreements Relating to Toronto Street Railway Company* (Toronto, 1891), in CTA.

41. *Toronto News,* May 8, 10, 18, 20, 26, 1886.

42. TCM, Report of the City Clerk, June 23, 1890; Toronto Empire, June 23, 1890.

43. *Toronto World,* May 18, 1891.

44. Sources for Tables 8 and 9: (a) population for both metropolitan areas in 1881 and 1891 was taken from George Nader, *Cities of Canada,* vol. 2 (Toronto: Macmillan, 1976), pp. 126, 203, with growth between the census intervals spread evenly over the decade; (b) passenger numbers were compiled from *Montreal Gazette* reports of Montreal City Passenger Company annual meetings and Pursley, *Street Railway of Toronto,* p. 131; (c) daily return trips were calculated on 6.5 days a week for the Montreal railway (to adjust for lower Sunday ridership) and 6 days for the Toronto system (which did not operate on Sunday); (d) the labour force figures were computed using the calculations of F. Denton and S. Ostry, *Historical Estimates of the Canadian Labour Force* (Ottawa: Queen's Printer, 1967), pp. 20–29. (the coefficient rises from 0.556 in 1881 to 0.563 in 1891, and once again the increase is distributed evenly over the series).

45. E. P. Thompson, "Time, Work-Discipline, and Industrial Capitalism," *Past and Present* 38 (1967): 56–97; Daniel Nelson, *Managers and Workers* (Madison: University of Wisconsin Press, 1975).

CHAPTER 3

1. On the invention of the telephone, see Robert V. Bruce, *Bell: Alexander Graham Bell and the Conquest of Silence* (Boston: Little, Brown, 1973); and David A. Hounshell, "Bell and Gray: Contrasts in Style, Politics and Etiquette," *Proceedings of the IEEE* 64 (1976): 1305–14. On arc lighting, see Harold Passer, *The Electrical Manufacturers, 1875–1900* (Cambridge, Mass.: Harvard University Press, 1953), pp. 11–74. On the development of incandescent lighting and the electric utilities industry, see T. P. Hughes, *Networks of Power: Electrification in Western Society, 1880–1930* (Baltimore, Md.: Johns Hopkins University Press, 1983). On electric street railway development, see Harold Passer, "Frank Julian Sprague: Father of Electric Traction, 1857–1934," in William Miller, ed., *Men in Business* (Cambridge, Mass.: Harvard University Press, 1952), pp. 212–37, and Passer, *Electrical Manufacturers,* pp. 216–75.

2. Edward Seidensticker, *Low City, High City* (New York: Alfred Knopf, 1983), p. 19; ibid., pp. 43–46, 80–82 for the contribution of trams and electric lights to the progress of "Civilization and Enlightment" in Meiji Japan.

3. Alfred D. Chandler, *The Visible Hand: The Managerial Revolution in American Business* (Cambridge, Mass.: Harvard University Press, 1977), pts. II, III, IV.

4. See, *inter alia,* E. B. Ogle, *Long Distance Please* (Toronto: Collins, 1979), pp. 278ff. for a chronology of telephone diffusion in Canada; William Patten, *Pioneering the Telephone in Canada* (Montreal, 1926); Passer, *Electrical Manufacturers,* pp. 19, 30, 114, 121; Passer, "Frank Julian Sprague," p. 228.

5. Hughes, *Networks of Power*, p. 29.

6. Alexander Graham Bell to his father, Melville Bell, March 10, 1876 quoted in Bruce, *Bell*, pp. 181.

7. Alexander Graham Bell to Melville Bell, Feb. 29, 1876, quoted in Bruce, *Bell*, p. 172.

8. Passer, *Electrical Manufacturers*, p. 83; Hughes, *Networks of Power*, pp. 28–40.

9. *New York Sun*, Oct. 10, 1878, quoted in Hughes, *Networks of Power*, p. 32.

10. Joseph Swan had demonstrated (but not patented) a carbon filament bulb with a short life considerably earlier: see Percy Dunseath, *A History of Electrical Engineering* (London: Faber & Faber, 1962), pp. 99–208.

11. Passer, *Electrical Manufacturers*, pp. 216–55.

12. This must be one of the most poignant moments in Canadian business history. The circumstances are recounted from Bell's perspective in Bruce, *Bell*, pp. 162–68, and from Brown's in J. M. S. Careless, *Brown of the Globe* (Toronto: Macmillan, 1963), vol. 2, pp. 343–45. The two key documents are to be found in PAC, George Brown Papers, George Brown to Anne Brown, Dec. 30, 1875, and Feb. 16, 1976. Bell almost missed his chance to patent his conception of the telephone in the United States by waiting for Brown's reply.

13. Edison used this now common expression in 1878 to describe the faults and difficulties that arise during the development phase: see Hughes, *Networks of Power*, p. 33.

14. Ibid., pp. 43–45, 55–57, 65–66.

15. Bruce, *Bell*, p. 281; Passer, "Frank Julian Sprague," p. 226.

16. Chandler, *Visible Hand*, pp. 200–203, 309–11, 426–33. See also Elisha P. Douglass, *The Coming of Age of American Business* (Chapel Hill: University of North Carolina Press, 1971), pp. 478–517; Passer, *Electrical Manufacturers*, pp. 321–68; John Brooks, *Telephone* (New York: Harper & Row, 1975), pp. 59–126.

17. Clarence Hogue, André Bolduc et Daniel Larouche, *Québec: Un Siècle d'électricité* (Montreal: Libre Expression, 1979), p. 24; MCA, Light Committee Files, Mar. 15, 1892: appropriations for the year were electric light $140,160, gaslight $12,920, additional lights $3,650, total $160,855.

18. *Lovell's Ontario Gazetteer and Directory, 1884–85* (Toronto, 1885), p. 1332; ibid., 1889–90, pp. 1384–85; *Dominion of Canada Business Directory* (Toronto: R. L. Polk, 1891), passim.

19. Bruce, *Bell*, pp. 199–211; Hogue et al., *Un Siècle*, pp. 19–20. Bell received some of his earliest business advice from a newspaper editor in Titusville, Pennsylvania.

20. Hughes, *Networks of Power*, p. 30; Bruce, *Bell*, pp. 188–98. For further analysis of Bell's consciously public, theatrical style, see Hounshell, "Bell and Gray." On the international expositions, see John Allwood, *The Great Exhibitions* (London: Studio Vista, 1977).

21. The quoted phrases are taken from titles of books about U.S. inventors written between the Civil War and the Great War (located in the Baker Library, Graduate School of Business Administration, Harvard University).

22. Tibor Skitovsky, *The Joyless Economy: An Inquiry into Human Satisfaction and Consumer Dissatisfaction* (New York: Oxford University Press, 1976), pp. 31–59, 108, 282–84.

23. Earl H. Kinmonth uses the phrase "character ethic" in *The Self-Made Man in Meiji Japanese Thought* (Berkeley: University of California Press, 1981), pp. 4–18. See also John G. Cawelti, *Apostles of the Self-Made Man in America* (New Brunswick, N.J.: Rutgers University Press, 1954); T. P. Hughes, Introduction to Samuel Smiles, *Selections for the Lives of the Engineers* (Cambridge, Mass.: MIT Press, 1966), pp. 1–29; and Allan Smith, "The Myth of the Self-Made Man in English Canada, 1850–1914," *Canadian Historical Review* 59 (1978): 189–219.

24. The most frequently cited evidence is Bell's 1878 letter to the English shareholders in which he likens the telephone to a gas company, with a central office linked to each house by mains, thus permitting "direct communication between any two places in the city." But he goes on to say, "Such a plan as this, though impracticable at the present moment, will, I firmly believe, be the outcome of the introduction of the telephone to the public." See Ithiel de Sola Pool, ed., *The Social Impact of the Telephone* (Cambridge, Mass.: MIT Press, 1977), pp. 156–57; and Ithiel de Sola Pool, *Forecasting the Telephone* (Norwood, N.J.: Ablex, 1983), p. 21.

25. Bruce, *Bell,* pp. 258–87.

26. Patten, *Pioneering,* pp. 19–45; Robert Collins, *A Voice from Afar* (Toronto: McGraw-Hill-Ryerson, 1977), pp. 65–84.

27. Patten, *Pioneering,* pp. 55–63.

28. Bruce, *Bell,* pp. 270–71; Chandler, *Visible Hand,* pp. 200–201; John Brooks, *Telephone* (New York: Harper & Row, 1975), pp. 59–73; R. J. Tosiello, "The Birth and Early Years of the Bell Telephone System, 1876–1880," Ph.D. thesis, Boston University, 1971. After trying and failing to overturn the Bell patents, and preoccupied with Jay Gould's threat to its own monopoly, Western Union chose to abandon the unproven telephone field to the upstart Bell Company in return for a percentage of all patent license fees and an undertaking by Bell to stay out of the telegraph field. Just as this book went to press there appeared two valuable new studies which further examine these developments: see George D. Smith, *The Anatomy of a Business Strategy: Bell, Western Electric and the Origins of the American Telephone Industry,* and Robert W. Garnet, *The Telephone Enterprise: The Evolution of the Bell System's Horizontal Structure* (both Baltimore: Johns Hopkins University Press, 1985), two volumes in the AT&T Series in Telephone History.

29. R. C. Fetherstonhaugh, *Charles Fleetford Sise, 1834–1918* (Montreal: Gazette Printing, 1944).

30. BCA, Sise Letterbooks, Sise to W. H. Forbes, Mar. 11, 1880. The pages of these letterbooks have been separated and filed with other correspondence in Boxes 2755-22, 23, 24.

31. Biographical information from *Lovell's Montreal Directory,* 1879–80, 1880–81 (including the advertisement for the Royal Canadian Insurance Company); *Dictionary of Canadian Biography,* vol. 11, pp. 559–60; and C. H. Mackintosh, ed., *The Canadian Parliamentary Companion and Annual Register, 1881* (Ottawa: Citizen Printing and Publishing, 1881).

32. BCA, Sise Letterbooks and Correspondence, Forbes to Sise, July 8, 1880. The key letters outlining the takeover negotiations are Forbes to Sise, Mar. 8, 1880; Sise to Forbes, Mar. 11, 13, 15, 20, 24, 25, 27, 31, April 9, 10, 16, 18, 19, 21, May 15, 17, 28, 29, June 2, 1880. Much of this correspondence has to do with setting up two companies in Canada, negotiations not discussed in the text. Forbes did not

think of Canada as simply a region of the United States; he insisted upon the creation of a patent-holding company (Company A) much like the National Bell Telephone Company in the United States, which would lease rights to local operating companies, in this case, the Bell Telephone Company of Canada (Company B). J. J. C. Abbott saw no need for this structure, as Company A's powers were possessed by Company B, but Forbes and Vail considered a patent-owning company under their control as a means of managing the Canadian situation without having to commit much capital to the operating company. In any event, Company A was folded into Company B in 1882 with American Bell taking stock in Canadian Bell for these patents.

33. BCA, Sise Letterbooks, Sise to Forbes, April 20, 1881.

34. See BCA, Sise Log Book no. 1, Oct. 1, 1881, April 14, 1882, May 7–June 9, 1884, for inspection tours of Maritime and Manitoba agencies. Baker in western Ontario, Neilson in Toronto, Ahearn in Ottawa, McFarlane in Quebec, Wainwright in Winnipeg and Wagstaff in the Maritimes were the principal agents.

35. Fetherstonhaugh, *Sise*, pp. 136–38; BCA, Sise Letterbooks, Sise to Baker, Sept. 1, 1880; Sise Log Book no. 1, May 12, 1881: "Baker here discussing affairs of Dept. Instructed him to cease opening in small towns and to stiffen rates."

36. BCA, Sise Letterbooks, Sise to Hugh Baker, March 9, 1883.

37. BCA, Sise Log Book no. 1, Jan. 7, 15, 1881; McFarlane Scrapbook no. 2, newspaper advertisement, 1885, and Bell Telephone Company circular, Feb. 1, 1887.

38. BCA, Sise Log Book no. 1, Nov. 20, 26, 1880, Jan. 24, 1881, May 11, 1882.

39. See BCA, Sise Log Book no. 1, Sept. 27, Oct. 1, 1881, Sept. 6, 1882, Dec. 4, 1883, Oct. 1, 1884, for authorization of lines.

40. Ibid., Oct. 1, 1881, Dec. 4, 1883, Oct. 1, 1884. On the telegraph merger of 1882, see Collins, *Voice from Afar,* "The Rise and Fall of a Boy Wonder," pp. 85–96; and Erastus Wiman, *The Union of the Telegraph Interests in Canada,* PAC, pamphlet, 1881, 2–300.

41. BCA, Correspondence, Forbes to Sise, July 13, 1880.

42. For an examination of the Bell Telephone Company in the literature dealing with multinational corporations, see Graham D. Taylor, "Charles F. Sise, Bell Canada and the Americans: A Study in Managerial Autonomy, 1880–1905," Canadian Historical Association, *Historical Papers,* 1982, pp. 11–30. Early in 1882, Western Union interests demanded two seats on the board; Forbes recommended adding Andrew Allan and Erastus Wiman to soothe Western Union sensibilities. Sise strongly objected: Wiman was *persona non grata* with the public and much of the Canadian business community after his handling of the telegraph merger, and a seat on the Bell board would allow him to interfere with expansion plans; as for Allan, "he and Mr. Hugh Mackay have not spoken for years and Mr. Mackay says plainly that he will not remain on the Board if Mr. Allan is there." Western Union remained without representation and shortly afterward quietly unloaded its Canadian Bell stock. Sise lost the dubious support of a large corporation, but he kept his company united. BCA, Sise Letterbooks, Sise to Forbes, Feb. 15, 16, 18, 1882; Log Book no. 1, Mar. 7, 1882: "Decided that no W.U. element was wanted on Board." Western Union had acquired its stock in Bell for the sale of its Maritime telephone exchanges.

43. *Statutes of Canada,* 1880, 43 Vic., c. 67, An Act to Incorporate the Bell Telephone Company of Canada.

44. Quebec, *Statutes,* 1881, 44–45 Vic., c. 66; Ontario, *Statutes,* 1882, 45 Vic. c. 71. Sise himself lobbied both legislatures for the passage of these bills; see BCA, Sise Log Book no. 1, June 19–28, 1881, Feb. 17, 1882.

45. Canada, Senate, *Debates,* 1882, April 26, May 5, pp. 438–39, 612–13; BCA, Sise Log Book no. 1, April 13, 20, May 4, 5, 1882. Hector Cameron, the member for Victoria North did the parliamentary work for the company; see BCA, Sise Letterbooks, Sise to J. E. Hudson, June 27, 1882. It is unlikely that anyone realized the full import of this declaration at the time.

46. BCA, Sise Log Book no. 1, Nov. 3, 1885.

47. BCA, Correspondence, S. C. Wood to Sise, Aug. 13, Oct. 30, 1884; Jan. 19, 20, 26, 1885. Wood, the company's Toronto lawyer, suspected that Taché's decision had been dictated by his minister. Sise and H. P. Dwight suspected that someone in Ottawa—that "eminent electrician"—was attempting to manoeuvre the government into taking over the telegraph and telephone lines and putting him at the head of the public corporation; see BCA, Sise Letterbooks, Sise to H. P. Dwight, April 1, 1882.

CHAPTER 4

1. Clarence Hogue et al., *Québec: Un Siècle d'électricité* (Montreal: Libre Expression, 1979), pp. 22–23.

2. E.g., Quebec, *Statutes,* 1881, 44 Vic. c. 70, An Act to Incorporate the Montreal Electric Light Company.

3. See Thomas P. Hughes, *Networks of Power* (Baltimore, Md.: Johns Hopkins University Press, 1983), pp. 47–78, for technology transfer to Great Britain and Germany. John Andre Millard, "The Diffusion of Electric Power Technology in England, 1880–1914," Ph.D. thesis, Emory University, 1981; Brian Bowers, *A History of Electric Light and Power* (London, Peter Peregrinus, 1982). See also John P. Mckay, *Tramways and Trolleys: The Rise of Urban Mass Transportation in Europe* (Princeton, N.J.: Princeton University Press, 1976), pp. 35–83.

4. PAO, T. L. Church Scrapbooks, undated clipping; TCM, July 19, 1883, communication from J. J. Wright.

5. HQA, REC, MB, March 28, April 9, June 23, 1884; Hogue et al., *Un Siècle,* pp. 28–31.

6. BCA, Correspondence, Hugh Neilson to Sise, April 28, 1884; Hogue et al., *Un siècle,* pp. 28–29.

7. HQA, REC, MB, Feb. 4, 23, 1887; BCA, Correspondence, H. P. Dwight to Sise, June 29, June 16, 1885, June 1, 1886.

8. HQA, REC, MB, Nov. 11, 12, 13, Dec. 12, 1884, Jan. 12, Feb. 5, 23, 1885, March 3, April 16, 27, May 5, July 7, Dec. 8, 1885, Jan. 5, Dec. 22, 1886, July 13, 20, 1887. The Ottawa plant sold in 1886 for $50,000 cash; see ibid., Jan. 12, Feb. 23, March 3, April 16, 27, 1886. A company agent sold the Halifax company without even consulting the board of Royal Electric, leaving them very much in the dark about the affair. In the end, $21,450 seemed to have been lost, and the lawyers were called in.

9. Ibid., Oct. 6, 1885, July 3, 1889.

10. In December, 1884, they had to stand behind another loan and submit personal notes of $4,000 each to the company. When the Bank of Montreal turned down a request to borrow $15,000 on the strength of Irvine's and Ross's stock in the company in 1885, five directors advanced $4,000 each at 7%. In March, 1886,

the board members put up $2,500 a head to pay a clearly unwarranted dividend largely to themselves. Irvine eventually asked to step down as treasurer because he was "not well enough known to banks"; see ibid., Nov. 27, Dec. 12, 15, 1884, May 26, June 2, 1885, Mar. 27, 1886, Oct. 20, 1886.

11. *Dominion of Canada Business Directory, 1891;* See also *Lovell's Ontario Gazetteer and Directory,* 1884–85, and 1889–90, especially the latter, pp. 1384–85 for the advertisement of the Ball Company listing all its installations.

12. HQA, REC, MB, Annual Meeting, April 1, 1890; April 15, June 22, July 2, Nov. 11, 1890.

13. Ibid., April 15, 1890; Hogue et al., *Un Siècle,* p. 41.

14. CGC, MB, Oct. 28, 1878.

15. CGA, 1881, Francis Clemow to W. H. Pearson, June 13, 1878. Ontario, *Statutes,* 1879, 42 Vic., c. 87; see also 1880, 43 Vic., c. 23, which gave these powers to all Ontario gas companies.

16. Hogue et al. *Un Siècle,* p. 31; Quebec, *Statutes,* 42–43 Vic., c. 81.

17. HQA, Montreal Gas Company, MB, Dec. 2, 1885, Oct. 23, 1888.

18. HQA, REC, MB, Sept. 16, 1890.

19. See Harold Passer, *The Electrical Manufacturers, 1875–1900* (Cambridge, Mass.: Harvard University Press, 1953), pp. 48–51, for a discussion of the technical details of gas–arc light competition. In the early 1880s, arc lights were between 15 and 18 times as expensive as gas lamps in New York City.

20. TCM, 1884, Appendix, Mayor's Inaugural Address; April 28, Aug. 25; Reports of the Committee on Fire and Gas, May 20, April 15, Aug. 25, Oct. 15, which include the relevant correspondence; TCM, 1885, Report of the Fire and Gas Committee, Dec. 8, 23.

21. MCM, June 19, 1882, Oct. 29, Nov. 12, Dec. 3, 10, 27, 1883, Jan. 14, Feb. 18, 1884. See also MCA, Light Committee MB, passim.

22. W. H. Atherton, *Montreal* (Montreal: S. J. Clarke, 1914), vol. 2, pp. 184–85; HQA, REC, MB, Feb. 15, March 2, May 4, 1886; MCA, Light Committee MB, Jan. 5, 20, Feb. 1, 16, March 26, April 15, May 10, 17, 1886; Hogue et al., *Un Siècle,* pp. 32–35.

23. HQA, REC, MB, Feb. 3, 1885, June 1, 4, Aug. 27, 1886.

24. CGC, MB, Sept. 17, 1888.

25. Thomas Edison, however, recognized the long-term advantages of low rates. In an April 7, 1891, letter to W. D. Marks, who was involved in an Edison lighting venture in Philadelphia, he observed: "To my mind the raising of the price from ¾¢ to 1¢ per lamp hour is a bid for competition. I am a believer in *insuring the permanency of an investment* by keeping prices so low that there is no inducement to others to come in and ruin it. There seems to be a law in commercial things as in nature. If one attempts to obtain more profit than general average he is immediately punished by competition"; quoted in Nicholas B. Wainwright, *History of the Philadelphia Electric Company, 1881–1961* (Philadelphia: Philadelphia Electric, 1961), p. 50.

26. Manitoba, *Statutes,* 1880, 43 Vic., c. 36, An Act to Incorporate the Manitoba Electric and Gas Light Company.

27. Public Archives of Nova Scotia, Halifax Gas Light Company, MB, Aug. 25, Sept. 9, 1887.

28. BCER, Vancouver Gas Company, MB, Nov. 1, 1887.

29. HQA, Montreal Gas Company, MB, Feb. 1, May 17, 1887.

30. CGC, MB, Dec. 17, 27, 31, 1888, Jan. 3, 7, 1889.

31. BCA, Sise Log Book no. 1, June 8, memorandum of October (n.d.), 1881.

32. CGC, MB, Oct. 26, 1885, Jan. 18, 1886, April 1, 4, 18, Oct. 31, 1887; TCM, 1887, March 17, April 12, and 1888, Appendix, T. H. Menzies to Mayor E. F. Clarke, Oct. 27; Ontario, *Statutes,* 1887, 50 Vic., c. 85. These issues are treated in more detail in our unpublished paper, "In Defence of Private Enterprise: Gas Supply in Toronto, 1840–1910"; and "The Rise of Civic Populism in Toronto, 1870–1920," in Victor Russell, ed., *Forging a Consensus: Historical Essays on Toronto* (Toronto: University of Toronto Press, 1984), pp. 192–237.

33. *Saturday Night,* Jan. 14, 21, 28, 1888; Menzies to Clarke, cited in n. 32.

34. CGC, MB, May 10, 20, 23, 27, 28, June 3, 7, 8, July 15, 1889; *Toronto World,* Feb. 5, May 28, June 4, 1889; *Saturday Night,* June 8, 1889; CM, 1889, June 24.

35. TCM, 1889, Appendix, Fire and Gas Committee Reports, Feb. 27, April 24, May 27; Mayor's Message, Oct. 1.

36. Atherton, *Montreal,* vol. 2, pp. 184–86. See also J. I. Cooper, *Montreal: A Brief History* (Montreal: McGill-Queens University Press, 1969), pp. 99–102.

37. MCA, Light Committee MB, June 1, 7, 19, Sept. 4, 25, Oct. 23, Nov. 28, 1888; HQA, REC, MB, Nov. 26, 1888.

38. MCA, Light Committee MB, Sept. 25, 1888.

39. Ibid., Dec. 4, 1888; MCM, Dec. 27, 1888; HQA, REC, MB, Dec. 15, 31, 1888.

40. See Hogue et al., *Un Siècle,* pp. 38–41, for charges and suspicion. Royal bought out Craig shortly afterward.

41. Thibaudeau received a bonus of $2,000 and 5% of profits. The company commenced paying a 6% dividend in 1889.

42. TCM, July 14, Oct. 13, 1890. See TCM, 1891, Appendix C, Mayor's Valedictory, Jan. 15, 1892, for a thorough review of the streetlighting issue, and Armstrong and Nelles, *The Revenge of the Methodist Bicycle Company* (Toronto: Peter Martin, 1977), pp. 121–28, for the subsequent streetlighting scandal of 1894.

43. HQA, REC, MB, Nov. 3, 1886.

44. Passer, *Electrical Manufacturers,* pp. 211–75; Alfred D. Chandler, *The Visible Hand* (Cambridge, Mass.: Harvard University Press, 1977), pp. 309–10, 426–33.

45. PAC, E. H. Bronson Papers, vol. 711, T. C. Keefer to Bronson, Feb. 27, 1890.

46. MUCTCA, CPR, MB, Nov. 3, 1886, June 22, 1887, March 8, May 3, 1888, March 3, 31, 1892.

47. Winnipeg City Archives, Council Communications, no. 1834, H. N. Ruttan, Report on the Storage Battery and Overhead Wire Systems of Electric Street Railways for the City of Winnipeg, 1891; see Council MB, Feb. 1, April 29, Dec. 28, 1891, for the debate on the street railway bylaw. See also H. W. Blake, *The Era of Street Cars in Winnipeg, 1881–1925* (Winnipeg, 1971).

48. OCM, Jan. 21, April 15, June 3, 1889; Ottawa City Archives, Special Committee MB, Committee on Street Railways, Dec. 26, 1888, Jan. 31, April 2, 9, 1889.

49. PAC, Bronson Papers, vol. 703, O. Mowat to Bronson, Feb, 6, 10, 1890; vol. 712, Memorial of the Municipal Convention, Nov. 12–14, 1889; *Ottawa Citizen,* Nov. 27, 1889; OCM, Message of Mayor Jacob Erratt, 1890.

50. PAC, Bronson Papers, vol. 703, A. MacLean to Mayor, Feb. 13, 1890; D. B. Mactavish to Bronson, Feb. 27, 1890; vol. 711, Resolution of the City of Ottawa, March 6, 1890; Ontario, *Statutes,* 1890, 53 Vic., c. 50. See also Peter Gillis, "E. H. Bronson and Corporate Capitalism," M.A. thesis, Queen's University, 1976, pp. 131–41.

51. *Ottawa Citizen,* April 22, 1890. See OCM, April 24, 1890, May 18, 1890, for reports of the street railway committee.

52. OCM, July 7, 14, Aug. 18, Oct. 6, 1890; Special Committee MB, Street Railway Committee, June 7, July 9, 1890; *Ottawa Citizen,* July 14, 15, 22, Aug. 18, 19, 21, Sept. 18, Oct. 10, 13, 1890.

53. See OCM, 1890, pp. 707–15, for text of Bylaw 1098, the Street Railway Agreement; *Ottawa Citizen,* Oct. 20, 1890.

54. This was also true in Hamilton in 1893 when a local syndicate fought off a proposal from a group of Toronto and Montreal financiers. M. F. Campbell, "Seventy years with Hamilton's Street Railway," *Wentworth Bygones* (1960): 16–22; H. I. Spanger, "A History of the Hamilton Street Railway Company," *Wentworth Bygones* 2 (1966): 22–23; R. Lucas, "The Hamilton Street Railway Strike of 1906," graduate research paper, York University, 1973, p. 4.

55. TCM, 1890, Appendix, Toronto Street Railway, Specifications for Tenders; CTA, Executive Committee Communications, 1891, Report on Tenders, W. T. Jennings, R. T. Coady, and C. R. W. Biggar, July 13, 1891. A detailed chronology can be found in CTA, "In the Matter of the Investigation Before His Honour Judge McDougall Pursuant to the Resolutions of City Council," Oct. 8, Nov. 13, 1894, *Evidence,* vol. 2, pp. 538–46. This franchise is dealt with at some length in Armstrong and Nelles, *Revenge,* pp. 35–48, and Gregory Kealey, *Toronto Workers Respond to Industrial Capitalism, 1867–1892* (Toronto: University of Toronto Press, 1980), pp. 274–90.

56. MCM, July 20, 1890; Feb. 15, Feb. 22, Mar. 14, 1892.

57. MUCTCA, MSR, MB, April 1, 28, May 12, 16, 17, 26, June 7, 23, July 7, 1892. MCM, June 28, July 4, 5, 8, 12, 19, 25, Aug. 8, 1892, Jan. 9, 1893. On July 19 one tender was withdrawn and three rejected by votes of 21 to 15. MUCTCA, MSR, MB, July 7, 20, 21, Aug. 11, 1892. For general accounts of Montreal transit, see MSR, *Annual Report,* 1910, pp. 24–42, "A Brief History of the Montreal Street Railway Company from 1861 to 1910"; J. M. Lajeunesse, *Histoire du transport en commune à Montréal* (Montreal: Appolon, 1933); and Omer S. A. Lavallée, *The Montreal City Passenger Railway Company* (Montreal: Canadian Railroad Historical Association, 1961).

58. See BCER, Vancouver Street Railway Company, MB and Letterbook for details. See also Patricia Roy, "The British Columbia Electric Railway Company, 1897–1928: A British Company in British Columbia," Ph.D. thesis, University of British Columbia, 1970, pp. 1–43.

59. On H. A. Everett's various promotions, see Melvin Holli, *Reform in Detroit* (New York: Oxford University Press, 1969); Graeme O'Geran, *A History of Detroit Street Railways* (Detroit: Conover Press, 1933); and Gerald Onn, "The His-

tory of the London Street Railway Company," M.A. thesis, University of Western Ontario, 1958.

60. Fred Angus, *Loyalist City Streetcars* (Toronto: Railfare Enterprises, 1979).

61. See our article "A Curious Capital Flow: Canadian Investment in Mexico, 1902-1911," *Business History Review* 58 (1984): 178-203.

62. On Whitney and Pearson, see Charles W. Cheape, *Moving the Masses* (Cambridge, Mass.: Harvard University Press, 1980), pp. 40-70, 107-25. For Halifax, see R. W. Brown, *Halifax: Birney Stronghold* (Montreal: Canadian Railway Historical Association, 1954); W. R. Bird, *Golden Jubilee Souvenir: 1908-1958* (Halifax: Amalgamated Association of Street, Electric, Railway and Motor Coach Employees of America, 1958); Nova Scotia, *Statutes*, 1889, 52 Vic., c. 135; 1890, 53 Vic., c. 193; 1895, 58 Vic., c. 107; Public Archives of Nova Scotia, Nova Scotia Light and Power Company Scrapbooks, Annual Reports; Halifax Council MB, July 16, 1895.

63. The Ontario Hydro Library has most of the issues of *Canadian Electrical News* for the 1890s. The proceedings of the annual meeting of the Canadian Electrical Association were usually printed in the October issue.

CHAPTER 5

1. J. P. Gould and C. E. Ferguson, *Microeconomic Theory* (Homewood, Ill.: Irwin-Dorsey, 1980), pp. 245-78; P. J. Garfield and W. F. Lovejoy, *Public Utility Economics* (Englewood Cliffs, N.J.: Prentice-Hall, 1964), pp. 15-26, 148-54.

2. See T. P. Hughes, *Networks of Power* (Baltimore, Md.: Johns Hopkins University Press, 1982), pp. 262-84, for a California example.

3. Manitoba, *Statutes*, 1892, 55 Vic., c. 56.

4. H. W. Blake, *The Era of Street Cars in Winnipeg, 1881-1955* (Winnipeg, 1971); Manitoba, *Statutes*, 1895, 58 & 59 Vic., c. 54; WESR, MB, vol. 1, May 7, 1894.

5. Manitoba Hydro Achives, Manitoba Electric and Gas Light Company, MB, vol. 2, Jan. 30, May 26, Aug. 4, 18, 1893, March 12, May 17, June 21, 1894, March 25, May 9, Dec. 18, 1895, Aug. 3, 1897; PAC, Charles Porteous Papers, vol. 26, Porteous to Wm. Mackenzie, June 29, 1897, and Porteous to W. G. Ross, Aug. 13, 1897; vol. 31, Manitoba Electric and Gas Light Company, undated memorandum showing work needed (worth $22,500).

6. WESR, MB, vol. 1, Dec. 16, 1899, June 1900; Manitoba Hydro Archives, North West Electric Company MB, vol. 1, passim; see also E. S. Russenholt, "The Power of a City: A History of the Development of Winnipeg's Hydro, 1890-1915," unpublished MS., ca. 1934, PAM, MG 9, 44, pp. 21-31.

7. PAC, Porteous Papers, vol. 2, Wm. Mackenzie to Charles Porteous, July 7, 1895.

8. As the eminently quotable Charles Porteous insisted in 1895, during one of Mackenzie's periodic takeover enthusiasms, "There is too much glass in the T. Ry house to do anything to invite stone throwing": ibid., vol. 24, Porteous to James Ross, April 23, 1895.

9. WESR, MB, vol. 2, April 3, 1900, June 23, Nov. 4, 13, 1903, Jan. 15, 1904,

Dec. 3, 1905; BCER, vol. 687, R. M. Horne-Payne to Johannes Buntzen, Aug. 26, 1898.

10. *Canadian Railway and Marine World,* Winnipeg Electric Railway Annual Report, 1905; PAC, Porteous Papers, vol. 22, Porteous to F. B. Morse, Feb. 21, Sept. 16, 1902.

11. WESR, MB, vol. 1, Aug. 2, 1904; vol. 2, July 26, 1904; Manitoba Hydro Archives, Winnipeg General Power Company MB, July 2, 22, 1902; PAC, Porteous Papers, vol. 12, F. B. Morse to Porteous, Dec. 16, 1903; vol. 17, F. B. Morse to Porteous, May 7, 1904.

12. Patricia Roy has written the definitive history of this company ("The British Columbia Electric Railway Company, 1897–1928: A British Company in British Columbia," Ph.D. thesis, University of British Columbia, 1970), from which she has published several articles including, "Direct Management from Abroad: The Formative Years of the British Columbia Electric Railway," *Business History Review* 47 (1974): 239–59, and "The Fine Arts of Lobbying and Persuading: The Case of the B.C. Electric Railway, 1897–1917," in D. S. Macmillan, *Canadian Business History: Selected Studies* (Toronto: McClelland & Stewart, 1971), pp. 239–54.

13. British Columbia, Legislative Assembly, *Journals,* 1896, Appendices, Petitions of the Consolidated Railway, Burnaby, South Vancouver, New Westminster, Richmond, and various ratepayer groups; BCER, Letterbook, J. Buntzen to Mayor of Vancouver, Jan. 22, 1896.

14. BCER, vol. 41, J. Buntzen to F. Hope, Feb. 8, 1899; British Columbia, *Statutes,* 1894–95, 57–58 Vic., c. 51; British Columbia, Legislative Assembly, *Journals,* 1894–95, Appendices. Similar legislation barring public competition with private enterprise was passed at about the same time in Manitoba, Ontario, and Quebec.

15. The details of these negotiations are covered in the work of Patricia Roy, cited in n. 12, and in our unpublished background paper, "Some Aspects of the BCER'S Relations with the City of Vancouver," pp. 7–24. The essential documentation is to be found in BCER, vol. 41 and Buntzen's London Letterbooks.

16. BCER, vol. 41, Buntzen to Hope, Sept. 14, Oct. 6, 1900 (both Private); Buntzen to Horne-Payne, Oct. 22, 1901 (Personal); VCA, City Clerk's Papers, Light, Railway and Tramway Committee MB, vol. 17, Agreement of Oct. 14, 1901, with the BCER.

17. BCER, Letterbook, Buntzen to E. A. Bennett, Oct. 27, 1897.

18. There is a large correspondence on the price war with the gas company and subsequent merger negotiations in BCER, esp. vol. 689, B. H. Binder to J. Buntzen, Jan. 15, 1902; Letterbook, Buntzen to Hope, Jan. 30, 1902; vol. 41, anonymous employee of Vancouver Gas to Buntzen, May 21, 1902 reporting internal financial affair of the gas company; Buntzen to Horne-Payne, Dec. 27, 1902 (Private); Horne-Payne to Buntzen, Oct. 8, 9, Nov. 21, 1902, Jan. 17, 22, 1903; Buntzen to Hope, Oct. 27, Nov. 5, 1903, Feb, 3, 1904.

19. BCER, Letterbook, Buntzen to Hope, June 22, July 14, 1904; Buntzen to B. H. Binder, May 25, 1905.

20. BCER, Letterbook, Buntzen to Hope, June 22, 1904.

21. Roy, "British Columbia Electric Railway Company," pp. 154–63; BCER,

vol. 41, Buntzen to Horne Payne, Jan. 20, 1902 (Private and Confidential), on the relations between Vancouver Power and the BCER.

22. Roy, "British Columbia Electric Railway Company," pp. 164–74; BCER, vol. 41, Horne-Payne to Buntzen, Mar. 21, 1900 (Private and Confidential), April 3, 1901 (Private and Confidential).

23. BCER, vol. 41, Buntzen to Wm. Mackenzie, cable, Aug. 24, 1904; Mackenzie to Buntzen, Aug. 27, 1904.

24. BCER, vol. 5, Z. A. Lash to R. H. Sperling, May 6, 1907; vol. 8, R. H. Sperling to Blake, Lash & Cassels, April 19, 1907; reply, June 10, 1907.

25. HQA, Montreal Gas Company MB, July 4, Oct. 17, 1893, April 9, Sept. 25, Oct. 19, 1894, July 18, 1895; Clarence Hogue et al., *Quebec: Un Siecle d'electricite* (Montreal: Libre Expression, 1979), pp. 57–60.

26. HQA contains MBs for most of these companies; see Hogue et al., *Un Siecle,* pp. 47–56.

27. HQA, Lachine Rapids Hydraulic and Land Company MB, Oct. 1, 4, 14, 1895, May 26, 1896.

28. Ibid., Oct. 1, 1897; Hogue et al., *Un Siècle,* pp. 53–57; *Canadian Electrical News,* January, 1899.

29. HQA, Chambly Manufacturing Company MB, 1891–1901; REC, MB, July 28, Aug. 25, Oct. 13, Dec. 28, 1891, April 25, 30, May 14, 1895, March 3, 30, May 6, Oct. 20, 1896, June 14, July 12, Aug. 23, Oct. 11, 13, 18, 1898, May 2, June 6, July 4, 1898; Hogue et al., *Un Siècle,* pp. 44–47, 60–61. Royal had examined and then rejected the Lachine Rapids hydraulic site in 1891.

30. On the transfer of hydroelectric technology to Quebec, see Robert Belfield, "The Niagara Frontier: The Evolution of Electric Power Systems in New York and Ontario, 1880–1935," Ph.D. thesis, University of Pennsylvania, 1981, pp. 53–63.

31. PAC, Porteous Papers, vol. 31, Brief Account of the Chambly Manufacturing Company, undated memorandum (probably 1905-7) from the disillusioned former president of Chambly.

32. HQA, REC, MB, Nov. 7, 9, 17, 1898, Sept. 5, 26, 28, Oct. 9, 24, 31, Dec. 9, 1899, Feb. 6, April 10, May 9, 22, June 12, July 11, 17, Nov. 27, Dec. 5, 1900; PAC, Porteous Papers, vol. 27, Porteous to Bank of Montreal, London, Nov. 12, 1900; vol. 30, James Ross to Porteous, July 27, 1900; vol. 31, Statement of Comparative Power Costs, 1900; Statement of Payment by Ross and Forget, undated; Memorandum, Chambly Contract with Royal Electric, undated; Memo re Cost of Power to Street Railway, undated; F. L. Wanklyn, General Manager of the Street Railway, to Porteous, April 26, 1900.

33. Hogue et al., *Un Siècle,* pp. 63–64; PAC, Porteous Papers, vol. 22, Porteous to James Ross, Birmingham, March 14, 26, 1901; vol. 27, Porteous to Royal Trust Company, April 23, 1901; Porteous to Rodolphe Forget, July 4, 1901; Porteous to H. S. Holt, July 4, 1901, and triplicate indenture.

34. HQA, Montreal Light, Heat and Power Company MB, July 23, 1902.

35. Hogue et al., *Un Siècle,* pp. 128–34; J. H. Dales, *Hydroelectricity and Industrial Development: Quebec, 1898–1940* (Cambridge, Mass.: Harvard University Press, 1957), pp. 50–55.

36. HQA, Montreal Light, Heat and Power Company, Executive Committee MB, Feb. 5, Mar. 11, 17, 1902.

37. In the process of reorganization, Chambly had been reduced to a mere paper corporation to collect rentals for the principals. If it worked, Forget and Ross received most of the benefits; if it didn't, Royal Electric—later Montreal Light, Heat and Power—bore all the risks. See PAC, Porteous Papers, vol. 31, Brief Account of the Chambly Manufacturing Company.

38. HQA, Montreal Light, Heat and Power Company, Executive Committee MB, Dec. 5, 1902, Jan. 29, March 7, 1903; MB, March 11, April 6, May 27, 1903; Lachine Rapids Hydraulic and Land Company MB, Dec. 9, 1902, Jan. 2, 19, April 29, May 5, 1903.

39. HQA, Montreal Light, Heat and Power Company MB, May 27, 1903.

40. PAC, Porteous Papers, vol. 16, E. R. Parrington to Porteous, July 13, 1900; MCA, Fire and Light Committee MB, June 15, 18, 1901; MCM, June 26, July 10, Sept. 3, Oct. 14, 21, 12, 1901.

41. We know a good deal about Holt's methods and strategy in this campaign because one of these attempts went awry. As instructed by Holt, Porteous obtained an option from E. A. Robert on his Buisson Point waterpower, but Robert had the document drafted in such a way that Montreal Light, Heat and Power was obliged to purchase the property at its full price if it failed to surrender its option within a specified time. When the time expired, Robert sued for the purchase price and won. Holt then sued Porteous, without success, for what he claimed was negligence. These lawsuits hung out all the dirty corporate linen in this policy of preemptive occupation. See PAC, Porteous Papers, vol. 17, Montreal Waterpower Survey, Nov. 29, 1901; vol. 30, where this whole sordid affair is recounted by Porteous in a Narrative History, Jan., 1907; vol. 31, documents relevant to the trials, including transcripts of testimony entered in Quebec Superior Court.

42. See, e.g., PAC, W. C. Hawkins Papers, Memo re Cataract Power Company and Group of Companies; and W. M. Cody, "Who Were the Five Johns," *Wentworth Bygones* 5 (1964): 14–17. For a comparison of monopoly development in Toronto and Montreal, see our article "Contrasting Development of the Hydro-Electric Industry in the Montreal and Toronto Regions, 1900–1930," *Journal of Canadian Studies* 18 (1983): 5–26.

43. BCA, Sise Letterbooks, Sise to W. A. Haskell, Boston, Jan. 28, 1885.

44. BCA, Sise Log Book no. 1, Feb. 1, 2, 1885; Correspondence, T. N. Vail to Sise, Jan. 27, 1885.

45. R. C. Fetherstonhaugh, *Charles Fleetford Sise* (Montreal: Gazette Printing, 1944), pp. 174–75; BCA, Correspondence, T. Ahearn to Sise, Nov. 4, 1885; Sise Letterbook, Sise to Hugh Mackay, Jan. 30, 1889; Sise Log Book no. 3, Nov. 1, 1888.

46. BCA, MB, Nov. 11, 1890, April 14, 1891, May 12, 1892, Feb. 13, 1895; Canada, House of Commons, *Select Committee Appointed to Inquire into the Various Telephone Systems in Canada and Elsewhere, Report* (Ottawa: King's Printer, 1905), vol. 2, p. 101; hereafter Telephone Committee, *Report*. See also BCA, Sise Log Book no. 5, Oct. 27, 1890: "Instructed Kent to make all at Peterboro free."

47. The main documents relating to this extraordinary episode are BCA, Correspondence, G. H. Wainwright to Sise, June 27, July 2, 1885; F. G. Walsh to Sise, Oct, 20, 25, 1885; and Sise Letterbook, Sise to G. H. Wainwright (Confidential), Oct. 26, Nov. 3, 1885; Sise to Wainwright and Walsh (Private and Confidential), April 20, 1886.

48. See Fetherstonhaugh, *Sise,* p. 171, and William Patten, *Pioneering the Telephone in Canada* (Montreal: 1926), pp. 90 and 122; BCA, MB Books, Dec. 5, 12, 1884; Feb. 4, Nov. 11, Dec. 14, 1885.

49. BCA, Correspondence, T. N. Vail to Sise, Feb. 17, 18, 1885; MB, June 12, 1888; Sise Log Book no. 3, Jan. 17, June 19, 1888.

50. British Columbia Telephone Company, New Westminster and Burrard Inlet Telephone Company MB, July 20, 1888, to June 11, 1901.

51. BCA, Sise Log Book no. 2, Nov. 18–Dec. 2, 1887; no. 3, May 2, Sept. 20, 1888; no. 4, Jan. 2–23, 1889; Letterbook, Sise to Hugh Mackay, Jan. 9, 20, 1889, Dec. 11, 1888; Sise to J. E. Hudson, April 25, Dec. 15, 1888; Correspondence, Hudson to Sise, Dec. 17, 1888; Mackay to Sise, Dec. 17, 1888, Feb. 8, 1889; New Brunswick Telephone Company MB, Aug. 20, Dec. 28, 1888, Feb. 12, 1889.

52. BCA, Sise Log Book no. 1, Feb. 11, March 30, May 5, 1885; MB, April 1, 1885. For a list of the agreements in force in 1905, see Telephone Committee, *Report,* vol. 3, Appendix B.

53. BCA, Sise Log Book no. 7, April 11, 1892.

54. TCM, 1891, June 12, July 6, 27; Report of the Committee of Works, May 7, 19, June 3; Appendix C, Agreement between the City of Toronto and the Bell Telephone Company, Sept. 17; BCA, Sise Log Book no. 6, April 25, June 8, 1891. For the day-to-day horsetrading and hand-holding associated with obtaining the Toronto contract, see BCA, Sise Log Book no. 6, 1891, esp. April 23, 24, 25, 27, May 4, 5, 6, 10, 11, 12, 16–27, June 3–13.

55. For the agreements, see BCA, MB, June 15, 1891 (Toronto), Feb. 9, 1892 (Hamilton), July 12, 1892 (London, Galt and Berlin). For a list of municipal contracts, see PAC, RG 46, Board of Railway Commissioners Papers, vol. 530, Exhibit 65, Jan. 7, 1907.

56. BCA, Correspondence, Erastus Wiman to Sise, Feb. 20, 1884.

57. BCA, Sise Letterbook, Sise to J. E. Hudson (Personal), Dec. 21, 1886, reporting a rumoured combination of the CPR and the Great North West Telegraph Company to compete with Bell in its major markets.

58. BCA, Sise Log Book no. 3, Nov. 2, 1888; Letterbook, Sise to J. E. Hudson, Oct. 22, 1888.

59. BCA, Sise Letterbook, Sise to J. E. Hudson, June 20, Aug. 7, 1890.

60. Ibid., Sise to J. E. Hudson, June 17, 19, 20, 1891.

61. Ibid., Sise to C. W. Williams, Jr., June 26, 1891.

62. Ibid., Sise to Irving A. Evans, Boston, March 26, 1891; Sise to C. W. Williams, June 26, 1891.

63. Ibid., Sise to J. E. Hudson, Feb. 10, 1891.

64. T. P. Hughes, *Networks of Power* (Baltimore, Md.: Johns Hopkins University Press, 1982), pp. 227–63; Leslie Hannah, *Electricity before Nationalization* (Baltimore, Md.: Johns Hopkins University Press, 1979).

CHAPTER 6

1. University of New Brunswick Archives, J. D. Hazen Papers, Hazen to Manning Doherty, July 18, 1912. MacKenzie was knighted in 1901.

2. Houston's *Annual Financial Review* (Toronto, 1906), pp. 338–39, Summary Statement of Capital in Electric Railways, June 30, 1905.

3. Ibid.; see listing of the CPR and Comparative Statement of the Chartered Banks, Dominion of Canada, pp. 60–61.

4. Canada, Senate, *Debates,* April 23, 1902, pp. 289–90. The unnamed company was the Sao Paulo Tramway, Light and Power Company, whose capitol was actually 6,000,000.

5. See MUCTCA, MSR, MB, May 30, July 25, 1895, for the last three calls on the $2,000,000 of common stock issued in March, 1894; April 25, 1897, for the terms of the additional $1,000,000 to be issued.

6. There is a particularly fine example of this process to be found in the Eleutherian Mills Historical Library, Pierre S. Du Pont Papers, 10, File 431, Box 1, in connection with the Forth Worth and Dallas Street Railway project attempted in 1901.

7. The phrase is from a letter by Charles Porteous to James Ross, July 21, 1896, PAC, Porteous Papers, vol. 19.

8. C. A. S. Hall, "Electrical Utilities in Ontario under Private Ownership, 1890–1914," Ph.D. thesis, University of Toronto, 1968, pp. 156–58, describes one such syndicate in the Electrical Development Company flotation. Numerous other examples can be found in the Porteous Papers and James Dunn Papers, both in PAC, and in the Lord Beaverbrook Papers, House of Lords Records Office. See our essay "A Curious Capital Flow: Canadian Investment in Mexico, 1902–1910," *Business History Review* 58 (1984): 178–203, for the application of this system to the foreign utilities flotations.

9. PAC, Porteous Papers, vol. 25, Porteous to James Ross, May 26, June 30, 1896; vol. 19, Porteous to James Ross, July 8, 1896.

10. Ibid., vol. 20, Porteous to E. Langham, Jan. 24, 1898.

11. BCER, vol. 41, Horne-Payne to Buntzen, Mar. 21, 1900 (Private and Confidential). The glowing statements and sustained dividends needed to raise money in England, reported in British Columbia, had an unsettling effect upon public opinion already excited by poor and indifferent service. See, e.g., Buntzen to Horne-Payne (Confidential), May 17, 1898.

12. Hall, "Electrical Utilities in Ontario," pp. 125–55.

13. Ibid., quoted on p. 162. See also Ian Drummond, "Canadian Life Insurance Companies and the Capital Market, 1890–1914," *Canadian Journal of Economics and Political Science* 28 (1962): 204–24.

14. Hall, "Electrical Utilities in Ontario," p. 161.

15. E. P. Neufeld, *The Financial System of Canada* (Toronto: Macmillan, 1972), p. 52.

16. Kenneth Buckley, *Capital Formation in Canada, 1896–1930* (Toronto: McClelland & Stewart, 1974); W. L. Marr and D. G. Paterson, *Canada: An Economic History* (Toronto: Macmillan, 1980), pp. 6, 9, 19, 226; Neufeld, *Financial System,* p. 60; Leroy O. Stone, *Urban Development of Canada* (Ottawa: Dominion Bureau of Statistics, 1968), p. 137.

17. Houston's *Annual Financial Review* (Toronto, 1905), p. 15.

18. *Canadian Electrical News,* Sept., 1895; this convention received daily coverage in the *Montreal Gazette* ("The Big Slot Machine," and "The Men of Nickels,") and the *Montreal Star,* October 14–21, 1895. See also *Canadian Engineer,* Nov., 1895. Photographs of the exhibits and a day-by-day commentary on the proceedings can be found in *Electric Railway Gazette,* Oct. 19, 1985.

19. W. G. Ross, "Development of Street Railways in Canada," *Railway and Shipping World,* April, 1901.

20. See *Railway and Shipping World,* Feb., 1905, July, 1906, Feb., April, July, Dec., 1908, July, 1909, for examples of these convention reports.

21. PAC, Porteous Papers, vol. 3, William Mackenzie to Porteous, May 9, 1896. See also BCER, vol. 41, Buntzen to Horne-Payne, May 17, 1898; vol. 687, Horne-Payne to Buntzen, Aug., 1898 (Private), commenting on his new policy in dispensing information.

22. Canada, Department of Railways and Canals, *Railway Statistics* (Ottawa, 1901-14). E.g., the Montreal Tramways Company submitted the same data for two years in succession.

23. PAC, Porteous Papers, vol. 25, Porteous to W. G. Ross, Aug. 13, 1896; vol. 19, Porteous to D. B. Hanna, Jan. 4, 1897 (Confidential); Porteous to Wm. Whyte, Winnipeg, Jan. 23, 1897.

24. Ibid., vol. 19, Porteous to James Gunn, June 18, 1896; Porteous to Mackenzie, Jan. 11, 1897. Note Porteous's interesting use of the upper case throughout this correspondence.

25. Ibid., vol. 20, Porteous to E. H. Keating, June 23, Nov. 14, 1898; Porteous to James Ross, June 21, 1898; vol. 21, Porteous to James Ross, Oct. 6, 1899.

26. The appointment of Wanklyn, e.g., "had a good effect on the price of the Stock and public feeling, and it will give the property better support from Mr. Angus and the Montreal men." Ibid., vol. 19, Porteous to Mackenzie, Jan. 11, 1897.

27. BCA, Correspondence File, Hamilton Revenue and Expenses Graph; Sise Log Book, no. 3, Jan. 3, 1888.

28. Ibid., Sise Log Book, no. 2, Dec., 1887.

29. Ibid., Sise Log Book, no. 3, May, 1888. By the turn of the century, according to Lewis B. Macfarlane (Telephone Committee, *Report,* vol. 1, pp. 830-31), there were probably 70 persons per telephone in Canada compared with 121 per telephone in the United States.

30. BCER, vol. 41, Buntzen to R. M. Horne-Payne, Feb. 23, 1900 (Personal).

31. PAC, Porteous Papers, vol. 20, Porteous to James Ross, Jan. 27, 1899.

32. W. Y. Soper, "The Model Electric Railway," *Canadian Engineer,* June, 1893, pp. 36-37, copied from *Street Railway Journal.*

33. Patricia Roy, "Direct Management from Abroad: The Formative Years of the British Columbia Electric Railway," *Business History Review,* 47 (1974): 239-59.

34. Toronto Metropolitan Library, Baldwin Room, Davenport Electric Railway and Light Company MB, and Weston, High Park and Toronto Street Railway Company; OHA, Metropolitan Railway Company MB, July 2, 1892; MUCTCA, Montreal Park and Island Railway Company MB, April 22, June 8, 1895; PAC, Porteous Papers, vol. 24, Porteous to James Ross, March 23, 1896; vol. 19, Porteous to James Ross, March 5, April 1, 1897. For the territorial agreement between the Montreal Street Railway and the Park and Island Railway, see the latter's MB, July 13, 1893, May 28, 1894.

35. PAC, Porteous Papers, vol. 25, Porteous to James Ross, April 23, 1985. For a full account of this legislation, see PAC, E. H. Bronson Papers, vol. 702, E. H. Bronson to A. G. Blair, Feb. 12, 1897.

36. MUCTCA, MSR, MB, June 26, 1897.

37. PAC, Porteous Papers, vol. 20, Porteous to James Ross, June 7, 1898. See also MUCTCA, Montreal Park and Island Railway MB, June 7, Sept. 15, 1898.

38. Paul-André Linteau, *Maisonneuve* (Montreal: Boréal Express, 1981), pp. 76–78, 128–35; MCM, June 29, Nov. 5, 1908.

39. Michael Doucet, "Mass Transit and the Failure of Private Ownership," *Urban History Review*, 3–77 (1977): 3–33; TCM, Board of Control Report, May 6, 1904; Committee on Legislation Report, March 28, 1905; Mayor's Message, Jan. 8, 1906; CTA, Board of Control Papers, Box 17, W. C. Chisholm to the Mayor and Board of Control, Nov. 3, 1906; Box 18, James Fullerton to W. C. Chisholm, April 29, 1907; Box 19, Ontario Railway and Municipal Board File, May 22, 1907; Board of Control MB, Jan. 11, April 1, 1910, Report of the Privy Council Decision.

40. The different policies adopted by these street railway companies are dealt with in greater detail in our paper "Street Railway Strategies in Three Canadian Cities: Montreal, Toronto and Vancouver," in G. A. Stelter and A. Artibise, eds., *Power and Place: Canadian Urban Development in the North American Context* (Vancouver: University of British Columbia Press, forthcoming).

41. Daily return trips were calculated by dividing the total paid fares by 6.5 days (338 per day) per week. Victoria had to be included with Vancouver because the passenger data submitted by the company in its annual return did not break the total down by city.

42. Toronto, Montreal, and Vancouver did not experience the same sort of suburban growth as Boston and Philadelphia, e.g., in the 1870s and 1880s; see S. B. Warner, Jr., *Streetcar Suburbs* (Cambridge, Mass.: Harvard University Press, 1962), and *The Private City* (Philadelphia: University of Philadelphia Press, 1968), and Theodore Hershberg, ed., *Philadelphia* (New York: Oxford University Press, 1981), pp. 128–203; Charles W. Cheape, *Moving the Masses* (Cambridge, Mass.: Harvard University Press, 1980), pp. 155–207.

43. T. P. Hughes, *Networks of Power* (Baltimore, Md.: John Hopkins University Press, 1982), pp. 175–261.

CHAPTER 7

1. For a more detailed working out of this idea in one city, see our essay "The Rise of Civic Populism in Toronto," in Victor Russell, ed., *Forging the Consensus: Essay on the History of Toronto* (Toronto: University of Toronto Press, 1984), pp. 192–237; for a comparison of the regulatory experience in two cities, see our "Contrasting Development of the Hydro-Electric Industry in the Montreal and Toronto Regions, 1900–1913," *Journal of Canadian Studies* 18 (1983): 5–27.

2. *Official Report of the Third Annual Convention of the Union of Canadian Municipalities* (Montreal: Witness Publishing, 1903), p. 3, quotes Lighthall's 1901 article in the *Montreal Herald*. See Sacvan Bercovitch, *The American Jeremiad* (Madison: University of Wisconsin Press, 1978).

3. PAC, W. D. Lighthall Papers, vol. 16, Notes for Presentation at the Quebec Legislature, Petition to the Lieutenant-Governor, 1901.

4. See ibid., Montreal Light, Heat and Power clipping file, 1901, for the detailed negotiations; PAC, Porteous Papers, vol. 22, Porteous to James Ross, March 26, 1901. The divisions within the Liberal party caused by this legislation are

discussed in Patrice Dutil, "L'Aigle et La Marmotte: The Liberal Party of Quebec, 1897–1905," graduate research paper, York University, 1984.

5. PAC, Lighthall Papers, vol. 14, Lighthall to Hon. S. N. Parent, Sept. 25, 1901 (Confidential with annotation); vol. 16, MS. of address before the Canadian Club of Toronto, October 17, 1904. See *Canadian Club Addresses, 1904–5* (Toronto, 1905) pp. 31–38 for the printed text.

6. PAC, Lighthall Papers, vol. 16, Lighthall to Howland, June 10, and reply, June 12, 1901 (also further correspondence between Lighthall and Howland dealing with the organization of the convention); vol. 14, Minutes of the First Dominion Municipal Convention, Toronto, Aug. 28, 1901, in Lighthall's hand (also file of newspapers clippings on the Toronto convention).

7. *Official Report of the Third Annual Convention,* pp. 4–5. See *Canadian Municipal Journal,* Oct., 1907, for the proceedings of the seventh annual convention.

8. *Official Report of the Third Annual Convention,* p. 12.

9. W. D. Lighthall, "Municipal Freedom," *Canadian Law Review,* 1905, p. 28, reprinted in *Canadian Municipal Journal,* April, May, 1905 (copy in PAC, vol. 3 of Lighthall Papers). On this subject, see the authors' "Private Property in Peril: Ontario Businessmen and the Federal System, 1898–1911," *Business History Review* 47 (1973): 158–76.

10. For a full account of the attack upon the Toronto and Hamilton bill see Christopher Armstrong, *The Politics of Federalism: Ontario's Relations with the Federal Government, 1867–1942* (Toronto: University of Toronto Press, 1981), pp. 85–100. See also Canada, House of Commons, *Debates,* July 7, 1903, p. 6092. Lighthall is quoted in *Official Report of the Third Annual Convention,* p. 22.

11. Lighthall, "Municipal Freedom," p. 29.

12. Coatsworth is quoted in *Canadian Municipal Journal,* Oct., 1907, pp. 420–21; Lighthall, "Municipal Freedom," p. 32.

13. PAC, Laurier Papers, W. D. Lighthall to Laurier, Jan. 30, 1905 (Confidential), 94261–3, *Canadian Club Addresses, 1904–5,* p. 35.

14. *Canadian Municipal Journal,* Oct., 1907, p. 420.

15. PAC, Laurier Papers, Lighthall to Laurier, Jan. 30, 1905 (Confidental), 94261–3. Later on, Lighthall distanced himself further from the most ardent exponents and argued for other means of control.

16. Asselin's views are quoted in Joseph Levitt, *Henri Bourassa and the Golden Calf: The Social Program of the Nationalists of Quebec, 1900–1914* (Ottawa: Editions de l'Université d'Ottawa, 1969) pp. 51–53. Levitt notes that Bourassa, the leading figure, was less enthusiastic about public ownership although convinced it was sometimes necessary. See also Dutil, "L'Aigle," pp. 72–83.

17. PAC, A. W. Wright Papers, vol. 1, Constitution of the Canadian Public Ownership League founded in Toronto, March, 1907, and Minutes of the Annual Meeting, March 9, 1908.

18. "Some suggestions as to Street Railway Problems," *Canadian Club Addresses, 1908–9* (Toronto, 1909), pp. 37–40, reprinted in Paul Rutherford, ed., *Saving the Canadian City* (Toronto: University of Toronto Press, 1974), pp. 59–64.

19. PAC, Laurier Papers, Laurier to Lighthall, Feb. 2, 1905 (Private), 94248–9; TCP, S. H. Blake to Thomas Caswell, June 29, 1891; *Grip,* Nov. 20, 1981.

20. TCM, 1890, Appendix, Report of the City Clerk, June 23; *Toronto World,*

June 16, 1890; TCM, 1895, Appendix C, Report of the City Clerk, June 1; VCA, Vancouver Council Minutes, July 9, 1895.

21. David Nord, "The Experts vs. The Experts: Conflicting Philosophies of Municipal Utility Regulation in the Progressive Era," *Wisconsin Magazine of History* 58 (1975): 219–36.

22. For a useful summary of the views of a number of these men, see David W. Allen, "The Arguments of Six Intellectuals for Municipal Ownership of Utilities, 1885–1910," unpublished research paper, Harvard University, 1966; for the kind of works in which these men developed their ideas, see, e.g., Edward W. Bemis, *Municipal Monopolies* (New York: Thomas Y. Crowell, 1899); Frank Parsons, *The City for the People, or the Municipalization of the City Government and of Local Franchises*, 2 vols. (Rochester, N.Y.: Gervaise Press, 1910–11).

23. At the 1907 convention, for instance, incoming president R. T. McIlreith introduced and had passed a resolution based upon the report of the National Civic Federation in the U.S. on municipal ownership, which McIlreith took to be an endorsement of the principle of regulated private ownership of utilities. See *Canadian Municipal Journal*, Oct., 1907, pp. 457–58 for the resolution, and R. T. McIlreith, "Public Utilities and Their Regulation," ibid., Jan., 1913, p. 17, for his interpretation.

24. For an account of the scandal and the investigation, see our *Revenge of the Methodist Bicycle Company* (Toronto: Peter Martin, 1977), pp. 121–28.

25. Richard McCormick, "The Discovery that 'Business Corrupts Politics': A Reappraisal of the Origins of Progressivism," *American Historical Review* 86 (1981): 247–74.

26. See, e.g., John Weaver, *Shaping the Canadian City* (Toronto: Institute of Public Administration, 1977) pp. 55–73; Alan Artibise, *Winnipeg; A Social History of Urban Growth, 1874–1914* (Montreal: McGill-Queen's University Press, 1975), pp. 43–58, 91–92; Winnipeg City Hall, Council Communications, 1906, no. 7832, Report of Voting on Bylaws, June 28; City of Ottawa, Minutes of Council, 1907, Votes on bylaws, Jan. 14; Dutil, "L'Aigle," pp. 65–97; Michel Gauvin, "The Reformer and the Machine: Montreal Civic Politics from Raymond Préfontaine to Médéric Martin," *Journal of Canadian Studies* 13 (1978): 16–26; MCA, *Charter of the City of Montreal adopted by the Council in the month of December, 1898 and Sanctioned by His Honour the Lieutenant Governor of the Province of Quebec, L. A. Jetté, on the 10th of March, 1899* corrected ed. with amendments as of Jan., 1924 (Montreal, 1924), pp. i–vi; Stephen Leacock, *The Arcadian Adventures of the Idle Rich* (1914; rpt. Toronto: McCelland & Stewart, 1959), and our piece, "The Great Fight for Clean Government," *Urban History Review* 2–76 (1976): 50–66.

27. See Armstrong and Nelles, "Rise of Civic Populism," pp. 198, 203–4, 211–12.

28. For a brief account of the several lawsuits involving the gas company, see TCM, 1903, Appendix C, re Consumers' Gas [Printed for the Information of Members of Council], n.d., and Appendix A, Report of Board of Control, March 28, 1903.

29. Ottawa City Archives, Special Committee MB, 1886–1908, Report of Electric Street Lighting Committee, Dec. 15, 1893; PAC, E. H. Bronson Papers, vol. 702, text of statement by Bronson, n.d., and vol. 703, clipping from *Ottawa*

Evening Journal, June 24, 1894, reporting statement by Bronson during the provincial election campaign defending his conduct; OCM, April 2, 1894.

30. OCM, May 14, 1894; PAC, Bronson Papers, vol. 724, Bronson to Levi Crannell, March 10, 1894; OCM, Jan. 8, 1900, April 15, June 17, 1901.

31. The company tried to get its charter amended in 1904 during the negotiations for the streetlighting contract, but the city successfully lobbied against this; see OCM, May 16, 1904, Feb. 9, 10, March 31, 1905; *Ottawa Free Press,* Feb. 9, 1905; Canada, House of Commons, *Debates,* March 22, 1905, 2953–6.

32. OCM, April 3, 17, 20, 1905; PAC, Bronson Papers, vol. 668, for newspaper clippings on the bylaw campaign; Ottawa City Archives, Elections of the City of Ottawa, 1891–1914, report on bylaw vote, May 18, 1905.

33. In the debate on the Ottawa Electric bill in 1905, parliamentarians referred specifically to the role of the UCM: Canada, House of Commons, *Debates,* March 22, 1905, 2956.

34. See Chap. 5.

35. Ontario, *Statutes,* 1899, 62 Vic., c. 26; see also K. C. Dewar, "State Ownership in Canada: The Origins of Ontario Hydro," Ph.D. thesis, University of Toronto, 1975, pp. 117–37.

36. Manitoba, *Statutes,* 1899, 62–63 Vic., c. 25; MCM, May 22, 1905; the question at issue in Montreal was a possible takeover of the gas company.

37. BCER, London Letterbook, no. 3, R. H. Sperling to B. H. Binder, Feb. 15, 1906.

38. For an account of the rise of the public power movement, see H. V. Nelles, *The Politics of Development: Forests, Mines Hydroelectric Power in Ontario, 1849–1914* (Toronto: Macmillan, 1974), pp. 237–306.

39. CTA, Board of Control Papers, Box 8, Urquhart to Ross, Jan. 31, 1903.

40. *Toronto World,* Feb. 18, 1903; Whitney is quoted by the *Toronto Globe,* April 20, 1905; PAO, Whitney Papers, Whitney to J. W. Lyon, Secretary-Treasurer, Western Ontario Municipalities' Power Union, Sept. 13, 1906 (Private). Toronto voted for the Hydro by 11,026 to 2,907; see TCM, 1906, Appendix C, Report of the City Clerk, Jan. 3, 1907; W. R. Plewman, *Adam Beck and the Ontario Hydro* (Toronto: Ryerson, 1947), p. 51.

41. OHA, Toronto Electric Light Company MB, May 2, Nov. 2, 21, 1907, Jan. 9, 1908; CTA, Board of Control Papers, Box 20, H. M. Pellatt to Mayor Emerson Coatsworth, Nov. 16, 1907; TCM, 1907, Appendix C, Report of the City Clerk, Jan. 3, 1908.

42. In the spring of 1911, with the new Toronto Hydro-Electric System almost completed and ready to operate, the city did offer to buy up Toronto Electric Light's $5,000,000 par value in common stock at 125% and to assume its $1,000,000 in bonded debt. But the shareholders chose instead to accept an offer of 135% for their stock from the Mackenzie syndicate: CTA, Board of Control Papers, Box 21, Pellatt to Mayor Joseph Oliver, Jan. 15, 1908; TCM, 1908, Appendix C, Mayor's Message, March 16; OHA, Toronto Electric Light Company MB, May 15, 1908; TCM, 1911, Appendix A, Report of Board of Control, March 17, 1911; OHA, Toronto Electric Light Company MB, March 17, April 7, 1911; OHA, Shareholders MB, April 8, 1911. From the time the power was switched on in Berlin in Oct., 1910, Ontario Hydro grew as follows (Plewman, *Adam Beck,* p. 186):

Year	Number of Municipalities	Horsepower Consumed
1910	8	750
1911	22	13,500
1912	33	30,000
1913	48	47,500
1914	82	82,500
1915	110	122,000

43. Winnipeg City Hall, Council Communications, 1906, no. 7832, report of voting on bylaws, June 28, 1906.

44. PAM, W. Sanford Evans Papers, Box 10, *Statement by Major Evans re Offer of the Company to Sell to the City of Winnipeg* (n.p., n.d. [July, 1911]); Winnipeg City Hall, Special Committee MB, 1909–11, Special Committee re Purchase of Street Railway, pp. 310–13; ibid., Council Minutes, Oct. 9, 1911.

45. C. O. White, "Saskatchewan Builds an Electrical System," Ph.D. thesis, University of Saskatchewan, 1968, pp. 26–32; Archives of Saskatchewan, Regina, MB, April 6, 1904. The owner of the plant, Gerald Spring Rice, offered to sell out, supported the bylaw approving the takeover in 1903, and accepted $14,000 for his property; see Max Foran, "Electric Power and Natural Gas in Calgary, 1890–1940: The Fruits and Follies of Institutional Pragmatism," paper presented to Conference on Canadian-American Urban Development, University of Guelph, Aug., 1982, p. 9; Glenbow Museum, Calgary MB, March 25, May 6, 1907 (microfilm); *Calgary Morning Albertan,* Feb. 23, 1911; *Canadian Transportation,* June, 1910, p. 497.

46. TCM, 1909, Appendix C, Report of the City Clerk, Jan. 4, 1910. In Jan., 1911, the voters approved spending $1,150,000 on the civic line; see TCM, 1910, Appendix C, Report of the City Clerk, Jan. 4, 1911 (which shows a vote of 14,609 to 4, 182); and *Report of Messrs. Jacobs and Davies on Street Railway Transportation in the City of Toronto, dated August 25th, 1910* (n.p., n.d.). In 1912, however, the voters rejected the plan to build a $5,400,000 subway system by a margin of 11,645 to 8,223; see TCM, 1911, Appendix C, Report of the City Clerk, Jan. 3, 1912.

47. BCER, London Letterbook, no. 17, Kidd to London, Jan. 16, 1918; Box 41, Buntzen to Horne-Payne, Oct. 22, 1901 (Personal). See our unpublished paper on this aspect of the BCER entitled, "On Influence."

48. For a more detailed examination of one cartoon campaign, using Samuel Hunter's works as an example, see our "Rise of Civic Populism in Toronto," pp. 216–23, 228–30.

49. See our "Contrasting Development."

50. J. E. Rea, "How Winnipeg Was Nearly Won," pp. 75–77, in A. R. McCormack and Ian Macpherson, eds., *Cities in the West: Papers of the Western Canada Urban History Conference, University of Winnipeg, October, 1974* (Ottawa: National Museums of Canada, 1975).

51. See our "Street Railway Strategies in Three Canadian Cities: Montreal, Toronto and Vancouver," in G. A. Stelter and Alan Artibise, eds., *Power and Place* (Vancouver: University of British Columbia Press, forthcoming).

52. CTA, City of Toronto Annexation Map, 1834–1914, shows 13 annexations between 1883 and 1893, then none for ten years, then another wave of 19 between 1903 and 1914. By contrast, Montreal took in only Hochelaga (1883), Saint-Jean Baptiste (1886), Saint-Gabriel (1887), and Côte Saint-Louis (1893) before 1900, followed by 16 suburban annexations from 1905 to 1916, leaving Lachine, Outremont, Verdun, and Westmount still independent; see Paul-André Linteau, *Maisonneuve* (Montreal: Boréal Express, 1981), p. 25.

53. Patricia Roy, "The Fine Arts of Lobbying and Persuading: The Case of the B.C. Electric Railway, 1897–1917," in D. S. Macmillan, ed., *Canadian Business History* (Toronto: McClelland & Stewart, 1972) pp. 239–54.

54. E.g., in 1908 the BCER extracted perpetual franchises from the government covering two suburban areas though the influence of R. G. Tatlow, Provincial Treasurer and member of the company's local advisory committee. It was this acutely embarrassing fact that helped to keep the cabinet from cancelling the franchises when a great stink arose over the issue in 1912 and afterward; see BCER, Box 43, BCER Vancouver to BCER London, Feb. 7, 1914, for Premier Richard McBride's admission that the deal had been made without his knowledge.

55. BCER, 76-1444, Sperling to Horne-Payne, Feb. 12, 1912 (Private); ibid., Box 713, Sperling to BCER London, March 15, 1912 (Private).

56. Nelles, *Politics of Development,* pp. 260–72, discusses Beck's effort to push the government into a more activist stance.

57. The differences between Ontario and Manitoba are discussed in H. V. Nelles, "Public Ownership of Electrical Utilities in Manitoba and Ontario, 1906–30," *Canadian Historical Review* 57 (1976): 461–84.

58. Nelles, *Politics of Development,* p. 287.

59. Ontario, *Statutes,* 1907, 7 Edw. VII, c. 37, voided all franchise rights acquired by utilities which had secured declarations of general advantage from parliament in Ottawa after Feb. 19, 1907; see Armstrong, *Politics of Federalism,* pp. 94–100.

60. *Canadian Engineer,* 35 (July 18, 1918): 59.

CHAPTER 8

1. Quoted in *The Independent Telephone Movement: Its Inception and Progress* (n.p., 1906), p. 59.

2. M. J. Trebilcock, R. S. Prichard, D. G. Hartle, and D. N. Dewees, *The Choice of Governing Instrument* (Ottawa: Economic Council of Canada, 1982) which is a critical commentary on the Economic Council of Canada, *Reforming Regulation* (Ottawa: Economic Council of Canada, 1981).

3. In 1892 an aggrieved former competitor of Bell Telephone had managed to insert a clause in a bill increasing its capitalization requiring Bell to seek approval from the Governor-General-in-Council (i.e., the federal cabinet) for any rate increases. See Canada, *Statutes,* 1892, 55–56 Vic., c. 67, An Act Respecting the Bell Telephone Company; and Canada, Senate, *Debates,* 1892, 187–96.

4. BCA, Correspondence, C. F. Sise to K. J. Dunstan, July 15, 1896; Robert Mackay to A. G. Blair, Feb. 26, 1897; C. F. Sise to T. Ahearn (Personal), Sept. 29, 1897; Robert MacKay to Wilfrid Laurier, April 2, 1897; C. F. Sise to A. G. Blair, April 3, 1897; C. F. Sise to David Mills, Feb. 1, 1898; Robert Mackay to David

Mills (Personal), Feb. 11, 1898; Sise Log Book no. 12, Jan. 24, Feb. 19, 20, 23, 1897; Log Book no. 13, Feb. 5, 11, 12, 14, March 2, 3, 23, 24, 26, 1898. In the cabinet A. G. Blair, president of the New Brunswick Telephone Company pushed for the increase. J. I. Tarte and William Mulock, representatives of Montreal and Toronto respectively, opposed it: see PAC, Laurier Papers, Israel Tarte to Laurier, June 27, 1898, 24577-8. See also TCM, 1897, Appendix A, Special Committee.

5. BCA, MB, Sept. 12, 1899; CTA, Board of Control Papers, Box 4, T. Caswell, city solicitor, to Mayor E. A. Macdonald, June 21, 1900; TCM, 1900, Appendix C, Board of Control Minutes, June 21.

6. BCA, MB, Sept. 11, 1900; TCM, 1901, Appendix A, Report of the Board of Control, April 20.

7. The progress of this suit can be followed in TCM, 1901, Feb. 14, March 25, April 18, June 5, 10, Sept. 4, Nov. 20; TCM, 1901, Appendix A, Board of Control Report no. 3, Feb. 22; TCM, 1902, Appendix A, and 1903, Appendix A; CTA, Board of Control Minutes, Nov. 16, Dec. 7, 1904.

8. CTA, Board of Control Minutes, Nov. 18, 1904.

9. TCM, 1900, June 11, Sept. 12; TCM, 1900, Appendix A, Report of Special Committee on Municipal Telephones, Oct. 19; TCM, 1901, Appendix A, Report of the Special Committee on Telephones, July 8.

10. TCM, 1904, Appendix A, Board of Control Report, June 17; CTA, Board of Control Papers, Box 10, City Solicitor's Report, May 5.

11. This brief account is based upon a large body of documents in the Ottawa City Archives, including council minutes, 1902–08, and the Special Committee of Council MB. See also *Canadian Railway and Marine World,* 1904 and 1907 issues.

12. See PAC, RG 46, Board of Railway Commissioners Papers, vol. 1, for the evidence; vol. 2, pp. 590ff. for the decision.

13. TCM, Appendix A, 1900, Report of the Special Committee on Municipal Telephones, Oct. 19, 1900; Appendix C, Mayor's Message; TCM, Appendix A, 1901, Report of the Special Committee on Telephones, July 8, 1901; TCM, Appendix A, 1904, Board of Control Report, June 17, 1904; Board of Control Papers, Box 10, City Solicitor's Report, May 25, 1904.

14. The best discussion of British telephone policy is still F. G. C. Baldwin, *History of the Telephone in the United Kingdom* (London: 1925), pp. 113–212.

15. Telephone Committee, *Report,* vol. 1, pp. 5–43.

16. See, e.g., Canadian Independent Telephone Association, *Proceedings,* vol. 1, 1905, and succeeding conventions. These sessions and Dagger's speeches were regularly reported in *Canadian Engineer* and *Canadian Municipal Journal.*

17. Canada, House of Commons, *Debates,* 1903, 5533-53.

18. On W. F. Maclean, see our *Revenge of the Methodist Bicycle Company* (Toronto: Peter Martin, 1977). The Bell Telephone Company kept a close eye on these efforts; see BCA, MB, June 9, 1903. See also Canada, House of Commons, *Debates,* 1902, 786-88.

19. Tony Cashman, *Singing Wires: The Telephone in Alberta* (Edmonton: Alberta Government Telephones, 1972), pp. 119–21. Both the Toronto Trades and Labour Council and the Toronto Board of Trade favoured public ownership of the telephone system; see PAC, Laurier Papers, Toronto Board of Trade Resolution, Sept. 29, 1904, 90162-3; and TCM Oct. 15, 1900, for the Trades and Labour Council resolution.

20. PAC, Laurier Papers, Robert Mackay to Laurier (Private and Confidential), April 8, 1897, 13823.

21. Ibid., William Mulock to Laurier (Private), June 15, 1904, 86826-6, and Mulock to Laurier, Feb. 24, 1905, 95099-100 (quotations from the latter). The school question concerned publicly funded Catholic education in the newly created provinces of Saskatchewan and Alberta, a highly contentious issue.

22. TCM, 1905, Mar. 27; Telephone Committee, *Report* vol. 1, p. 12, 118, 217-18.

23. See Telephone Committee, *Report,* vol. 1, pp. 5-43, for Dagger; pp. 703-13 for Mayor Urquhart; pp. 659-66, 746-53 for W. D. Lighthall.

24. BCA, Sise Log Book no. 20, March 14, 1905; AT&T Letterbook, Charles Sclater to Frederick P. Fish, March 15, 1905; K. Dunstan Letterbook, Dunstan to L. B. McFarlane, March 22, 1905.

25. BCA, Sise Log Book no. 20, Mar. 28, April 11, 20, May 3, 5, 6 ("Transferred $50,000 from Special a/c. Pringle & Guthrie ha and ta [code for amounts] contingent on successful results"), 8, 9, 17, June 2, 1905; AT&T Letterbook, C. F. Sise to F. P. Fish, April 24, May 12, 22, 1905.

26. BCA, MB, April 11, 1905; Telephone Committee, *Report,* vol. 1, pp. 622-67, 764-88, 803-41. As a fascinating irrelevancy, it is perhaps worth recording that during this inquiry both W. F. Maclean and William Mulock refused to pay their telephone bills: AT&T Letterbook, C. F. Sise to F. P. Fish, May 24, June 14, 1905.

27. BCA, Sise Log Book no. 20, July 13, 1905; AT&T Letterbook, C. F. Sise to F. P. Fish, July 19, 1905.

28. BCA, AT&T Letterbook, C. F. Sise to F. P. Fish, Oct. 9, 1905; Sise Log Book no. 20, Oct. 7, 1905; K. Dunstan Letterbook, Dunstan to C. F. Sise, Oct. 18, 1905.

29. BCA, AT&T Letterbook, C. F. Sise to F. P. Fish, May 24, 1905.

30. BCA, Sise Log Book no. 20, Sept. 22, Oct. 7, 9, 10 (for a list of $6,750 in legal retainers), 20, Nov. 8, 1905. Through all of this, Sise not only wrote in considerable detail to Fish in Boston but regularly visited Boston to discuss strategy in person.

31. BCA, AT&T Letterbook, C. F. Sise to F. P. Fish, Oct. 11, 1905. For a cryptic account of this cabinet shuffle, see O. D. Skelton, *The Life and Letters of Sir Wilfrid Laurier* (Toronto: Oxford University Press, 1921), vol. 2, pp. 252-53.

32. PAC, Laurier Papers, Memorandum from the Minister of Justice in Reference to the Telephone and Telegraph Bill, undated (Session of 1903), 68724-68768.

33. Ibid., Memorandum Thomas Ahearn to Laurier, undated (1905), 93142a-93142b reporting the testimony of H. L. Webb on the failure of public ownership in Britain; Laurier to William Ross, Sept. 26, 1906, 114016-7 denying the Intercolonial analogy.

34. BCA, Sise Log Book no. 20, Dec. 19, 1905; AT&T Letterbook, C. F. Sise to F. P. Fish, Jan. 24, Mar. 12, 22, 29, 1906.

35. Canada, House of Commons, *Debates,* 1906 March 8, 706; March 28, 751-8; June 25, 6088-6119; June 26, 6205ff; July 5, 7067-7105.

36. See BCA, AT&T Letterbook, C. F. Sise to F. P. Fish, May 2, 16, 25, June 20, 1906, for Bell's partially successful attempt to remove the requirement of con-

nection for all competitors; Sise Log Book no. 21 for regular reports from "Inspirator" regarding the progress of the bill; Canada, *Statutes,* 1906, 6 Edw. VII, c. 42, for the Railway Act amendments; at the same session 6 Edw. VII, c. 61 authorized an increase of Bell Telephone's capital to thirty million dollars.

37. BCA, AT&T Letterbook, C. F. Sise to F. P. Fish, June 21, 23, 25, 27, 28, July 10, 1906.

38. Ibid., C. F. Sise to F. P. Fish, June 27, 1906.

39. Theodore N. Vail, *Views on Public Questions* (New York, 1913), p. 156. See also Douglas D. Anderson, "State Regulation of Electric Utilities," in James Q. Wilson, ed., *The Politics of Regulation* (New York: Basic Books, 1980), pp. 4–10.

40. BCA, Sise Log Book no. 13, Jan. 20, 25, 1898.

41. PAM, Winnipeg Board of Trade, MB no. 1, Nov. 8, 1894. See also BCA, AT&T Letterbook, Sise to F. P. Fish, June 23, 1906.

42. See R. C. Fetherstonhaugh, *Charles Fleetford Sise* (Montreal: Gazette Printing, 1944), p. 208, Sise Log Book no. 22, May 9, 1907.

43. BCA, Letterbook, Sise to F. H. Phippen, June 2, 1899 (Confidential).

44. BCA, AT&T Letterbook, Sise to F. P. Fish, April 4, June 8, 1904.

45. Winnipeg City Archives, Council Communications no. 7554, 1905, J. Ambrose, City Electrician to Sir William Mulock, June 7, 1905. For political background to the Manitoba insurrection, see Philip Lee Eyler, "Public Ownership and Politics in Manitoba, 1900–1915," M.A. thesis, University of Manitoba, 1972, pp. 29–66. See also James Mavor, *Government Telephones: The Experience of Manitoba, Canada* (New York: Moffat, Yard, 1916), 13–35.

46. See Manitoba, Legislative Assembly, *Journals,* 1904–5, Jan. 26, 1905 for report of Private Bills Committee.

47. BCA, AT&T Letterbook, Sise to F. P. Fish, June 9, 28, Dec. 23, 1905; Sise Log Book no. 21, Jan. 11, 1906.

48. BCA, Sise Log Book no. 20, July 28, Dec. 23, 1905; no. 21, Jan. 11, 1906.

49. BCA, AT&T Letterbook, Notes of a Conference with Mr. Fish, July 31 and Aug. 1, 1905; Sise Log Book no. 20, Sept. 21, Nov. 17, Dec. 28, 1905.

50. BCA, Sise Log Book no. 20, Oct. 23, 1905; no. 21, Jan. 5, 1906; AT&T Letterbook, Sise to F. P. Fish, Nov. 14, 1905; Jan. 24, 1906.

51. PAM, Colin Campbell Papers, Resolutions and Memorial of the Legislative Assembly of Manitoba Respecting Public Telephones, Winnipeg, 1906; Resolution appointing the Select Committee, Jan. 29, 1906; Report of the Select Committee on the Telephone System, Feb. 27, 1906. Campbell was also stunned by the lawyer's bill. Wallace Nesbitt wanted $1,000 for his adverse opinion; see PAM, Campbell Papers, Wallace Nesbitt to Campbell, Jan. 8, 1906. Manitoba tried to retain the famous Blake law firm in Toronto, but Bell got there first; see BCA, Sise Log Book no. 21, Jan. 11, 1906, for S. H. Blake's opinion on behalf of Bell.

52. Manitoba, *Statutes,* 1906, 5–6 Edw. VII, c. 89, An Act Respecting Government Telephone and Telegraph Systems, and c. 90, An Act Respecting Municipal Telephone Systems; PAM, Campbell Papers, Speech by the Hon. C. H. Campbell in moving the resolutions, and Second Reading of the Bills Respecting Government and Municipal Telephone Systems, March 1, 1906; BCA, Sise Log Book no. 21, Jan. 25, 1906; AT&T Letterbook, Sise to F. P. Fish, March 12, May 2, 1906.

53. PAM, United Farmers of Manitoba Papers, Box 2, Manitoba Grain

Growers Association MB, 1903–6 (telephones do not appear to have been discussed at the February conventions in either 1905 or 1906; the executive committee was concerned mainly with the Grain Act, transportation, grain grading and inspection, the lumber combine, and the price of coal); Union of Manitoba Municipalities MB, Nov. 7, 25, 1905; Campbell Papers, Campbell to J. H. Howden, Nov. 15, 1905; Eyler, "Public Ownership," p. 51; BCA, AT&T Letterbook, Sise to F. P. Fish (Private), Dec. 22, 1905.

54. BCA, AT&T Letterbook, Sise to F. P. Fish, Feb. 17, 1906 (Private); Lawrence Macfarlane to Lafleur, MacDougall, Macfarlane & Pope, Feb. 17, 1909 (Private and Confidential); Sise to T. N. Vail, Feb. 23, 1909.

55. PAM, Attorney General's Letterbook, Colin Campbell to F. Dagger, Aug. 21, 1906; Attorney General's Department, Deputy Minister's Letterbook, Campbell to Dagger, Jan. 29, 1906. Dagger drafted Campbell's speech to the Canadian Independent Telephone Association delivered in the fall of 1906.

56. PAM, Attorney General's Department, Deputy Minister's Letterbook, Campbell to Wilfrid Laurier, Mar. 29, 1906; Campbell to D. W. Bole, April 17, 1906; BCA, Sise Log Book no. 21, Oct. 6, 13, 1906; AT&T Letterbook, memorandum of discussion, W. C. Scott and C. F. Sise, Montreal, Oct. 6, 1906.

57. A trade paper, the *Western Municipal News,* which appeared in January, 1906, was full of propaganda about the telephone issue; see PAM, Union of Manitoba Municipalities MB, Nov. 14, 1906. The official results of the plebiscites are reported in the *Manitoba Free Press,* Feb. 12, 1907; BCA, AT&T Letterbook, Sise to F. P. Fish, Dec. 14, 21, 1906 reports the results.

58. Eyler, "Public Ownership," pp. 55–56; Mavor, *Government Telephones,* pp. 24–25.

59. Manitoba, *Sessional Papers,* 1908, no. 4, copies of government correspondence with Bell Telephone Company of Canada relating to the Purchase by the Government of the Property and Rights of the said Company in the Province of Manitoba; R. P. Roblin to Sise, Mar. 11, 1908; Sise to Roblin, Mar. 16, 1907.

60. Cashman, *Singing Wires,* pp. 137–43; Alberta Government Telephone Archives, clippings from *Calgary Herald,* Jan. 12–June 12, 1907; notes from Calgary Council Minutes, Jan. 14, Mar. 11, April 6, 8, June 3, 1907; BCA, MB, June 12, 1907.

61. Alberta Government Telephone Archives, clipping from *Strathcona Plain Dealer,* Oct. 1, 1907.

62. Ibid., clipping from *Calgary Eye Opener,* Feb. 3, 1907.

63. Eyler, "Public Ownership, p. 48. Even into 1907 and 1908 the Manitoba Grain Growers MB is silent on the telephone issue.

64. BCA, Sise Log Book no. 22, May 8, June 17, July 4, 11, Aug. 17, 1907. Alberta, *Sessional Papers,* 1909, no. 12, Correspondence Regarding the Purchase of the Bell Telephone Company's Long Distance Lines and Telephone Exchanges in the Province of Alberta; S. Edwards to C. F. Sise, June 10, 1907; Sise to Edwards, June 20, 1907.

65. BCA, AT&T Letterbook, Sise to T. N. Vail, Aug. 15, 1907.

66. John Brooks, *Telephone* (New York: Harper & Row, 1975), pp. 102–26; A. D. Chandler, *The Visible Hand* (Cambridge, Mass.: Harvard University Press, 1977), p. 202.

67. See BCA, Sise Log Book no. 21, Oct. 10, 1906, for the $5,000,000 capital

programme authorized for 1907–8; AT&T Letterbook, Sise to T. N. Vail, Aug. 9, 15, 1907, enclosing copies of correspondence with Roblin and a memorandum on Bell's Manitoba business; Sise Log Book no. 22, Nov. 8, 1907.

68. BCA, Sise Log Book no. 22, Oct, 2, 4, 5, 23, Nov. 13, 1907; Letterbook, Sise to H. D. Warren (a new director from Toronto), Nov. 8, Dec. 9, 1907 (both Personal).

69. BCA, AT&T Letterbook, Sise to T. N. Vail, Oct. 3, 7, 1907; Sise to W. R. Driver, Treasurer, AT&T, Oct. 18, Dec. 11, 1907; Sise to T. N. Vail, Dec. 24, 1907; Sise Log Book no. 22, Dec. 2, 7, 1907. The correspondence with the Government of Manitoba is printed in Manitoba, *Sessional Papers,* 1908, no. 4, pp. 356–64. See also BCA, C. F. Sise Private Letterbook, Sise to Clive Pringle, Nov. 21, 23, 1907 (Private and Confidential), specifying the conditions of the sale.

70. University of Alberta Archives, Alex Rutherford Papers, W. H. Cushing to Rutherford, March 27, 1908; Cushing to Rutherford, March 29, 1908; Alberta Government Telephone Archives, Professor Herdt's Valuation, April 15, 1908; Memorandum of Agreement between Bell Telephone Company and the Province of Alberta, April 16, 1908; Alberta, *Sessional Papers,* 1909, no. 12 for relevant correspondence; BCA, MB, April 6, 8, May 13, 1908. In Saskatchewan the transfer to provincial hands was delayed by a provincial election and a good deal of internal debate regarding the best method of organizing a public telephone service; See the Archives of Saskatchewan, Walter Scott Papers, for extensive correspondence with Bell Officials between 1906 and 1909 on this question; see also the J. A. Calder Papers for correspondence with Bell special agent W. C. Scott; BCA, MB, Sept. 9, 1908, April 14, 1909; Duff Spafford, "Telephone Service in Saskatchewan," M.A. thesis, University of Saskatchewan, 1961, pp. 5–19.

71. BCA, AT&T Letterbook, Sise to F. P. Fish, Sept. 2, 1902.

72. BCA, MB, April 6, 1908.

73. Trebilcock et al., *Governing Instrument,* pp. 21–35.

74. See on this point Wilson, *Politics of Regulation,* pp. 357–94.

CHAPTER 9

1. In Alberta, e.g., the courts held that the PUC could not override franchises and raise rates above the maximum prescribed: Provincial Archives of Alberta, Premier's Papers, Box 26, J. E. Brownlee to Herbert Greenfield, Feb. 21, 1922.

2. For reviews of this literature, see Thomas K. McCraw, "Regulation in America: A Review Article," *Business History Review* 49 (1975): 159–83; Richard Posner, "Theories of Economic Regulation," *Bell Journal of Economics and Management Science* 5 (1974): 335–57; Douglas D. Anderson, *Regulatory Politics and Electric Utilities* (Boston: Auburn House, 1981); James Q. Wilson, ed., *The Politics of Regulation* (New York: Basic Books, 1980), pp. 357–63; and Bruce Owen and Ronald Braeutigam, *The Regulation Game* (Cambridge, Mass.: Ballinger, 1978), pp. 9–18. The capture theory is most succinctly expressed by Gabriel Kolko, *The Triumph of Conservatism* (Chicago: Quandrangle Books, 1963); and George Stigler, "The Theory of Economic Regulation," *Bell Journal of Economic and Management Science* 2 (1971): 3–21.

3. In 1916, British Columbia Telephone acquired a federal charter in order to

come under Ottawa's jurisdiction; BCER, London Letterbook, George Kidd to BCER, Jan. 18, 1916.

4. Ibid., vol. 39, Kidd to BCER, Mar. 5, 1921.

5. Canada, *Sessional Papers,* 1888, no. 8A, Report of the Royal Commission on Railways (Ottawa: MacLean, Roger, 1888), p. 10.

6. Ibid., 1902, no. 20A, S. J. McLean, Reports upon Railway Commissions, Railway Rate Grievances and Regulative Legislation, Feb. 10, 1899, Jan. 17, 1902; Arthur W. Wright, "An Examination of the Role of the Board of Transport Commissioners as a Regulatory Tribunal," M.A. thesis, Carleton University, 1962, pp. 1–37.

7. For a brief account of the legal context of regulation in the United States, see Alfred E. Kahn, *The Economics of Regulation: Principle and Institutions,* vol. 1, *Economic Principles* (New York: John Wiley, 1970), pp. 3–11, 36–39. In Canada, of course, the doctrine of the legislature's supremacy also averted some problems that arose in the U.S.

8. National Civic Federation, *Municipal and Private Ownership of Public Utilities: Report of the Commission on Public Ownership and Operation,* 3 vols. (New York: National Civic Federation, 1907); the Introduction by Edward A. Moffett in vol. 1 describes the information of the commission and is followed by report itself (the quotation is from pp. 25–26) and the dissent.

9. See, *inter alia,* Forrest McDonald, *Let There Be Light: The Electric Utility Industry in Wisconsin, 1881–1955,* (Madison: University of Wisconsin, 1957), pp. 114–25; Governor Charles Evans Hughes of New York oversaw the creation of a PUC in New York in the same year.

10. Beck made this statement at a hearing on a plan by American-backed interests to dam the entire flow of the river above Cornwall, Ontario; see J. Castell Hopkins, *The Canadian Annual Review of Public Affairs, 1910* (Toronto: Annual Review Publishing, 1911), p. 147; and PAC, Laurier Papers, 166394a–166618, Transcript of Hearing of International Waterways Commission on Application of Long Sault Development Company to Dam the St. Lawrence, February 8–9, 1910.

11. Beck said this at the opening of Hydro's second generating plant; quoted in W. R. Plewman, *Adam Beck and the Ontario Hydro* (Toronto: Ryerson, 1947), p. 179.

12. A full account may be found in H. V. Nelles, *The Politics of Development* (Toronto: Macmillan, 1974), pp. 288–303.

13. Rates are given in Toronto Hydro-Electric System, *Annual Report of the Toronto Electric Commissioners,* 1914; a 1911 survey of 26 houses from 4 to 12 rooms revealed that Toronto Electric Light had been forced to reduce its rates an average of 36% to meet the competition, but that its rates were still higher than the THES by 12% in 20 cases, almost identical in 3, and lower in 3 by 5% to 15%; see PAC, Kerry and Chace Papers, vol. 92, "How City and T.E.L. Co's. Charges Compare" (extracted from *Toronto News,* July 3, 1911).

14. Between 1915 and 1917, THES residential lighting rates per KWH fell from 3.86¢ to 2.70¢; commercial lighting rates from $2.86¢ to 2.16¢; commercial power rates from 1.23¢ to 0.80¢. See Toronto Hydro-Electric System, *Annual Reports of the Toronto Electric Commissioners,* 1915–17.

15. TCM, 1914, Appendix A, Mayor's Message Relating to Reduction of

Hydro-Electric Rates, June 1, 1914; Toronto-Hydro Electric System, Extracts from the Minutes of the Toronto Electric Commissioners, December 11, 31, 1914.

16. OHA, Toronto Electric Light Company, Shareholders' MB, Feb. 9, 1909.

17. BCER, vol. 40, Kidd to R. M. Horne-Payne, March 1, 1917.

18. Plewman, *Adam Beck*, pp. 199–211. Christopher Armstrong, *The Politics of Federalism* (Toronto: University of Toronto Press: 1981), pp. 76–84, gives a brief account of these events.

19. Plewman, *Adam Beck*, pp. 258–60.

20. Ontario, *Statutes*, 1906, 6 Edw. VII, c. 31. See Brian C. Elkin, "The Ontario Railway and Municipal Board, 1906–1914: A Study of a Regulatory Agency under the Whitney Administration," graduate research paper, York University, 1977.

21. Ontario Railway and Municipal Board, *Annual Report*, 1906, pp. 53–55; PAO, Sir James P. Whitney Papers, Whitney to James Leitch, Nov. 20, 1906 (Private).

22. Ontario Railway and Municipal Board, *Annual Report*, 1908, p. 102.

23. Ibid., 1910, p. 11; Elkin, "Ontario Railway and Municipal Board," pp. 26–32.

24. Manitoba, *Sessional Papers*, 1910, Appendix A, Evidence Taken before the Public Accounts Committee, pp. 703–9.

25. *Manitoba Free Press*, quoted in G. E. Britnell, "Public Ownership of Telephones in the Prairie Provinces," M.A. thesis, University of Toronto, 1934, p. 41.

26. Britnell, "Public Ownership," pp. 45–47; Philip Eyler, "Public Ownership and Politics in Manitoba, 1900–1915," M.A. thesis, University of Manitoba, 1972, p. 118. These events receive a much more partisan treatment in James Mavor, *Government Telephones* (New York: Moffat, Yard, 1916), pp. 36–114.

27. Britnell, "Public Ownership," pp. 118–20. Testimony given before the Royal Commission may be found in PAM, Royal Commission re Manitoba Telephones, 1912, typescript. AT&T commissioned Professor James Mavor of the University of Toronto to write a long "Confidential Report on the Telephone Systems of Manitoba, Saskatchewan and Alberta" for $2,050 in 1914. This manuscript, stripped of its more favourable chapters dealing with Saskatchewan and Alberta, was published after a sprightly rewrite in 1916 as *Government Telephones* (see n. 26). In its final polemical form it constituted a devastating expose of the utter failure of public ownership of telephones. See Mavor MS., Baker Library, Harvard University, YCPM, M461.

28. Manitoba, *Sessional Papers*, 1912, no. 19, Interim Report of the Telephone Inquiry; Britnell, "Public Ownership," p. 50; Eyler, "Public Ownership," p. 119.

29. Manitoba, *Sessional Papers*, 1913, no. 15, Fifth Annual Report of the Manitoba Government Telephones, pp. 733–54; Eyler, "Public Ownership," p. 120.

30. The abortive attempt to return to the status quo is documented in BCA, "Proposed Operation of Government Telephone Service," 1912, 19675.

31. E.g., PAM, Colin H. Campbell Papers, Letterbook, Campbell to Public Service Commission, New York City, Jan. 24, 1912.

32. J. E. Rea, "How Winnipeg Was Nearly Won," in A. R. McCormack and Ian Macpherson, eds., *Cities in the West* (Ottawa: National Museums of Canada, 1975), pp. 74–87. In Roblin's defence it should be noted that the original bill did

not make it compulsory for municipal enterprises to place themselves under the PUC's control.

33. H. V. Nelles, "Public Ownership of Electrical Utilities in Manitoba and Ontario, 1906-30," *Canadian Historical Review* 57 (1976): 467-69; Rea, "How Winnipeg Was Nearly Won," sees Reese as an agent for Sir William Mackenzie, but the evidence is unclear.

34. Manitoba, *Statutes*, 1912, 2 Geo. V., c. 66.

35. Britnell, "Public Ownership," pp. 54-56; Eyler, "Public Ownership," p. 127; see also H. A. Innis, *Problems of Staple Production in Canada* (Toronto: University of Toronto Press, 1933), pp. 67-69.

36. Manitoba, *Sessional Papers*, 1914, no. 31, Report on the Projected Hydro-Electric System For the Province of Manitoba by the Public Utilities Commissioner, H. A. Robson, pp. 907-21. Robson was also a shareholder of the private company. See WESR, MB 2, Stock Allotment, March 10, 1902, Nov. 26, 1903, Sept. 21, 1907.

37. Manitoba, *Sessional Papers*, 1915, no. 34, Third Annual Report of the Manitoba Public Utilities Commission, pp. 739-40.

38. PAC, RG 89, vol. 14, file 6060-7, J. B. Challies to W. W. Cory, March 10, 1915. Challies was head of the Waterpowers Branch of the Interior Department. When Robson resigned in the fall of 1915, he noted that Winnipeg Hydro enjoyed tremendous advantages over private companies in that it did not have to pay taxes, dividends, or interest charges. See PAM, R. A. C. Manning Papers, file 11, clipping from the *Manitoba Evening Free Press*, Nov. 5, 1915.

39. Nova Scotia, *Statutes*, 1903, 3 Edw. VII, c. 33; 1903-4, 3 & 4 Edw. VII, c. 26; 1907, 7 Edw. VII, c. 40; 1909, 9 Edw. VII, c. 1; Nova Scotia, Legislative Assembly, *Debates and Proceedings*, March 4, 1909, pp. 75-78. See also W. J. Dalton, "Public Utility Regulation in Nova Scotia," M.A. thesis, University of Toronto, 1954, pp. 10-13.

40. For a fuller account of these events, see Christopher Armstrong and H. V. Nelles, "Getting Your Way in Nova Scotia: 'Tweaking' Halifax, 1909-1917," *Acadiensis* 5 (1976): 105-31.

41. Nova Scotia, Legislative Assembly, *Debates and Proceedings*, March 3, 1914, pp. 85-86.

42. The power to value properties and control the issue of securities was not contained in the original 1909 legislation but added by amendment in 1912; see Nova Scotia, *Statutes*, 1912, 2 Geo. V, c. 64. See also Nova Scotia, *Sessional Papers*, 1913, no. 27, Report of the Board of Commissioners of Public Utilities.

43. These estimated profits are calculated in Armstrong and Nelles, "Getting Your Way in Nova Scotia," pp. 127-29.

44. Nova Scotia, Legislative Assembly, *Debates and Proceedings*, May 8, 1914, p. 671.

45. To add insult to injury, the funds raised to develop the Gaspereau were lent to another Robert-controlled company, the Montreal Tramways; see Nova Scotia Tramways and Power Company, MB 1, April 15, 1917, held by Nova Scotia Power Corporation.

46. Saint John, *Minutes of the Common Council* (hereafter Saint John Council Minutes), Jan. 4-11, 1904, Reports of the Special Committee on Civic Telephone Service.

47. *Canadian Transportation,* Sept., 1906, p. 566; New Brunswick Telephone Company MB, Sept. 6, 1906; Central Telephone Company MB, Sept. 25, 1906, in possession of New Brunswick Telephone Company.

48. Saint John Council Minutes, March 9, 1907; New Brunswick, Legislative Assembly, *Journals,* Report of the Committee on Corporations, March 12, 1907.

49. New Brunswick, Legislative Assembly, *Journals,* Report of the Committee on Corporations, March 12, 1907, p. 6; New Brunswick Telephone Company MB, Feb. 6, 1908.

50. New Brunswick, *Synoptic Report of the Proceedings of the Legislative Assembly,* Feb. 18, 1910, pp. 19–20.

51. Ibid., Feb. 28, 1910, p. 50; March 24, 1910, pp. 209–10.

52. PANB, Board of Commissioners of Public Utilities, New Brunswick Telephone file, Telephone Rate Case, 1911, Transcript of Hearings, March 22–31, June 19–20, 1911. For H. A. Powell's arguments in summing up for the city, see pp. 707–38.

53. Ibid., A. P. Barnhill summing up for the company, June 19, 1911, p. 1.

54. New Brunswick Telephone Company MB, May 16, 1912.

55. PANB, Board of Commissioners of Public Utilities, New Brunswick Telephone file, Transcript of New Brunswick Telephone hearings, January 21–June 18, 1920, p. 106.

56. Ibid., p. 9.

57. Ibid., p. 187; New Brunswick Telephone Company MB, July 15, 1920.

58. See PAC, RG 46 Board of Railway Commissioners Papers, vol. 19, pp. 3075, 3097–98, 3142, 3222–23 for Sise's views.

59. Ibid., p. 3142.

60. Ibid., pp. 3550–3868.

61. Board of Railway Commissioners, *Fourth Annual Report* (Ottawa, 1909), p. 6; the peculiar disposition of this case may be followed in succeeding annual reports.

62. *Statutes of Canada,* 1908, 7–8 Edw. VII, c. 61.

63. Board of Railway Commissioners, *Seventh Annual Report* (Ottawa, 1912), pp. 289–93.

64. On the unpopularity of Montreal Light, Heat and Power, see Clarence Hogue et al. *Québec: Un Siècle d'électricité* (Montreal: Libre Expression, 1979), pp. 67–69; for a list of tramway franchises, see MCA, Board of Commissioners Minutes, Jan. 8, 1915.

65. Quebec, *Statutes,* 1909, 9 Edw. VII, c. 16; *Montreal Gazette,* April 12, 16, 20, May 6, 17, 18, 19, 1909; coverage of the final debate on the bill was somewhat scanty as it coincided with a sensational assault by journalist Olivar Asselin upon one of Gouin's ministers who had attacked Asselin for an exposé he had published.

66. See PAC, Sir Lomer Gouin Papers, vol. 20, Report of the Proceedings of the City Council anent Bill no. 143 before the Provincial Legislature, entitled "An Act to Incorporate the Montreal Tramways Company" (extract from MCM, special meeting, Feb. 24, 1911), and Memorial to Sir Lomer Gouin from the Fair Franchise League, Feb. 26, 1916, to which is attached "History of the Montreal Tramways Co." by A. Falconer, K.C.; Quebec, *Statutes,* 1911, 1 Geo. V, c. 77; the quotation is from the resolution passed by the city council.

67. Quebec, *Sessional Papers,* 1913, no. 14, Report of the Public Utilities Commission, July 25, 1912, Schedule A, Case no. 50.

68. Quebec, *Sessional Papers,* 1916, no. 14, Report of the Public Utilities Commission for the year ending June 30, 1914, Appendix B, Case no. 79. MCM March–June, 1914, are filled with complaints about the tram service; see also Montreal Tramways Company, *Annual Report,* 1914.

69. Quebec, *Sessional Papers,* 1912, no. 66, Report of the Public Utilities Commission for 1911, Case no. 25; HQA, Montreal Light Heat and Power Company MB, July 17, Dec. 18, 1911; Quebec, *Statutes,* 1911, 1 Geo. V, c. 14.

70. HQA, Montreal Light, Heat and Power Company MB, April 15, 1908, April 19, 1909, Feb. 21, April 18, 1910, April 30, 1911, May 16, 1912, June 16, 1913, May 21, 1914.

71. HQA, Civic Investment and Industrial Company MB, May 31, 1916, Feb. 18, 1918.

72. BCER, R. H. Sperling Private Letterbook, Sperling to BCER London, April 10, 1912 (Private); Sperling to R. M. Horne-Payne, June 5, 1912.

73. Provincial Library of British Columbia, Royal Commission on Municipal Government, *Evidence and Documents* (1912), typescript; British Columbia, *Report of the Royal Commission on Provincial Government, 1912* (Victoria: King's Printer, 1913), pp. 18-19.

74. Provincial Archives of British Columbia, Sir Richard McBride Papers, Box 138, Sargison to McBride, Sept. 28, 1913; BCER, Box 43, R. H. Sperling to R. F. Hayward, Dec. 12, 1913; BCER London to BCER Vancouver, Jan. 6, 1914.

75. BCER, Box 43, Sperling to McBride, Jan. 8, 1914 (Private and Confidential); Sperling memorandum of conference with Premier McBride, Jan. 13, 1914. Patricia E. Roy, "Regulating the British Columbia Electric Railway: The First Public Utilities Commission in British Columbia," *B.C. Studies* 11 (1971); 3-20, interprets the company as being more favourable toward a PUC. Despite some vacillation and differing views between London and Vancouver, the company remained fundamentally hostile to the idea throughout the period.

76. BCER, Box 43, Sperling to R. F. Hayward, Dec. 12, 1913; N. N. Todd, president, Galt, Preston and Hespler Street Railway, to A. A. Burrows, Jan. 15, 1914; E. L. Milliken to A. A. Burrows, Feb. 3, 1914; W. Saville to R. H. Sperling, Macrh 23, 1914; H. G. Mathews to J. V. Armstrong, Jan. 21, 1914; E. P. Coleman to Burrows, Jan. 15, 1914; J. W. Crosby, manager, Halifax Electric Tramway, to Burrows, Jan. 15, 1914; A. A. Burrows to J. V. Armstrong, Jan. 15, 1914; Box 44, W. Saville to George Kidd, March 28, 1914.

77. BCER, Box 43, F. R. Glover to George Kidd, June 13, 1914; Box 44, M. Urwin to Kidd, Sept. 23, 1914.

78. BCER, Box 44, M. Urwin to George Kidd, Jan. 15, 1915; London Letterbook no. 12, Kidd to BCER London, April 29, 1915. Box 44, W. Saville to Kidd, March 28, and Urwin to Kidd, July 30, 1915, deal with personnel and organization; London Letterbook no. 12, Kidd to BCER London, July 3, 1915, notes the need to thwart competition.

79. BCER, London Letterbook no. 13, Kidd to Sperling, Dec. 16, 1915. Later, Kidd concluded that however disagreeable and unpopular Bowser was, the company could probably expect more from him than from the Liberals, who were likely

to advocate public ownership of utilities, and so should support the Conservatives in the general election: "On the whole, therefore, I think we should be better off with the devil we know"; see *ibid.,* no. 14, Kidd to BCER London, April 26, 1916. See also Patricia Roy, "The Fine Arts of Lobbying and Persuading: The Case of the B.C. Electric Railway," in David S. Macmillan, ed., *Canadian Business History* (Toronto: McClelland & Stewart, 1972), pp. 239–54.

80. BCER, Box 43, M. Urwin to R. H. Sperling, March 5, 1914 (Private).

CHAPTER 10

1. Quoted in Emerson P. Schmidt, *Industrial Relations in Urban Transportation* (Minneapolis: University of Minnesota Press, 1937), p. 131.

2. Wayne Roberts, "Studies in the Toronto Labour Movement," Ph.D. thesis, University of Toronto, 1978, p. 166.

3. Quoted from the text of the Toronto Railway Company response to 1902 union demands, *Labour Gazette,* June, 1902, p. 36.

4. Examples are quoted in Richard Lucas, "The Hamilton Street Railway Strike of 1906," graduate research paper, York University, 1973, p. 25.

5. Desmond Morton, "Aid to the Civil Power: The Canadian Militia in Support of the Social Order, 1867–1914," *Canadian Historical Review* 51 (1970): 424–25.

6. Our composite of a typical street railway strike has been built up from the following accounts: Robert Babcock, "The Saint John Street Railwaymen's Strike and Riot, 1914," *Acadiensis* 11 (1982): 3–28; Howard Brown, "The Toronto Street Railway Workers: Relations between Government, Company, and Union, 1886–1921," graduate research paper, York University, 1979; Jessie I. Carlson, "The Winnipeg Electric Railway Strike of 1906," undergraduate research paper, University of Manitoba, 1973; Lucas, "Hamilton Street Railway Strike"; Jean Morrison, "Community and Conflict: A Study of the Working Class and its Relationships at the Canadian Lakehead," M.A. thesis, Lakehead University, 1974; Bryan Palmer, "Give Us The Road And We Will Run It: The Social and Cultural Matrix of an Emerging Labour Movement," in G. Kealey and P. Warrian, eds., *Essays in Canadian Working Class History* (Toronto: McClelland & Stewart, 1976), pp. 106–24; L. C. Pitcairn, "The Strike of the Amalgamated Union of Street Railway Employees, No. 99, against the Winnipeg Electric Railway Company, 1910," undergraduate research paper, University of Manitoba, 1973; Roberts, "Toronto Labour Movement"; Patricia Roy, "The British Columbia Electric Railway and Its Street Railway Employees: Paternalism in Labour Relations," *BC Studies* 16, (1973): 3–24; and published reports in the *Labour Gazette.* Wherever possible, strike records have been examined in the Strike and Lockout Files of the Department of Labour, PAC, RG 27, vols. 294–436.

7. *Labour Gazette,* May, June, Oct., 1906; Roy, "BCER and Its Employees," pp. 9–10; BCER, Sperling Private Letterbook, 1913, passim; Schmidt, *Industrial Relations,* chs. 9, 10.

8. *Labour Gazette,* Dec., 1902, Jan., 1903; Elaine Bernard, *The Long-Distance Feeling: A History of the Telecommunications Workers* (Vancouver: New Star, 1982).

9. Canada, Department of Labour, *Report of the Royal Commission on a*

Dispute respecting Hours of Employment between the Bell Telephone Company of Canada, Ltd., and Operators at Toronto, Ont. (Ottawa, 1907), pp. 12–17, 27; Joan Sangster, "The 1907 Bell Telephone Strike: Organizing Women Workers," *Labour/Le Travailleur* 3 (1978), 109–130.

10. *Report of the Royal Commission* pp. 38–97; BCA, AT&T Letterbook, C. F. Sise to Frederick P. Fish, Feb. 20, 1907, reports the incident; L. B. Macfarlane to C. F. Sise, Feb. 20, 1907. The draft report and correspondence between the commissioners can be found in PAC, RG 27, vol. 68.

11. *Labour Gazette,* May, June, Aug., 1903; for gas industry examples, see PAC, RG 27, vol. 300, file 3510; vol. 305, file 47; vol. 323, files 336, 336a; vol. 294, file 2862.

12. PAC, RG 27, vol. 296, files 3184, 3197.

13. Data on utilities strikes have been compiled from the annual report on strikes and lockouts published in the February or March issues of the *Labour Gazette* each year, 1901–30; files on individual strikes begin in PAC, RG 27 after 1907. All 138 strikes in the sector have been checked against these records where available.

14. Schmidt, *Industrial Relations,* pp. 82–84; see also U.S. Bureau of Labor, Bureau of Labor Statistics, *Street Railway Employment in the United States* (Washington, D.C.: Government Printing Office, 1917), pp. 193–203; Charles F. Marsh, *Trade Unionism in the Electric Light and Power Industry* (Urbana: University of Illinois Press, 1928), p. 100.

15. Schmidt, *Industrial Relations,* pp. 121–63; University of British Columbia, Special Collections, Pioneer 101 Division of the Amalgamated Association of Street Railway and Electrical Workers Papers, MB; BCER, Letterbook 4, J. Buntzen to F. A. Shand, Secretary of Division 101, April 27, Aug. 31, 1899.

16. H. A. Logan, *Trade Unions in Canada* (Toronto: Macmillan, 1948), pp. 95–99.

17. PAC, Bronson Papers, vol. 238, John W. Weccard, General Manager, American Detective Agency, Chicago, to Bronson, April 18, 1905, describes his company's services. See also WESR, MB, July 26, 1906: "Moved by Mr. Whyte and seconded by Mr. Sutherland that the Thiel Company's account amounting to $21,481.35 for handling the strike be authorized for payment."

18. Pitcairn, "Strike of the Amalgamated Union of Street Railway Employees."

19. See *Railway and Shipping World,* Sept., 1903, April 1905, for details of the plan; *Labour Gazette,* July, 1903, pp. 343–45.

20. Schimdt, *Industrial Relations,* pp. 96–97; Marsh, *Trade Unionism,* p. 87.

21. On the origins of the Hydro pension plan, see OHA, Files OR946 and 946.11, and esp. Professor M. A. Mackenzie to F. A. Gaby, Jan. 22, 1919.

22. University of British Columbia Library, Special Collections, Pioneer 101 Division Papers, minutes of special meeting Aug. 9, 1902, to receive international president W. D. Mahon; BCER, Box 41, Buntzen to R. M. Horne-Payne, Aug. 24, 1902; Patricia Roy, "BCER and Its Employees," pp. 3–24. Horne-Payne proposed a profit-sharing scheme in 1900; the Board approved it in 1902, and it went into effect in 1903. See BCER, Box 2, for the profit-sharing file; Box 41, Horne-Payne to Buntzen, Mar. 21, 1900; Directors' MB, Aug. 6, 1902. See also *Labour Gazette,* Oct., 1905.

23. *Labour Gazette,* July, 1902, Mar., 1903.

24. BCER, Box 41, Buntzen to Horne-Payne, Oct. 28, 1902.

25. Logan, *Trade Unions in Canada,* pp. 610–14; F. H. Leacy, M. C. Urquhart and K. A. H. Buckley, eds., *Historical Statistics of Canada,* 2d ed., (Ottawa: Statistics Canada, 1984), Series E 175–77.

26. The best description of the occupational hierarchy in the street railway industry is to be found in U.S. Bureau of Labor, *Street Railway Employment,* pp. 11–16. Toronto Transit Commission Archives, "Memorandum on Wages of the Toronto Railway Company, 1891 to 1921 and Copies of Agreements between the Toronto Railway Company and its Trainmen, Motor and Truck Repairmen, Shedmen, Car Cleaners, from 1902 to the Expiration of its Franchise," typescript.

27. BCER, Box 41, Buntzen to Horne-Payne, Aug. 24, 1902; Box 665, R. H. Sperling to Buntzen, Sept. 17, Dec. 19, 1907; Buntzen to Sperling, Aug. 14, Oct. 30, 1907.

28. Roy, "BCER and Its Employees," pp. 5–7; University of British Columbia, Special Collections, Pioneer 101 Division Papers, MB, Feb. 23, March 2, 26, June 8, 15, 29, 1910.

29. BCER, Box 31, Thiel Detective Agency File beginning May 29, 1911; spies sent among the men to check for dishonesty, and the appointment of an American manager who shook up operations to improve efficiency, exacerbated industrial relations. The Sperling Private Letterbook and Box 51 contain most of the correspondence on strike preparations, negotiations, appointment of a conciliation board, and ultimate settlement.

30. BCER, London Letterbook, G. Kidd to London, Aug. 7, 1915, enclosing the notice.

31. Terry Copp, *The Anatomy of Poverty: The Conditions of the Working Class in Montreal* (Toronto: McClelland and Stewart, 1974); Michael Piva, *The Conditions of the Working Class in Toronto, 1900–1921* (Ottawa: University of Ottawa Press, 1979); Eleanor Bartlett, "Real Wages and the Standard of Living in Vancouver, 1901–29," *BC Studies* 51 (1981): 3–62.

32. Marsh, *Trade Unionism,* p. 11, 304–5.

33. Paul Craven, *"An Impartial Umpire": Industrial Relations and the Canadian State* (Toronto: University of Toronto Press, 1980), p. 290.

34. PAC, RG 27, vol. 88 for correspondence between Mackenzie King and Judge Winchester, who wanted a stronger report; *Report of the Royal Commission,* p. 37.

35. Sangster, "Bell Telephone Strike," pp. 123–24; Craven, *Impartial Umpire,* p. 289.

36. Craven, *Impartial Umpire,* p. 298.

37. See, e.g., Michael J. Piva "The Toronto District Labour Council and Independent Political Action: Factionalism and Frustration, 1900–1921," *Labour/ Le Travailleur* 4 (1979): 118.

38. Glenbow Archives, Calgary Trades and Labour Council Papers MB, May 29, 1913; clipping, *Calgary News-Telegram,* Dec. 6, 1915.

39. PAC, RG 27, vol. 322, file 244.

40. Ibid., Vol. 302, file 73.

41. Quoted in Jean Morrison, "Community and Conflict," p. 253; see also pp. 224–53, and Morrison's article "Ethnicity and Violence: The Lakehead Freight Handlers before World War I," in Kealey and Warrian, *Canadian Working Class History,* pp. 143–60.

42. *Ottawa Citizen,* June 24, 1920, comments on the low fares in Toronto.

43. Newspaper accounts and official reports of the foregoing strikes can be found in PAC, RG 27, vol. 307, file 109; vol. 309, files 140, 142, 159; vol. 316, file 255; vol. 327, file 161. See also *Canadian Transportation,* Nov., 1921, p. 605.

44. OHA, "Wages-Niagara Development" files, memorandum from H. G. Acres to Sir Adam Beck, April 22, 1919; Acres to F. A. Gaby, May 13, 1919.

45. Ibid., "Memorandum of Discussion with Labour representatives on April 30, 1919"; George Pay to Beck, March 17, 1919.

46. Ibid., Sir William Hearst to Beck, March 26, 1918.

47. Ibid., two draft statements dated c. April, 1920.

48. Toronto Hydro-Electric System, Excerpts of Minutes, April 9, May 9, 15, 28, June 25, July 20, 1914; April 26, 1917; Oct. 24, 31, Dec. 27, 1918; Jan. 3, June 5, 12, July 3, Aug. 5, Sept. 8, Nov. 21, 1919; April 27, May 6, 14, June 25, July 9, 23, 1920; Toronto-Hydro Electric System, *Labour, 1915, Statement of the Toronto Electric Commissioners under the Industrial Disputes and Investigation Act, Minority Report of the Arbitrators under the Industrial Disputes and Investigation Act* (n.p., 1915).

49. Toronto Hydro-Electric System, Excerpts of Minutes, March 21, May 6, 13, 20, 27, June 3, 10, 17, July 8, 1921; Toronto Hydro-Electric System, *Annual Report of the Toronto Electric Commissioners, 1920.* When the THES refused to appoint a representative to the board, Ottawa did so, but eventually disbanded it on the advice of its lawyers.

50. *Toronto Electric Commissioners v. Snider* (1925), A.C. 396; for an account of the dispute that led to the final lawsuit, see *Canadian Transportation,* Sept., 1923, p. 431; Oct., 1923, p. 490; Jan., 1924, p. 39; May, 1924, p. 249.

CHAPTER 11

1. This problem is anticipated in Thomas Conway, "The Decreasing Financial Returns upon Urban Street Railway Properties," *Annals of the American Academy of Political and Social Science* 37 (1911): 14-30, and documented in, *inter alia,* the Massachusetts *Report of the Street Railway Investigation Commission on the Problems Relating to the Street Railways of the Commonwealth* (Boston: Wright & Potter, 1918); American Electric Railway Association, *Electric Railways: Recommendations Made by Investigating Committees and Commissions* (Washington, D.C.: 1919) and *Argument and Brief Submitted to the Federal Electric Railways Commission* (New York, 1919); *Proceedings and Final Report of the Federal Electric Railways Commission* (Washington, D.C.: 1920), 3 vols.; and Delos F. Wilcox's dissenting *Analysis of the Electric Railway Problem* (New York, 1921).

2. MCA, Board of Commissioners' MB, April 11, 18, 24, June 13, 28, July 24, Sept. 20, 1911; Feb. 22, 1912; MCM, Mar. 19, Sept. 24 (Special Committee), Oct. 8, 1912; MCA, Board of Commissioners' MB, Oct. 19, 1912, Jan. 23, 1913.

3. MCM, March 25, April 7, 1913, for the newspaper campaign; Oct. 13, 21, 1913, for resolutions protesting unilateral action by the Board of Commissioners; and Nov. 24, Dec. 15, 1913, for protests from the Montreal Citizens' Association and the Trades and Labour Council regarding the extension of the tramway franchise. The crucial negotiations between the board and the company in 1914 can be followed in the Board of Commissioners' MB, esp. Jan. 7, Feb. 20, March 4, 17, Nov. 10 (presentation of the draft contract), 1914.

4. MCA, Board of Commissioners' MB, Nov. 16, 1914, Jan. 18, Mar. 8, 26, 27, May 5, June 1, 2, 8, 10, 11, 1915; Richard D. Harlan, "Municipal Patriotism," March 29, 1915, in Canadian Club of Montreal, *Addresses* (Montreal, 1915), pp. 273–88.

5. MCA, Board of Commissioners' MB, E. A. Robert to the Mayor and Board of Commissioners, June 17, 1915.

6. Quebec, *Statutes,* 1916, 7 Geo. V, c. 60. On service interruptions, see Quebec, *Sessional Papers,* 1917–18, Report of the Public Utilities Commission for the Year Ending June 30, 1917, Appendix A, no. 224.

7. Commission des tramways de Montréal, *Rapport sur le contrat, 28 janvier 1918* (Montreal, 1918), pp. 10–13.

8. Ibid., p. 12, for the main recommendation, p. 14 for the valuation (details in appendices). For commentaries, see "The Montreal Tramways System," *Canadian Municipal Journal,* Jan., 1921, p. 20; and Lt. Col. J. E. Hutcheson, General Manager, Montreal Tramways Co., "Practical Operation of a Service at Cost Contract," *Canadian Railway and Marine World,* March, 1921, pp. 150–53. This pioneering agreement, variously cited as an exemplary solution or a fate to avoid, was explicitly commended by the Federal Electric Railways Commission in its *Proceedings and Final Report,* p. 27–28. Wilcox (*Analysis,* pp. 216–17, 456–63), who favoured stringent application of the service-at-cost principle, found the Montreal formulae too generous to the company and deplored its authoritarianism. See also Harlow C. Clark, *Service at Cost Plans* (New York: American Electric Railway Association, 1920).

9. The first annual report of the Montreal Tramways Commission, 1918–29, shows fare increases to 6¢ (with variations for certain tickets) and general wage increases introduced May 1, June 30, 1918, and July 1, 1919. Quebec, *Statutes,* 1918, 8 Geo. V, c. 84, ratified the contract in a general amendment to the Montreal City Charter and established the permanent commission. The company accepted the contract on Jan. 26, 1918; see MUCTCA, Montreal Tramways Company MB no. 1, Jan. 26, 1918. For the city protest, see MCM, June 25, 1918. On the fiscal impotence of the city, see the devastating Bureau of Municipal Research, *Report on Montreal* (New York, 1918), passim; Wilcox, *Analysis,* p. 463.

10. Ross Eckert and G. W. Hilton, "The Jitneys," *Journal of Law and Economics* 15 (1972): 283–325; *Canadian Railway and Marine World,* March, 1915, p. 106.

11. BCER, London Letterbook no. 11, George Kidd to BCER London, Jan. 28, 1915.

12. *Canadian Railway and Marine World,* Nov., 1915, p. 96.

13. Ibid., June, 1915, p. 229; Dec., 1916, p. 501; BCER, London Letterbook, no. 16, George Kidd to BCER London, May 17, 1917.

14. BCER, London Letterbook no. 12, George Kidd to BCER London, Mar. 22, 1915.

15. BCER, London Letterbook no. 14, Kidd to BCER London, April 25, May 12, 1916.

16. BCER, London Letterbook no. 15, Kidd to BCER London, Dec. 9, 14, 1916; Box 60, A. T. Goward to George Kidd, Dec. 1, 1916; Box 40, memorandum, J. Buntzen on Clause 5 of the Vancouver Incorporation Act, Dec. 12, 1916.

17. BCER, Box 40, R. M. Horne-Payne to George Kidd, Jan. 4, 1917 (Personal); Horne-Payne to Kidd, Jan. 12, 1917.

18. BCER, Box 40, George Kidd to Horne-Payne, Dec. 15, 1916, Mar. 1, 1917; Box 60, W. G. Murrin to Kidd, Jan. 18, 1917.

19. British Columbia Archives, Pamphlet Collection, *The City of Vancouver Desires to be Freed from the Shackles of the B.C. Electric Railway Co. Limited* (n.p., n.d.), prepared by Alderman Gale.

20. Parliamentary Library of British Columbia, Clerk of the House Papers, 1917, no. 30, Frank Stacpoole (parliamentary agent for the BCER) to E. F. Jones, Solicitor for Vancouver, Mar. 28, 1917; BCER, Box 60, Statement by George Kidd, April 17, 1917 (also printed as a pamphlet); Box 60, file 1461, list of the companies who wired protests, 1917.

21. BCER, Box 40, Horne-Payne to Kidd, Jan. 22, 1917; Box 60, Kidd memorandum, Feb. 28, 1917; memorandum from G. Porter (Confidential), Feb. 28, 1917; memorandum from J. Buntzen, March 27, 1917; Box 40, Kidd to Horne-Payne, March 27, 1917; memorandum from J. Buntzen, April 12, 1917; Buntzen to Horne-Payne, April 12, 1917.

22. BCER, London Letterbook no. 16, Kidd to BCER London, May 17, 19, 1917.

23. BCER, Box 40, Horne-Payne to Kidd, May 26, 1917 (Private).

24. *Canadian Railway and Marine World,* July, 1917, p. 283; Aug., 1917, p. 324; PAC, RG 27, vol. 307, file 108.

25. VCA, City Clerk's Papers, vol. 63, City Clerk to George Kidd, June 19, 1917, forwarding resolution asking for a Royal Commission.

26. PAC, Adam Shortt Papers, M 1599, H. C. Brewster to Shortt, June 20, 1917; BCER, Box 40, Kidd to Horne-Payne, June 7, 9, 18, 20, 23, 1917; PAC, Shortt Papers, Deputy Provincial Secretary, British Columbia to Shortt, July 12, 1917 and Attorney General to Shortt, July 12, 1917. The quotations are taken from C. Berger, *The Writing of Canadian History* (Toronto: Oxford University Press, 1976), p. 21, and S. E. D. Shortt, *The Search For An Ideal* (Toronto: University of Toronto Press, 1976), p. 103.

27. PAC, Shortt Papers, M 1597, Shortt to Beth Shortt, Mar. 13, 26, 1917.

28. BCER, G. Kidd to Horne-Payne, Aug. 24, 1917 (Private and Confidential).

29. To ensure its consideration without delay, the company had a version of the report printed up immediately. It was not issued in official form as a government document until 1918. See PAC, Shortt Papers, M 1597, Kidd to Shortt, Nov. 23, Dec. 1, 4, 5, 6, 1917; Horne-Payne to Shortt, Dec. 21, 1917 (Personal).

30. See, *inter alia,* BCER, Box 40, Horne-Payne to Kidd, Jan. 4, 1918 (Private); London Letterbook no. 17, Kidd to Horne-Payne, Jan. 14, 15, 1918; Box 51, R. H. Sperling to BCER London, Jan. 15, 1918; *Documents in Connection with the City Charter Amendments* (Vancouver, 1918), 2 vols.; VCA, Council MB, July 18, 1918, and Bridges and Railway Committee MB; BCER, Box 40, Report on the B.C. Electric Railway Company's Position with Regard to the City of Vancouver, Aug. 3, 1918; Box 39, Kidd to BCER London, Sept. 18, 1918 (Private and Confidential); Box 44, memorandum by George Kidd re Meeting with Premier Oliver, Oct. 10, 1918; London Letterbook no. 17, Kidd to BCER London, Oct. 11, Nov. 1, 27, 1918; Box 44, Kidd to Premier John Oliver, Dec. 6, 27, 1918; London Letterbook no. 18, Kidd to London, Jan. 7, 9, 20, April 3, 26, 1919; VCA, Board of Trade MB, March 6, 1919; British Columbia, Legislative Assembly, *Journals,* 1919, Bill 69, March 24, 25, 27, 28, 29; *Canadian Railway and Marine World,* April, 1919, p. 209; May, 1919, p. 262; Nov. 1919, p. 608.

31. BCER, Box 81, Kidd to BCER London, Oct. 4, 1919; Box 39, Kidd to BCER London, Oct. 10, 11, 1919; Box 81, L. G. McPhillips to Kidd, Oct. 9, 18, 1919; Kidd to Mayor Gale, Oct, 30, 1919.

32. BCER, Box 39, Kidd to Horne-Payne, Nov. 6, 10, 1919 (Private).

33. BCER, Box 55, Kidd to W. G. Murrin, April 8, 1920; Kidd to Col. A. T. Thompson, April 9, 1920; London Letterbook no. 19, Kidd to BCER London, April 13, 1920; British Columbia, Legislative Assembly, *Journals,* 1920, Bill 94, April 8, 10, 14, 17, 1920; *Canadian Railway and Marine World,* May, 1920, p. 255.

34. BCER, Box 55, H. H. Stevens to George Kidd, April 16, 1920; A. T. Goward to Kidd, May 3, 4, 8, 10, 12, 13, 1920; Kidd to London, June 11, 1920; *Statutes of Canada* 1920, 10–11 Geo. V, c. 65.

35. The campaign for federal incorporation began in Sept., 1920, and lasted more than two years, producing an enormous deposit of correspondence in BCER, esp. Boxes 40, 55, 56, and London Letterbook no. 20. See also PAC, H. H. Stevens Papers, vol. 2.

36. Direct negotiations with the City of Vancouver and other municipalities began on Feb. 14, 1921, and went on for over a year. These talks can be followed day to day in BCER; in VCA, Council MB, City Clerk's Papers, Minutes of the Bridges and Railways Committee; and in the Provincial Archives of British Columbia, Attorney General's Records, File R 277-3.

37. City and company came to terms in May, 1922, and the provincial government confirmed the new contract in December; see, *inter alia,* BCER, Box 40, Kidd to Horne-Payne, Dec. 19, 1922. Meanwhile, the company kept up its unsuccessful campaign in Ottawa for a federal charter.

38. BCER, Box 56, memorandum, April 3, 1922: Street Car Fares in Principal Canadian Cities:

	Cash	Ticket
Calgary	10¢	7.5¢
St. John	10	8.3
Regina	10	7.5
Saskatoon	10	6.5
Edmonton	7	6.25
Winnipeg	7	6.25
Halifax	7	6.25
Montreal	7	6.25
Vancouver	6	5.83
Hamilton	5	4.16
Ottawa	5	5
Toronto	7	6.25

39. J. E. Rea, "The Politics of Conscience: Winnipeg After the Strike," *Historical Papers,* 1971, pp. 276–78, and "The Politics of Class: Winnipeg Council, 1919-1945," in C. C. Berger and G. R. Cook, eds., *The West and the Nation* (Toronto: McClelland & Stewart, 1976), pp. 232–49; A. B. McKillop, "Citizen and Socialist: The Ethos of Political Winnipeg, 1919-1935," M.A. thesis, University of Manitoba, 1970; Paul Phillips, "Power Politics: Municipal Affairs and Seymour James Farmer, 1909-1924," in A. R. McCormack and I. Macpherson, eds., *Cities in the West* (Ottawa: National Museums of Canada, 1975), pp. 159–80; and H. V.

Nelles, "Public Ownership of Electrical Utilities in Manitoba and Ontario, 1906-1930," *Canadian Historical Review* 57 (1976): 461-84.

40. Manitoba, *Sessional Papers*, 1920, Eighth Annual Report of the Manitoba Public Utilities Commission, pp. 3-4; *Canadian Railway and Marine World*, June, 1915, p. 234; Oct., 1916, p. 422; May, 1917, p. 198; March, 1918, p. 116; June, 1918, p. 253; March, 1919, p. 140; Nov., 1919, p. 608; May, 1921, pp. 265-66.

41. University of Manitoba Archives, J. W. Dafoe Papers, vol. 2, Dafoe to Clifford Sifton, Nov. 9, and Sifton to Dafoe, Nov. 13, 1922. Dafoe concluded: "The situation is an awkward one . . . I have no doubt in the world that it is the intention of the citizens of this town to take over the Street Railway and if circumstances compel us to take a stand there is in my judgement no question about the course we shall pursue, that is that we should keep in touch with the mass of the public opinion of this city. The . . . Board of Trade, the Manufacturers' Assn., and the Employers' Assn., are all practically solid behind the street railway but when it comes to voting or to buying newspapers they don't amount to very much." To this the financier and utilities promoter, who was also owner of the newspaper, replied: "You are aware that I do not agree with the current cant about Municipal Ownership, nor have I yet been able to see how it advantages the people of a City to pay a higher fare on a municipally owned Railway than they do on a privately owned Railway. However, my opinions . . . are of no account. . . . My interests are purely and entirely located in the *Free Press* Office and I desire to see that the course taken will most surely conduce to the prosperity of the *Free Press*."

42. Winnipeg City Hall, Council MB, Oct. 5, 1925, Report of the Special Committee on the Purchase of the Street Railway, pp. 884-97; *Canadian Railway and Marine World*, May, 1922, p. 254; Sept., 1922, pp. 476-97; Feb., 1923, p. 84; April, 1923, p. 180.

43. *Canadian Railway and Marine World* March, 1925, p. 132; Feb., 1926, p. 88.

44. TCM, 1913, Appendix C, Mayor's Message re Street Railways, Oct. 13; 1914, Appendix A, Mayor's Message, Feb. 9, and Appendix C, Mayor's Message, Sept. 21. See also M. J. Doucet, "Mass Transit and the Failure of Private Ownership," *Urban History Review*, 1977, pp. 3-33.

45. Doucet, "Mass Transit," pp. 24-25.

46. Ibid., pp. 31-32; Howard Brown, "The Toronto Railway Workers: Relations between Government, Company, and Union, 1886-1921," graduate research paper, York University, 1979, pp. 72-96.

47. Bion J. Arnold, *Report on the Traction Improvement and Development of the Toronto Metropolitan District* (Toronto, 1912); C. R. Barnes et al., *Report to the Ontario Railway and Municipal Board on a Survey of Traffic Requirements in the City of Toronto* (Toronto, 1914); and Toronto Civic Transportation Committee, *Report on Radial Entrances and Rapid Transit for the City of Toronto*, 2 vols., (Toronto, 1915).

48. M. Montgomery, "Cleaning Up the Mackenzie Power and Utility Interests in Ontario," graduate research paper, York University, 1977, pp. 6-12, 25.

49. Doucet, "Mass Transit," pp. 28-33. See Toronto Transportation Commission, *Wheels of Progress* (Toronto, 1953); and L. H. Pursley, *The Toronto Trolley Car Story, 1921-1961* (Los Angeles: Electric Railway Publications, 1961), for a year-by-year account.

50. W. R. Plewman, *Adam Beck and the Ontario Hydro* (Toronto: Ryerson, 1947), pp. 157–314; Merrill Denison, *The People's Power* (Toronto: McClelland & Stewart, 1960), pp. 117–56; H. V. Nelles, *The Politics of Development* (Toronto: Macmillan, 1974), pp. 362–75, 399–425; Christopher Armstrong, *The Politics of Federalism* (Toronto: University of Toronto Press, 1981), pp. 76–84.

51. After arbitration proceedings lasting more than a year and a half, the city of Toronto acquired the Toronto Railway Company for $13 million. Hydro offered $27 million, Mackenzie asked $45 million for his remaining assets, and the arbitrators decided upon $32,734,000, of which the city of Toronto had to pay $6,900,000 for the assets it acquired. See CTA, *The Toronto Railway Award,* Jan. 30, 1923; *Agreement between the Toronto Railway Company and the Hydro-Electric Power Commission of Ontario,* Aug. 15, 1922; and other pertinent documents.

52. Dominion Bureau of Statistics, *Street Car Fares and Index Numbers* (Ottawa: King's Printer, 1927, 1931).

CHAPTER 12

1. PAC, RG 46, Board of Railway Commissioners Papers, vol. 54, 1911, Ingersoll Rate Case; vol. 62, 1911, Toronto Case; vol. 68, 1912, Montreal Case; vol. 104, 1915, Toronto Case.

2. BCA, *Annual Reports,* 1907–19; PAC, RG 46, vol. 140, Montreal Argument Summarized, p. 1074.

3. BCA, MB, Oct. 13, 1915; May 10, July 12, 1916, May 9, 1917, Feb. 13, 1918, July 9, 1919. See also the debate on revisions to the Railway Act in Canada, House of Commons, *Debates,* esp. June 27, 1919; Canada, Senate, *Debates,* June 6, 17, 1919; and *Statutes of Canada,* 1919, 9–10 Geo. V, c. 68. The House sought to strike out the phrase "compensation if any" from the clause giving the Railway Commissioners power to order physical connection, on the grounds that it implied that compensation was normally required. The Senate insisted upon leaving the phrase in.

4. BCA, MB, July 10, Sept. 11, 1918.

5. Ibid., Sept. 11, 1918, letter from Mr. Bethell, New York Director.

6. PAC, RG 46, vol. 139, 140, 144, 145, Case 955, 1919 Bell Telephone Rate Case Transcripts; Sise, vol. 140, p. 447; Osler, vol. 145, p. 3673.

7. Ibid., vol. 529, Exhibit 15, Hagenah & Erickson, *In Re Application of the Bell Telephone Company of Canada For Increased Rates, Tolls and Charges* (Montreal, 1919); Exhibit 38, Report of Francis Dagger, *In Re Application of the Bell Telephone Company for Increased Rates, Tolls and Charges* (Toronto, 1919).

8. Ibid., vol. 140, pp. 517, 521–22.

9. Ibid., pp. 1832, 522–27; vol. 145, pp. 3352–68.

10. Ibid., vol. 529, Exhibit 38; vol. 144, pp. 2622–2714, 3056ff.

11. Ibid., vol. 140, p. 1156; vol. 145, pp. 3488–3519, 3625–26.

12. Ibid., vol. 139, pp. 3785–3888; vol. 144, pp. 2410–2619; Hagenah allowed for a depreciation rate even higher than the charge by Bell.

13. Ibid., vol. 145, pp. 3563–73.

14. Board of Railway Commissioners, *Judgments, Orders, Regulations and Rulings,* vol. 9 (Ottawa: King's Printer, 1920), Case 955, pp. 69, 70, 72, 93, 96, 98.

15. BCA, MB, May 14, 1919.

16. Ibid., June 11, 1919.

17. Ibid., July 9, Sept. 10, Oct. 8, 1919, April 14, July 14, 1920.

18. See PAC, RG 46, vol. 174, pp. 1456–1553, for summary arguments by F. H. Phippen and Glyn Osler for the Bell Telephone Company.

19. See the report in *Canadian Municipal Journal,* March, 1921, pp. 80–81.

20. Board of Railway Commissioners, *Judgments, Orders, Regulations and Rulings,* vol. 11 (Ottawa: King's Printer, 1922), Case 955, pp. 35–51; BCA, MB, April 13, 1921.

21. BCA, MB, Aug. 10, Sept. 14, 1921.

22. See PAC, RG 46, vols. 181, 182, 187, 188, for transcripts of these hearings; Reid, vol. 181, pp. 10492, 10640–41, 10746, 10637.

23. See ibid., vol. 181. pp. 10522, 19747; vol. 188, p. 18665, for Carvell's rejoinders.

24. Ibid., vol. 181, pp. 10675–76; vol. 187, pp. 18494–566.

25. Board of Railway Commissioners, *Judgments, Orders, Regulations and Rulings,* vol. 11 (Ottawa: King's Printer, 1922), pp. 440–59. This judgement was reproduced in its entirety in the Board's *Annual Report,* 1922, in Canada, House of Commons, *Sessional Paper* no. 33, pp. 10–12, 46–53.

26. Saskatchewan Archives, Walter Scott Papers, A. J. Anderson to Scott, Oct. 15, 1910; Scott to Anderson, Oct. 31, 1910.

27. Nova Scotia, *Sessional Papers,* 1913, First Annual Report of the Board of Commissioners of Public Utilities; 1919, Annual Report of the Board of Commissioners of Public Utilities.

28. PANB, Board of Commissioners of Public Utilities, New Brunswick Telephone File, Telephone Rate Case, 1911, Transcript of Hearings.

29. New Brunswick Telephone Company MB, Shareholders' Meeting, May 16, 1912.

30. Nova Scotia, Legislature, *Journals,* 1924, Part II, Appendix 27, Report of the Public Utilities Board, p. 118ff.

31. PANB, Board of Commissioners of Public Utilities Papers, New Brunswick Telephone Company File, Transcripts of the 1920 Hearings, Jan. 21–June 18, 1920, p. 9.

32. Tony Cashman, *Singing Wires* (Edmonton: Alberta Government Telephones, 1972), pp. 265–66.

33. PAC, RG 46, vol. 178, British Columbia Telephone Rate Case, May 18–20, 1921.

34. Dominion Bureau of Statistics, *Telephone Statistics,* (Ottawa: King's Printer, annual after 1919); and *Telephone Rates and Index Numbers* (Ottawa: King's Printer, 1927, 1931, 1933).

35. John Fox, of the York University Institute of Social Research Statistical Consulting Service, performed multiple regression analysis of the data presented in Table 36. The correlation of income and telephone use presents almost a textbook case in statistical analysis, despite the paucity of data. Fox's results also indicate a slight increase in per capita telephone use over time. There is no evidence to suggest that income had a different effect in different provinces. Overall, an additional $1.00 in per capita income was associated with a 0.00017818 increase in telephones per capita.

36. Thomas Grindlay, *The Independent Telephone Industry in Ontario: A History* (Toronto: Ontario Telephone Service Commission, 1975), pp. 26–29.

37. CTA, Board of Control Papers, Box 55a, no. 498, memorandum from

T. L. Church, Sept. 25, 1920, for municipal pressure on Beck; BCA, MB, Oct. 9, 1912, May 12, July 14, 1915, Aug. 9, 1917.

38. New Brunswick Telephone Company MB, March 12, 1912.

39. BCA, MB, April 12, 1922, Jan. 10, 1923.

40. James Mavor, "Confidential Report on the Telephone Systems of Manitoba, Saskatchewan and Alberta," 1914, MS., in Baker Library, Harvard University, YCPM, M461; Harold Innis, *Problems of Staple Production in Canada* (Toronto: Ryerson, 1933), p. 72. Provincial Archives of Alberta, Attorney General's Records, Box 8, file T.G. 69.187, gives comparative rates, while Alberta Government Telephone Archives, memorandum, Feb. 20, 1934, gives the financial history of AGT. See also Duff Spafford, "Telephone Service in Saskatchewan," M.A. thesis, University of Saskatchewan, 1961, pp. 70–123 (quotation from p. 121).

41. AGT Archives, memorandum, Feb. 20, 1934, File re Rural Line Sales; Provincial Archives of Alberta, Premiers' Papers, Box 36, Rural Investment Statistics; Collection of Rural Accounts; General Manager J. D. Baker to Premier John Brownlee, July 6, 1933; pamphlet, "Sale of Rural Lines to Privately Owned Companies, 1933". See also Cashman, *Singing Wires,* pp. 273–365.

42. See Neil H. Wasserman, *From Invention to Innovation, Long Distance Telephone Transmission at the Turn of the Century* (Baltimore: Johns Hopkins University Press, 1985) which appeared just as this manuscript went to press.

43. E. B. Ogle, *Long Distance Please: The Story of the TransCanada Telephone System* (Toronto: Collins, 1979), pp. 44–92.

CHAPTER 13

1. T. P. Hughes, *Networks of Power* (Baltimore, Md.: John Hopkins University Press. 1983), pp. 404–60.

2. Stanley Mallach, "The Origins of the Decline of Urban Mass Transportation in the United States, 1890–1930," *Urbanism Past and Present,* 81 (1979): pp. 1–17; Donald F. Davis, "Mass Transit and Private Ownership: An Alternative Perspective on the Case of Toronto," *Urban History Review,* 3–78 (1978): pp. 60–98; Montreal Tramways Company, *Annual Report,* 1931, p. 15, shows that traffic on 232 U.S. street railways was consistently lower than in Montreal for 1928–31; John F. Due, *The Intercity Electric Railway Industry in Canada* (Toronto: University of Toronto Press, 1966), pp. 37–38 gives figures for miles of line in service each year.

3. A. E. Safarian, *The Canadian Economy in the Great Depression* (Toronto: McClelland & Stewart, 1970), pp. 46–52; K. H. Buckley, *Capital Formation in Canada, 1896–1930* (Toronto: McClelland & Stewart, 1974), pp. 81–87, 104.

4. See Eugene Lewis, *Pubic Entrepreneurship: Toward a Theory of Bureaucratic Political Power* (Bloomington: Indiana University Press, 1980); for another notable figure who behaved much like Beck—Robert Moses of New York—see Robert A. Caro, *The Power Broker* (New York: Random House, Vintage Books, 1975).

5. Quoted in Robert B. Belfield, "The Niagara Frontier: The Evolution of Electric Power Systems in New York and Ontario, 1880–1935," Ph.D. thesis, University of Pennsylvania, 1981, p. 266.

6. Richard Schmalensee, *The Control of Natural Monopolies* (Lexington, Mass.: D. C. Heath, 1979), pp. 85–100. For a slightly different view, see L. De-Alessi, "An Economic Analysis of Government Ownership and Regulation," *Public*

Choice 19 (1974): 1-42; L. DeAlessi, "Some Effects of Ownership on the Wholesale Prices of Electric Power," *Economic Inquiry* 13 (1975): 526-38.

7. OHA, File A1950-21, Report of the Joint Municipal Rate Committee, Sept. 29, 30, 1909; cost comparisons are in A1936-4, "Memorandum of Certain Comparative Costs of Electrical Service in Ontario and the State of New York." The origins of rural electrification in Ontario are described in Keith Fleming, "The Uniform Rate and Rural Electrification Issues in Ontario Politics, 1919-1923," *Canadian Historical Review* 64 (1983): 494-518.

8. See Christopher Armstrong, *The Politics of Federalism* (Toronto: University of Toronto Press, 1981), pp. 160-77.

9. J. H. Dales, *Hydroelectricity and Industrial Development* (Cambridge, Mass.: Harvard University Press, 1957) pp. 40-1, 202-3.

10. See Dales, *Hydroelectricity,* pp. 104-23; the comparative revenue estimates are from his Table 3, p. 45.

11. Patricia Roy, "The British Columbia Electric Railway Company, 1897-1928: A British Company in British Columbia," Ph.D. thesis, University of British Columbia, 1970, pp. 347-49; on American holding companies, see Sidney A. Mitchell, *S. Z. Mitchell and the Electrical Industry* (New York: Farrar, Straus & Cudahy, 1960), esp. pp. 76-80; see also Alfred D. Chandler, *The Visible Hand* (Cambridge, Mass.: Harvard University Press, 1977), passim; and Alfred D. Chandler and Herman Daems, ed., *Managerial Hierarchies: Comparative Perspectives on the Rise of Modern Industrial Enterprise* (Cambridge, Mass.: Harvard University Press, 1981).

12. The plan to sell the transmission line in 1923 is described in the *Canadian Engineer* 44 (Feb. 20, 1923): 264, and power zoning in *Canadian Transportation,* Sept., 1925, p. 463. For the Seven Sisters affair, see John Kendle, *John Bracken: A Political Biography* (Toronto: University of Toronto Press, 1979) pp. 68-103 and H. V. Nelles, "Public Ownership of Electrical Utilities in Manitoba and Ontario, 1906-30," *Canadian Historical Review,* 57 (1976): 475-83; the quotation is from PAM, John Bracken Papers, Personal, Box 28, notes for speech, n.d.

13. On Halifax, see Christopher Armstrong and H. V. Nelles, "Getting Your Way in Nova Scotia: 'Tweaking' Halifax, 1909-17," *Acadiensis* 5 (1976): 105-31, and our unpublished paper "Public versus Private Power in Halifax: The Tale of One City."

14. On Saint John, see our unpublished paper "The Distribution of Hydroelectric Power in Saint John, New Brunswick, 1917-23."

15. The origins of Calgary Power are described in the our "Competition vs. Convenience: Federal Administration of Bow River Waterpowers, 1906-13," in Henry C. Klassen, ed. *The Canadian West* (Calgary: Comprint Publishing, 1977), pp. 163-80. The rest of the story is exhaustively detailed in the records of the federal Interior Department; see PAC, RG 84, File B39-5. On the province's plans, see Provincial Archives of Alberta, Premiers' Papers, Box 42, A. G. Christie to J. E. Brownlee, n.d. [Aug., 1929].

16. See Clinton O. White, *Power for a Province: A History of Saskatchewan Power* (Regina: Canadian Plains Research Center, 1976), pp. 18-114; (p. 92 is quoted).

17. U.S. Bureau of the Census, *Central Electric Light and Power Stations, 1912, 1927* (Washington, D.C.: Government Printing Office, 1915, 1930).

18. Hughes, *Networks of Power,* p. 462.

19. New Brunswick, Legislative Assembly, *Synoptic Report,* March 26, 1920, pp. 80–89.

20. Dunning is quoted in White, *Power for a Province,* p. 23.

21. Christie's report is cited in n. 15, above; from the same source, see R. G. Reid to John Brownlee, Aug. 15, 1929.

22. PAC, W. L. M. King Papers, Memorandum by R. H. Coats, Dominion Bureau of Statistics, "Probable Line of Future Canadian Progress-Industry and the Tariff-Immigration" (Confidential), n.d. [1929], C44543-50; OHA, Bin 12-2-049, file 148, G. H. Ferguson to C. A. Magrath, May 3, 1930.

23. By comparison, government-owned and cooperative generating stations in the United States had only 5.5% of total installed capacity in 1932, the number of municipally owned plants having peaked at over 3,000 in 1923 and then declined. See Edison Electric Institute, *Historical Statistics of the Electrical Utility Industry* (n.p., n.d.), p. 12, which also shows that nonmunicipal public agencies possessed no more than 33% of public generating capacity prior to 1938, by which time government plants still accounted for less than 10% of total capacity. On the number of municipal plants, see H. B. Dorau, *The Changing Character and Extent of Municipal Ownership in the Electric Light and Power Industry* (Chicago: Institute for Research in Land Economics and Public Utilities, 1930), p. 18.

24. For an extended analysis, see Christopher Armstrong and H. V. Nelles, "Contrasting Development of the Hydro-Electric Industry in the Montreal and Toronto Regions, 1900-1930," *Journal of Canadian Studies* 18 (1983): 5-27. On the failure of the public power movement in Quebec, see Patricia Dirks, "Dr. Phillippe Hamel and the Public Power Movement in Quebec City, 1929-1934: The Failure of a Crusade," *Urban History Review,* vol. x, no. 1 (1981): 17-29.

25. The quotation comes from Nova Scotia Tramways and Power Company MB, Special Directors' Meeting, Feb. 16, 1923, Report of Stone and Webster on operations for 1922-23 (in the possession of the Nova Scotia Power Commission).

26. See Christopher Armstrong and H. V. Nelles, "Private Property in Peril: Ontario Businessmen and the Federal System, 1898-1911," *Business History Review* 47 (1973): 158-76. For a list of all declarations of general advantage 1867-1961, see Annexe to Andrée Lajoie, *Le Pouvoir déclaratoire du Parlement: Augmentation discretionnaire de la compétence fédérale au Canada* (Montreal: Presses de l'Université de Montréal, 1969), pp. 123-51.

27. PAM, John Bracken Papers, Box 29, Deputy Attorney General John Allen to Bracken, Feb. 15, 1928; on the BCER's efforts, see Chap. 11.

28. Armstrong, *Politics of Federalism,* pp. 160-77, provides a full account.

29. See Nelles, "Public Ownership," pp. 472-78.

30. See PAC, RG 84, file B39-8, vol. 4, memorandum from J. B. Harkin to R. A. Gibson, Aug. 29, 1925, for criticism of the provincial request from the Commissioner of Parks.

31. Belfield, "The Niagara Frontier," pp. 25-26, 317-18, 345-46, 363-71.

32. On the abortive projects of the 1920s, see Armstrong, *Politics of Federalism,* pp. 166-70.

CONCLUSION

1. W. L. Hall, Nova Scotia, Legislative Assembly, *Debates,* May 7, 1914, p. 656.

2. William Letwin, *Law and Economic Policy in America* (New York: Random House, 1965), pp. 18–52. The British jurisprudence on the question of monopolies and combination in restraint of trade reviewed by Letwin applies equally to Canada.

3. James Willard Hurst, *The Legitimacy of the Business Corporation* (Charlottesville: University Press of Virginia, 1970), p. 58.

4. The State Electricity Commission of Victoria was modelled to some extent upon the Ontario Hydro-Electric Power Commission, but outside of that state, private enterprise remained strong in Australia. See C. Armstrong and H. V. Nelles, "The State and the Provision of Electricity in Canada and Australia, 1880–1965," in D. C. M. Platt and Guido di Tella, eds., *Argentia, Australia and Canada: Studies in Comparative Development, 1870–1965* (London: Macmillan, 1985), pp. 207–30.

5. N. G. Butlin, A. Barnard, and J. J. Pincus, *Government and Capitalism: Public and Private Choice in Twentieth Century Australia* (Sydney: Allen & Unwin, 1982). It cannot be argued with the same force in the Canadian context that in the process of capital formation, particularly the importation of capital from abroad, state intervention compensated for a comparatively weak private sector, as was the case in Australia.

6. For a detailed elaboration of this point see Ken Cruikshank, "Law versus Common Sense: Judicial Regulation of Railway Shipping Contracts, 1850–1910," graduate research paper, York University, 1984.

7. F. A. Knox, C. L. Barber, and D. W. Slater, *The Canadian Electrical Manufacturing Industry* (Ottawa: Royal Commission on Canada's Economic Prospects, 1955), pp. 1–11.

8. See, e.g., Douglas D. Anderson, *Regulatory Politics and Electrical Utilities* (Boston: Auburn House, 1981), p. 61, and Thomas McCraw, *Prophets of Regulation* (Cambridge, Mass.: Harvard University Press, 1984), pp. 300–309.

Index